CODE OF ALABAMA
1975

With Provision for Subsequent Pocket Parts

Prepared under the Supervision of

The Legislative Council
Jerry L. Bassett, Code Commissioner

by

The Editorial Staff of the Publishers

Under the Direction of

D. S. Tussey, R. W. Walter, W. L. Jackson, M. A. Sancilio, J. H. Runkle, and L. A. Burckell

---

VOLUME 13A

1995 REPLACEMENT VOLUME

---

*Including Acts through the 1995 Regular Session
and annotations taken through Southern Reporter,
Second Series, Volume 652, page 1133*

THE MICHIE COMPANY
Law Publishers
Charlottesville, Virginia
1995

Preface

The general and permanent laws of the State of Alabama, as enacted during the 1995 Regular Session of the Legislature which are contained in the 1995 Cumulative Supplement to certain volumes of the Code and in the 1995 Replacement Volumes of the Code, although operative on their effective dates, will not be adopted and incorporated into the Code of Alabama 1975 until the passage of the annual codification act. The annual codification act is usually passed the year following the current legislative session. As to previous years' codification acts, see Volume 1 of this set.

User's Guide

In order to assist both the legal profession and the layman in obtaining the maximum benefit from the Code of Alabama, a User's Guide has been included in Volume 1. This guide contains comments and information on the many features found within the Code of Alabama intended to increase the usefulness of this set of laws to the user. See Volume 1 of this set for the complete User's Guide.

Scope of Annotations

The annotations contained in this volume are derived from the following sources:

Southern Reporter, Second Series, through volume 652, p. 1133.

Federal Reporter, Third Series, through volume 51, p. 287.

Federal Supplement, through volume 879, p. 1340.

Federal Rules Decisions, through volume 160, p. 274.

Bankruptcy Reporter, through volume 179, p. 985.

Supreme Court Reporter, through volume 115, p. 1731.

Opinions of the Clerk of the Supreme Court of Alabama.

Table of Titles

In Addition, This Publication Contains

Table of Contents

VOLUME 13A

TITLE 17.

Elections.

TITLE 17.

ELECTIONS.

TABLE OF CONTENTS

CHAPTER 4. REGISTRATION.

Article 1. General Provisions.

Article 2. Boards of Registrars.

Article 3. Purging of Registration Lists.

Article 4. Registration of Absentee Electors.

Division 1. General provisions.

Division 2. Electors attending institutions of higher learning.

Article 5. General Provisions.

CHAPTER 9. VOTING MACHINES.

CHAPTER 10. ABSENTEE VOTING.

TABLE OF CONTENTS

CHAPTER 11. IDENTIFICATION OF VOTERS.

CHAPTER 12. CHALLENGE OF VOTERS.

CHAPTER 13. COUNTING OF VOTES.

CHAPTER 14. CANVASSING RETURNS; DECLARATION OF RESULTS.

Article 1. County Elections.

Article 2. State Elections.

CHAPTER 15. CONTESTING ELECTIONS.

Article 1. General Provisions.

Article 2. Legislature, Judicial or County Offices.

Article 2. Contest of Elections.

CHAPTER 23. MISCELLANEOUS OFFENSES.

CHAPTER 24. ELECTRONIC VOTE COUNTING SYSTEMS.

Article 1. The 1983 Election Reform Act.

CODE OF ALABAMA

TITLE 17.

ELECTIONS.

TABLE OF CONTENTS

CHAPTER 1.

GENERAL PROVISIONS.

1

Cross references. — As to establishment of segregated, separate political funds by businesses and corporations, see § 10-1-2. As to giving aid or contribution to political party or candidate by corporation or association, see § 10-2A-70. As to municipal elections generally, see § 11-46-1 et seq. As to elections regarding sale and distribution of alcoholic beverages within counties, see § 28-2-1 et seq.

Cited in Haas v. McCrary, 399 So. 2d 298 (Ala. 1981).

§ 17-1-1. Applicability of title to primary elections and county or municipal elections.

All of the provisions of this title shall apply to all primary elections and all elections by counties or municipalities held in this state, except in cases where the provisions of this title are inconsistent or in conflict with the provisions of a law governing special primary, county or municipal elections. (Code 1907, § 432; Code 1923, § 522; Code 1940, T. 17, § 1.)

Cross references. — As to primary elections generally, see § 17-16-1 et seq.

Right of suffrage a political privilege controlled by state. — The right of suffrage and the right to hold an office under authority of the state, unlike the right of a citizen to engage in a gainful occupation, is not considered, as a general rule, a privilege or immunity belonging to a citizen of the United States, nor an inherent or natural right existing in the absence of constitutional provision or legislative enactment. It is rather considered as a political privilege or civil right under the control of the state, which it may regulate or restrict, so long as the right of suffrage is not denied to any person on account of race, color or previous condition of servitude. Ex parte Bullen, 236 Ala. 56, 181 So. 498 (1938).

Cited in State ex rel. Austin v. Black, 224 Ala. 200, 139 So. 431 (1932); Ex parte Brassell, 261 Ala. 265, 73 So. 2d 907 (1954); United States v. Parker, 236 F. Supp. 511 (M.D. Ala. 1964); United States v. Alabama, 252 F. Supp. 95 (M.D. Ala. 1966).

Collateral references. — 29 C.J.S., Elections, §§ 111-129.

§ 17-1-2. Duty of sheriff to preserve order at elections.

The sheriff of each county shall, on each day of election, be present in person or by deputy at all election precincts where elections are held in the county, and he shall preserve good order; and, in order that every elector who desires to vote may do so without interference or interruption, such sheriff or his deputy may specially deputize a sufficient force to act at all election precincts on the day of any election that he may deem necessary.

Any sheriff or deputy who wilfully or corruptly fails to perform any duty imposed by this section must, on conviction, be fined not less than $1,000.00 nor more than $5,000.00, and be imprisoned in the penitentiary for not less than two nor more than five years, at the discretion of the jury; and, upon conviction, the office of such sheriff is thereby vacated. (Code 1876, §§ 281, 4282; Code 1886, §§ 377, 4181; Code 1896, §§ 1633, 4688; Code 1907, §§ 412, 6785; Code 1923, §§ 502, 3903; Code 1940, T. 17, §§ 2, 299.)

§ 17-1-3. How tie vote decided.

In all elections where there is a tie between the two highest candidates for the same office, for all county or precinct offices, it shall be decided by lot by the sheriff of the county in the presence of the candidates; and in the case of the office of circuit judge, senator, representative or any state officer not otherwise provided for, the Secretary of State shall, in the presence of the Governor, and such other electors as may choose to be present, decide the tie by lot. (Code 1876, § 297; Code 1886, § 395; Code 1896, § 1652; Code 1907, § 428; Code 1923, § 518; Code 1940, T. 17, § 3.)

Collateral references. — 29 C.J.S., Elections, § 244.
26 Am. Jur. 2d, Elections, §§ 315, 335.

§ 17-1-4. Probate judge's duties to devolve upon circuit court in event of failure to perform.

In the event the judge of probate of any county is unable, or neglects, fails or refuses to perform the duties prescribed in this title, the duties, responsibilities, penalty and authority of the judge of probate shall devolve upon the judge of the circuit court of the county. (Code 1896, § 1614; Code 1907, § 429; Code 1923, § 519; Code 1940, T. 17, § 4.)

§ 17-1-5. Neglect of duties by probate judge.

Any judge of probate or other officer on whom the duty of a judge of probate may have been temporarily devolved, who wilfully and knowingly neglects, fails or refuses to perform any of the duties prescribed in this title, shall be guilty of a misdemeanor, and, on conviction, shall be fined not less than $100.00 unless otherwise provided in this title. (Code 1896, § 4683; Code 1907, § 6811; Code 1923, § 3929; Code 1940, T. 17, § 324.)

§ 17-1-6. Arrest of electors attending, going to or returning from elections.

An elector must not be arrested during his attendance at elections, or while going to or returning therefrom, except for treason, felony or breach of the peace or for a violation on that day of any of the provisions of the election law. For such breach of the peace the sheriff or his deputy may arrest without process and commit to jail until the offender shall give bond with good and sufficient sureties, to be approved by the sheriff, for his appearance at the next session of the circuit court to answer any indictment which may be found against him. (Code 1876, § 282; Code 1886, § 378; Code 1896, § 1634; Code 1907, § 298; Code 1923, § 369; Code 1940, T. 17, § 20.)

§ 17-1-7. Right of city, county and state employees to participate in political activities; improper use of position or state property, time, etc., for political activities.

(a)(1) No person in the employment of any city, whether classified or unclassified, shall be denied the right to participate in city, county, or state political activities to the same extent as any other citizen of the State of Alabama, including endorsing candidates and contributing to campaigns of his or her choosing.

(2) No person in the employment of any county, whether classified or unclassified, shall be denied the right to participate in city, county, or state

political activities to the same extent as any other citizen of the State of Alabama, including endorsing candidates and contributing to campaigns of his or her choosing.

(3) No person in the employment of the State of Alabama, whether classified or unclassified, shall be denied the right to participate in city, county, or state political activities to the same extent as any other citizen of the State of Alabama, including endorsing candidates and contributing to campaigns of his or her choosing. Notwithstanding the foregoing, any person within the classified service shall comply with Section 36-26-38.

(4) All persons in the employment of any city, county, or state shall have the right to join local political clubs and organizations, and state or national political parties.

(5) All persons in the employment of any city, county, or state shall have the right to publicly support issues of public welfare, circulate petitions calling for or in support of referendums, and contribute freely to those of his or her choosing.

(b) No person shall attempt to use his or her official authority or position for the purpose of influencing the vote or political action of any person. Any person who violates this subsection (b) shall be guilty of a felony and punishable by a fine not to exceed ten thousand dollars ($10,000) or imprisonment in the state penitentiary for a period not to exceed two years, or both.

(c) No person in the employment of the State of Alabama, a county, or a city whether classified or unclassified, shall use any state, county, or city funds, property or time, for any political activities. Any person who is in the employment of the State of Alabama, a county, or a city shall be on approved leave to engage in political action or the person shall be on personal time before or after work and on holidays. It shall be unlawful for any officer or employee to solicit any type of political campaign contributions from other employees who work for the officer or employee in a subordinate capacity. It shall also be unlawful for any officer or employee to coerce or attempt to coerce any subordinate employee to work in any capacity in any political campaign or cause. Any person who violates this section shall be guilty of the crime of trading in public office and upon conviction thereof, shall be fined or sentenced, or both, as provided by Section 13A-10-63.

(d) Notwithstanding subsection (c), any employee of a county or a city, whether in the classified or unclassified service, who qualifies to seek a political office with the governmental entity with which he or she is employed, shall be required to take an unpaid leave of absence from his or her employment, or use accrued overtime leave, or use accrued vacation time with the county or city from the date he or she qualifies to run for office until the date on which the election results are certified or the employee is no longer a candidate or there are no other candidates on the ballot. For purposes of this subsection, the term "employing authority" means the county commission for county employees or the city council for city employees. Any employee who violates this subsection shall forfeit his or her employment position. In no event shall this subsection apply to elected officials.

(e) When off duty, out of uniform, and acting as a private citizen, no law enforcement officer, firefighter, or peace officer shall be prohibited from engaging in city, county, or state political activity or denied the right to refrain from engaging in political activity so long as there is compliance with this section. (Acts 1978, No. 819, p. 1194; Code 1975, § 11-80-6; Acts 1983, No. 83-497, p. 696, § 2; Acts 1995, No. 95-378, § 1.)

The **1995 amendment,** effective July 24, 1995, in subsection (a), in subdivision (1), inserted "city" preceding "county," and substituted "or" for "and"; in subdivision (2), inserted "county" following "city" and substituted "or" for "and"; in subdivision (3), deleted "provided, however" following "choosing" at the end of the first sentence, and added "Notwithstanding the foregoing" preceding "any person" at the beginning of the second sentence; in subsection (c), in the first sentence inserted "a county, or a city" and inserted "county, or city," substituted "a county, or city shall" for "must" following "State of Alabama" in the second sentence, and in the last sentence, deleted "the provisions of" following "Any person who violates" and substituted "crime of trading" for "crime or trading"; added subsections (d) and (e); and made nonsubstantive changes.

Code Commissioner's note. — This section was originally codified as § 11-80-6.

Acts 1983, No. 83-497, § 1, declares that this act shall be known as the Equality of Citizenship Act.

In 1995, the Code Commissioner inserted "this subsection" for "subsection (d) of this act" in subsection (d) because the deleted language was surplusage.

Personnel board's restriction did not indicate irreconcilable inconsistency with section. — Rule 2, the personnel board's restriction concerning political activities, did not indicate an irreconcilable inconsistency with this section; those provisions of Rule 2 which were in direct conflict with this section were expressly repealed, and those provisions which

could be reconciled — i.e., the personnel board's ability to lawfully prohibit employees from participating in political activities involving the same political subdivision in which they were employed — remained in full force and effect. Kirby v. Mobile County Comm'n, 564 So. 2d 447 (Ala. Civ. App. 1990).

Personnel board's restriction did not prohibit activities guaranteed by section. — Rule 2, which was personnel board's restriction concerning political activities, was not overbroad and did not prohibit certain political activities which are guaranteed under Ala. Const. Art. I, § 4, and protected by this section; this section does not circumscribe the ability of the county or the personnel board to limit or restrict the participation of county employees in county politics or political activities; furthermore, because employee's rights were not adversely affected by the features of the rules he alleged to have been overbroad, he lacked standing to challenge the alleged overbreadth of the rule. Kirby v. Mobile County Comm'n, 564 So. 2d 447 (Ala. Civ. App. 1990).

Cited in Still v. Personnel Bd., 406 So. 2d 860 (Ala. 1981); City of Huntsville v. Certain, 453 So. 2d 715 (Ala. 1984); Williams v. Killough, 474 So. 2d 680 (Ala. 1985).

Collateral references. — 62 C.J.S., Municipal Corporations, §§ 508, 566, 578, 700; 67 C.J.S., Officers, § 54(*l*).

26 Am. Jur. 2d, Elections, § 387; 63 Am. Jur. 2d, Public Officers and Employees, §§ 198, 285.

Validity, construction, and effect of state statutes restricting political activities of public officers or employees, 51 ALR4th 702.

CHAPTER 2.

ELECTIVE OFFICERS.

§ 17-2-1. State and county officers who are elected by the people.

The following officers in this state shall be elected by the qualified electors thereof: Governor, Lieutenant Governor, Attorney General, Auditor, Secretary of State, Treasurer, Commissioner of Agriculture and Industries, public service commissioners, senators and representatives in the Legislature, chief justice and associate justices of the Supreme Court, judges of the courts of appeals, circuit courts and district courts, district attorneys, judges of the probate court, sheriffs, coroners, clerks of the circuit courts, deputy circuit clerks in the counties for which they are provided, tax assessors, tax collectors, county treasurers in counties of more than 56,000 population, as provided by law, members of county commissions, constables, representatives in Congress, United States senators, electors for President and Vice-President of the United States and such other officers as may be required by law to be elected by the people, when not otherwise specially provided for. (Code 1876, § 243; Code 1886, § 338; Code 1896, § 1573; Code 1907, § 331; Code 1923, § 413; Code 1940, T. 17, § 65.)

§ 17-2-2. Holding of general election.

General elections throughout the state shall be held for Governor, Lieutenant Governor, Attorney General, Auditor, Secretary of State, Treasurer, Commissioner of Agriculture and Industries, three public service commissioners, no two of whom shall be elected from the same congressional district, chief justice and associate justices of the Supreme Court, judges of the courts of appeals and electors for President and Vice-President of the United States, United States senators and such other officers as may be required by law to be elected by the voters of the entire state; for a member of Congress in each congressional district; judges of the circuit court in each judicial circuit; judges of the district courts in each district; district attorneys in each judicial circuit, a senator in each senatorial district; a representative in the Legislature in each house district; a judge of the probate court, sheriff, clerks of the circuit courts, deputy circuit clerks in counties for which they are provided, tax assessor, tax collector, a county treasurer in counties of more than 56,000 population, as provided by law, coroner and members of the county commission in each county and constables in each precinct of the county. (Code 1876, § 244; Code 1886, § 339; Code 1896, § 1574; Code 1907, § 332; Code 1923, § 414; Code 1940, T. 17, § 66.)

§ 17-2-3. Time of general elections.

The Governor, Lieutenant Governor, Attorney General, Auditor, Secretary of State, Treasurer, Commissioner of Agriculture and Industries, senators and representatives in the Legislature, and a sheriff, tax assessor and tax collector in each county and one coroner in all counties having a coroner, and other officers not otherwise provided for, shall be elected on the first Tuesday after the first Monday in November, 1978, and every fourth year thereafter. A president of the public service commission shall be elected on the first Tuesday after the first Monday in November, 1980, and every fourth year thereafter. Two associate public service commissioners shall be elected on the first Tuesday after the first Monday in November, 1978, and every fourth year thereafter. (Code 1876, § 245; Code 1886, § 340; Code 1896, § 1575; Code 1907, § 333; Code 1923, § 416; Code 1940, T. 17, § 68.)

Cross references. — As to terms of office of governor and other executive officers, see § 36-3-1. As to terms of office of sheriffs and coroners, see § 36-3-4. As to term of office of county tax assessors, see § 36-3-5. As to term of office of county tax collectors, see § 36-3-6. As to members of public service commission, see also, § 37-1-3.

Action to have elections declared illegal for discrimination, offices declared vacant and unexpired terms filled dismissed. — See McGill v. Ryals, 253 F. Supp. 374 (M.D.

Ala.), appeal dismissed, 385 U.S. 19, 87 S. Ct. 212, 17 L. Ed. 2d 17 (1966).

Trial court's decision not to consider ballots because oaths of those voters were defective and the voters did not testify at trial to cure the defects was proper. Williams v. Lide, 628 So. 2d 531 (Ala. 1993).

Cited in Hadnott v. Amos, 320 F. Supp. 107 (M.D. Ala. 1970), aff'd, 401 U.S. 968, 91 S. Ct. 1189, 28 L. Ed. 2d 318 (1971).

Collateral references. — 29 C.J.S., Elections, § 77.

§ 17-2-4. When county officers elected.

Members of county commissions, one county treasurer in all counties having a county treasurer and one constable for each election precinct shall be elected on the first Tuesday after the first Monday in November, 1980, and every fourth year thereafter. (Code 1876, § 341; Code 1886, § 1577; Code 1896, § 1576; Code 1907, § 334; Code 1923, § 417; Code 1940, T. 17, § 69.)

Cross references. — As to terms of office of county officers generally, see § 36-3-4.

Action to have elections declared illegal for discrimination, offices declared vacant and unexpired terms filled dismissed. — See McGill v. Ryals, 253 F. Supp. 374 (M.D. Ala.), appeal dismissed, 385 U.S. 19, 87 S. Ct.

212, 17 L. Ed. 2d 17 (1966).

Cited in Clarke v. Jack, 60 Ala. 271 (1877); Leigh v. State, 69 Ala. 261 (1881); State ex rel. Melton v. Slaughter, 196 Ala. 699, 71 So. 417 (1916); State ex rel. Benefield v. Cottle, 254 Ala. 520, 49 So. 2d 224 (1950).

§ 17-2-5. County boards of education.

At the general election of state and county officers in November, 1978, and biennially thereafter, a member or members of the county board of education shall be elected for a term of six years to succeed those whose term or terms of office shall expire at that time. Each member shall hold office until his successor has been elected and qualified. (Acts 1915, No. 220, p. 281; Code 1923, § 418; Code 1940, T. 17, § 70.)

Cited in United States v. Dallas County Comm'n, 548 F. Supp. 794 (S.D. Ala. 1982); United States v. Dallas County Comm'n, 548 F. Supp. 875 (S.D. Ala. 1982).

§ 17-2-6. Justices of the Supreme Court.

A chief justice and two associate justices of the Supreme Court shall be elected on the first Tuesday after the first Monday in November, 1976, and every six years thereafter; three associate justices shall be elected on the first Tuesday after the first Monday in November, 1978, and every six years thereafter, and three associate justices shall be elected on the first Tuesday after the first Monday in November, 1980, and every six years thereafter. The justices of the Supreme Court shall hold office for a term of six years and until their successors are elected and qualified. (Code 1876, § 247; Code 1886, § 342; Code 1896, § 1578; Code 1907, § 335; Code 1923, § 419; Code 1940, T. 17, § 71; Acts 1969, No. 602, p. 1087, § 2.)

Constitution. — As to term of office of justices, see Constitution 1901, Amendment No. 328, § 6.15.
Cross references. — For other provision as to composition and election of supreme court justices, see § 12-2-1. As to terms of office of judicial officers generally, see § 36-3-2.

§ 17-2-7. Circuit and probate judges; judges of the courts of appeals.

The judges of the circuit, district and probate courts, the judges of the courts of appeals and clerks of the circuit court shall be elected on the first Tuesday after the first Monday in November, 1982, and every sixth year thereafter. (Code 1876, § 247; Code 1886, § 342; Code 1896, § 1578; Code 1907, § 336; Code 1923, § 420; Code 1940, T. 17, § 72.)

Constitution. — As to term of office of judges, see Constitution 1901, Amendment No. 328, § 6.15.
Cross references. — In regard to judges of courts of appeals, see §§ 12-3-2, 12-3-3. As to terms of office of judicial officers generally, see § 36-3-2.
Terms of office created by local acts are not affected by this section. Betts v. Ballentine, 172 Ala. 325, 55 So. 814 (1911).
Action to have elections declared illegal for discrimination, offices declared vacant and unexpired terms filled dismissed. — See McGill v. Ryals, 253 F. Supp. 374 (M.D. Ala.), appeal dismissed, 385 U.S. 19, 87 S. Ct. 212, 17 L. Ed. 2d 17 (1966).
Cited in Macon County v. Abercrombie, 9 Ala. App. 147, 62 So. 449 (1913).

§ 17-2-8. Deputy circuit clerks in counties having more than five circuit judges.

In all counties having more than five circuit judges, there shall be elected, at each election when clerks of the circuit court are elected, a deputy circuit clerk, who shall hold office during the term of the circuit clerk of such county and until his successor is elected and qualified. (Acts 1915, No. 686, p. 741; Code 1923, § 421; Code 1940, T. 17, § 73; Acts 1953, No. 511, p. 646.)

§ 17-2-9. District attorneys.

One district attorney for each judicial circuit shall be elected on the first Tuesday after the first Monday in November, 1980, and every sixth year thereafter, and their terms shall be six years and until their successors are elected and qualified. (Code 1923, § 422; Code 1940, T. 17, § 74.)

Constitution. — As to term of office of district attorneys, see Constitution 1901, Amendment No. 328, § 6.20.

Cross references. — See also, § 12-17-180. As to terms of office of district attorneys, see § 36-3-3.

Action to have elections declared illegal for discrimination, offices declared vacant and unexpired terms filled dismissed. — See McGill v. Ryals, 253 F. Supp. 374 (M.D. Ala.), appeal dismissed, 385 U.S. 19, 87 S. Ct. 212, 17 L. Ed. 2d 17 (1966).

§ 17-2-10. When presidential electors and congressmen elected.

Electors for President and Vice-President of the United States shall be elected on the first Tuesday after the first Monday in November, 1980, and every fourth year thereafter. A member of Congress from each congressional district shall be elected on the first Tuesday after the first Monday in November, 1978, and every second year thereafter. (Code 1876, § 248; Code 1886, § 343; Code 1896, § 1579; Code 1907, § 338; Code 1923, § 423; Code 1940, T. 17, § 75.)

Cross references. — See also § 17-20-2.
Cited in Lewis v. Bruton, 74 Ala. 317 (1883).

§ 17-2-11. United States senators.

At the general election to be held on the first Tuesday after the first Monday in November, 1978, and each six years thereafter, a senator of and from the State of Alabama in the Senate of the United States shall be elected by the people for a term of six years, beginning on the third day of January next after his election. At the general election to be held on the first Tuesday after the first Monday in November, 1980, and every six years thereafter, a senator of and from the State of Alabama in the Senate of the United States shall be elected by the people for a term of six years, beginning on the third day of January next after his election. (Acts 1915, No. 410, p. 364; Code 1923, § 424; Code 1940, T. 17, § 76; Acts 1942, Ex. Sess., No. 3, p. 10.)

Cross references. — As to proceedings upon occurrence of vacancy in office of United States senator, see § 36-9-7 et seq.

CHAPTER 3.

QUALIFICATIONS OF ELECTORS.

§§ 17-3-1 through 17-3-8. Repealed by Acts 1978, No. 584, p. 667, § 34, effective April 27, 1978.

Cross references. — For present provisions relative to qualifications of voters, see § 17-3-9 et seq.

§ 17-3-9. Qualifications of electors generally.

Any person possessing the qualifications of an elector set out in Article 8 of the Constitution of Alabama, as modified by federal law, and not laboring under any disqualification listed therein, shall be an elector, and shall be entitled to register and to vote at any election by the people. (Code 1876, § 224; Code 1886, § 319; Code 1896, § 1556; Code 1907, § 290; Acts 1920, No. 5, p. 4; Code 1923, § 361; Code 1940, T. 17, § 12; Acts 1953, No. 330, p. 385; Code 1975, § 17-3-1; Acts 1978, No. 584, p. 667, § 1.)

Code Commissioner's note. — Acts 1978, No. 584, p. 667, repealed §§ 17-3-1 through 17-3-8 and enacted §§ 17-3-9 through 17-3-13 in place thereof. Historical citations from the repealed sections have been placed following the corresponding sections in the 1978 enactment.

Construction. — The rule that mandatory provisions of election law are generally to be construed as only directory, in proceedings attacking the election after it is held, is applicable to provisions relating to the duties and acts of election officials, but not to the qualifications of electors. Ex parte Bullen, 236 Ala. 56, 181 So. 498 (1938) (decided under former § 17-3-1).

Federal protection. — Although the particular qualifications one must possess in order to exercise the right to vote are left to the states — as long as that exercise is within the constitutional framework — the power to protect citizens who are qualified to vote, but not allowed to vote solely because of their color, is confided in the United States government. United States v. Penton, 212 F. Supp. 193 (M.D. Ala. 1962) (decided under former § 17-3-1).

Good moral character. — If the applicant has not been convicted of a felony, a crime involving moral turpitude or a disqualifying crime as defined by the Alabama Constitution, and if he is neither a dope addict nor a habitual drunkard, he shall be deemed to be of good moral character. United States v. Penton, 212 F. Supp. 193 (M.D. Ala. 1962) (decided under former § 17-3-1).

Domicile of the elector is a mixed question of law and fact, dependent upon the intention and acts of the elector. Gray v. Main, 309 F. Supp. 207 (M.D. Ala. 1968) (decided under former § 17-3-1).

Physical presence is by no means an absolute prerequisite in determining a person's residence or domicile for the purposes of voting; the Alabama supreme court has also observed that voting is indicative of intention in determining domicile. Gray v. Main, 309 F. Supp. 207 (M.D. Ala. 1968) (decided under former § 17-3-1).

Domicile of married women. — When a woman marries and enters into the family relation at the domicile of the husband, this domicile becomes the domicile of the wife. Wilkerson v. Lee, 236 Ala. 104, 181 So. 296 (1938) (decided under former § 17-3-1).

If the husband, at the time of marriage, has merely a temporary abode in the county where they live, being a resident and qualified voter of another county, and husband and wife establish no family residence facto et animo prior to the date of the election, the wife would still be a legal voter in her home town. Wilkerson v. Lee, 236 Ala. 104, 181 So. 296 (1938) (decided under former § 17-3-1).

The term "issues" as contained in section 17-4-124 refers to those factual issues involving qualifications, as defined in this section such as residence, age, and conviction of crime. It would appear that the legislature intended that, on appeal, the fact finder, whether the judge or jury, would decide only factual issues. State v. Taylor, 415 So. 2d 1043 (Ala. 1982).

No rejection for technical errors in filling out application. — An applicant may not be rejected or denied for technical or inconsequential errors or omissions made by him in filling out the application. United States v. Penton, 212 F. Supp. 193 (M.D. Ala. 1962) (decided under former § 17-3-1).

Failure to sign in appropriate places. — An applicant may not be rejected on the ground that he has failed to sign the oath, the supplemental oath or the spaces for the applicant's name in the supplemental application. The registrars are under a duty to have the applicant sign in the appropriate places unless he refuses to do so. United States v. Penton, 212 F. Supp. 193 (M.D. Ala. 1962) (decided under former § 17-3-1).

Local statutory provision against invalidation of city election by technicalities does not deal with qualification of electors, which is left to be controlled by this chapter. Ex parte Bullen, 236 Ala. 56, 181 So. 498 (1938) (decided under former § 17-3-1).

Burden of proof of qualifications. — See Black v. Pate, 136 Ala. 601, 34 So. 844 (1903).

Civil Rights Act violated. — Under the evidence presented it was concluded that the acts of a county board of registrars constituted violations of the Civil Rights Act of 1960. United States v. Penton, 212 F. Supp. 193 (M.D. Ala. 1962) (decided under former § 17-3-1).

As well as fourteenth and fifteenth amendments. — Under the facts presented it was concluded that the discriminatory acts and practices of a county board of registrars constituted deprivations of the rights secured by the fourteenth and fifteenth amendments to the federal Constitution of the United States. United States v. Penton, 212 F. Supp. 193 (M.D. Ala. 1962) (decided under former § 17-3-1).

Registration of negro applicants ordered. — Registration board which was held to have followed discriminatory practices was ordered to register those negro applicants who were possessed of all the qualifications and none of the disqualifications to register to vote at the time they applied for and were deprived registration. United States v. Penton, 212 F. Supp. 193 (M.D. Ala. 1962) (decided under former § 17-3-1).

Collateral references. — 29 C.J.S., Elections, §§ 14-35.

25 Am. Jur. 2d, Elections, § 52 et seq.

State voting rights of residents of military establishments. 34 ALR2d 1193.

What constitutes "conviction" within constitutional or statutory provision disfranchising one convicted of crime. 36 ALR2d 1238.

Residence or domicile of student or teacher for purpose of voting. 98 ALR2d 488, 44 ALR3d 797.

Elections: effect of conviction under federal law or law of another state or country, on right to vote or hold public office. 39 ALR3d 303.

§ 17-3-10. Restoration of right to vote upon pardon.

Any person who is disqualified by reason of conviction of any of the offenses mentioned in Article VIII of the Constitution of Alabama, except treason and impeachment, whether the conviction was had in a state or federal court, and who has been pardoned, may be restored to his citizenship with right to vote by the State Board of Pardons and Paroles when specifically expressed in the pardon. If otherwise qualified, such person shall be permitted to register or reregister as an elector upon submission of a copy of the pardon document to the board of registrars or deputy registrars of the county of his residence. (Code 1907, § 294; Acts 1920, No. 5, p. 4; Code 1923, § 365; Acts 1939, No. 275, p. 426; Code 1940, T. 17, § 16; Code 1975, § 17-3-5; Acts 1978, No. 584, p. 667, § 2.)

Cross references. — As to pardons generally, see § 15-22-20 et seq.

Legislative intent for requiring notice, by certified mail, of the board's intention to strike a person's name from the registration list is two-fold: (1) to provide an elector with a reasonable opportunity to prevent his disfranchisement by offering proof that he had not been convicted of the disqualifying offense, and (2) to apprise an elector of the fact of his disqualification, thus providing him an incentive to seek the restoration of his right to vote. Williams v. Lide, 628 So. 2d 531 (Ala. 1993).

State board of pardons and paroles had authority to restore citizenship and political rights of one convicted in federal court of a felony, as against contention that a pardon by President of United States was essential to restore the lost rights. Hogan v. Hartwell, 242 Ala. 646, 7 So. 2d 889 (1942).

And form of pardon order immaterial. — Fact that pardon order issued by state board of pardons and paroles purporting to restore citizenship and political rights of one convicted in federal court was in form of a certificate would not render pardon order ineffective. Hogan v. Hartwell, 242 Ala. 646, 7 So. 2d 889 (1942).

Reregistration unnecessary. — One who was a registered elector prior to his conviction in federal court of a felony, and who thereafter secured a pardon order from the state board of pardons and paroles restoring his citizenship and political rights, was not required to reregister as a voter to be eligible to hold a public office since the board of registrars had not stricken his name from the registration list. Hogan v. Hartwell, 242 Ala. 646, 7 So. 2d 889 (1942).

"Prima facie" case for contestant. — Evidence that contestee, who was elected city commissioner, had been convicted in federal court of a felony, and, punishment imposed of a fine of $250 and imprisonment in penitentiary for one year and a day, and that fine was duly paid and sentence suspended, standing alone, would establish a "prima facie case" in favor of contestant, in election contest, on ground of contestee's ineligibility to hold the office. Hogan v. Hartwell, 242 Ala. 646, 7 So. 2d 889 (1942).

Collateral references. — 29 C.J.S., Elections, § 33.

Offenses and convictions covered by pardon. 35 ALR2d 1261.

§ 17-3-11. Residence not acquired or lost by temporary absence.

No person shall lose or acquire a residence either by temporary absence from his or her place of residence without the intention of remaining or by navigating any of the waters of this state, the United States or the high seas, without having acquired any other lawful residence, or by being absent from his place of residence in the civil or military service of the state or the United States. (Code 1876, § 226; Code 1886, § 321; Code 1896, § 1558; Code 1907, § 295; Acts 1920, No. 5, p. 4; Code 1940, T. 17, § 17; Code 1975, § 17-3-6; Acts 1978, No. 584, p. 667, § 3.)

This section is but a recognition of established principles concerning domicile. Ex parte Phillips, 275 Ala. 80, 152 So. 2d 144 (1963); Gray v. Main, 309 F. Supp. 207 (M.D. Ala. 1968); State ex rel. Rabren v. Baxter, 46 Ala. App. 134, 239 So. 2d 206 (1970).

Domicile defined. — Domicile is that place where a man has his true, fixed and permanent home and principal establishment, and to which whenever he is absent he has the intention of returning. State ex rel. Rabren v. Baxter, 46 Ala. App. 134, 239 So. 2d 206 (1970).

Requirements for acquiring domicile. — In order to acquire a domicile of choice there must be both an abandonment of the former domicile with no present intention of return, and the establishment of another place of residence with the intention to remain permanently, or at least for an unlimited time; and the intent to remain permanently may be inferred from the intent to remain for an unlimited time. State ex rel. Rabren v. Baxter, 46 Ala.

App. 134, 239 So. 2d 206 (1970).

In order to displace the former original domicile by the acquisition of one of choice, actual residence and intent to remain at the new one must concur. State ex rel. Rabren v. Baxter, 46 Ala. App. 134, 239 So. 2d 206 (1970).

A voter who has acquired a legal residence, been duly registered as a voter of the county and precinct or ward and paid his poll tax therein for the year in which the election is held may retain such residence until he has abandoned and removed therefrom with the intent to become a resident elsewhere. Wilkerson v. Lee, 236 Ala. 104, 181 So. 296 (1938).

Temporary absence does not forfeit right to vote. — Temporary absence from one's residence for the purposes of his employment and the like, without the intent to abandon the home town and acquire a domicile elsewhere permanently, or for an indefinite time, does not forfeit his right to vote. Wilkerson v. Lee, 236 Ala. 104, 181 So. 296 (1938). See also State v.

Hallett, 8 Ala. 159 (1845); Boyd v. Beck, 29 Ala. 703 (1857); Griffin v. Wall, 32 Ala. 149 (1858).

Assignment of reserve officer to foreign country. — A second lieutenant in the reserve corps on inactive duty was ordered by the Procurement and Assignment Service of the United States to report for duty as a civilian in another country. The court held that this did not amount to a forfeiture of his original domicile since the move was not of his own free will. This section is but a legislative declaration of the same principle. Ex parte Weissinger, 247 Ala. 113, 22 So. 2d 510 (1945).

Assignment of domicile by operation of law. — Since every person must have a domicile, the law assigns to persons incapable of acquiring a domicile through choice, a domicile by operation of law. This first domicile so assigned is the domicile of origin. The place of the birth of a person is considered as his domicile of origin, if at the time of his birth it is the domicile of his parents. A domicile of origin, as in the case of domicile of choice, when once established is continuing until another domicile is acquired. State ex rel. Rabren v. Baxter, 46 Ala. App. 134, 239 So. 2d 206 (1970).

A domicile once acquired continues until a new domicile is effectuated. State ex rel. Rabren v. Baxter, 46 Ala. App. 134, 239 So. 2d 206 (1970).

A domicile, once acquired, is presumed to exist until a new one has been gained "facto et animo." State ex rel. Rabren v. Baxter, 46 Ala. App. 134, 239 So. 2d 206 (1970).

Presumption favors original domicile as against acquired domicile. — Where facts are conflicting, the presumption is strongly in favor of an original, or former, domicile, as against an acquired one. State ex rel. Rabren v. Baxter, 46 Ala. App. 134, 239 So. 2d 206 (1970).

One who asserts a change of domicile has the burden of establishing it. State ex rel. Rabren v. Baxter, 46 Ala. App. 134, 239 So. 2d 206 (1970).

Collateral references. — 29 C.J.S., Elections, §§ 19-21.

25 Am. Jur. 2d, Elections, §§ 70-77.

§ 17-3-12. Selection of precinct of residence when place of residence located partly in two or more counties, districts or precincts.

When the place of residence of any person is located partly in two or more counties, districts or precincts, such persons may select the county, district or precinct of their residence, and to that end may file a statement in writing in the office of the judge of probate of the county selected, setting forth the locality of their residence and the lines passing through the same, together with the county, district or precinct selected for residence, which statement, when filed and recorded, shall establish the residence of the person filing it in the county, district or precinct of their selection. (Code 1896, § 1559; Code 1907, § 296; Acts 1920, No. 5, p. 4; Code 1923, § 367; Code 1940, T. 17, § 18; Code 1975, § 17-3-7; Acts 1978, No. 584, p. 667, § 4.)

Effect of selection of one county as residence. — This section does not apply to a person residing on the line between two counties who has prior to the passage of this act selected one county and precinct as his residence. Danforth v. Nabors, 120 Ala. 430, 24 So. 891 (1898).

Where a person resides in different counties in different seasons of the year, he will be a legal voter in that county which he considers his place of residence. State v. Judge, etc., 13 Ala. 805 (1848).

Section abrogates case law rules. — This section was enacted to abrogate the artificial and technical rules existing under case law. Woodall v. City of Gadsden, 278 Ala. 634, 179 So. 2d 759 (1965); Hobbie v. Vance, 292 Ala.

367, 294 So. 2d 743 (1974).

This section abrogates the strict common-law rules to the extent that a person can be considered a liner for voting purposes if the boundary line goes through any part of his dwelling house just so long as part of the house was on one side and part on the other, regardless of the size of either part. Hobbie v. Vance, 292 Ala. 367, 294 So. 2d 743 (1974).

Applies wherever political line divides residence. — The legislature did not intend to provide a remedy only when the home of the person was situated on a county or precinct line, but rather it was intended to apply in any case where a political line is so drawn that the residence is situated partly on one side and partly on another. Woodall v. City of Gadsden,

278 Ala. 634, 179 So. 2d 759 (1965); Hobbie v. Vance, 292 Ala. 367, 294 So. 2d 743 (1974).

When person is not a liner. — If the line in question does not pass through the dwelling house so that part of the house lies partly in one county, precinct or district and the other part lies in a different county, precinct or district, then the person living in that house is not a liner and is a citizen and elector of the county, precinct or district in which the dwelling house is situated. Hobbie v. Vance, 292 Ala. 367, 294 So. 2d 743 (1974).

§ 17-3-13. Liners between counties, districts and precincts.

Any person who may be declared to be a liner between counties, districts or precincts, and shall have fixed his or her citizenship according to law and that may be hereafter provided in such cases, shall be construed a citizen and elector of the county, district or precinct in which he or she so fixes his or her citizenship, for all the purposes of this title. (Code 1907, § 297; Acts 1920, No. 5, p. 4; Code 1923, § 368; Code 1940, T. 17, § 19; Code 1975, § 17-3-8; Acts 1978, No. 584, p. 667, § 5.)

When person is not a liner. — If the line in question does not pass through the dwelling house so that part of the house lies partly in one county, precinct or district and the other part lies in a different county, precinct or district, then the person living in that house is not a liner and is a citizen and elector of the county, precinct or district in which the dwelling house is situated. Hobbie v. Vance, 292 Ala. 367, 294 So. 2d 743 (1974).

Cited in Perloff v. Edington, 293 Ala. 277, 302 So. 2d 92 (1974).

Collateral references. — 29 C.J.S., Elections, §§ 53, 54.

CHAPTER 4.

REGISTRATION.

Collateral references. — 25 Am. Jur. 2d, Elections, § 95 et seq.

ARTICLE 1.

GENERAL PROVISIONS.

§§ 17-4-1 through 17-4-24. Repealed by Acts 1978, No. 584, p. 667, § 34, effective April 27, 1978.

Code Commissioner's note. — Acts 1977, No. 607, p. 812, § 9901, as amended, (Criminal Code) effective January 1, 1980, also repealed §§ 17-4-9, 17-4-16 and 17-4-21.

Cross references. — For present provisions as to registration generally, see § 17-4-120 et seq.

§§ 17-4-25, 17-4-26. Renumbered.

Code Commissioner's note. — Sections 17-4-25 and 17-4-26, as set out in the original 1975 Code, have been transferred and renumbered as §§ 17-4-138 and 17-4-139, respectively.

ARTICLE 2.

BOARDS OF REGISTRARS.

§§ 17-4-40 through 17-4-47. Repealed by Acts 1978, No. 584, p. 667, § 34, effective April 27, 1978.

Cross references. — For present provisions as to boards of registrars, see § 17-4-150 et seq.

§ 17-4-48. Expenditure of county funds for office space, etc., for board of registrars; employment and compensation of clerks. Repealed by Acts 1978, No. 584, p. 667, § 35, effective April 27, 1978.

Cross references. — For present provisions as to expenditure of county funds for office space, etc., for boards of registrars, see § 17-4-159.

§ 17-4-49. Transferred.

Code Commissioner's note. — Section 17-4-49, has been transferred and renumbered as § 17-4-160.

ARTICLE 3.

PURGING OF REGISTRATION LISTS.

§§ 17-4-60 through 17-4-67. Repealed by Acts 1978, No. 584, p. 667, § 34, effective April 27, 1978.

Cross references. — For present provisions as to purging of registration lists, see §§ 17-4-132, 17-4-133, and 17-4-180, et seq.

ARTICLE 4.

REGISTRATION OF ABSENTEE ELECTORS.

Division 1.

General provisions.

§§ 17-4-80 through 17-4-83. Repealed by Acts 1978, No. 584, p. 667, § 35, effective April 27, 1978.

Cross references. — For present provisions as to registration of absentee electors, see § 17-4-134.

Division 2.

Electors attending institutions of higher learning.

§§ 17-4-100 through 17-4-103. Repealed by Acts 1978, No. 584, p. 667, § 35, effective April 27, 1978.

Cross references. — For present provisions as to registration of absentee electors, see § 17-4-134.

ARTICLE 5.

GENERAL PROVISIONS.

Code Commissioner's note. — Acts 1978, No. 584, p. 667, repealed §§ 17-4-1 through 17-4-24 and enacted §§ 17-4-120 through 17-4-137 in place thereof. Historical citations from the repealed sections have been placed following the corresponding sections in this article.

§ 17-4-120. Registration deadline.

(a) The boards of registrars in the several counties of the state or their deputies shall not register any person as a qualified elector within 10 days prior to any election; provided, that the boards shall maintain open offices during business days in such 10-day period and on election day during the hours of voting.

(b) The provisions of this section shall not apply in any county having a population of not less than 600,000 inhabitants according to the 1970 or any succeeding federal decennial census, and any currently effective local law or general law of local application providing for a deadline on registration in such county shall remain in full force and effect and shall not be repealed by operation of this section. (Acts 1950, 4th Ex. Sess., No. 6, p. 45; Code 1975, § 17-4-4; Acts 1978, No. 584, p. 667, § 14.)

Cited in Gray v. Main, 309 F. Supp. 207 (M.D. Ala. 1968).

Collateral references. — 29 C.J.S., Elections, § 39.

§ 17-4-121. Certificate of registration.

The registrars shall issue to each person registered a certificate of registration. (Code 1896, § 1565; Code 1907, §§ 307, 321; Acts 1920, No. 78, p. 124; Code 1923, §§ 378, 390; Acts 1939, No. 112, p. 144; Code 1940, T. 17, §§ 29, 42; Code 1975, § 17-4-23; Acts 1978, No. 584, p. 667, § 15.)

Collateral references. — 29 C.J.S., Elections, §§ 38, 46, 50.

§ 17-4-122. Examination and oath of applicants to register; applications not public records; political parties may obtain voter registration information.

The board of registrars shall have power to examine, under oath or affirmation, all applicants for registration, and to take testimony touching the qualifications of such applicants, but no applicant shall be required to answer any question, written or oral, not related to his qualifications to register. In order to aid the registrars to judicially determine if applicants to register have the qualifications to register to vote, each applicant shall be furnished by the board a written application, which shall be uniform in all cases with no discrimination as between applicants, the form and contents of which application shall be prescribed by the Supreme Court of Alabama and be filed by such court with the Secretary of State of the State of Alabama. The application shall be so worded that there will be placed before the registrars information necessary or proper to aid them to pass upon the qualifications of each applicant. The application shall be completed in writing, in the presence of the board or of a deputy registrar. There shall be incorporated in such application an oath to support and defend the Constitution of the United States and the Constitution of the State of Alabama and a statement in such oath by the applicant disavowing belief in or affiliation with any group or party which advocates the overthrow of the government of the United States or the State of Alabama by unlawful means. The application and oath shall be duly signed and sworn to by the applicant before a member or deputy of the board. If the applicant is unable to read or write, then he shall be exempt from the above stated requirements which he is unable to meet and in such cases a member or deputy of the board shall read to the applicant the application and oath herein provided for and the applicant's answers thereto shall be written down by such board member or deputy, and the applicant shall be registered as a voter if he meets all other requirements herein set out. Each member or deputy of the board is authorized to administer the oaths to be taken by applicants and witnesses. The applications of persons applying for registration shall not become public records as public records are defined under the laws of the State of Alabama, nor shall the board or its deputies disclose the information contained in such applications and written answers, except with the written consent of the person who filed the answer or pursuant to the order of a court of competent jurisdiction in a proper proceeding. Provided, however, that political parties as defined in Section 17-16-2, shall be authorized to obtain all voter registration information in the possession of boards of registrars or probate judges concerning registered voters in their jurisdictions. The boards of registrars or probate judges may collect the actual cost, if any, of providing said information. Provided, however, that nothing herein shall prohibit acts pertaining to individual counties which further provide for the availability of such voter information. (Code 1907, § 311; Acts 1920, No. 78, p. 124; Code 1923, § 380; Code 1940, T. 17, § 31; Acts 1953, No. 754, p. 1016, § 1; Acts 1959, 1st Ex. Sess., No. 54, p. 98; Acts 1961, Ex. Sess., No. 320, p. 2380, §§ 9, 10; Acts 1965, 1st Ex. Sess., No. 288, p. 396, § 1; Code 1975, § 17-4-7; Acts 1978, No. 584, p. 667, § 17; Acts 1985, 2nd Ex. Sess., No. 85-929, p. 228.)

Code Commissioner's note. — By order dated February 11, 1991, the Alabama Su-preme Court approved the Alabama voter registration form set out below:

Alabama Voter Registration Application

COUNTY: _____

Cnty ___ City ___
Prct ___ Prct ___ In ___ Out ___

COMPUTER REGISTRATION NO _____

NAME OF APPLICANT (PLEASE PRINT)   **DATE OF APPLICATION**

LAST   FIRST   MIDDLE OR MAIDEN   MONTH   DAY   YEAR

RESIDENCE ADDRESS _____   **GIVE LOCATION**

House or Apt No & Street Id Rural Route & Box No   CITY OR TOWN   STATE   ZIP

Mailing Address if Different   DAYTIME PHONE

APPLICANT'S PLACE OF BIRTH   **DATE OF BIRTH**

CITY OR TOWN   COUNTY   STATE   FOREIGN COUNTRY   AGE   MONTH   DAY   YEAR

SOCIAL SECURITY NO. SEX (Circle One)   **RACE** (Circle One)

MALE FEMALE WHITE BLACK ASIAN AM INDIAN HISPANIC OTHER

PLACE OF LAST REGISTRATION   If Naturalized Citizen,
                                        Give Date and Number
ADDRESS   CITY   COUNTY   STATE

Have You Ever Been Convicted of   YES   NO
any Felony? If Yes and If Pardoned,   Are You Currently Under a Judgment of
Give Date and Number _____   Mental Incompetence? (Circle One)   YES   NO

DATE APPROVED _____   I SOLEMNLY SWEAR OR AFFIRM TO SUPPORT
                                         AND DEFEND THE CONSTITUTIONS OF THE
                                         UNITED STATES AND THE STATE OF ALABAMA
_____   AND FURTHER DISAVOW ANY BELIEF OR AFFILI-
                                         ATION WITH ANY GROUP WHICH ADVOCATES
Board Member or Deputy Registering   THE OVERTHROW OF THE GOVERNMENTS OF
                                         THE UNITED STATES OR THE STATE OF ALA-
_____   BAMA BY UNLAWFUL MEANS AND THAT THE
                                         INFORMATION CONTAINED HEREIN IS TRUE. SO
Board Member   HELP ME GOD.

_____

Board Member

Form VR0001 1/16/90   _____
                                         SIGNATURE OF APPLICANT

21

Cited in Williams v. Wright, 249 Ala. 9, 29 So. 2d 295 (1947).

Collateral references. — 29 C.J.S., Elections, § 43.

§ 17-4-123. Refusal of registration — Authorized; notice required.

Any person making application to the board of registrars for registration who fails to establish by evidence to the reasonable satisfaction of the board of registrars that he or she is qualified to register, may be refused registration. The board shall give written notice to each applicant deemed unqualified, within 10 days of its refusal to register him, stating the specific reason for such refusal. (Code 1907, § 313; Acts 1920, No. 78, p. 124; Code 1923, § 382; Code 1940, T. 17, § 33; Code 1975, § 17-4-10; Acts 1978, No. 584, p. 667, § 18.)

Notice. — In an action alleging discriminatory registration practices on the part of a county registration board, a federal court ordered that an applicant whose application is rejected or denied must be notified of that fact within 10 days from the date of his application. The notice must contain the specific reasons for the rejection or denial. United States v. Penton, 212 F. Supp. 193 (M.D. Ala. 1962).

Failure and refusal by a registration board to notify rejected applicants or the arbitrary rejection of negro applicants on technical, insubstantial and inconsequential grounds constitute a denial of due process of law and an abridgment of privileges and immunities of citizens under the Constitution of the United States. United States v. Penton, 212 F. Supp. 193 (M.D. Ala. 1962).

The limitation of reasonableness contained in this section goes far to bring a proper use of the written questionnaire furnished each applicant for registration into compliance with the federal Constitution. United States v. Atkins, 323 F.2d 733 (5th Cir. 1963).

Collateral references. — 29 C.J.S., Elections, § 43.

§ 17-4-124. Refusal of registration — Appeal.

Any person to whom registration is denied shall have the right of appeal, without giving security for costs, within 30 days after such denial, by filing a petition in the circuit court in the county in which he or she seeks to register, alleging that he or she is a citizen of the United States over the age of 18 years having the qualifications as to residence prescribed by law and entitled to register to vote under the provisions of the Constitution of Alabama, as amended. Upon the filing of the petition, the clerk of the court shall give notice thereof to the district attorney authorized to represent the state in said county, who shall appear and defend against the petition on behalf of the state. The issues shall be tried in the same manner and under the same rules that other cases are tried in such court and by a jury, if the petitioner demands it. The registrars shall not be made parties and shall not be liable for costs. An appeal will lie to the Supreme Court in favor of the petitioner if taken within 42 days from the date of the judgment. Final judgment in favor of the petitioner shall entitle him or her to registration as of the date of his or her application to the registrars. (Code 1907, § 315; Acts 1920, No. 78, p. 124; Code 1923, § 384; Code 1940, T. 17, § 35; Acts 1953, No. 754, p. 1016, § 3; Code 1975, § 17-4-11; Acts 1978, No. 584, p. 667, § 19.)

This section applies only when an applicant has been denied registration because the applicant was found to be unqualified. State v. Taylor, 415 So. 2d 1043 (Ala. 1982).

The remedy provided by this section is not purely of an administrative nature; it is of a type of proceeding traditionally considered judicial. Mitchell v. Wright, 154 F.2d 924

(5th Cir.), cert. denied, 329 U.S. 733, 67 S. Ct. 96, 91 L. Ed. 633 (1946), rev'g 62 F. Supp. 580 (M.D. Ala. 1945), and holding that jurisdiction of federal court was not ousted because appellant, who was denied registration, had failed to exhaust his administrative remedy in the state courts of Alabama.

Right determined by status at time of application. — Under this section the right of one to be registered is determined by the status of an applicant at the time of the application for registration. Hawkins v. Vines, 249 Ala. 165, 30 So. 2d 451 (1947).

State has no right of appeal to supreme court where judgment was in favor of plaintiff. State v. Crenshaw, 138 Ala. 506, 35 So. 456 (1903).

Burden on applicant. — The pleader, in stating his case on appeal, has the burden of showing that the board, in whom was vested the discretion of determining an applicant's qualifications, had erroneously refused him

registration. Hawkins v. Vines, 249 Ala. 165, 30 So. 2d 451 (1947).

The term "issues" as contained in this section refers to those factual issues involving qualifications, as defined in section 17-3-9, such as residence, age, and conviction of crime. It would appear that the legislature intended that, on appeal, the fact finder, whether the judge or jury, would decide only factual issues. State v. Taylor, 415 So. 2d 1043 (Ala. 1982).

Time for appeal. — An appeal from an order of board of registrars denying registration as an elector taken on December 31 when application, if denied at all, must have been denied on or prior to October 16, was too late under statute requiring appeal to be taken within 30 days. Madison v. Nunnelee, 246 Ala. 325, 20 So. 2d 589 (1945).

Collateral references. — 29 C.J.S., Elections, § 46.

25 Am. Jur. 2d, Elections, § 104.

§ 17-4-125. Registration required only once; exceptions.

No person heretofore registered and no person hereafter registered shall again be required to register unless he or she has changed the county of his or her residence, or was convicted of a disqualifying criminal offense and was subsequently pardoned with restoration of the right to vote expressed in the pardon, or was declared non compus mentis (incompetent), but has subsequently had those disabilities removed, or was stricken from the registered voter list for failure to vote at least once in four years. (Code 1907, § 316; Acts 1920, No. 78, p. 124; Code 1923, § 385; Code 1940, T. 17, § 36; Code 1975, § 17-4-12; Acts 1978, No. 584, p. 667, § 21.)

Change of residence. — Under this section a registered voter, who changes his legal residence from one county to another must register in the county of his new residence in order to be entitled to vote therein. Shepherd v. Sartain, 185 Ala. 439, 64 So. 57 (1913).

But a voter registered in a county is not required to register on changing his residence to another precinct of the same county. Sellers v. Commissioners' Court, 165 Ala. 338, 51 So. 795 (1910).

§ 17-4-126. Forms and notices.

The Department of Finance shall, at the expense of the state, have prepared and furnished to the Secretary of State and by him to be furnished to the boards of registrars in the several counties a sufficient number of forms and notices necessary to carry out their lawful functions.

The cost of the publication of the notices required to be given by the registrars shall be paid by the state. The bills therefor shall be rendered to the Director of Finance and approved by him. (Code 1896, § 1568; Code 1907, § 317; Acts 1920, No. 78, p. 124; Code 1923, § 386; Code 1940, T. 17, § 37; Code 1975, § 17-4-13; Acts 1978, No. 584, p. 667, § 22.)

Cross references. — See also § 17-4-137.
Collateral references. — 25 Am. Jur. 2d,
Elections, § 109.

§ 17-4-127. Voting in precinct, etc., where elector's name does not appear on official list.

It shall be unlawful for any elector to cast his or her ballot during any general election, primary election, municipal election or special election in any precinct, any district, any ward or any other subdivision where his or her name does not duly appear upon the official list of such precinct, district, ward or subdivision. All ballots cast in any election contrary to the provisions of this section are hereby declared illegal and, upon a contest duly instituted, such ballots shall be excluded in determining the final result of any election; provided, that nothing in this section shall prevent any qualified elector residing in said precinct, ward or voting district from voting after presenting a proper certificate from the board of registrars, or from voting a challenge ballot with the proper officials of said box or voting place. (Acts 1947, No. 482, p. 331, § 2; Code 1975, § 17-4-18; Acts 1978, No. 584, p. 667, § 23.)

Casting of challenge ballots without making oath cured by electors' testimony at trial. — Whatever defects existed as a result of the voters' casting challenge ballots without first making the required oath were cured by the electors' sworn testimony at trial as to their qualifications. The obvious purpose of the challenge procedure is to provide a mechanism to prevent those who are not qualified from voting. Surely that end was more fully served by the challenged electors when in open court they gave sworn testimony as to their eligibility to vote and were subject to cross-examination than it would have been by their making to the prescribed oath. Hawkins v. Persons, 484 So. 2d 1072 (Ala. 1986).

Cited in Williams v. Lide, 628 So. 2d 531 (Ala. 1993); United States v. Jones, 846 F. Supp. 955 (S.D. Ala. 1994).

§ 17-4-128. Voters in territory transferred to another county.

Every qualified elector of the State of Alabama who resides in territory which has been detached from one county and added to an adjoining county of the State of Alabama shall be entitled to have his name added to the list of the qualified electors of said county to which the territory wherein he resides has been added. (Acts 1932, Ex. Sess., No. 172, p. 199; Code 1940, T. 17, § 39; Code 1975, § 17-4-19; Acts 1978, No. 584, p. 667, § 24.)

§ 17-4-129. Lists of registered voters to be published.

The judge of probate shall publish a correct alphabetical list of qualified electors by precinct, district or subdivision wherein each elector is registered to vote, in some newspaper with general circulation in the county, on or before the twentieth day preceding the regularly scheduled primary election. Such list shall be accompanied by a certificate that said lists contain the names of all qualified electors registered as of the date shown on the list certified by the board of registrars. Such list shall further state that any elector whose name was inadvertently omitted from the list shall have 10 days in which to have his or her name entered upon the lists of qualified voters. If within 10 days any voter shall reasonably satisfy the board of registrars by proper proof that any name should be added to the list, the board shall add such name to the list. The supplemental list of registered voters inadvertently omitted from the original list shall be published once in a newspaper of general circulation in the county on or before the seventh day preceding the date of the primary election. Only in 1978, in any county which has duly published a list of qualified voters prior to August 4, 1978, the probate judge shall prepare and publish in some newspaper with a general circulation in said county, an alphabetical listing, as hereinabove required, only on or before the seventh day preceding the date of the primary election. In 1978, in any such county, this list, together with the list published prior to August 4, 1978, shall be the official list of voters qualified in each of the precincts, districts, wards or other subdivisions within such county. (Acts 1920, No. 78, p. 124; Code 1923, § 387; Acts 1927, No. 289, p. 274; Code 1940, T. 17, § 38; Acts 1947, No. 482, p. 331, § 1; Code 1975, § 17-4-14; Acts 1978, No. 380, p. 343; Acts 1978, No. 584, p. 667, § 25; Acts 1978, 2nd Ex. Sess., No. 5, p. 1601.)

Code Commissioner's note. — Acts 1978, No. 380, p. 343, which amended former § 17-4-14 prior to its repeal by Acts 1978, No. 584, p. 667, provided as follows:

"Only in 1978, in any county which has published a list of qualified voters prior to April 6, 1978, the probate judge shall prepare and publish in some newspaper with a general circulation in said county, an alphabetical listing as hereinabove [former § 17-4-14] required, only on or before the seventh day preceding the date of the primary election. In 1978, in such county, this list, together with the list published prior to April 6, 1978, shall be the official list of voters qualified in each of the precincts, districts, wards or other subdivisions within such county."

Error in placing name on list as qualified elector is subject to correction in list made subsequently thereto, and failure to correct is subject to review by mandamus. Malone v. Jones, 219 Ala. 236, 122 So. 26 (1929).

But elector cannot require probate judge by mandamus to enter his name on list of qualified electors without having first offered proper proof of eligibility in accordance with requirement of this section. Malone v. Jones, 219 Ala. 236, 122 So. 26 (1929).

Cited in United States v. Jones, 846 F. Supp. 955 (S.D. Ala. 1994).

Collateral references. — 29 C.J.S., Elections, §§ 47-50.

§ 17-4-130. Poll lists.

The board of registrars shall, when registration is closed before a primary, general, or special election, certify to the judge of probate any additions, deletions, corrections or changes from the list previously prepared and submitted to the judge. From these lists the judge shall prepare correct alphabetical lists of the qualified electors registered by precincts, by districts or by subdivisions thereof where the precinct has been divided or subdivided, if not within a city or incorporated town, and by wards and other subdivisions, if within a city or incorporated town, and no others, which lists shall be certified by the board thereof officially to be full and correct copies of the lists of registered electors for each of said political subdivisions, as the same appears from the records of the board, and shall deliver the same to the judge of probate for distribution to the officers of election. The judge of probate shall deliver or cause to be delivered to the inspectors in each precinct, each district, each ward or each other subdivision one copy of the list prepared for such box or voting place immediately preceding every general, primary or special election, and the delivered list shall contain only the names of persons qualified to vote at such box or voting place; except, that for purposes of information only, there may be delivered to such inspectors lists prepared for other boxes or voting places. The list published in the newspaper before each primary election shall not be used as the poll list.

The judge of probate shall certify a copy of each such poll list to the Secretary of State and shall provide a copy to the board of registrars. Both the board of registrars and the judge of probate shall keep a current copy of such lists open and subject to public inspection. (Code 1896, § 1567; Code 1907, § 319; Acts 1920, No. 78, p. 124; Code 1923, § 388; Code 1940, T. 17, § 40; Acts 1947, No. 482, p. 331, § 3; Code 1975, § 17-4-15; Acts 1978, No. 584, p. 667, § 26.)

Declaratory relief was properly denied to newspaper which had requested public inspection of precinct registration lists stored in locked voting machines, where it was conceded that the lists sought were in fact "lists of the persons voting" within the meaning of § 17-7-17, which proscribes the unlawful use of poll lists. Advertiser Co. v. Hobbie, 474 So. 2d 93 (Ala. 1985).

Cited in United States v. Jones, 846 F. Supp. 955 (S.D. Ala. 1994).

Collateral references. — 29 C.J.S., Elections, §§ 47-50.

§ 17-4-131. Information of deaths, incompetency and convictions to be furnished to boards of registrars.

In addition to all other duties now required by law, the several registrars of vital statistics for each of the several registration districts of this state shall furnish to the board of registrars of the county in which such district is located, once each month, a report of the death of all persons over 18 years of age who resided in such registration district.

In addition to all other duties now required by law, the judges of probate of the several counties of this state shall furnish to the board of registrars of their respective counties, once each month, a list of all residents of the county, 18 years of age or over, who have been declared mentally incompetent.

In addition to all other duties required by law, the clerks of the circuit and district courts of this state shall furnish to the board of registrars of each county, once each month, a list of all residents of that county who have been convicted of any offense mentioned in Section 182 of the Constitution of 1901. Any person who willfully fails to perform such duties shall forfeit the sum of $100.00 for each such failure. Such sum may be recovered in an action by law by any citizen of the county in which the officer acts, one half to his own use and one half to the use of the state. (Acts 1935, No. 434, p. 914; Code 1940, T. 17, § 45; Code 1975, § 17-4-61; Acts 1978, No. 584, p. 667, § 27.)

§ 17-4-132. Purgation of registration lists; transfer of names to precinct to which elector has moved; failure to perform duties.

The board of registrars shall purge the registration list whenever it receives and confirms information that a person registered to vote in that county has died, become a nonresident of the state or county, been declared mentally incompetent, been convicted of any offense mentioned in Section 182 of the Constitution since being registered or otherwise become disqualified as an elector. A person convicted of a disqualifying offense must be notified by certified mail of the board's intention to strike his name from the list. No person convicted of a disqualifying crime may be stricken from the poll list while an appeal from the conviction is pending. Notice of the names of all other persons proposed to be stricken from the list shall be published in some newspaper published in the county.

On the date set in the notice, or at a later date to which the case may have been continued by the board, the board shall proceed to consider the case of such elector whose name it proposes to strike from the registration list and determine the same. Any person whose name is stricken from the list may appeal from the decision of the board, without giving security for costs, and a trial by jury may be had; and the board shall forthwith certify the proceedings to the circuit clerk, who shall docket the case in the circuit court.

When the board has sufficient evidence furnished it that any elector has permanently moved from one precinct to another within the county, it shall transfer the name of such elector to the registration list of the precinct to which such elector has moved, and shall give notice by mail to such elector if the elector has not requested the change of registration.

Any member or deputy of the board of registrars who neglects or willfully refuses to perform the duties herein required of him shall be guilty of a misdemeanor and on conviction shall be punished by a fine of not more than $500.00 and may also be imprisoned in the county jail, or sentenced to hard labor for the county, for not more than six months. (Code 1907, §§ 323, 326; Acts 1920, No. 78, p. 124; Code 1923, §§ 392, 395; Acts 1927, No. 289, p. 274; Acts 1935, No. 460, p. 989; Code 1940, T. 17, §§ 44, 48; Code 1975, §§ 17-4-60, 17-4-63; Acts 1978, No. 584, p. 667, § 28.)

Cross references. — As to boards of registrars of municipalities and counties conducting an identification program of electors eligible to vote in municipal elections, see § 11-46-4. As to purging the lists of registered voters, see art. 7, ch. 4, T. 17.

The last sentence of this section amounts to nothing more than a directive. No penalty is directly or by reference to other code sections tied in with it. Mitchell v. State, 32 Ala. App. 467, 27 So. 2d 30 (1945), modified, 248 Ala. 169, 27 So. 2d 36 (1946).

As to prosecution for criminal conspiracy for attempting to secure an unauthorized transfer of registered electors from one precinct to another, see Mitchell v. State, 32 Ala. App. 467, 27 So. 2d 30 (1945), modified, 248 Ala. 169, 27 So. 2d 36 (1946). See also notes to § 13-9-24.

The presence or absence of a person's name on the voter registration list does not necessarily determine the right to vote. Williams v. Lide, 628 So. 2d 531 (Ala. 1993).

Cited in Gray v. Main, 309 F. Supp. 207 (M.D. Ala. 1968).

Collateral references. — 29 C.J.S., Elections, § 48.

§ 17-4-133. Reason for striking elector's name from registration list required to be recorded.

When the name of any elector is stricken from the registration list, the records maintained by the board of registrars must show the reason for striking the elector from the list. (Code 1907, § 330; Acts 1920, No. 78, p. 124;

Code 1923, § 399; Code 1940, T. 17, § 52; Code 1975, § 17-4-67; Acts 1978, No. 584, p. 667, § 29.)

Collateral references. — 29 C.J.S., Elections, § 48.

§ 17-4-134. Electors temporarily out of the county may register.

The following persons shall be entitled to register to vote by mail if they possess the qualifications of an elector and are not disqualified from voting under the Constitution and laws of Alabama, namely, members of the armed forces of the United States, persons employed outside the United States, persons absent because of attendance at institutions of higher learning and the spouses and children of such persons; provided, that such persons shall be entitled to register by mail only in the counties where they were residents prior to entering the status which makes them eligible for such registration.

An application for absentee registration shall be in writing and shall be filed with the board of registrars of the county in which the elector resides. The board shall furnish the applicant a written application in the same form as that provided other applicants and any additional application deemed necessary to determine eligibility to register, which application shall be answered by the applicant without assistance and shall be verified before a commissioned officer of the armed forces of the United States or any person authorized to administer oaths and take affidavits. Such application shall be filed with the records of the board. The board may take other testimony respecting the applicant and the truthfulness of any information furnished by him. Any additional testimony so taken shall be reduced to writing and shall be sworn to by the witness before a member or clerk of the board or anyone authorized to administer oaths. (Acts 1969, No. 604, p. 1092, §§ 1, 2; Acts 1971, No. 2426, p. 3868, §§ 1, 2; Code 1975, §§ 17-4-80, 17-4-81, 17-4-100, 17-4-101; Acts 1978, No. 584, p. 667, § 32.)

Collateral references. — 25 Am. Jur. 2d, Elections, §§ 100, 107.

§ 17-4-135. Notice of previous registration to be given.

When a person makes application for registration before a county board of registrars, it shall be the duty of that board, if the elector has been previously registered before in any other county or state, to notify the registrar of voters in the county or state of his previous registration that such elector has applied for and been registered as an elector in the county where such application for registration is made.

When the notice required in this section is received by the board of registrars of any county where such person had been previously registered, it shall be the duty of the board of registrars receiving such notice to remove forthwith the name of such person from the list of qualified electors of the county of previous registration, and such person shall thereafter be disqualified to vote in any election held in any county of previous registration unless he shall be duly reregistered. (Acts 1949, No. 27, p. 39, §§ 1, 2; Code 1975, § 17-4-22; Acts 1978, No. 584, p. 667, § 33.)

Collateral references. — 29 C.J.S., Elections, § 52.
25 Am. Jur. 2d, Elections, § 110.

§ 17-4-136. Rules and regulations of boards of registrars.

The board of registrars may make such rules and regulations as it deems proper for the receipt of applications for registration and the accomplishing in as expedient a manner as possible the registration of those entitled to register, but no person shall be registered until a majority of the board of registrars has passed favorably upon such person's qualifications. (Acts 1920, No. 78, p. 124; Code 1923, § 400; Code 1940, T. 17, § 53; Code 1975, § 17-4-24; Acts 1978, No. 584, p. 667, § 30.)

Members of boards are state officers. — The members of the boards of registrars of the different counties of Alabama are state officers. Mitchell v. Wright, 69 F. Supp. 698 (M.D. Ala. 1947).

Rules and regulations have force and effect of law. — Under this section the rules and regulations, once established by the board of registrars, have the force and effect of law, and are to be complied with the same as if they were statutory before an applicant is registered as a qualified elector. Mitchell v. Wright, 69 F. Supp. 698 (M.D. Ala. 1947).

And one who has not complied with them is not entitled to register. — A person is not entitled to registration as an elector in Alabama who does not possess the required qualifications, possesses none of the disqualifications and has complied with the rules and regulations prescribed by the board of registrars. Mitchell v. Wright, 69 F. Supp. 698 (M.D. Ala. 1947).

But they must be applied equally. — All rules and regulations established by the board of registrars must be applied to all persons equally and without discrimination. Mitchell v. Wright, 69 F. Supp. 698 (M.D. Ala. 1947).

Where an applicant for registration as an elector in Alabama fails to comply with the legal requirements, it is not a denial of constitutional rights to deny registration because of failure to comply with prescribed requirements, if such requirements are made of all persons applying for registration, irrespective of race, color or previous condition of servitude. Mitchell v. Wright, 69 F. Supp. 698 (M.D. Ala. 1947).

Registration cannot be denied merely because of color. — The right to register as an elector in Alabama, where all the constitutional and statutory requirements are met, and where all the rules and regulations have been complied with, cannot be denied a citizen merely because he is a member of the negro race. Mitchell v. Wright, 69 F. Supp. 698 (M.D. Ala. 1947).

Rule requiring supporting affidavit of elector was reasonable. — Rule requiring that applicant for registration furnish to board, with his application, a supporting affidavit of some qualified elector residing in the county was fair, just and reasonable, and failure to comply therewith justified a denial of registration. Williams v. Wright, 249 Ala. 9, 29 So. 2d 295 (1947).

Collateral references. — 29 C.J.S., Elections, § 43.

§ 17-4-137. Secretary of State to furnish forms and supplies to boards of registrars.

The Secretary of State shall furnish to each board of registrars the necessary forms and supplies for effectuating the purposes of this chapter, and the expense incurred thereby shall be paid out of the State Treasury. The several counties shall pay all other reasonable and necessary expenses incurred by the boards in carrying out the provisions of this chapter. (Acts 1978, No. 584, p. 667, § 31.)

Cross references. — See also § 17-4-126.

§ 17-4-138. Clerical assistants and help for judge of probate and certain boards of registrars.

The judge of probate may employ such assistants and clerical help as may be necessary to complete and properly prepare the list of qualified electors which the judge of probate is required to furnish the election inspectors. The judge of probate shall receive or such assistants shall be paid out of the county treasury by warrants, drawn by the county commission on certificate of the probate judge, accompanied by the certificates of the person being paid, showing the amount is due under the provisions of this chapter, but the entire amount spent for the preparation of such lists shall not exceed a sum equal to the amount obtained by multiplying the number of names on said list by $.05 for the preparation of such list. The judge of probate in all counties having a population of not less than 100,000 nor more than 350,000, according to the last or any subsequent federal census, is hereby authorized and directed to employ a clerk to assist the board of registrars of said county. The duties of said clerk shall be to submit to the board of registrars revised election lists of said county by placing all persons in their proper ward or precincts and eliminating therefrom all deceased, nonresident and fictitious persons named upon said roll and those convicted of crime, and shall further attend to all clerical work of the board of registrars. Such clerk shall be paid a compensation out of the county treasury, of not more than $250.00 per month, to be fixed by the judge of probate.

The board of registrars shall be furnished with not less than 450 square feet of office space by the county governing body. The chairman of the board of registrars is hereby authorized to purchase all necessary office equipment and hire all necessary part time or full time clerical help to perform its prescribed duties.

At the discretion of the board of registrars, voting machines may be placed in their office. (Acts 1920, No. 78, p. 124; Code 1923, § 402; Acts 1927, No. 289, p. 274; Acts 1931, No. 251, p. 293; Code 1940, T. 17, § 55; Acts 1951, No. 385, p. 677; Acts 1959, 2nd Ex. Sess., No. 54, p. 220; Code 1975, § 17-4-25; Acts 1979, No. 79-465, p. 847; Acts 1981, No. 81-640, p. 1057.)

Code Commissioner's note. — This section was originally codified as § 17-4-25.

Present wording of this section does not distinguish between judges paid on fee system and those not paid on the fee system. Presently, all probate judges are entitled to receive compensation of five cents per name for the preparation of lists of qualified electors. A proposed amendment which would provide that only probate judges who receive compensation on the fee system and prepare lists of qualified electors shall receive five cents per name for preparation of such lists would remove this form of compensation from probate judges not compensated on the fee system. The proposed change clearly would reduce the compensation of probate judges who are not compensated on the fee system for work performed in preparation of lists of qualified electors. It, therefore, contravenes Ala. Const., amendment 328, § 6.09(d) and is unconstitutional. Opinion of Justices, 407 So. 2d 122 (Ala. 1981).

Local act as to Morgan county not repealed. — The 1979 general act, which amended § 17-4-25, renumbered as this section, did not impliedly repeal the provisions of the 1943 local act which fixed the compensation of the probate judge in Morgan county, nor did it repeal the provisions in the 1943 act making it the duty of the clerks in the probate judge's office to prepare the list of electors. Day v. Morgan County Comm'n, 487 So. 2d 856 (Ala. 1986).

Discretion in making contract employing assistants and fixing amount of compensation is left with the probate judge. Alldredge v. Bailey, 29 Ala. App. 44, 191 So. 647 (1939).

Where amount ascertained and certified by probate judge. — Where claimant was employed by judge of probate to complete and properly prepare list of qualified electors to be furnished election inspectors and claimant completed and prepared such list and presented original certificate of judge of probate accompanied by claimant's certificate, each being properly sworn to together with claim for compensation to the board of finance and control, showing amount due claimant for making the list, there was nothing left for the board of finance to do but to pay the amount ascertained and certified by the probate judge and the claimant who did the work. Alldredge v. Bailey, 29 Ala. App. 44, 191 So. 647 (1939).

§ 17-4-139. Unlawful registration.

Any person who registers for another, or who knowingly and wilfully registers or procures the registration of any person not possessing the qualifications of an elector, or who registers more than once, and any registrar who enters the name of any person on the list of registered voters without such person having made application in person under oath on a form provided for that purpose, or who knowingly registers any person more than once, or who knowingly enters a name upon the registration list as the name of a voter, without anyone of that name applying to register, shall be guilty of a felony, and, upon conviction thereof, shall be imprisoned in the penitentiary for not less than one nor more than five years. (Code 1907, § 6795; Code 1923, § 3913; Code 1940, T. 17, § 308; Code 1975, § 17-4-26.)

Code Commissioner's note. — This section was originally codified as § 17-4-26.

Cited in Mitchell v. State, 32 Ala. App. 467, 27 So. 2d 30 (1945).

Collateral references. — 29 C.J.S., Elections, § 342.

26 Am. Jur. 2d, Elections, § 375.

ARTICLE 6.

BOARDS OF REGISTRARS.

Code Commissioner's note. — Acts 1978, No. 584, p. 667, repealed article 2 of this chapter and enacted §§ 17-4-150 through 17-4-159 in place thereof. Historical citations from the repealed sections have been placed following the corresponding sections in this article.

§ 17-4-150. Qualifications and appointment of registrars; chairman.

(a) Registration shall be conducted in each county by a board of three reputable and suitable persons to be appointed, unless otherwise provided by law, by the Governor, Auditor, and Commissioner of Agriculture and Industries, or by a majority of them acting as a board of appointment, and who must be also qualified electors and residents of the county and who shall not hold an elective office during their term. One of the members shall be designated by the Board of Appointment as chair of the board of registrars for each county.

31

(b) Notwithstanding the provisions of subsection (a), the Legislature may provide by local law for the appointment of additional members to the board of registrars for a county that has two courthouses.

(c) The provisions of this section shall not apply in any county having a population of not less than 600,000 inhabitants according to the 1970 or any succeeding federal decennial census, and any currently effective local law or general law of local application providing for the appointment of any member of the board of registrars in the county shall remain in full force and effect and shall not be repealed by operation of this chapter. (Code 1896, § 1561; Code 1907, § 300; Acts 1920, No. 78, p. 124; Code 1923, § 370; Acts 1932, Ex. Sess., No. 157, p. 177; Code 1940, T. 17, § 21; Code 1975, § 17-4-40; Acts 1978, No. 584, p. 667, § 6; Acts 1992, No. 92-223, p. 551, § 1.)

List constituting official register. — Registration list made in book furnished by secretary of state under provisions of former § 17-4-13 returned to judge of probate by registrars under former § 17-4-17, and containing alphabetical list of registered voters, must be held to be official register of qualified voters at election, in view of this section. Davis v. Teague, 220 Ala. 309, 125 So. 51 (1929).

The board of registrars of Jefferson county is an independent agency of the state for a state-wide purpose rather than a county authority and its appointment of one of its members as a clerk thereof is not subject to the requirements of the civil service board having jurisdiction over employees of the county. Garner v. McCall, 235 Ala. 187, 178 So. 210 (1938).

Right of chairman to retain salary received under unconstitutional appointment. — Appointee to office of chairman of board of registrars of Jefferson county, whose right to office had been challenged in quo warranto proceedings on ground of unconstitutionality of the 1932 amendment of this section under which appointment was made, but whose right thereto had been upheld and affirmed by the supreme court, was an "officer de jure" as respects right to retain compensation received up to time his right to office was subsequently successfully challenged on different constitutional ground. Cooper v. Hawkins, 234 Ala. 636, 176 So. 329 (1937).

Collateral references. — 29 C.J.S., Elections, § 42.

§ 17-4-151. Terms of office; removal from office.

The registrars so appointed under this article may be removed at the will of the appointing board, or a majority of the members thereof, at any time, with or without cause, and without giving their reasons therefor; and if not so removed, the registrars may hold office for four years from the time of their appointment and until their successors are appointed. (Code 1907, § 301; Acts 1920, No. 78, p. 124; Code 1923, § 371; Code 1940, T. 17, § 22; Code 1975, § 17-4-41; Acts 1978, No. 584, p. 667, § 7.)

Collateral references. — 29 C.J.S., Elections, § 42.

§ 17-4-152. Filling of vacancies.

If one or more of the persons appointed on such board of registration shall refuse, neglect or be unable to qualify to serve, or if a vacancy or vacancies occur in the membership of the board of registrars, from any cause, the Governor, Auditor and Commissioner of Agriculture and Industries, or a majority of them acting as a board of appointment, shall make other appointments to fill such board. (Code 1896, § 1571; Code 1907, § 302; Acts 1920, No. 78, p. 124; Code 1923, § 372; Code 1940, T. 17, § 23; Code 1975, § 17-4-42; Acts 1978, No. 584, p. 667, § 8.)

Collateral references. — 29 C.J.S., Elections, § 42.

§ 17-4-153. Compensation and allowances for registrars; treatment as state employees; reduction of county supplement upon implementation of 1994 act barred.

(a) Each registrar shall receive a salary in the amount of $60 per day for each day's attendance upon business of the board, to be paid by the state and disbursed to the county commissions and disbursed by the county commissions to each registrar on order of a quorum of the board of registrars of the county. The State Comptroller shall issue to each county commission on a monthly basis an amount sufficient to fund these payments plus the employer share of the social security or Federal Insurance Corporation Act tax. The county commission will provide to the State Comptroller an invoice itemized to reflect payments made. If a legal holiday falls on a day the board is to be in session, and the courthouse of the county is closed for the holiday, the board of registrars shall be compensated for the holiday. Each registrar shall receive a mileage allowance equal to the amount allowed state employees or employees of the county, whichever is greater, for official travel in the course of attending the business of the board, including attending continuing education programs. Travel and other expenses shall be paid by the county commissions to the boards of registrars and the state shall reimburse the county commissions based on a written request submitted by the county commissions to the State Comptroller.

(b) The provisions of this section regarding travel mileage shall not apply in any county having a population of 600,000 or more inhabitants according to the 1970 or any succeeding federal decennial census, and any currently effective local law or general law of local application regarding travel mileage for registrars in the county shall remain in full force and effect and shall not be repealed by operation of this chapter.

(c) Members of the boards of registrars of this state are hereby declared to be state employees for the purposes of Chapter 28 of Title 36.

(d) Members of the boards of registrars of this state shall be treated as equals with other state and county employees in regard to social security protection and benefits.

(e) All payments by a county to any member of a county board of registrars (except for mileage or reimbursement for expenses) shall be treated for social security purposes equally with payments by that county to other county employees of the county.

(f) The State Office for Social Security and the State Comptroller and each county commission are directed to take all necessary action to insure that members of the boards of registrars of this state are treated as other state and

33

county employees in regard to social security protection and benefits as provided in Chapter 28 of Title 36, including, if necessary, amending the federal-state agreement referred to in Chapter 28 of Title 36, to implement the intent of the Legislature as expressed herein.

(g) No county commission may reduce the current county supplement upon the effect of this section by implementation of Acts 1994, No. 94-693. (Code 1896, § 1570; Code 1907, § 303; Acts 1920, No. 78, p. 124; Code 1923, § 373; Acts 1933, Ex. Sess., No. 8, p. 6; Code 1940, T. 17, § 24; Acts 1947, No. 531, p. 388; Acts 1951, No. 874, p. 1512; Acts 1973, No. 1206, p. 2029; Code 1975, § 17-4-43; Acts 1978, No. 584, p. 667, § 9; Acts 1982, No. 82-541, p. 892, § 1; Acts 1987, No. 87-577; Acts 1988, No. 88-659, p. 1056, § 1; Acts 1993, No. 93-640, p. 1096, § 1; Acts 1994, No. 94-693, p. 1333, § 1.)

The **1993 amendment,** effective May 13, 1993, rewrote the fifth sentence of subsection (a) which formerly read: "Each registrar shall receive $.20 per mile for official travel in the course of registration in the county"; in subsection (b), deleted "not less than" following "population of," inserted "or more," and substituted "the county" for "such county"; and substituted "the county" for "such county" in subsection (e).

The **1994 amendment,** effective May 3, 1994, in subsection (a), substituted "$60" for "$50" in the first sentence, and substituted "the holiday" for "such holiday" in the fourth sentence, added subsection (g), and made nonsubstantive changes.

For case dealing with former provisions as to compensation of registrars, see St. Clair County v. Smith, 112 Ala. 347, 20 So. 384 (1896).

Collateral references. — 29 C.J.S., Elections, § 44.

§ 17-4-154. Oath of office; registrars designated as judicial officers.

Before entering upon the performance of the duties of his office, each registrar shall take the same oath as required by the judicial officers of the state, which oath may be administered by any person authorized to administer oaths. The oath shall be in writing and subscribed by the registrar, and filed in the office of the judge of probate of the county. Said registrars are judicial officers and shall act judicially in all matters pertaining to the registration of applicants. (Code 1907, § 304; Acts 1920, No. 78, p. 124; Code 1923, § 374; Code 1940, T. 17, § 25; Code 1975, § 17-4-44; Acts 1978, No. 584, p. 667, § 10.)

Collateral references. — 29 C.J.S., Elections, § 42.

§ 17-4-155. Quorum.

The action of a majority of the board of registrars shall be the action of the board, and a majority of the board shall constitute a quorum for the transaction of all business. (Code 1907, § 314; Acts 1920, No. 78, p. 124; Code 1923, § 383; Code 1940, T. 17, § 34; Code 1975, § 17-4-45; Acts 1978, No. 584, p. 667, § 20.)

§ 17-4-156. Sessions of boards; working days of registrars; special registration sessions.

(a) Each member of the board of registrars in the Counties of Chambers, Cherokee, Clarke, Clay, Cleburne, Conecuh, Coosa, Crenshaw, Dallas,

Escambia, Geneva, Hale, Henry, Lawrence, Limestone, Lowndes, Perry, Sumter, Washington, and Wilcox may meet a maximum of 120 working days each fiscal year beginning October 1, 1984, and thereafter; each member of the board of registrars in the Counties of Barbour, Blount, Butler, Covington, Fayette, Greene, Lauderdale, Lee, Marengo, Pickens, Pike, Randolph, Talladega, and Winston may meet a maximum of 168 working days each fiscal year beginning October 1, 1984, and thereafter, except in the Counties of Lee and Pike each board of registrars may meet up to an additional 30 session days each fiscal year, at the discretion of the chairman of the county commission, beginning October 1, 1985, and thereafter and such days shall be paid from the respective county funds; each member of the board of registrars in Tallapoosa County may meet a maximum of 220 working days each fiscal year beginning October 1, 1994, and thereafter; each member of the board of registrars in the Counties of Dale, Franklin, Houston, Marion, Marshall, Bullock, Macon, St. Clair, and Tuscaloosa may meet a maximum of 216 working days each fiscal year beginning October 1, 1984, and thereafter; and each member of the boards of registrars in the Counties of DeKalb, Elmore, Jackson, Russell, and Shelby may meet a maximum of 167 working days each fiscal year beginning October 1, 1984, and thereafter.

(b) In the Counties of Choctaw, Coffee, Colbert, Cullman, and Monroe, each member of the board of registrars may meet a maximum of 199 working days each fiscal year beginning October 1, 1984, and thereafter.

(c) Each member of the board of registrars of Etowah, Autauga, and Bibb Counties may meet a maximum of 187 working days each fiscal year. Each member of the board of registrars of Walker County may meet a maximum of 180 days each fiscal year and each member of the board of registrars of Lamar County may meet a maximum of 140 days each fiscal year.

(d) Each member of the board of registrars in the Counties of Baldwin, Calhoun, Chilton, Madison, Mobile, Montgomery, and Morgan are authorized to meet not more than five days each week for the purpose of carrying out their official duties. Jefferson County, which is now operating under the provisions of local bills, shall be exempted from the provisions of this section. Provided, however, that where the words "each year" are used in the local acts the words mean "each fiscal year beginning October 1, 1984, and thereafter."

(e) The actual number of working days to be used as session days shall be determined by a quorum of the board according to the needs of the county.

(f) As many as 25 of the allotted working days may be used for special registration sessions (i.e., those sessions held away from the courthouse in the several precincts of the county or sessions held on Saturday or between the hours of 5:00 P.M. and 9:00 P.M.). Notice of any special session scheduled by the board shall be given at least 10 days prior to the special session by (1) bills posted at three or more public places in each election precinct affected, if the session involves precinct visits, and (2) advertisement once a week for two successive weeks in a newspaper published in the county or by radio or television announcements on a local station, or both by newspaper or announcement. (Acts 1978, No. 584, p. 667, § 11; Acts 1978, 2nd Ex. Sess., No. 23,

p. 1701; Acts 1984, 1st Ex. Sess., No. 84-785, p. 168; Acts 1984, 1st Ex. Sess., No. 84-800, p. 215; Acts 1985, No. 85-527, p. 635; Acts 1985, No. 85-533, p. 642; Acts 1985, No. 85-591, p. 919, § 1; Acts 1986, No. 86-495, p. 938, § 1; Acts 1988, 2nd Ex. Sess., No. 88-985, p. 711; Acts 1990, No. 90-640, p. 1195; Acts 1994, No. 94-248, p. 462, § 1; Acts 1994, No. 94-249, p. 463, § 1; Acts 1994, No. 94-530, p. 963, § 1; Acts 1994, No. 94-560, p. 1030, § 1.)

The 1994 amendments. — The first 1994 amendment, by Acts 1994, No. 94-248, § 1, effective March 22, 1994, in subsection (a), deleted "St. Clair" following "Randolph" and inserted "St. Clair" following "Macon"; in subsection (f), added "by newspaper or announcement" to the end; and made nonsubstantive changes.

The second 1994 amendment, by Acts 1994, No. 94-249, § 1, effective March 22, 1994, in subsection (a), deleted "Marion" following "Lee" and inserted "Marion" following "Marshall"; and made nonsubstantive changes.

The third 1994 amendment, by Acts 1994, No. 94-530, § 1, effective April 21, 1994, in subsection (a), deleted "Blount" and "Marengo" from the list of counties whose boards of registrars may meet a maximum of 120 working days each fiscal year, inserted "Blount" and "Marengo" into the list of counties whose boards of registrars may meet a maximum of

168 working days each fiscal year, and inserted "each member of the board of registrars in Tallapoosa County may meet a maximum of 220 working days each fiscal year beginning October 1, 1994, and thereafter"; substituted "and Bibb" for "Bibb, and Tallapoosa" in the first sentence of subsection (c); deleted "shall" preceding "mean 'each fiscal year' " in the last sentence of subsection (d); in subsection (f), deleted "which special sessions are hereby authorized" at the end of the first sentence, substituted "shall" for "must" in the second sentence, and inserted "special" and "by newspaper or announcement" in the second sentence; and made nonsubstantive changes.

The fourth 1994 amendment, by Acts 1994, No. 94-560, § 1, effective April 21, 1994, in subsection (a) deleted "Talladega" following "Sumter", and inserted "Talladega" following "Randolph"; and made nonsubstantive changes.

§ 17-4-157. Time and place of meeting in counties with two or more courthouses.

Where there are two or more courthouses in any county, the board of registrars shall divide the time equally between the courthouses for the purpose of holding regular sessions for registering voters and shall give notice accordingly. (Code 1907, § 310; Acts 1920, No. 78, p. 124; Code 1923, § 379; Code 1940, T. 17, § 30; Code 1975, § 17-4-6; Acts 1978, No. 584, p. 667, § 16.)

§ 17-4-158. Deputy registrars.

Each board may appoint deputy registrars to aid it in its performance of its lawful duties. Any person serving as a deputy registrar shall be trained by the board of registrars and shall serve without compensation. The board shall provide deputy registrars with all necessary registration forms, and when such forms are completed, the deputy registrar shall return them to the office of the board of registrars before the close of business on the next business day. (Acts 1978, No. 584, p. 667, § 13.)

Cited in Clark v. Marengo County, 469 F. Supp. 1150 (S.D. Ala. 1979); United States v. Dallas County Comm'n, 548 F. Supp. 794 (S.D. Ala. 1982); United States v. Dallas County Comm'n, 548 F. Supp. 875 (S.D. Ala. 1982); United States v. Marengo County Comm'n, 731 F.2d 1546 (11th Cir. 1984).

§ 17-4-159. Expenditure of county funds for supplies, office space, etc.; clerical personnel of boards.

All county governing bodies are authorized and directed to expend county funds for supplies, equipment, telephone service, office space and clerical help as may be necessary to carry out the purposes and provisions of this chapter. Any clerical personnel who work under the direction of the board of registrars shall be selected by the board of registrars, and the compensation shall be set by the county governing body. (Acts 1965, No. 829, p. 1557; Code 1975, § 17-4-48; Acts 1978, No. 584, p. 667, § 12.)

§ 17-4-160. Duty to visit four-year colleges and universities for purpose of registering voters.

(a) The board of registrars in each county shall visit each four-year college or university, whether public or private, having an enrollment of 500 or more, which is located therein, at least once between March 1 and April 30 of each year for the purpose of registering voters, and shall remain there for one full working day, weekends and holidays excepted. They shall give at least 12-days notice of the time and place where they will attend to register applicants for registration, by bills posted at three or more public places and by advertisement once a week for three consecutive weeks in a campus newspaper, if there is one published on the campus. Each college or university affected by the provisions of this section shall provide space and accommodations for said board of registrars on their campus.

(b) Each member of the board of registrars shall be entitled to receive their usual salary and per diem for attending the meetings of the board of registrars provided for in this section.

(c) The provisions of this section shall not be construed to repeal or supersede any provision of the general or any local law relative to meetings of registrars.

(d) This section shall not apply to Etowah County. (Acts 1977, No. 769, p. 1327, §§ 1, 2, 3, 5; Code 1975, § 17-4-49.)

Code Commissioner's note. — This section was originally codified as § 17-4-49.

Collateral references. — Validity of college or university regulation of political or voter registration activity in student housing facilities. 39 ALR4th 1137.

ARTICLE 7.

PURGING OF REGISTRATION LISTS.

Cross references. — As to purging the lists of registered voters, see § 17-4-132.

Division 1.

General Provisions.

§ 17-4-180. County board of registrars to purge disqualified electors.

The board of registrars of each county is hereby directed to purge the names of those qualified electors where there is reasonable evidence that these electors are deceased or have otherwise become disqualified from voting in the county. (Acts 1984, No. 84-389, p. 896, § 1.)

Purpose. — The legislature intended by 1984 Ala. Acts No. 389, codified as sections 17-4-180 to 17-4-191, to repeal 1965 Ala. Acts No. 36 (First Special Session), so as not to have a dual and conflicting system on the subject, and the later statute prevails as the last expression of the legislative will. Buskey v. Mobile County Bd. of Registrars, 501 So. 2d 447 (Ala. 1986).

Voter need reidentify only after his name purged. — Under 1984 Ala. Acts No. 389, a voter need reidentify only after his name has been purged because of reasonable evidence that he has become ineligible. Thus, not only did Act No. 389 drastically change the standard under which purging was to occur, but it also changed completely the voter's requirement for reidentification. Buskey v. Mobile County Bd. of Registrars, 501 So. 2d 447 (Ala. 1986).

§ 17-4-181. Board of registrars to meet in August to purge lists.

The board of registrars shall meet during the month of August for the purpose of purging the registration lists and the names of all persons who have failed to reidentify themselves in the manner herein prescribed. (Acts 1984, No. 84-389, p. 896, § 2.)

§ 17-4-182. Electors to reidentify themselves; notice of reidentification; when eligible by mail.

Each voter whose name appears on the list of electors to be removed shall reidentify himself by appearing in person before a registrar or deputy registrar, or by appearing before the judge of probate, or either of the clerks in the office of the judge of probate, or through his or her representative before the board of registrars in regular session except that the following persons shall be entitled to reidentify by mail if they possess the qualifications of an elector and are not disqualified from voting under the Constitution and laws of Alabama: members of the armed forces of the United States, persons employed outside the United States, persons absent because of attendance at an institution of higher learning, and the spouses and children of such persons. The board of registrars shall notify such persons who are eligible for reidentification by mail as to how they can reidentify themselves. Electors eligible to reidentify by mail shall have their eligibility verified before a commissioned officer of the armed forces of the United States, or any person authorized to administer oaths and take affidavits, or before two witnesses who are 18 years old or older. (Acts 1984, No. 84-389, p. 896, § 3.)

§ 17-4-183. Publication of names to be struck from list.

The names of persons to be struck from the list of registered voters shall be listed by precinct and in alphabetical order and published in a newspaper of general circulation in the county once each in two consecutive weeks prior to August each year. (Acts 1984, No. 84-389, p. 896, § 4.)

§ 17-4-184. Only electors disqualified or not reidentified to be removed.

The board shall not remove the name of any elector, known by any member of said board, or made known to the said board by another qualified elector, or duly representative of the elector whose name is to be stricken, to be a legal resident of the county not known to be suffering from any disqualification. In purging the list of qualified electors, the board of registrars shall remove only the names of those persons who have not reidentified in the manner prescribed herein. (Acts 1984, No. 84-389, p. 896, § 5.)

§ 17-4-185. Records to show reason for striking elector from list; removal for failure to reidentify not permanent disqualification.

When the name of any elector is struck from the registration list, the records maintained by the board of registrars must show the reason for striking the elector from the list. No such person whose name is removed from the list of qualified electors for failure to reidentify shall cease permanently to be a qualified elector nor be subject to reregistration, but shall be subject only to the requirement that he or she reidentify as prescribed herein. (Acts 1984, No. 84-389, p. 896, § 6.)

§ 17-4-186. Procedure for having name restored to list of qualified electors; limitation of provisions.

Any qualified elector of the county who shall have his name omitted or removed from the list of qualified electors in the county for failure to appear and reidentify himself and who has not otherwise been reidentified as herein provided shall be entitled to have his name restored to the list of qualified electors by written affidavit or appearing in person before a registrar, or deputy registrar, or at the office of the board of registrars or at the office of the judge of probate, certifying that he or she is in fact a bonafide registered voter of that county; provided, however, that any qualified elector can be reidentified on election day; provided further, however, that this division shall not be construed or applied to impair or deny the right to vote in person or by absentee ballot of any person or of the spouse or child of any person who is in active duty of any of the armed forces of the United States of America and stationed, and as to the spouse or child, who is living with her or his husband or wife, mother or father, as the case may be, outside of the county, or who is living outside the county while attending a college or university or other institution of higher education or who is employed outside of the United States during the period of time from May 21, 1984; and provided further that the provisions of this division shall not restrict the board of registrars from purging the registration lists as provided in Section 17-4-132. (Acts 1984, No. 84-389, p. 896, § 7.)

Cross references. — As to provision for the disposition of records and forms after elections, see § 17-4-230 et seq.

§ 17-4-187. Board to maintain permanent list of qualified electors.

The board of registrars shall maintain a permanent list of all qualified electors by precinct and by race. (Acts 1984, No. 84-389, p. 896, § 8.)

Cited in Harris v. Graddick, 615 F. Supp. 239 (M.D. Ala. 1985).

§ 17-4-188. Per diem for board members; appointments to fill board vacancies.

Each member of the board of registrars shall receive $50.00 per day, for each day's attendance upon the special sessions of the board required under the provisions of this division; but if such special session is held on the same day a regular session is required to be held under the laws of this state, registrars shall receive only one per diem allowed for performing their regular duties, it being the intent and purpose of this division that registrars shall be entitled to receive only one per diem allowance for one day's service. If one or more of the members of the board shall refuse, neglect, or be unable to serve, or if a vacancy or vacancies occur in the membership of the board from any cause, the Governor, State Auditor, and Commissioner of Agriculture and Industries, or a majority of them, shall forthwith make other appointments to fill such membership positions. (Acts 1984, No. 84-389, p. 896, § 9; Acts 1988, No. 88-659, p. 1056, § 1.)

§ 17-4-189. Appointment of deputy registrars; terms, duties, compensation, etc.

To assist in the reidentification required by this division, in the registration of electors and in the board's continuing performance of its lawful duties, each board of registrars shall appoint in accordance with Section 17-4-157, at least one or more deputy registrars in each precinct in the county for a four-year term or for the remainder of an unexpired term. A deputy registrar's term of appointment shall run concurrently with that of the board. Deputy registrars shall be free to accept applications to reidentify and register any elector at any time, up to 10 days prior to an election. Any person serving as a deputy registrar shall be trained by the board of registrars and shall not be entitled to compensation. County governing bodies may authorize the boards of registrars to appoint additional deputy registrars, not to exceed six (6), to help as may be needed in periods of heavy registration, not to exceed 10 registration days, resulting from the implementation of the National Voter Registration Act of 1993. County governing bodies are authorized to provide additional clerical help as needed. Each deputy registrar appointed for this purpose shall receive a salary in the amount of $40.00 per day and shall be paid by the state as provided for in Section 17-4-153. The board shall provide deputy registrars with all necessary forms to perform their duties, and when such forms are completed, deputy registrars shall return them to the office of the board of registrars as the board may require, but not later than five working days. (Acts 1984, No. 84-389, p. 896, § 10; Acts 1994, 1st Ex. Sess., No. 94-826, p. 158, § 1.)

The 1994, 1st Ex. Sess., amendment, effective May 9, 1994, inserted "accept applications to" in the second sentence, added "and shall not be entitled to compensation" in the third sentence, and added the present fourth and fifth sentences.

§ 17-4-190. County commission to furnish board of registrars with supplies, equipment, etc.

The county commission of each county is hereby authorized, directed, and required to furnish the county board of registrars with the supplies, equipment, printed forms, stationery and newspaper advertisements necessary for the performance of their duties as herein provided. (Acts 1984, No. 84-389, p. 896, § 11.)

§ 17-4-191. Penalties for making false statements to board, etc.

Any person who willfully makes a false statement to the board of registrars, or any duly authorized person, in reidentifying himself as a qualified elector in the manner provided herein shall be guilty of perjury, and upon conviction thereof shall be punished by a fine of up to $500.00 or up to one year in prison. (Acts 1984, No. 84-389, p. 896, § 12.)

Division 2.

Statewide Voter File Maintenance Process.

Effective date. — The act which added this division becomes effective January 1, 1996.

§ 17-4-200. County boards of registrars to use process; exceptions; publication of registered voters' names.

The county boards of registrars throughout the state shall use the voter file maintenance process prescribed in this division in lieu of any voter list purge procedures heretofore provided by law except where the purge procedures are necessary to remove from a list of registered voters the names of voters who are deceased, voters convicted of disqualifying crimes and voters adjudged as mentally incompetent by a court of competent jurisdiction. Publication of the names of registered voters pursuant to this chapter, may be by general circulation newspaper. (Acts 1995, No. 95-769, § 1.)

§ 17-4-201. When maintenance activities to be conducted; notice to registered voters; updating voter list; suspense file; names removed from voter list.

(a) Beginning in January, 1996, and each year thereafter during the month of January, the county boards of registrars shall conduct voter list maintenance activities in lieu of the purge activities which were heretofore conducted in the month of August.

(b) Beginning in January, 1997, and in January of every fourth year thereafter, the boards of registrars shall mail a nonforwardable notice to all registered voters in the county. The notice shall be designed and provided for the boards of registrars by the Secretary of State. The notice shall be sent on a postcard providing general information on elections. The notice shall be mailed to the last known address of the voter appearing on the voter registration list. If the notice is returned to the boards of registrars indicating that the voter may have relocated, the board shall send a forwardable notice to the registered voter on which the voter may confirm his or her current address. The forwardable notice shall be mailed no later than 90 days after receipt of the returned nonforwardable notice. The boards of registrars shall record and maintain the dates on which the nonforwardable notice was returned to the board and the date on which the forwardable notice was mailed to the registered voter.

(c) The boards of registrars shall update the voter list for the county using the information reported to the board by the registered voters on the address confirmation cards provided for in subsection (b). If the registered voter does not respond to the forwardable notice on which the registered voter may confirm his or her address within 90 days on the date on which the notice was mailed or if the forwardable notice is returned to the board as undeliverable, the boards of registrars shall place the name of the registered voter on the inactive list of registered voters and in a suspense file in the office of the board. The suspense file shall contain all of the following information:

(1) The name of the registered voter.

(2) The last known address of the registered voter.

(3) The social security number or other personal identification number of the registered voter.

(4) The date on which the name of the registered voter was placed in the suspense file.

(d) The name of a registered voter who does not vote or appear to vote in one of the next two federal elections held after his or her name is placed in the suspense file shall be removed from the voter list.

(e) The names of persons to be removed from the list of registered voters shall be listed by precinct and in alphabetical order and published in a newspaper of general circulation in the county once a week for two consecutive weeks in November or December of each year commencing in November 1996. (Acts 1995, No. 95-769, § 2.)

§ 17-4-202. State to reimburse county commissions certain costs associated with process.

The state shall reimburse each county commission for all the postage costs associated with voter lists maintenance activities provided for in this division and one-fourth of the cost of the publication of the names of persons to be removed from the list of registered voters as required in Section 17-4-201. The reimbursement shall be made from the Election Expenses Account in the State Treasury upon approval by the Secretary of State on warrants drawn by the State Comptroller. (Acts 1995, No. 95-769, § 3.)

§ 17-4-203. Judge of probate to have access to current list of registered voters; no state entities to pay costs for access to list.

The judge of probate shall have access to and be provided with the current list of registered voters within his or her county at no cost within seven days after making the request. If computer access to the list of registered voters is available, upon request for access, the judge of probate shall be provided with immediate on-line availability to the list. No agency, department, or office of the State of Alabama shall pay any cost associated with printing or computer access to a list of registered voters available to a judge of probate under this section. (Acts 1995, No. 95-769, § 4.)

§ 17-4-204. Construction with Division 1.

This division shall be cumulative and supplemental to Act 84-389 now appearing as Division 1 of this article. Except as provided in subsections (a) and (b) of Section 17-4-201, this division shall not amend, repeal, or supersede Act 84-389 now appearing as Division 1 of this article. (Acts 1995, No. 95-769, § 5.)

ARTICLE 8.

STATEWIDE VOTER REGISTRATION FILE,
VOTER REGISTRATION ADVISORY
BOARD, AND DIRECTOR OF
VOTER REGISTRATION.

Effective date. — The act which added this article became effective May 11, 1989.

Code Commissioner's note. — Section 7 of Acts 1989, No. 89-649 provides: "The provisions of this [article] are supplemental. It shall be construed in pari materia with other laws regulating elections; however, those laws or parts of laws which are in direct conflict or inconsistent herewith are hereby repealed."

Cross references. — As to provisions for the disposition of records and forms after elections, see § 17-4-230 et seq.

§ 17-4-210. Purge of voter registration list; establishment of statewide voter registration file; creation of Voter Registration Advisory Board; composition; qualifications and appointment of members; duties.

Every county that has not conducted and completed a purge of its voter registration list pursuant to the provisions of Article 7 of this chapter since January 1, 1984, shall conduct and complete such purge no later than December 15, 1992. Only when every county has completed a voter registration list purge in compliance with the aforementioned mandate, the State of Alabama shall provide, through the Voter Registration Advisory Board and Director of Voter Registration as established herein, for the establishment, operation and maintenance of a centralized statewide voter registration file, effective no later than January 1, 1993, as a service to the board of registrars. Such file shall include the following information:

(1) The names, addresses, and voting locations of all registered voters of this state.

(2) The minutes of the meetings of the Voter Registration Advisory Board, as established under this article.

(3) Information such as may be deemed necessary by the Voter Registration Advisory Board or the Director of Voter Registration, as established herein, in order to ensure honesty, fairness, and integrity in the lists of qualified voters maintained by the various county boards of registrars.

As an oversight board for such system, there is hereby created and established a State Voter Registration Advisory Board composed of nine members, to be appointed as follows:

Three members by the Governor for terms of four years of which one must be Black.

Three members by the Commissioner of Agriculture and Industries for terms of four years of which one must be Black.

Three members by the State Auditor for terms of four years of which one must be Black.

Such appointments shall be made no later than September 30, 1989. Persons appointed to the Voter Registration Advisory Board shall have knowledge of the workings of voter registration and election laws and shall receive no compensation for their services other than reimbursement for traveling and other expenses actually incurred in the performance of their official duties. Such expenses shall be paid in the manner and amount as is provided for other state officers and employees and persons traveling on official business for state departments and agencies. Such appointees shall meet within 30 days after their appointments to select one of their number as chairperson who shall serve for two years. Thereafter, the Voter Registration Advisory Board shall elect a new chairperson every four years. The Voter Registration Advisory Board shall meet regularly at least once during each quarter and at such special meetings as may be called, from time to time, by the chairperson. Such appointees, if reappointed after the conclusion of their original terms, shall then serve for new terms of four years after the conclusion of their original terms and shall be eligible for reappointment. Whenever any vacancy occurs on the Voter Registration Advisory Board, for any reason, a successor shall be appointed by the original appointing state official, whether the Governor, Commissioner of Agriculture and Industries, or State Auditor, to serve on the Voter Registration Advisory Board for the remaining period of the unexpired term.

The Voter Registration Advisory Board shall have the following duties:

(1) To oversee the statewide voter registration file created in this article;

(2) To advise and consult with the Director of Voter Registration, as established in this article, concerning the statewide voter registration file maintenance system created in this article;

(3) To recommend to the Legislature and the Governor any needed improvements or legislation in regard to the statewide voter registration file;

(4) To make studies of conditions and problems pertaining to voter identification and registration in the state;

(5) To keep abreast of the latest developments in the field of voter identification and registration; and

(6) To promote honesty, fairness, and integrity in lists of qualified voters, the voter registration process, and the election process in the State of Alabama. (Acts 1989, No. 89-649, p. 1279, § 1.)

§ 17-4-211. Director of Voter Registration; selection by board; compensation; removal; duties and responsibilities.

The Board of Appointment provided for in Section 17-4-150 shall unanimously select a Director of Voter Registration who shall serve at the pleasure of such board. Said director, who shall serve as a member of the unclassified service of the state, shall be a confidential assistant to said Board of Appointment. Said director, whose salary and benefits shall be set by the said Board of Appointment out of funds appropriated for such purpose, may be removed from such position at any time, with or without cause, by a unanimous vote if the said Board of Appointment, for any reason, revokes their appointment of the individual to such position. Said Director of Voter Registration shall work at the direction of the said Board of Appointment. Said director shall have the following duties:

(1) To keep the minutes of the meetings of the Voter Registration Advisory Board, conduct the day-to-day business activities of the Voter Registration Advisory Board and give progress reports on such activities at its meetings;

(2) To serve as a liaison between the state, the Board of Appointment set forth in Section 17-4-150, and the county boards of registrars on implementation of existing and future laws pertaining to voter registration;

(3) To provide to the county boards of registrars such information as would allow them to determine which names should be stricken by them from voter lists in accordance with state law;

(4) To provide assistance to the county boards of registrars in determining the names of any person or persons who are deceased, who are no longer

qualified to vote in the election district where registered due to removal of his or her residence from the county in which he or she is registered, or from the State of Alabama, who has been convicted of a disqualifying crime, or who is otherwise no longer qualified to vote as may be provided by law;

(5) To establish and maintain a statewide voter registration file including all registered voters of the state as such information is reported to the Director of Voter Registration by the boards of registrars or judges of probate of the various counties;

(6) To maintain all information furnished to the Director of Voter Registration relating to the inclusion or deletion of names from the lists of registered voters;

(7) To acquire by purchase, lease, or contract, the use of such equipment as is required to establish a fully centralized statewide voter registration file which will allow the computerization of all of the offices of the boards of registrars throughout the state upon legislative approval of funds for such computerization, the communication of necessary information between the boards of registrars and the Director of Voter Registration; storage and instant comparison of names and other identifying information contained in voter lists, automatically identifying duplicate entries, produce in printed forms selected names or lists of names with identifying information, and do such other tasks as may be designated for it by the Director of Voter Registration;

(8) To promulgate procedures and prepare forms necessary to properly carry out such duties set forth herein;

(9) To secure from each county voter registration information and from any state department, agency, board, bureau, or commission, or from any other sources, information regarding the death, conviction of disqualifying crime, or removal of residence from the county or state of any registered voter;

(10) To furnish, at a reasonable charge and within 14 days of receipt of the request, voter registration lists limited to the names, addresses, and political subdivisions or voting places to candidates for election or political party nomination to further their candidacy, political party committees or officials thereof for political purposes only, incumbent officeholders to report to their constituents; nonprofit organizations which promote voter participation and registration for that purpose only; and for no other purpose and to no one else; failure to furnish the requested voter registration list within 14 days of receipt of request shall result in no charge to the requesting entity and said cost shall be absorbed by the Director of Voter Registration;

(11) To perform such duties pertaining to voter registration as may be assigned by the members of the Board of Appointment set forth in Section 17-4-150; and

(12) To employ persons, subject to the State Merit System laws and entitled to the rights of benefits thereunder, as may be necessary to carry out the provisions of this article. (Acts 1989, No. 89-649, p. 1279, § 2.)

§ 17-4-212. Information to be provided director by state departments or agencies.

To continuously and automatically identify the names of persons to be purged from the voters' list, the appropriate state departments or agencies shall provide to the Director of Voter Registration, as such information is recorded by said departments, the names and identifying information set out below of any person age 18 or older who:

(1) Have died, with date of birth and social security number (if such number is known), last known address with county of residence, and date of death, as provided by the Bureau of Vital Statistics of the State Health Department; and

(2) Have been convicted of a felony with date of birth and social security number (if such number is known), last known address with county of residence, and date of conviction, as provided by the Alabama criminal justice information systems. (Acts 1989, No. 89-649, p. 1279, § 3.)

§ 17-4-213. Procedure for striking voter from registration list; placement on inactive list; reidentification with local board; voting by voter on inactive list.

Any voter who fails to vote for four years in his or her county shall have his or her name automatically struck from the voter registration list and placed on an inactive voter list by the local board of registrars. Once on such inactive list, said voter must reidentify with the local board of registrars in order to again have his or her name placed on the active voter registration list. Provided, however, that if a voter on the inactive list goes to his or her polling place to vote on an election day and identifies himself or herself to the poll's official responsible for the voter registration list, such voter shall be permitted to vote. (Acts 1989, No. 89-649, p. 1279, § 4.)

§ 17-4-214. Duties of boards of registrars; penalty.

(a) In order to establish the statewide voter file and to ensure its continued accuracy, it shall be the duty of the boards of registrars, on forms or in a manner prescribed by the Director of Voter Registration:

(1) To provide said director the name, social security number (if such number is known), date of birth, address, political subdivision or voting place of each registered voter in their respective counties within one month after a written request from said director;

(2) To provide said director the name, social security number (if such number is known), date of birth, address, political subdivision or voting place, place of previous registration, if applicable, and date of registration of each newly registered voter as such voter is registered;

(3) To provide to said director the name, social security number (if such number is known), date of birth, address, political subdivision or voting place and date of reidentification of every voter who reidentifies, pursuant to Article 7 of this chapter.

(b) Members of local boards of registrars and members of county commissions who fail to comply with the provisions of this article in their representative capacities as such registrars and commissioners shall be guilty of a Class A misdemeanor and punished as prescribed by law. (Acts 1989, No. 89-649, p. 1279, § 5.)

§ 17-4-215. Applicability of Article 7 to registration, reidentification and purging of voters.

All voter registration, voter reidentification, and the purging of voters from the voter roll shall be done pursuant to Article 7 of this chapter. (Acts 1989, No. 89-649, p. 1279, § 6.)

ARTICLE 9.

DISPOSITION OF RECORDS AND FORMS AFTER ELECTION.

§ 17-4-230. Definitions.

For purposes of this article, unless the context plainly indicates otherwise, the following terms shall have the meanings respectively ascribed to them by this section:

(1) CLERK'S POLL LIST. The list of voters that is written by a clerk at the polling place pursuant to Section 11-46-39 or 17-8-34.

(2) LIST OF REGISTERED VOTERS. The list of registered voters, sometimes called the list of qualified voters, that is provided for each polling place by the city clerk in municipal elections and by the judge of probate in all other elections.

(3) STATEMENT OF CANVAS or CERTIFICATE OF RESULT. The vote totals recorded at the polling places on forms provided for that purpose in accordance with Sections 17-13-6, 17-9-33, 17-16-32, 11-46-116 and 11-46-123.

(4) VOTERS' POLL LIST. The numbered list that is signed by the voter at the polling place.

(5) VOTER REIDENTIFICATION FORM. A form that is approved by the Alabama Director of Voter Registration for use at the polling place pursuant to Section 17-4-186. (Acts 1990, No. 90-557, p. 947, § 1.)

§ 17-4-231. Disposition of records and forms after close of polls.

After the close of the polls in all primary, special, general and municipal elections held in the state, the records and forms produced at the polling places shall be returned as follows:

(1) The list of registered voters and the voter reidentification forms shall be sealed in an envelope addressed to the board of registrars and the inspectors and any poll watchers present shall sign across the seal. The board of registrars shall hold the list of registered voters as a public record while using it to update their voter histories in accordance with Article 8 of this chapter. The list shall then be returned to the city clerk in municipal elections and the judge of probate in all other elections.

(2) One copy of the affidavits of challenged voters and witnesses shall be placed in an envelope addressed to the district attorney as required by Section 17-12-4.

(3) The voters' poll list, the clerk's poll list and all records required by law to be sealed in a voting machine or sealed in a ballot box shall be sealed in an envelope labeled "RECORDS OF ELECTION" and the inspectors and any poll watchers present shall sign across the seal. The "records of election" envelope shall be sealed in the ballot box or voting machine and remain there during the period of time for the initiation of election contest. The "records of election" envelope shall be removed and returned to the city clerk in municipal elections and the sheriff in all other elections to be retained in accordance with state and federal law. (Acts 1990, No. 90-557, p. 947, § 2.)

ARTICLE 10.

STATE IMPLEMENTATION OF NATIONAL VOTER REGISTRATION ACT OF 1993.

Effective date. — The act which added this article became effective May 9, 1994.

§ 17-4-250. Secretary of State: Chief state elections official.

(a) The Secretary of State shall be the primary state official for federal contact for the implementation of the National Voter Registration Act of 1993. The Secretary of State is the chief state elections official.

(b) The State Department of Public Safety shall integrate voter registration into driver's license application and renewal or updating procedures.

(c) The state through the Secretary of State's Office shall allow citizens to register to vote by mail. The voter registration application may be designed by the Secretary of State provided it meets the requirements of the National Voter Registration Act of 1993. The Secretary of State may, however, choose to use federally prescribed forms.

(d) State agencies which provide food stamps, Medicaid, services related to Women and Infant Children program (WIC), services related to Aid to Families with Dependent Children (AFDC), and agencies providing services to the disabled shall provide voter registration opportunities to their clientele in accordance with the National Voter Registration Act of 1993.

(e) Recruitment offices of the armed forces of the United States shall provide voter registration opportunities to their clientele in accordance with the National Voter Registration Act of 1993.

(f) Other public offices and agencies which may provide the voter registration services provided by the National Voter Registration Act of 1993 include public libraries, public schools, offices of municipal clerks, probate offices, state and local revenue offices, unemployment compensation offices, offices providing services to the disabled other than those required in (d) to provide voter registration services, and federal and nongovernmental offices which agree to provide the voter registration services.

(g) Voter registration, confirmation documents, and any other documents necessary to be prescribed by the Secretary of State to meet the requirements of the National Voter Registration Act of 1993 shall be prepared and furnished as provided for in Sections 17-4-126 and 17-4-137. (Acts 1994, 1st Ex. Sess., No. 94-826, p. 158, § 2.)

§ 17-4-251. Additional personnel.

The Secretary of State may hire a computer programmer and other necessary personnel to carry out the additional responsibilities placed on his or her office by state implementation of the National Voter Registration Act of 1993. The programmer and other personnel employed shall be under the State Merit System. (Acts 1994, 1st Ex. Sess., No. 94-826, p. 158, § 3.)

§ 17-4-252. Dissemination of information on voter registration.

The Director of Voter Registration shall ensure that all applicants obtain requested voter lists in a timely manner. Methods shall be established for the transmission of tapes, discs, or lists to any applicant. Hindrances shall not be created or devised to delay transmission of tapes, discs, or lists to any applicant. Except as provided in this section, there shall be a uniform charge for the production of voter lists. The costs of the basic electronic copy of the statewide file shall be reasonable as determined by the Office of Voter Registration and a fee schedule shall be conspicuously posted in the office of the director. Costs of printed copies of lists are as otherwise provided by law. Access to the lists and voter history information contained on the central computer in the Office of Voter Registration is accessible to anyone making application, except social security numbers which are not to be released. Proceeds from the sale of tapes, discs, lists, labels, or other materials from the Office of Voter Registration shall be retained by the Director of the Office of Voter Registration for use in the Office of Voter Registration. Upon application and without charge legislators shall be furnished up to two free printed copies of the voter lists for their districts during a legislative quadrennium and resale of the lists shall be strictly prohibited. (Acts 1994, 1st Ex. Sess., No. 94-826, p. 158, § 5.)

§ 17-4-253. State voter file computer.

It shall be the responsibility of the board of registrars to enter in a timely manner the names of the electors who vote in each election into the state voter file computer as maintained by the Office of Voter Registration. (Acts 1994, 1st Ex. Sess., No. 94-826, p. 158, § 6.)

§ 17-4-254. Voter Registration Fund.

There is established a separate trust fund in the State Treasury to be known as the Voter Registration Fund. All receipts collected under this act by the Office of Voter Registration are to be deposited in this fund. The receipts shall be disbursed only by warrant of the State Comptroller drawn upon the State Treasury supported by itemized vouchers approved by the Director of Voter Registration. No funds shall be withdrawn or expended except as budgeted and allotted according to Sections 41-4-80 to 41-4-96, inclusive, and 41-19-1 to 41-19-12, inclusive, and only in amounts as stipulated in the general appropriations act or other appropriations acts. (Acts 1994, 1st Ex. Sess., No. 94-826, p. 158, § 7.)

§ 17-4-255. Inter-agency agreements.

The Secretary of State shall promulgate rules and regulations and prescribe forms as shall be necessary to implement the National Voter Registration Act of 1993 in Alabama on January 1, 1995, including any rules, regulations, and forms necessary for the administration of the act by state departments and agencies. The Director of the Office of Voter Registration shall work in close cooperation and coordination with the Secretary of State and under his or her direct supervision for the implementation of the National Voter Registration Act of 1993. The Secretary of State is further authorized to enter into inter-agency agreements with other government agencies for the implementation of the National Voter Registration Act of 1993. (Acts 1994, 1st Ex. Sess., No. 94-826, p. 158, § 8.)

§ 17-4-256. Penalties.

Violation of this article shall be a Class C misdemeanor punishable as provided by law. (Acts 1994, 1st Ex. Sess., No. 94-826, p. 158, § 10.)

CHAPTER 5.

PRECINCTS, DISTRICTS AND POLLING PLACES.

REPEALED.

§§ 17-5-1 through 17-5-13. Repealed by Acts 1989, No. 89-952, p. 1874, § 12, effective June 1, 1989.

CHAPTER 5A.

PRECINCTS.

§ 17-5A-1. Purpose.

It is the purpose of this chapter to provide for participation by the State of Alabama in programs of the Bureau of the Census of the United States Department of Commerce which provide for furnishing census information to the states for purposes of reapportionment, pursuant to federal laws for that purpose. It is further the purpose of this chapter to reduce voter confusion and facilitate the election process in Alabama. (Acts 1989, No. 89-952, p. 1874, § 1.)

§ 17-5A-2. Definitions.

For purposes of this chapter, the following terms shall have the definitions ascribed to them:

(1) PRECINCT. A geographical subdivision of a county having clearly visible, definable and observable physical boundaries which are based upon criteria established and recognized by the Bureau of the Census of the United States Department of Commerce for purposes of defining census blocks for its decennial census. A "precinct" shall be the smallest geographical area for purposes of holding national, state or county-wide elections. A "precinct" is also sometimes referred to as a "voting district" by the Census Bureau and other agencies.

(2) CENSUS BUREAU. The Bureau of the Census of the United States Department of Commerce, or any successor bureau or department which conducts an official decennial census of the United States.

(3) TASK FORCE or REAPPORTIONMENT TASK FORCE. The joint legislative task force on reapportionment.

(4) ELECTRONIC VOTE COUNTING STATUTES. Sections 17-24-1 through 17-24-11, or any rule or regulation adopted pursuant thereto, or any subsequent statute providing county governing bodies with methods of electronic vote tabulations for election purposes. (Acts 1989, No. 89-952, p. 1874, § 2.)

§ 17-5A-3. Establishment of precincts; boundaries; precinct map; co-ordination with reapportionment task force; adjustments of boundaries.

(a) The governing body of each county shall establish precincts, define the territorial limits for which each precinct is established, prescribe their boundaries, and designate the precincts. The governing body of each county shall, by resolution, adopt the establishment and boundaries of each precinct in accordance with the timetable as set forth herein.

(b) Each precinct shall be a contiguous, compact area having clearly defined and clearly observable boundaries coinciding with visible features readily distinguishable on the ground such as designated highways, roads, streets, or rivers or be coterminous with a county boundary.

(c) Each county governing body shall provide and maintain at all times a suitable map showing the current geographical boundaries with designation of precincts and a legal description of the geographical boundaries of each precinct. Each county governing body shall send a copy of each map, with description attached, to the county board of registrars, the probate judge and the reapportionment task force. All features, names, titles, and symbols on the map shall be clearly shown and legible. Each map sheet shall indicate the date of the base map or the date of last revision.

(d)(1) In complying with the provisions of this section for the establishment of precincts and the prescription of their boundaries, each county governing body and the board of registrars shall coordinate with the reapportionment task force or their designees, pursuant to their authority to submit a plan for census data for reapportionment under the provisions of Section 199 of the State Constitution, and shall adopt or adjust precinct boundaries as may be necessary to comply with this section.

(2) Each county governing body shall by resolution adopt a proposal for the establishment or adjustment of precinct boundaries, in compliance with this section, no later than June 1, 1989, provided that any establishment of a precinct or adjustment of a precinct boundary to comply with this section shall be effective for the following purposes at the following times:

a. Not later than January 1, 1990, for the purpose of establishing block boundaries for the 1990 federal decennial census.

b. Not later than April 1, 1991, for all other election purposes. (Acts 1989, No. 89-952, p. 1874, § 3.)

§ 17-5A-4. Voting districts; designated voting places; voting machines; division of precincts; filing of boundaries; naming of precincts.

(a) Except as may be provided further by local election laws or by the electronic vote counting statutes, the counties in this state, as divided pursuant to this chapter into election precincts and the boundaries of such precincts shall so remain until changed by order of the county governing body, but the county governing body, at its first regular meeting in March in each even-numbered year beginning 1990, shall subdivide any election precinct in which there are more than 300 qualified voters and paper ballots are used or in which there are more than 600 qualified voters and voting machines are used into voting districts or shall divide alphabetically the list of qualified voters in such precincts into groups and assign each qualified voter a designated voting place and a designated box or voting machine in such precinct so as to provide a box for every person legally entitled to vote at which not more than 300 paper ballots will be cast or a machine at which not more than 600 votes by voting machines will be cast.

(b) Except as may be provided further by local election laws or by the electronic vote counting statutes, the county governing body, at its first regular meeting in March in each even-numbered year beginning in 1990, shall in their respective counties examine the registration and official list of voters as the same is on file in the office of the judge of probate of said county, and if it shall appear from such examination and from other available sources of information that there is in any election precinct as constituted pursuant to this chapter in which paper ballots are used more than 300 legal voters, or that there is in any election precinct as constituted pursuant to this chapter in which voting machines are used more than 600 legal voters, they shall immediately either divide said precinct into voting districts so that no one district shall contain over 300 legal voters where paper ballots are used or 600 legal voters where voting machines are used or establish two or more places or provide additional boxes or voting machines at established polling places in such precinct and shall separate the list of qualified registered voters in said precinct, as shown by the list on file in the office of the probate judge in said county, into groups in alphabetical order so that no group in a precinct in which paper ballots are used shall contain more than 300 qualified registered voters or in a precinct where voting machines are used more than 600 qualified registered voters and shall designate the place and box or machine in such precinct at which each qualified voter shall cast his ballot.

(c) Whenever any election precinct has been subdivided into voting districts, pursuant to subsection (a) or (b) hereof, the county governing body making such subdivision shall immediately cause a description of the boundaries of said voting districts to be filed in the office of the judge of probate and shall post a copy thereof at the county courthouse.

(d) Such precincts shall be named and designated by the county governing body numerically or alphabetically or by a combination thereof in a manner that will be uniform statewide as determined by the association of county commissions and approved by the reapportionment task force. (Acts 1989, No. 89-952, p. 1874, § 4.)

§ 17-5A-5. Designation of voting places; installation of voting boxes or machines; filing of voting places, etc.; publication; county voting centers; change of voting places.

(a) Except as may be provided further by local election laws or by the electronic vote counting statutes, the county governing bodies shall designate the places of holding elections in the precincts established hereunder, and, whenever the county has alphabetically divided the list of registered qualified voters of a precinct into groups, it shall designate not only the voting place but also the number of boxes or voting machines at each voting place in the precinct, being sure that it designates a box or machine for each group of qualified voters. The county governing body is hereby specifically authorized to provide for installing as many boxes or machines as are needed in each precinct, and such boxes or machines may be installed at one designated voting place or there may be more than one voting place designated and such number of boxes or machines installed at each place as needed to provide for the voters authorized to vote at each such place. The county governing body shall file with the judge of probate of the county along with a copy of its order fixing the boundaries of a precinct, the names of places designated for voting, indicating in those precincts in which the voters have been alphabetically divided into groups the voting places and boxes or voting machine at which each alphabetical group shall vote and shall also post such list of voting places at the county courthouse.

(b) The judge of probate, within five days after the county governing body of any county files with him the boundaries of such election precincts and the names of the voting places therein, shall give notice of the same by publishing the same in some newspaper of general circulation published in said county and shall have the same posted by the sheriff at the courthouse and at two public places in said election district of such precinct. Such notice must describe such election precincts by its number and must specify the place therein where elections are to be held.

(c) Where election precincts have been subdivided into voting districts hereunder, no voter in any election held thereafter shall vote at any place other than the voting district in which said voter is at such time registered as a qualified elector; provided further, however, that any county may, by local law, establish voting centers by combining voters from two or more precincts in order to create a voting center in order to facilitate, or reduce costs, for elections.

(d) Except as may be provided further by local election laws or by the electronic vote counting statutes, whenever places of voting are once designated and established as required by this chapter, the voting places for precincts shall not be changed within three months before an election is to be held; and, whenever the boundaries of election precincts are changed, the county governing body shall forthwith designate and establish at least one voting place for every 300, or 600 where voting machines are used, voters in each election precinct so created. Places of voting shall be the same for all elections, whether primary, general or special, or federal, state, district, or county.

(e) The courthouse is the place of holding elections in the precinct in which it is situated unless another place for that purpose is designated by the county governing body. Elections must be held at such places in the other precincts as may be designated hereafter by the county governing body. (Acts 1989, No. 89-952, p. 1874, § 5.)

§ 17-5A-6. List of voters for each voting place.

The judge of probate shall prepare a separate, correct alphabetical list of all the names of qualified electors or voters for each voting place from the list compiled and filed in the probate office, pursuant to Sections 17-4-129 and 17-4-130, for all elections hereafter held in this state, whether primary, general or special, or federal, state, district, county or municipal, and shall certify separately for each voting place, to the election officials appointed for holding election, each of which election official shall be an elector qualified to vote only in the box at the place for which he or she is chosen to serve, a list containing only the names of the voters or qualified electors entitled to vote at such voting place; provided, that as regards municipal elections, the mayor of the city or town shall cause to be made and certified such lists; provided further, that nothing in this section shall prevent a series of lists of names of voters or electors of other voting places from being certified by the judge of probate on the same general list for information. A vote cast at a place other than the voting place at which the voter is entitled to vote shall be illegal. (Acts 1989, No. 89-952, p. 1874, § 6.)

§ 17-5A-7. Authority to change configuration, boundaries, etc., of election precincts; procedure; copy of resolution and map to be sent to reapportionment task force.

(a) The county governing body shall have sole authority to change the configuration, boundaries, or designation of an election precinct. Any change so determined shall be adopted by resolution of the county governing body.

(b) After June 1, 1989, a county governing body shall only change a precinct by dividing the precinct into two or more precincts except when in order to make it more convenient for voters to vote, or to facilitate the administration of the election process, or to accomplish reapportionment, it becomes necessary to consolidate all or part of a precinct with adjacent precincts, a part or parts may be consolidated.

(c) Except as may be provided further by local election laws or by the electronic vote counting statutes, whenever at any general or primary election in any election precinct over 300 votes shall have been cast by paper ballot or 600 by voting machines, the county governing body shall readjust the boundary lines of said election precincts or shall separate the list of qualified registered voters in such precinct into alphabetical groups of not more than 300 when paper ballots are used or 600 when voting machines are used and may divide or consolidate any number of precincts and resubdivide the same in order that not more than 300 voters shall be contained in any one precinct and authorized to vote at one box when paper ballots are used, or not more than 600 voters shall be contained in any one precinct in which voting machines are used and voters are authorized to vote at only one place.

(d) In changing any precinct boundary, the county governing body shall comply with the requirements of Section 17-5A-3.

(e) Within 30 days after the adoption of any resolution as provided in this section, the county governing body shall send to the reapportionment task force a certified copy of the resolution and a copy of a map showing the new precinct boundaries together with a written description of such boundaries. (Acts 1989, No. 89-952, p. 1874, § 7.)

§ 17-5A-8. Reapportionment task force as liaison with Bureau of Census; assistance to counties.

(a) The reapportionment task force, or its designees, shall serve as the state liaison with the United States Bureau of the Census on all matters related to the tabulation of population and other census information for purposes of reapportionment. The reapportionment task force may submit to the bureau, on behalf of the state, a plan identifying the geographic areas for which specific tabulations of population or other census information are desired for reapportionment purposes, in accordance with criteria established by the United States Secretary of Commerce, and may supply such other information as may be required by the Census Bureau or the Secretary of Commerce in order to furnish the state such tabulations.

(b) The reapportionment task force shall furnish the county governing bodies and the county boards of registrars such information and assistance as is necessary in order to enable them to comply timely with the Census Bureau requirements. (Acts 1989, No. 89-952, p. 1874, § 8.)

§ 17-5A-9. Cooperation with reapportionment task force; penalty.

All state and county agencies and officials shall cooperate with the reapportionment task force in carrying out the purposes of this chapter and shall cooperate with the reapportionment task force in the development of all information, maps, and other data as is needed to comply with requirements of the Census Bureau. Failure to comply with the provisions of this chapter shall be a Class B misdemeanor punishable as prescribed by law. (Acts 1989, No. 89-952, p. 1874, § 9.)

§ 17-5A-10. Inapplicability to municipal elections.

The provisions of this chapter shall have no effect on the conduct of municipal elections of this state. It is further specifically provided that nothing herein contained shall be construed to require any municipality to establish single or multiple representation districts for the election of municipal officials in this state. It is further provided that all general or local provisions of law regarding the conduct of municipal elections are hereby expressly preserved. (Acts 1989, No. 89-952, p. 1874, § 10.)

CHAPTER 6.

ELECTION OFFICERS.

§ 17-6-1. Who appoints; number.

The judge of probate, sheriff and clerk of the circuit court, or a majority of them, acting as an appointing board, must, not more than 20 nor less than 15 days before the holding of any election in their county, appoint from the qualified electors of the respective voting places, excluding members of a candidate's immediate family to the second degree of kinship by affinity or consanguinity or any member of a candidate's political committee as prescribed by Section 17-22A-4, three inspectors and two clerks for each place of voting, and returning officer for each precinct, to act at the place of holding elections in each precinct. (Code 1876, § 259; Code 1886, § 352; Code 1896, § 1588; Code 1907, § 347; Code 1923, § 437; Code 1940, T. 17, § 120; Acts 1980, No. 80-725, p. 1467.)

Cited in Ex parte State ex rel. Tucker, 236 Ala. 284, 181 So. 761 (1938); Ex parte Register, 257 Ala. 408, 60 So. 2d 41 (1952); Gray v. Main, 309 F. Supp. 207 (M.D. Ala. 1968); Taxpayers & Citizens v. Cleburne County, 287 Ala. 116, 248 So. 2d 711 (1971); Mobile County Republican Executive Comm. v. Mandeville, 363 So. 2d 754 (Ala. 1978); Clark v. Marengo County, 469 F. Supp. 1150 (S.D. Ala. 1979); Harris v. Conradi, 675 F.2d 1212 (11th Cir. 1982); Harris v. Graddick, 593 F. Supp. 128 (M.D. Ala. 1984); United States v. Marengo County Comm'n, 731 F.2d 1546 (11th Cir. 1984); Harris v. Graddick, 615 F. Supp. 239 (M.D. Ala. 1985); Vintson v. Anton, 786 F.2d 1023 (11th Cir. 1986); Haughton v. McCollum, 530 So. 2d 758 (Ala. 1988).

Collateral references. — 29 C.J.S., Elections, § 59.

25 Am. Jur. 2d, Elections, § 39 et seq.

§ 17-6-2. Notice of appointment.

The sheriff shall notify such inspectors and returning officers and clerks of their appointment and publish a list of them in some newspaper published in the county. (Code 1907, § 348; Code 1923, § 438; Code 1940, T. 17, § 121.)

§ 17-6-3. When county officers not eligible for appointing boards; notice of ineligibility; serving on board when ineligible.

When the judge of probate, sheriff or clerk of the circuit court is a candidate for election to any office at that election, he shall not serve on the appointing board. The judge of probate shall certify to the clerk or register of the circuit court the fact of the candidacy of any member of the appointing board immediately after the certificate of nomination, or petition, as provided in Section 17-7-1, is filed with him.

Any probate judge who shall fail to certify to the clerk or register of the circuit court the fact of the candidacy of himself, the clerk of the circuit court or the sheriff, thus rendering them ineligible to serve as members of the appointing board of election managers, in the manner and time he is required to so certify such fact under the election laws of this state, shall be guilty of a misdemeanor, and, upon conviction, shall be fined not less than $50.00 nor more than $100.00.

Any probate judge, sheriff or circuit clerk who shall act as a member of the appointing board of election managers while he is a candidate for public office, shall be guilty of a misdemeanor, and, upon conviction, shall be fined not less than $50.00 nor more than $100.00. (Code 1907, §§ 349, 6812, 6813; Code 1923, §§ 439, 3930, 3931; Code 1940, T. 17, §§ 122, 325, 326.)

Cited in Ex parte Register, 257 Ala. 408, 60 So. 2d 41 (1952); Mobile County Republican Executive Comm. v. Mandeville, 363 So. 2d 754 (Ala. 1978).

Collateral references. — 29 C.J.S., Elections, § 58.

§ 17-6-4. Replacement of ineligible member of appointing board; compensation of board members.

Upon receiving the certificate provided for in Section 17-6-3, the clerk or register of the circuit court shall forthwith and without delay appoint a qualified elector to take the place of each member of the appointing board who is a candidate for election, and shall cause the elector so appointed to be informed of his appointment; but no person shall be appointed who is a candidate for any office to be voted for in that election.

Any person serving as a member of the appointing board shall receive $4.00 for such service.

The person so appointed shall perform all the duties and be vested with all the powers of the regular members of the appointing board, and shall take an oath to faithfully perform his duties. (Code 1907, § 350; Code 1923, § 440; Code 1940, T. 17, § 123.)

Cited in Ex parte Register, 257 Ala. 408, 60 So. 2d 41 (1952); Mobile County Republican Executive Comm. v. Mandeville, 363 So. 2d 754 (Ala. 1978).

§ 17-6-5. Proceedings when clerk or register disqualified.

When the clerk or register of the circuit court is disqualified from any cause to perform the duties herein prescribed, the judge of probate shall certify the fact of the candidacy of the judge of probate, sheriff or circuit clerk to the governor, who shall forthwith appoint a qualified elector to act in the place of each of said officers who is a candidate for election, who shall take an oath to faithfully discharge his duties. (Code 1907, § 351; Code 1923, § 441; Code 1940, T. 17, § 124.)

Cited in Ex parte Register, 257 Ala. 408, 60 So. 2d 41 (1952); Mobile County Republican Executive Comm. v. Mandeville, 363 So. 2d 754 (Ala. 1978).

§ 17-6-6. Political parties furnish lists from which appointments are made.

Each political party or organization having made nominations may, by the chairman of its state or county executive committee or nominees for office, furnish the appointing board a list of not less than three names of qualified electors from each voting place, and from each of said lists an inspector and clerk shall be appointed for each voting place; provided, that where there are more than two lists filed, the appointments shall be made from the lists presented by the two political parties having received the highest number of votes in the state in the next preceding regular election, if each of said parties present a list. (Code 1896, § 1595; Code 1907, § 352; Code 1923, § 442; Code 1940, T. 17, § 125.)

This section is not unconstitutional on its face, is not proved to be unconstitutionally applied and is not in violation of the Voting Rights Act of 1965. Hadnott v. Amos, 295 F. Supp. 1003 (M.D. Ala. 1968), rev'd on other grounds, 394 U.S. 358, 89 S. Ct. 1101, 22 L. Ed. 2d 336 (1969).

For general discussion relative to constitutionality of this section, see Harris v. Conradi, 675 F.2d 1212 (11th Cir. 1982).

As to constitutionality of practices of appointing board, see Harris v. Conradi, 675 F.2d 1212 (11th Cir. 1982).

Statute does not require appointment of election officers in equal proportion. — Statute controlling manner of appointment of election officers who serve in general elections does not require the appointment of election officers in equal proportion nor does it establish any mathematical formula for such appointments; it simply requires the appointing board to make its selection of election officers from lists provided by the two major political parties. Mobile County Republican Executive Comm. v. Mandeville, 363 So. 2d 754 (Ala. 1978).

The legislature did not intend to require the appointment of election officers in equal proportion nor did it establish any mathematical formula for such appointments. This section simply requires the appointing board to make its selection of election officers from lists provided by the two major political parties. Harris v. Conradi, 675 F.2d 1212 (11th Cir. 1982).

Cited in Harris v. Graddick, 593 F. Supp. 128 (M.D. Ala. 1984); Vintson v. Anton, 786 F.2d 1023 (11th Cir. 1986).

§ 17-6-7. Failure of officers of election to attend.

On the failure of any inspector or returning officer to attend at the hour of 8:00 A.M., such inspector and returning officers as may be present may complete the number. If none of the inspectors appointed are present, the returning officer of a precinct shall appoint three inspectors to act, who, in every instance, shall be qualified electors who are entitled to vote at the polling place and who shall appoint from the qualified electors at such polling place such clerks as may be necessary to fill places of those failing to attend; and, if there should be no inspector or returning officer present at the polling place by the hour of 8:00 A.M., then any three qualified electors who are entitled by law to vote at that polling place at the election then to be held may open the polls and act as inspectors during the election and appoint clerks to fill the places of those absent in the manner hereinabove provided.

Any manager or clerk appointed such by the appointing board who shall fail to attend an election without a lawful excuse shall, on conviction, be fined not more than $100.00. (Code 1876, § 262; Code 1886, § 355; Code 1896, § 1591; Code 1907, §§ 359, 6814; Code 1923, §§ 449, 3932; Code 1940, T. 17, §§ 132, 327.)

The absence of one of the election officers does not void the election. Lee v. State, 49 Ala. 43 (1873).

Collateral references. — 29 C.J.S., Elections, § 192.

§ 17-6-8. Poll watchers.

Each political party or organization having candidates nominated may, by the chairman of the county executive committee or nominees for office or beat committeeman, name a watcher who shall be permitted to be present at the place where the ballots are cast from the time the polls are opened until the ballots are counted and certificates of the result of the election signed by the inspectors. The said watcher shall be permitted to see the ballots as they are called during the count. The watcher shall be sworn to faithfully observe the rule of law prescribed for the conduct of elections. (Code 1907, § 353; Code 1923, § 443; Code 1940, T. 17, § 126.)

Cited in Harris v. Conradi, 675 F.2d 1212 (11th Cir. 1982); Vintson v. Anton, 786 F.2d 1023 (11th Cir. 1986).

§ 17-6-9. Inspectors and clerks appointed.

If no lists are furnished as provided in Section 17-6-6, the appointing board shall appoint inspectors, two of whom shall be members of opposing political parties, if practicable, and shall appoint clerks from opposing political parties, if practicable. (Code 1852, § 201; Code 1867, § 243; Code 1876, § 264; Code 1886, § 357; Code 1896, § 1593; Code 1907, § 362; Code 1923, § 452; Code 1940, T. 17, § 135.)

Cited in Harris v. Conradi, 675 F.2d 1212 (11th Cir. 1982).

Collateral references. — 29 C.J.S., Elections, § 59.

§ 17-6-10. Oaths of election officers.

Before entering upon their duties, inspectors and clerks must take an oath to perform their duties at the election according to law, and such oath may be administered by any person authorized by law to administer oaths or by any one of the inspectors. (Code 1852, § 202; Code 1867, § 244; Code 1876, § 265; Code 1886, § 358; Code 1896, § 1597; Code 1907, § 369; Code 1923, § 459; Code 1940, T. 17, § 142.)

Collateral references. — 29 C.J.S., Elections, § 61.

§ 17-6-11. Sheriff designated returning officer.

The sheriff of each county or the person discharging the duties of such office is the returning officer for his county. (Code 1876, § 260; Code 1886, § 353; Code 1896, § 1589; Code 1907, § 356; Code 1923, § 446; Code 1940, T. 17, § 129.)

Collateral references. — 29 C.J.S., Elections, § 229.

§ 17-6-12. Appointment of acting returning officer in absence of regular officer.

If the returning officer is not present at the hour appointed, the inspectors or those acting as such must appoint from the qualified electors one to serve during the election. (Code 1876, § 263; Code 1886, § 356; Code 1896, § 1592; Code 1907, § 361; Code 1923, § 451; Code 1940, T. 17, § 134.)

§ 17-6-13. Compensation of election officers; counties where compensation prescribed by other provisions.

The returning officer, the inspectors, and clerks shall each be entitled to $50. The several claims shall be paid as preferred claims, out of moneys in the county treasury not appropriated, on proper proof of service rendered. In all counties in which the compensation of election officials is prescribed by local law or general law of local application at an amount in excess of the amount prescribed, the compensation of the election officials shall not be increased or decreased. Those counties in which compensation of election officials is set at an amount in excess of $5 per day, but less than $50 per day, the provision of the local law or general law of local application relative thereto is superseded and the compensation prescribed shall be the total compensation of election officials in the counties. (Code 1876, § 290; Code 1886, § 386; Code 1896, § 1643; Code 1907, § 419; Code 1923, § 509; Code 1940, T. 17, § 198; Acts 1943, No. 311, p. 299; Acts 1947, No. 127, p. 38; Acts 1970, Ex. Sess., No. 30, p. 2652; Acts 1981, No. 81-674, p. 1099; Acts 1993, No. 93-639, p. 1095, § 1.)

The 1993 amendment, effective May 13, 1993, in the first sentence, deleted "and" following "officer," substituted "$50" for "$25.00," and deleted "and the returning officer, in addition, to $.25 a mile in going to the courthouse and returning to the place of holding the election" at the end of the sentence; deleted "otherwise" preceding "appropriated" in the second sentence; in the third sentence, deleted "However" preceding "in all," deleted "hereinabove" preceding "prescribed," substituted "the election" for "such election," and deleted "hereby, but in those" following "decreased"; and in the last sentence, inserted "compensation of," deleted "compensation" following "officials'," substituted "less than $50" for "not as much as

$25.00," deleted "hereby" preceding "superseded," deleted "hereinabove" preceding "prescribed," and substituted "the counties" for "such counties."

Election expense a preferred claim. — The fact that election expense is an involuntary expense of county makes such expense a preferred claim against the county, taking precedence over general and voluntary obligations. Abrasley v. Jefferson County, 241 Ala. 660, 4 So. 2d 153 (1941).

Cited in State ex rel. Austin v. Black, 224 Ala. 200, 139 So. 431 (1932).

Collateral references. — 29 C.J.S., Elections, § 63.

§ 17-6-14. Failure of officers to perform duty.

If any inspector, clerk or other officer on whom any duty is imposed by the election laws wilfully neglects to perform such duty, or is guilty of any corrupt conduct in the execution of the same, and no other punishment is provided for such neglect, or conduct, he must, on conviction, be fined not less than $100.00 nor more than $1,000.00; but no person shall be deemed an inspector, clerk or officer, within the meaning of this section, until he first shall have taken an oath well and truly to discharge the duties of such office, to the best of his ability, or until he shall have performed some of the duties pertaining to such office. The failure or refusal of any person to accept office, or his failure or refusal to discharge and perform the duties of such office at any time after his appointment thereto, and prior to his taking the oath of such office, and before he shall have discharged and performed any of the duties thereof, shall not, in either event, be deemed a violation of this section. (Code 1876, § 4284; Code 1886, § 4183; Code 1896, § 4690; Code 1907, § 6787; Code 1923, § 3905; Code 1940, T. 17, § 301.)

Collateral references. — 29 C.J.S., Elections, §§ 339-347.

§ 17-6-15. Officer or employee of city acting as election officer.

No officer or employee of any city or town shall act in the capacity of election officer, returning officer, marker or watcher, or as a deputy sheriff in conducting any town or city election; and any person violating any provision of this section shall be guilty of a misdemeanor, and, upon conviction, shall be fined not less than $50.00 and may also be imprisoned in the county jail or sentenced to hard labor for the county for not more than 12 months. (Acts 1915, No. 62, p. 202; Code 1923, § 3936; Code 1940, T. 17, § 331.)

§ 17-6-16. Officers consuming intoxicating liquors during election.

Any inspector, clerk, watcher or returning officer who drinks any intoxicating liquors while any election is being held, shall be guilty of a misdemeanor, and, upon conviction, shall be fined not less than $50.00. (Code 1907, § 6799; Code 1923, § 3917; Code 1940, T. 17, § 312.)

CHAPTER 7.

CONDUCT AND MANAGEMENT OF ELECTIONS GENERALLY.

Collateral references. — Criticism or disparagement of character, competence, or conduct of candidate for office as defamation. 37 ALR4th 1088.

§ 17-7-1. Persons entitled to have names printed on ballots; failure of Secretary of State to certify nominations.

(a) The following persons shall be entitled to have their names printed on the appropriate ballot for the general election, provided they are otherwise qualified for the office they seek:

(1) All candidates who have been put in nomination by primary election and certified in writing by the chair and secretary of the canvassing board of the party holding the primary and filed with the probate judge of the county, in the case of a candidate for county office, and the Secretary of State in all other cases, on the day next following the last day for contesting the primary election for that office if no contest is filed. If a contest is filed, then the certificate for the contested office must be filed on the day next following the date of settlement or decision of the contest.

(2) All candidates who have been put in nomination by any caucus, convention, mass meeting, or other assembly of any political party or faction and certified in writing by the chair and secretary of the nominating caucus, convention, mass meeting, or assembly and filed with the probate judge, in the case of a candidate for county office, and the Secretary of State in all other cases, on or before 5:00 P.M. six days after the second primary election.

(3) Each candidate who has been requested to be an independent candidate for a specified office by written petition signed by electors qualified to vote in the election to fill the office when the petition has been filed with the probate judge, in the case of a county office and with the Secretary of State

in all other cases, on or before 5:00 P.M. six days after the second primary election. The number of qualified electors signing the petition shall equal or exceed three percent of the qualified electors who cast ballots for the office of Governor in the last general election for the state, county, city, district, or other political subdivision in which the candidate seeks to qualify.

(b) With regard to the 1992 election cycle for candidates for the United States House of Representatives only, and only if the Legislature adopts an approved congressional reapportionment plan in the 1992 Regular Session, candidates shall be certified or qualified on or before 5:00 p.m. 29 days before the first primary election.

(c) The Secretary of State must, not later than 45 days after the second primary, certify to the probate judge of each county in the state, in the case of an officer to be voted for by the electors of the whole state, and to the probate judges of the counties composing the circuit or district in case of an officer to be voted for by the electors of a circuit or district, upon suitable blanks to be prepared by him or her for that purpose, the fact of nomination or independent candidacy of each nominee or independent candidate or candidate of a party who did not receive more than 20 percent of the entire vote cast in the last general election preceding the primary who has qualified to appear on the general election ballot. The probate judge shall then prepare the ballot with the names of each candidate qualified under the provisions of this section printed on the ballot. The probate judge is prohibited from causing to be printed on the ballot the name of any independent candidate who was a candidate in the primary election of that year. (Code 1896, §§ 1606, 4674; Code 1907, §§ 372, 6773; Code 1923, §§ 462, 3891; Acts 1935, No. 188, p. 238; Acts 1935, No. 424, p. 894; Code 1940, T. 17, §§ 145, 287; Acts 1945, No. 79, p. 76; Acts 1971, No. 2324, p. 3746; Acts 1977, 1st Ex. Sess., No. 69, p. 1493, §§ 2, 4; Acts 1982, No. 82-611, p. 1109, § 1; Acts 1992, No. 92-152, p. 262, § 1; Acts 1995, No. 95-786, § 1.)

The **1995 amendment,** effective August 9, 1995, in subsection (a), substituted "six days after the second primary election" for "60 days before the date of the first primary election" in subdivision (2), and rewrote subdivision (3); and in the first sentence of subsection (c), substituted "45 days" for "six days," and inserted the language beginning "or candidate of a party" and ending "preceding the primary."

Cross references. — As to certification of names of candidates for President and Vice-President, see § 17-19-2.

Current system of statewide elections of federal judges does not violate the Voting Rights Act. — Where plaintiffs' claim was that current system of statewide elections of federal judges violated § 2 of the Voting Rights Act, and where final judgment implemented appointment procedure for created judicial seats, although opponents maintained that this situation violated state law, which allows all qualified candidates to appear on the general elec-

tion ballot, this argument was fallacious because candidates were only entitled to run for positions that exist. The proposed settlement temporarily removed supreme court open seats from the electoral process under some circumstances, thereby removing any right to appear on the ballot. White v. Alabama, 867 F. Supp. 1519 (M.D. Ala. 1994).

Deadline provisions placed unconstitutional burden on parties. — Deadline provisions having the effect of requiring a minor party to submit its qualifying petitions and nominate its candidates seven months prior to the election placed an unconstitutional burden on such a party and its candidates in attempting to access the Alabama ballot. New Alliance Party v. Hand, 933 F.2d 1568 (11th Cir. 1991).

Ballot to contain names of all candidates not declining. — In the absence of written notice by a candidate that he will not accept the nomination, given to the judge of probate not less than 20 days before the election as provided by § 17-8-2, the ballot shall contain the names of all candidates nominated by mass meeting and other means. Herndon v. Lee, 281 Ala. 61, 199 So. 2d 74 (1967).

When announcement of candidacy occurs. — Announcement of candidacy occurs at the time of the filing of the certificate of nomination pursuant to this section. Hadnott v. Amos, 320 F. Supp. 107 (M.D. Ala. 1970), aff'd, 401 U.S. 968, 91 S. Ct. 1189, 28 L. Ed. 2d 318 (1971), 405 U.S. 1035, 92 S. Ct. 1304, 31 L. Ed. 2d 576 (1972).

The act of probate judge in printing ballots and inserting names of nominees at a primary is ministerial, and the fact that the certificate must show a compliance with the law in unambiguous language does not involve a judicial inquiry so as to give the courts jurisdiction. Boyd v. Garrison, 246 Ala. 122, 19 So. 2d 385 (1944).

Right of judge to inquire into nominations. — Where the certificate of nomination presented to probate judge was ambiguous and indicated that nominations were made by committees with the significant omission of the time when nominations were made, the probate judge, even acting in a ministerial capacity, had the right to make further inquiry to ascertain if statute had been complied with. Kinney v. House, 243 Ala. 393, 10 So. 2d 167 (1942).

And to decline to print names on ballots. — Since this section contains no provision that a certificate of nomination should be conclusive, where it appeared to the probate judge, even acting as a ministerial officer, that the nominations were contrary to statute, he had the right to decline to print the names on the ballots and leave the matter to the courts. Kinney v. House, 243 Ala. 393, 10 So. 2d 167 (1942).

Mandamus lies against probate judge. — Mandamus will lie to compel the probate judge to place the candidate's name on the ballot. Dunn v. Dean, 196 Ala. 486, 71 So. 2d 709 (1916).

Cited in Waid v. Pool, 255 Ala. 441, 51 So. 2d 869 (1951); Opinion of Justices, 418 So. 107 (Ala. 1982); Bostwick v. Harris, 421 So. 2d 492 (Ala. 1982); Godfrey v. Oswalt, 428 So. 2d 40 (Ala. 1983).

Collateral references. — 29 C.J.S., Elections, §§ 7(3), 135-138, 355(1).

25 Am. Jur. 2d, Elections, § 128 et seq.

§ 17-7-2. Certificates of nomination to be preserved by probate judge.

The probate judge shall cause to be preserved all certificates and petitions of nomination filed in his office under the provisions of this chapter for six months after the election for which such nominations are made. (Code 1896, § 1610; Code 1907, § 392; Code 1923, § 482; Code 1940, T. 17, § 168.)

Collateral references. — 29 C.J.S., Elections, §§ 135-138.

§ 17-7-3. Falsely making or fraudulently destroying certificates of nomination. Repealed by Acts 1977, No. 607, p. 812, § 9901, effective January 1, 1980.

§ 17-7-4. Suppressing nomination.

Any person who suppresses any nomination which has been duly filed, shall be guilty of a felony, and, on conviction, must be imprisoned in the penitentiary not less than one nor more than five years. (Code 1896, § 4676; Code 1907, § 6775; Code 1923, § 3893; Code 1940, T. 17, § 289.)

Collateral references. — 29 C.J.S., Elections, § 327.

§ 17-7-5. Notice of election.

The sheriff must give notice at least 30 days before each election by publication in some newspaper in the county, if any is published therein and, if not, by writings posted at the courthouse door and at three other public places in the county, of the time of holding and the offices to be filled by such election. Such notice shall consist only of the date of the election and the officers to be voted for or subjects to be voted on. (Code 1876, § 261; Code 1886, § 354; Code 1896, § 1590; Code 1907, § 357; Code 1923, § 447; Code 1940, T. 17, § 130.)

This section is not applicable to proposed amendments to the Constitution. In re Opinions of the Justices, 238 Ala. 150, 192 So. 905 (1939).

Governs publication of notice of general elections. — The law governing the publication of the notice of general elections is contained in this section. In re Opinion of Justices,

252 Ala. 199, 40 So. 2d 330 (1949).

Cited in Carson v. Hornsby, 402 So. 2d 931 (Ala. 1981).

Collateral references. — 29 C.J.S., Elections, §§ 73, 74.

26 Am. Jur. 2d, Elections, § 193 et seq.

What is "public place" within requirement as to posting of election notices. 90 ALR2d 1210.

§ 17-7-5.1. Time of holding elections.

Every polling place shall open for voting no later than 8:00 A.M. and shall close no earlier than 6:00 P.M. nor later than 8:00 P.M. and shall remain open for voting for not less than 10 consecutive hours. The precise hours of voting for each polling place, within these limits, shall be prescribed by the county commission. (Acts 1979, No. 79-616, p. 1086, § 1.)

Failure to keep the polls open during the hours specified does not render votes cast illegal. Patton v. Watkins, 131 Ala. 387, 31 So. 93 (1901).

§ 17-7-6. When inspectors, clerks, etc., to meet, open polling place, etc.

When paper ballots are used, the inspectors, clerks and returning officers appointed shall meet at the place of holding elections in the several precincts for which they have been appointed not later than 15 minutes before the hours of voting in the county commence and shall open the several polling places at the time designated. (Code 1907, § 358; Code 1923, § 448; Code 1940, T. 17, § 131; Acts 1979, No. 79-616, p. 1086, § 2.)

Cross references. — As to time of holding elections see § 17-7-5.1.

Collateral references. — 29 C.J.S., Elections, §§ 76, 78, 199.

§ 17-7-7. No adjournment.

After the polls have been opened, no adjournment or recess shall be taken until the certificate of the result of the election is signed. (Code 1907, § 360; Code 1923, § 450; Code 1940, T. 17, § 133.)

Collateral references. — 29 C.J.S., Elections, §§ 77, 80.

§ 17-7-8. Booths and place for holding election to be provided.

The sheriff of each county, at the expense of the county or, in case of a municipal election, the mayor or other chief executive officer, at the expense of the municipality shall provide at each polling place in all municipalities of over 3,000 inhabitants, a room or covered enclosure and, in such room or covered enclosure, shall provide booths or compartments, one booth or compartment for each 100 or fraction of 100 over 50 electors registered in the ward or wards in such municipality for that election and shall furnish each booth or compartment with a shelf or table for the convenience of the electors in the preparation of their ballots. Each booth or compartment shall be so arranged that it will be impossible for one elector at a shelf or table in one compartment to see an elector at a shelf or table in another compartment in the act of marking his ballot. Each voting shelf or table shall be kept supplied with conveniences for marking the ballots. In all other voting places other than in municipalities of over 3,000 inhabitants, no booths or compartments shall be required. (Code 1896, § 1616; Code 1907, § 388; Code 1923, § 478; Code 1940, T. 17, § 164.)

Collateral references. — 29 C.J.S., Elections, § 195.

§ 17-7-9. Removing, etc., booth, convenience or card of instruction.
Repealed by Acts 1977, No. 607, p. 812, § 9901, effective January 1, 1980.

§ 17-7-10. Hours polls to be open.
Repealed by Acts 1979, No. 79-616, p. 1086, § 3, effective July 30, 1979.

§ 17-7-11. Proclaiming polls open.

The inspectors, before they commence receiving ballots, must cause it to be proclaimed aloud at the place of voting that the election is opened. (Code 1876, § 272; Code 1886, § 367; Code 1896, § 1619; Code 1907, § 397; Code 1923, § 487; Code 1940, T. 17, § 173.)

§ 17-7-12. Voting without registration and taking oath.

Any person voting at any county or state election who has not registered and taken and subscribed to the registration oath, must, on conviction, be fined not less than $100.00 nor more than $1,000.00, or imprisoned in the county jail, or sentenced to hard labor for the county for not less than one nor more than six months. (Code 1876, § 4291; Code 1886, § 4186; Code 1896, § 4693; Code 1907, § 6789; Code 1923, § 3907; Code 1940, T. 17, § 303.)

§ 17-7-13. Elector must vote in county and precinct of residence.

At all elections by the people of this state the elector must vote in the county and precinct of his residence and nowhere else and must have registered as provided in this title; and, if any elector attempts to vote in any precinct other than that of his residence, his vote must be rejected, except as provided in Section 17-3-2. (Code 1876, § 273; Code 1886, § 368; Code 1896, § 1620; Code 1907, § 398; Code 1923, § 488; Code 1940, T. 17, § 174.)

Section is mandatory. — Where the Constitution and statute prescribe essential qualifications of electors and fix the place where elector must exercise his franchise, such provisions are mandatory and vote cast at any other place is illegal. Ex parte Bullen, 236 Ala. 56, 181 So. 498 (1938).

And applies to elections of city commissioners. — The constitutional and statutory provisions governing residence of electors and place of voting do not conflict with statutes governing commission form of city government, and hence are applicable to elections of city commissioners. Ex parte Bullen, 236 Ala. 56, 181 So. 498 (1938).

Collateral references. — 29 C.J.S., Elections, § 13.

§ 17-7-14. When registration certificate not required.

Electors whose names appear on the list of registered voters may vote without producing their registration certificate. (Code 1907, § 363; Code 1923, § 453; Code 1940, T. 17, § 136.)

Collateral references. — 29 C.J.S., Elections, §§ 38, 46.

§ 17-7-15. Voter to sign name on poll list; exceptions.

In every election held in this state, the voter himself shall sign his name on one of the poll lists or lists of persons who vote in the election, required by law to be maintained at each polling place; and no person shall record on this list the name of any voter for him, except where the voter, because of physical handicap, is unable to write his own name on the poll list; in which case an election official shall write the name of such voter on said list together with the cause of assistance and shall sign his own name on the poll list on the same line with the name of the voter. If the voter is unable to sign his name because of illiteracy, his name shall be written for him and the voter shall make his mark upon the poll list, in the presence of any of the election officials, and the election official witnessing the act shall record his name, as witness, on the same line with the name of the voter.

Any person who wilfully and intentionally signs on the poll list the name of any person other than himself, including any signing by mark, in violation of the provisions of this section, shall, upon conviction, be sentenced to imprisonment in the penitentiary for a period of not less than one nor more than five years. (Acts 1953, No. 201, p. 266, §§ 1, 2.)

Technical violation of section. — Where the evidence established that 25 couples, 50 husbands and wives, signed in for one another, this was a technical violation of this section, but one which the plaintiffs conceded to have been unobjectionable. Gray v. Main, 309 F. Supp. 207 (M.D. Ala. 1968).

Collateral references. — 29 C.J.S., Elections, §§ 171, 340, 352.

§ 17-7-16. Poll list to be sealed.

The poll list shall be sealed in an envelope before the inspectors begin to count the vote and shall not be opened. (Code 1907, § 367; Code 1923, § 457; Code 1940, T. 17, § 140.)

§ 17-7-17. Unlawful use of poll list.

Any election officer or any other person who makes a copy of the poll list or any memoranda therefrom, or list of the persons voting, or the number of their ballots, or discloses the number of such voter's ballot, shall be guilty of a misdemeanor, and upon conviction, shall be fined not less than $200.00. (Code 1907, § 6806; Code 1923, § 3924; Code 1940, T. 17, § 319.)

The plain meaning of this section can be gleaned from its words; therefore, the statute should be construed in accordance with that meaning. Advertiser Co. v. Hobbie, 474 So. 2d 93 (Ala. 1985).

Effect of section 17-15-4. — The sheriff nor any other person has authority to furnish a copy of the poll list, except as provided by § 17-15-4, which makes the judge of probate an exception to the provisions of this section. Sartain v. Gray, 173 Ala. 472, 55 So. 922 (1911), wherein it was held that this section does not abrogate § 17-15-4.

Color coding poll list. — A plan calling for color coding of the official voting list to indicate in which party's primary those voting participated does not violate this section. Haughton v. McCollum, 530 So. 2d 758 (Ala. 1988).

Declaratory relief was properly denied to newspaper which had requested public inspection of precinct registration lists stored in locked voting machines, where it was conceded that the lists sought were in fact "lists of the persons voting" within the meaning of this section, which proscribes the unlawful use of poll lists. Advertiser Co. v. Hobbie, 474 So. 2d 93 (Ala. 1985).

Cited in Gray v. Main, 309 F. Supp. 207 (M.D. Ala. 1968).

§ 17-7-18. Proximity of persons to polling place.

Except as electors are admitted to vote and persons to assist them as herein provided, and except the sheriff or his deputy, the inspectors, returning officer, clerks of elections and watchers, no person shall be permitted within 30 feet of the polling place. (Code 1896, § 1621; Code 1907, § 371; Code 1923, § 461; Code 1940, T. 17, § 144.)

Local law which prohibited distribution of election campaign materials within 600 feet of a polling place was in conflict with this section, and violated the uniformity provisions of the Alabama Constitution. Kiel v. Purvis, 510 So. 2d 190 (Ala. 1987).

Collateral references. — 29 C.J.S., Elections, § 144.

§ 17-7-19. Loitering about polling place; standing in line of voters after having voted.

Any person who loiters in, around or about a polling place on election day for the purpose of discouraging qualified electors from entering the voting place, or from voting, or whoever having voted enters or stands in a line or file of voters waiting to vote, is guilty of a misdemeanor and upon conviction shall be fined not less than $25.00 nor more than $500.00. (Acts 1966, Ex. Sess., No. 158, p. 183.)

§ 17-7-20. Designating certain officers by number.

In all primary and general elections of associate justices of the Supreme Court of Alabama, justices of the courts of appeals of Alabama, judges of the circuit and district courts and associate members of the public service commission, wherein two or more of such justices, judges or officers are to be elected at the same time, each of such places to be filled shall be designated by number. (Acts 1927, No. 348, p. 409; Code 1940, T. 17, § 146.)

§ 17-7-21. Announcements and ballots to contain number of office sought.

Every candidate for the offices mentioned in Section 17-7-20 shall, in the announcement of his candidacy, designate the number of the office for which he is a candidate, and the ballots of such election shall be numbered accordingly. (Acts 1927, No. 348, p. 409; Code 1940, T. 17, § 147.)

Collateral references. — 29 C.J.S., Elections, §§ 153, 155, 334(2).

CHAPTER 8.

BALLOTS.

Collateral references. — 26 Am. Jur. 2d, Elections, §§ 202-224.

§ 17-8-1. Elections must be by official ballot.

In all elections held in this state on any subject which may be submitted by law to the vote of the people and for all or any state, county, district or municipal officers, the voting shall be by official ballot printed and distributed as provided in this chapter, except when the form of the ballot is otherwise prescribed by law, or when the use of voting machines is authorized, and no ballot shall be received or counted in any election except it be provided as prescribed by law; but this section shall not apply to elections held for trustees of public schools or other local elections which are otherwise specifically provided for. (Code 1896, § 1605; Code 1907, § 389; Code 1923, § 479; Code 1940, T. 17, § 165.)

This section is mandatory to the extent that an official ballot is essential to the validity of the enumerated elections and that balloting on ex parte slips of paper submitted by individual voters or furnished by other unauthorized persons is illegal, will not be counted and, if such was the balloting, there, of necessity, could be no election, hence void. Walker v. Junior, 247 Ala. 342, 24 So. 2d 431 (1945).

Statutory provisions relative to the preparation and distribution of the ballots for an election must be strictly adhered to and a provision that none but official ballots be counted is mandatory. Walker v. Junior, 247 Ala. 342, 24 So. 2d 431 (1945).

And failure of substantial compliance invalidates ballot. — As a general proposition, when the statute expressly declares how the ballot shall be prepared, distributed, marked and identified by the officers charged with such duties and provides that ballots which do not so conform shall not be counted, a failure of substantial compliance with such mandatory provisions invalidates the ballot. Walker v. Junior, 247 Ala. 342, 24 So. 2d 431 (1945).

This section gives the directions and declares what the consequences of neglecting their observance shall be, and ballots for an election, prepared and distributed by unauthorized parties omitting the names of candidates duly nominated, in total disregard of the requirements, are void. Walker v. Junior, 247 Ala. 342, 24 So. 2d 431 (1945).

So that if only unofficial ballots were used election would be void. — If the only ballots made available to the voters and permitted to be used were those prepared by unauthorized persons, containing the names of only one set of nominees and omitting the names of the other nominees and though some voters requested the right to cast their votes on the alleged official ballot and this was refused, then no legal ballots were cast, and under this section none should have been counted. If this was the status, no officers were legally elected and the election was void. Walker v. Junior, 247 Ala. 342, 24 So. 2d 431 (1945), holding, however, that the evidence should be excluded for the court had no authority to declare, in an election contest proceeding, the election void when no legal votes were cast. See § 17-15-1.

Where no official ballot furnished. — The court raises but does not decide the question as to whether a ballot proposed by the voter may be used in case no official ballot is furnished in Bryce v. Burke, 172 Ala. 219, 55 So. 635 (1911).

Cited in Black v. Pate, 130 Ala. 514, 30 So. 434 (1901); Opinion of Justices No. 305, 442 So. 2d 42 (Ala. 1983).

Collateral references. — 29 C.J.S., Elections, § 154.

§ 17-8-2. Contents; withdrawal of name.

The ballots printed in accordance with the provisions of this chapter shall contain the names of all candidates nominated by caucus, convention, mass meeting, primary election or other assembly of any political party or faction, or by petition of electors and certified as provided in Section 17-7-1, but the name of no person shall be printed upon the ballots who, not less than 20 days before the election, notifies the judge of probate in writing, acknowledged before an officer authorized by law to take acknowledgments, that he will not accept the nomination specified in the certificate of nomination or petition of electors. The name of each candidate shall appear but one time on said ballot and under only one emblem. (Code 1896, § 1607; Code 1907, § 373; Acts 1909, No. 110, p. 277; Code 1923, § 463; Code 1940, T. 17, § 148.)

This section is not unconstitutional on its face, is not proved to be applied in an unconstitutional manner and does not violate the Voting Rights Act of 1965. Hadnott v. Amos, 295 F. Supp. 1003 (M.D. Ala. 1968), rev'd on other grounds, 394 U.S. 358, 89 S. Ct. 1101, 22 L. Ed. 2d 336 (1969).

Ballot to contain names of all candidates not declining. — See note to § 17-7-1.

Discriminatory application violated

fourteenth amendment. — Where the secretary of state rejected a political party's donkey emblem in 1968 because of a preexisting donkey emblem used by another party, and accepted a third and a fourth parties' eagle emblems in 1970 in spite of the preexisting eagle emblem of another party, discriminatory standards were applied which violated the provisions of the fourteenth amendment to the Constitution of the United States which guarantees equal protection of the laws to all citizens.

Hadnott v. Amos, 320 F. Supp. 107 (M.D. Ala. 1970), aff'd, 401 U.S. 968, 91 S. Ct. 1189, 28 L. Ed. 2d 318 (1971), 405 U.S. 1035, 92 S. Ct. 1304, 31 L. Ed. 2d 576 (1972).

Probate judge of Jefferson county held unauthorized to reject as party's nominee for constable name of one certified after primary by chairman of county executive committee. Blackwell v. Hawkins, 226 Ala. 149, 145 So. 477 (1932).

§ 17-8-2.1. Political parties not included on ballot unless requirements met.

(a) No political party, except those qualified as a political party under Title 17, chapter 16, shall be included on any general election ballot unless:

(1) The party shall have filed with the Secretary of State or other appropriate official six days after the second primary election a list of the signatures of at least three percent of the qualified electors who casts ballots for the office of Governor in the last general election for the state, county, city, district or other political subdivision in which the political party seeks to qualify candidates for office; and unless

(2) The party shall have fulfilled all other applicable requirements of federal, state or local laws.

(b) The provisions of this section are supplemental to the provisions of Title 17, chapter 16, and other laws regarding the conduct of elections in Alabama, and shall repeal only those laws or parts of laws in direct conflict herewith. (Acts 1982, No. 82-572, p. 1064, §§ 1, 2; Acts 1995, No. 95-786, § 1.)

The 1995 amendment, effective August 9, 1995, in subdivision (a)(1), substituted "six days after the second primary election" for "at the same time set by law in section 17-16-11, for candidates in primary elections to qualify," and substituted "three percent" for "one percent."

Constitutionality. — The levels of support required by this section, in conjunction with §§ 17-16-2 and 17-16-3, are constitutional. Libertarian Party v. Wallace, 586 F. Supp. 399 (M.D. Ala. 1984).

Deadline provisions placed unconstitutional burden on parties. — Deadline provisions having the effect of requiring a minor party to submit its qualifying petitions and nominate its candidates seven months prior to the election placed an unconstitutional burden on such a party and its candidates in attempting to access the Alabama ballot. New Alliance Party v. Hand, 933 F.2d 1568 (11th Cir. 1991).

This section, in conjunction with §§ 17-16-2 and 17-16-3 provides a two-track system by which a political party may have its name placed on a ballot for statewide and local elections: (1) a candidate of the party must have garnered at least 20 percent of votes cast in the last general election; or (2) the party must gather one percent of the signatures of qualified electors who cast ballots for governor in the last general election. If the office sought requires a statewide vote, the percentage requirements apply statewide; but if the party is seeking only a local office, the percentage requirements apply to the local political unit only. The secretary of state, who is responsible for monitoring and implementing the level of support requirements, has also adopted the policy that if a party is qualified statewide it is also qualified, without further filings, for all local offices throughout the state. Libertarian Party v. Wallace, 586 F. Supp. 399 (M.D. Ala. 1984).

States have an important interest in protecting their electoral processes through restrictions that eliminate fraudulent or frivolous candidacies, ensure efficient election procedures, and minimize voter confusion as the result of overcrowded ballots. States may therefore require that a political party demonstrate a certain level of support among the electorate before it may obtain a place on the ballot. Such restrictions, however, substantially implicate constitutionally protected liberties under the first amendment and the equal protection clause of the fourteenth amendment. Therefore, states must adopt the least drastic means to achieve their ends. Libertarian Party v. Wallace, 586 F. Supp. 399 (M.D. Ala. 1984).

Alabama does not substantially restrict who may sign the access ballot petitions. There are no political affiliation restrictions for those who sign the petitions; there are no time limits on when the petition drive may begin; and there are no geographic restrictions on where the signatures may come from. Furthermore, if a party qualifies for the ballot statewide, it automatically qualifies for all local offices. Libertarian Party v. Wallace, 586 F. Supp. 399 (M.D. Ala. 1984).

§ 17-8-3. Uniform ballots at each polling place; electors for President and Vice-President.

There shall be provided at each polling place at each election at which public officers are voted for, but one form of ballot for all the candidates for public office, and every ballot shall contain the names of all candidates whose nominations for any office specified on the ballot have been duly made and not withdrawn, as provided in this chapter, together with the title of the office, arranged in tickets under the titles of the respective political parties or independent bodies as certified in the certificates of nomination. When electors for the President and Vice-President of the United States are to be elected, the names of the candidates for President and Vice-President shall be listed on the ballot, but not the names of the electors. (Code 1907, § 378; Code 1923, § 468; Code 1940, T. 17, § 153.)

The provision that every ballot shall contain the title of the office being voted for must be strictly adhered to and a failure to substantially comply with the provision invalidates the ballot. State ex rel. Smith v. Deason, 264 Ala. 596, 88 So. 2d 674 (1956).

There is no provision of law which justifies the addition to the printed ballot of the name of an office to be filled not appearing on the official ballot. The office to be voted for cannot be added to the ballot by a voter and the name inserted of one for whom he wishes to vote. State ex rel. Smith v. Deason, 264 Ala. 596, 88 So. 2d 674 (1956).

Collateral references. — 29 C.J.S., Elections, § 156.

§ 17-8-4. Printing and design.

All ballots shall be printed in black ink on clear book paper, and every such ballot printed in accordance with the provisions of this chapter shall contain a party device for each political party represented on the ticket. The arrangement of the ballot shall in general conform substantially to the plan hereinafter given, and in all cases the party columns must be placed in alphabetical order, beginning on the left of the ballot. The list of candidates of the several parties shall be printed in parallel and perpendicular columns, each column to be headed by the chosen device of such party and the party name or other designation in such order as the Secretary of State may direct. The number of columns shall exceed by one the number of separate tickets of candidates to be voted for at the polling place for which the ballot is provided, and in the appropriate place the words vote for one (or two or other number, as the case may be) to indicate the number which may be elected to each office. On the right of each ballot shall be a column in which shall be printed only the titles of the office for which candidates may be voted for by the electors at the polling places for which the ballot is printed. Said column is designated as "blank column," and in such column the voting spaces shall be omitted, but in all other respects such blank column shall be a duplicate of the political party columns upon such ballot. (Code 1896, § 1611; Code 1907, § 379; Code 1923, § 469; Code 1940, T. 17, § 154.)

Effect of words "Vote for One." — Fact that official ballot contained printed words "Vote for One" in space provided to vote for two candidates for justices of the peace did not deprive electors of privilege of voting for two candidates, and vote for person whose name was written in proper place on ballot by elector must be counted, tabulated and reported to board of supervisors by precinct election inspectors. Reed v. State ex rel. Davis, 234 Ala. 306, 174 So. 498 (1937).

Cited in White v. Frink, 274 Ala. 49, 145 So. 2d 435 (1962).

Collateral references. — 29 C.J.S., Elections, § 158.

§ 17-8-5. Write-in votes; listing of independent candidates; form of ballots.

The elector may write in the column under the title of the office the name of any person whose name is not printed upon the ballot for whom he may desire to vote. In case of nomination by independent bodies, the ballot shall be so arranged that at the right of the last column for party nomination the several tickets of the names of the independent candidates shall be printed in one or more columns according to the space required, having above each of the tickets the political or other names selected to designate such independent nominations. The ballot herein provided shall be substantially in the following form:

Names of Officers To Be Voted for	(Emblem) Democratic O*	(Emblem) Republican O*	(Emblem) Independent O*
State: Governor .... Vote for One	( ) Wm. D. Jelks	( ) J. W. Smith	( ) Richard Roe ( ) John Doe ( ) David Moore
Lieutenant Governor .... Vote for One	( ) R. M. Cunningham	( ) Chas. P. Lane	( ) Samuel Jones
Congressional: Representative in Congress — First Congressional District	( ) Geo. W. Taylor	( ) Morris Wickersham	
Presidential: Electors of President and Vice-President Vote for One	( ) Harry S. Truman, President and Alben W. Barkley, Vice-President	( ) Thomas E. Dewey, President and Earl Warren, Vice-President	
Legislative: State Senator, First District .... Vote for One	( )..........................	....	....
Representative .... Vote for Two	( ).......................... ( )..........................	( ).......................... ( )..........................	( ).......................... ( )..........................
District Attorney, Third Judicial Circuit .... Vote for One	( )..........................	( )..........................	( )..........................
County: Sheriff .... Vote for One	( )..........................	( )..........................	( )..........................

Names of Officers To Be Voted for	(Emblem) Democratic O*	(Emblem) Republican O*	(Emblem) Independent O*
Judge of Probate .... Vote for One	( )........................	( )........................	( )........................
Beat: Constable .... Vote for One	( )........................	( )........................	( )........................

(Code 1907, § 380; Code 1923, § 470; Code 1940, T. 17, § 155.)

Erasure of name and substitution. — In Wilkerson v. Cantelou, 165 Ala. 619, 51 So. 799 (1910), it was held that an elector may erase the name of the democratic candidate and substitute therefor the name of an independent candidate for whom he wishes to vote instead of using the blank column as provided for under this section.

Cited in White v. Frink, 274 Ala. 49, 145 So. 2d 435 (1962).

Collateral references. — 29 C.J.S., Elections, §§ 1(10), 132, 133, 158, 159, 168.

§ 17-8-6. Party emblem — Submission; approval.

Each political party shall, by its state party convention or state executive committee, adopt, prepare and file with the Secretary of State, at least 60 days before each election for state officers, by engraving or otherwise, at least 150 copies of an emblem to be printed at the top of the column of such ballot assigned to such party, as a distinctive and characteristic heading thereof; and such emblem shall not be more than one inch and a half square. No party shall adopt an emblem similar in appearance to an emblem already adopted by another political party or organization, and the Secretary of State shall, upon the presentation or offer to him of any emblem which in his opinion is so like any other emblem already filed as to be likely to mislead any voter, forthwith notify the committee or any officer thereof or any person sending or offering such emblem of such similarity or resemblance and shall require such party, organization or committee to adopt, prepare and file another emblem. The emblem, once adopted, prepared and filed as aforesaid, shall continue the emblem of the party adopting the same until it is changed by the same or like authority as prepared, adopted and filed the original emblem, and the changed emblem, as prepared and adopted, if filed and accepted by the Secretary of State as in case of the original emblem. (Code 1907, § 374; Code 1923, § 464; Code 1940, T. 17, § 149.)

Collateral references. — 29 C.J.S., Elections, §§ 159, 173.

§ 17-8-7. Party emblem — Certification to probate judge.

The Secretary of State shall, immediately after an emblem has been filed in his office, certify to each judge of probate in the state the fact of the adoption of said emblem by the political party filing the same, with a proof copy thereof. (Code 1907, § 375; Code 1923, § 465; Code 1940, T. 17, § 150.)

§ 17-8-8. Party emblem — Prohibited designs.

The coat of arms or seal of any state or the United States, or the national flag, or the likeness of any person, living or dead, or religious emblem or symbol of any secret or fraternal organization or society, or the symbol of any industrial organization or a representation of a coin or the currency of the United States shall not be used as an emblem. (Code 1907, § 376; Code 1923, § 466; Code 1940, T. 17, § 151.)

§ 17-8-9. Party emblem — Use when party is divided.

When there is a division of any political party and each faction claims the party emblem, the judge of probate shall at once certify the fact to the chairman of the state executive committee of that party, who shall within 10 days notify the judge of probate which ticket is entitled to the party emblem, and the judge of probate shall be governed by the decision of said chairman, whereupon the other factions may file with the judge of probate an emblem to be used in that election only. (Code 1907, § 377; Code 1923, § 467; Code 1940, T. 17, § 152.)

§ 17-8-10. Designation of different offices of same classification.

Whenever nominations for two or more offices of the same classification are to be made, or whenever candidates are to be elected to two or more offices of the same classification at the same primary, general, special or municipal election, each office shall be separately designated by number on the official ballot as "Place No. 1," "Place No. 2," "Place No. 3" and so forth; and the candidates for each place shall be separately nominated or elected, as the case may be. In the case of primary elections, the designations required herein shall be made by the state executive committee of the political party holding the election. Each candidate for nomination for such office shall designate in the announcement of his candidacy and in his request to have his name placed on the official primary ballot the number of the place for which he desires to become a candidate. The name of each qualified candidate shall be printed on the official ballot used at any such election beneath the title of the office and the number of the place for which he is seeking nomination or election. No person shall be a candidate for more than one such place; provided, that this provision shall not apply to counties having a population of 500,000 or more according to the last or any subsequent federal census, except as to judicial officers and members of Congress. (Acts 1961, Ex. Sess., No. 221, p. 2234, § 1.)

§ 17-8-11. Secret ballot.

Every voter in Alabama shall have the right to vote a secret ballot, and that ballot shall be kept secret and inviolate. (Acts 1939, No. 209, p. 361; Code 1940, T. 17, § 156.)

The statutory provisions for the preservation of the secrecy of the ballot are for the protection of the voter against the conduct of others, and in no manner is intended as restrictive of any voluntary act of his own. United States v. Executive Comm. of Democratic Party, 254 F. Supp. 543 (N.D. Ala. 1966).

Presence of federal observers when voter receives assistance. — See United States v. Executive Comm. of Democratic Party, 254 F. Supp. 543 (N.D. Ala. 1966).

Jury venire questions would infringe upon secrecy of ballot. — Requiring an answer to question of whether members of jury venire had voted for county sheriff who was subsequently called as a defense witness would have infringed upon the right of the venire members to maintain the secrecy of the ballot. McLeod v. State, 581 So. 2d 1144 (Ala. Crim. App. 1990).

Collateral references. — 29 C.J.S., Elections, § 1(1).

26 Am. Jur. 2d, Elections, § 236.

§ 17-8-12. Disclosing votes by inspectors, clerks, etc.

Any inspector, clerk or other person who discloses how any elector voted shall be guilty of a misdemeanor, and, on conviction, shall be fined not less than $100.00 nor more than $500.00, and may be also sentenced to hard labor for the county for not more than six months. (Code 1896, § 4681; Code 1907, § 6798; Code 1923, § 3916; Code 1940, T. 17, § 311.)

§ 17-8-13. Numbering of ballots.

Each ballot shall be numbered by one of the inspectors to correspond to the number of the voter voting the same on the poll list. A voter may write his name on the ballot. The number corresponding with the voter's name on the poll list must be plainly entered in the square on the bottom of the ballot 52 the voter. (Code 1907, § 354; Code 1923, § 444; Code 1940, T. 17, § 127.)

Purpose of section. — The system of numbering the ballots, as provided for in this section, is intended to furnish a means for the discovery of frauds and irregularities in election, but to be used only in a legally instituted contest thereof. Sartain v. Shepherd, 173 Ala. 474, 55 So. 919 (1911).

Which is not mandatory. — The statutory provision requiring ballots to be numbered is not mandatory and the ballot may be counted although not numbered. Montgomery v. Henry, 144 Ala. 629, 39 So. 507 (1905). See also Lee v. State, 49 Ala. 43 (1873).

Cited in Harris v. Conradi, 675 F.2d 1212 (11th Cir. 1982).

Collateral references. — 29 C.J.S., Elections, § 171.

§ 17-8-14. Number of ballot boxes, and by whom provided.

The judge of probate, sheriff and clerk of the circuit court of each county in this state shall provide one ballot box and, where it is deemed necessary, shall provide more than one. (Code 1876, § 258; Code 1886, § 351; Code 1896, § 1587; Code 1907, § 346; Code 1923, § 436; Code 1940, T. 17, § 89; Acts 1956, 1st Ex. Sess., No. 141, p. 201, § 5.)

Collateral references. — 29 C.J.S., Elections, § 194.

§ 17-8-15. Procedure to vote straight party ticket.

If the elector desires to vote a straight ticket, that is, for each and every candidate for one party for whatever office nominated, he shall mark a cross mark (x) in the circle under the name of the party at the head of the ticket. (Code 1896, § 1622; Code 1907, § 381; Code 1923, § 471; Code 1940, T. 17, § 157.)

Ballots marked opposite but after the candidate's name instead of as provided for by this section should be rejected. Black v. Pate, 130 Ala. 514, 30 So. 434 (1901).

§ 17-8-16. Procedure to vote for one candidate not on party ticket.

When only one candidate is to be elected to any office and the elector desires to vote for a candidate not on his party ticket, he may make a cross mark (x) before the name of the candidate for whom he desires to vote on the other ticket. (Code 1907, § 382; Code 1923, § 472; Code 1940, T. 17, § 158.)

§ 17-8-17. Procedure to vote for two or more candidates on different tickets.

When two or more candidates are to be elected to the same office and he desires to vote for candidates on different tickets for such office, he may make a cross mark (x) before the names of the candidates for whom he desires to vote on the other ticket and must also erase an equal number of names of candidates on his party ticket for the same office for whom he does not desire to vote. (Code 1907, § 383; Code 1923, § 473; Code 1940, T. 17, § 159.)

§ 17-8-18. Procedure to vote split ticket.

If the elector desires to vote a split ticket, that is, for candidates of different parties, he may make a cross mark (x) in the voting space before the name of each candidate for whom he desires to vote on whatever ticket he may be. (Code 1907, § 384; Code 1923, § 474; Code 1940, T. 17, § 160.)

Collateral references. — 29 C.J.S., Elections, § 182.

§ 17-8-19. Procedure when straight ticket does not contain names of all officers.

If the ticket marked in the circle for a straight ticket does not contain the names of candidates for all offices for which the elector may vote, he may vote for candidates for such offices so omitted by making a cross mark (x) before the names of candidates for such offices on other tickets, or by writing the names, if they are not printed, upon the ballot in the blank column under the title of the office. (Code 1907, § 385; Code 1923, § 475; Code 1940, T. 17, § 161.)

Cited in Reed v. State ex rel. Davis, 234 Ala. 306, 174 So. 498 (1937).

§ 17-8-20. Procedure to vote for person whose name not on ballot.

If the elector desires to vote for any person whose name does not appear upon the ballot, he can so vote by writing the name in the proper place on the blank column. (Code 1907, § 386; Code 1923, § 476; Code 1940, T. 17, § 162.)

Ballot must be legal. — The ballot must be a legal one for the vote to count. Walker v. Junior, 247 Ala. 342, 24 So. 2d 431 (1945).

Cited in Reed v. State ex rel. Davis, 234 Ala. 306, 174 So. 498 (1937); State ex rel. Smith v. Deason, 264 Ala. 596, 88 So. 2d 674 (1956).

Collateral references. — 29 C.J.S., Elections, §§ 118, 156, 175, 177, 180.

Validity of write-in vote where candidate's surname only is written in on ballot. 86 ALR2d 1025.

Elections: validity of state or local legislative ban on write-in votes. 69 ALR4th 948.

§ 17-8-21. Procedure to vote blank for any officer on ticket.

The elector can vote blank for any office on his party ticket by making a cross mark (x) in the circle at the top of the ticket and striking out with pencil or pen the name or names of candidates he does not desire to vote for on the ticket. (Code 1907, § 387; Code 1923, § 477; Code 1940, T. 17, § 163.)

§ 17-8-22. Ballot for constitutional amendment.

Whenever a constitutional amendment is submitted to a vote of the qualified electors the substance or subject matter of each proposed amendment shall be so printed that the nature thereof shall be clearly indicated. Following each proposed amendment or other public measure on the ballot shall be printed the word "Yes" and immediately under that shall be printed the word "No." The choice of the electors shall be indicated by a cross mark made by him or under his direction opposite the words expressing his desire. (Code 1896, § 1608; Code 1907, § 390; Code 1923, § 480; Code 1940, T. 17, § 166.)

Cross references. — As to elections regarding amendments to the Constitution generally, see § 17-17-1 et seq.

This section wisely follows the exact requirements of the Constitution as to the ballots to be used in voting for constitutional amendments. Reality Inv. Co. v. City of Mobile, 181 Ala. 184, 61 So. 248 (1913).

Collateral references. — 29 C.J.S., Elections, §§ 79, 329.

§ 17-8-23. Ballots to be paid for by counties and cities.

The printing and delivery of the ballots and cards of instructions to voters shall in municipal elections be paid for by the several cities and towns and in all other elections by the several counties respectively. (Code 1896, § 1609; Code 1907, § 391; Code 1923, § 481; Code 1940, T. 17, § 167.)

County's function. — Notwithstanding statutes placing financial burden of elections on county, county in corporate capacity has no function to perform in respect thereto.

Wilkinson v. Henry, 221 Ala. 254, 128 So. 362 (1930).

Collateral references. — 29 C.J.S., Elections, §§ 153, 155, 334(2).

§ 17-8-24. Ballots to be bound together, etc.

All ballots for use in each precinct shall be fastened together in convenient numbers in books or blocks in such manner that each ballot may be detached and removed separately. Each ballot shall have attached to it a stub of sufficient size to enable one of the inspectors to write or stamp his name or initials thereon and so attached to the ballot that when the same is folded the stub can be detached therefrom without injury to the ballot or exposing the contents thereof. (Code 1896, § 1612; Code 1907, § 393; Code 1923, § 483; Code 1940, T. 17, § 169.)

§ 17-8-25. Number of ballots per voter.

There shall be provided for each voting place at least 50 ballots for each 50 registered electors at that place. (Code 1896, § 1613; Code 1907, § 394; Code 1923, § 484; Code 1940, T. 17, § 170; Acts 1991, No. 91-583, p. 1073, § 1.)

Collateral references. — 29 C.J.S., Elections, §§ 155, 157.

§ 17-8-26. Performance of duties under chapter for municipal elections.

In case of any municipal election held at a time different from a general state or federal election, the duties herein prescribed for the judge of probate in respect to receiving nominations, printing and distributing ballots and cards of instructions shall be discharged under the same sanctions by the mayor or other chief executive officer of the city or town. (Code 1896, § 1615; Code 1907, § 395; Code 1923, § 485; Code 1940, T. 17, § 171.)

Cited in Walker v. Junior, 247 Ala. 342, 24 So. 2d 431 (1945).

Collateral references. — 29 C.J.S., Elections, §§ 1(2), 1(7), 54, 77, 99, 108, 210(1).

§ 17-8-27. Delivery of ballot to voter.

Each elector, upon entering the polling place, shall be given one ballot by the inspectors. Before delivering the ballot to the elector, at least one of the inspectors shall write or shall have already written his name or the initials of his name on the stub attached to the ballot. (Code 1896, § 1622; Code 1907, § 399; Code 1923, § 489; Code 1940, T. 17, § 175.)

§ 17-8-28. Forging inspector's name on ballot. Repealed by Acts 1977, No. 607, p. 812, § 9901, effective January 1, 1980.

§ 17-8-29. Assistance in casting; number of electors in polling place; length of time elector may stay in polling place.

Any elector applying to vote who shall state to any of the inspectors that by reason of his inability to write the English language or by reason of blindness or the loss of the use of his hand or hands he is unable to prepare his ballot may have the assistance of any person he may select. In such case said elector must remain within the polling place and the inspector shall send for the person selected; if the person cannot be found, then such elector may select any other person. An elector who prepares his ballot alone or with the assistance of another shall be permitted to prepare it at any point in the polling place. Any person called in to assist an elector in preparing his ballot shall retire when the elector retires.

No more than 10 electors shall be allowed in the polling place at the same time. No elector shall remain more than five minutes in, nor shall he be permitted to take his ballot from the polling place.

In cities or towns of more than 3,000 inhabitants, each elector on receiving the ballot shall forthwith and without leaving the polling place retire alone to one of the booths or compartments provided for that purpose, and there prepare his ballot in the manner herein provided. Any elector applying to vote in such city or town who shall state under oath to any of the inspectors, which said oath may be administered by any one of the inspectors, that by reason of his inability to write the English language or by reason of blindness or the loss of the use of his hand or hands he is unable to prepare his ballot may have the assistance of any person he may select. In such case, said elector must remain within the polling place, and the inspector shall send for the person selected. If the person cannot be found, then such elector may select any other person, and, thereupon, said elector and the person so selected shall retire to a booth or compartment, and there the person so selected shall render said elector all such assistance in the preparation of said ballot as he may require, so that the same may be voted for the candidate of his choice, in the manner herein provided. In all other respects, said elector shall vote as is required of other electors.

No candidate for election shall act as assistant to any elector in the preparation of his ballot. When all the booths or compartments are occupied and other electors are waiting to vote, no elector shall occupy a booth or compartment for a longer time than five minutes. No elector shall be allowed to occupy a booth or compartment already occupied by another, nor speak or converse with anyone except as herein provided while in the polling place. After having voted or declined or failed to vote within five minutes, the elector shall immediately withdraw from the polling place and go beyond the prohibited distance and shall not enter the polling place again. (Code 1896, §§ 1623, 1627; Code 1907, §§ 400, 401; Code 1923, §§ 490, 491; Code 1940, T. 17, §§ 176, 177.)

This section violates § 2 of the Voting Rights Act. — This section authorizes assistance not only for voters who cannot write the English language but also for physically disabled voters. The additional disability provision does not, however, save this section from censure under the federal Voting Rights Act of 1965, § 2, as amended, 42 U.S.C. § 1973, because white poll officials have recently used this section, even with the disability provision, to deny assistance to black voters who clearly needed it. This section's assistance provisions must therefore fall in their entirety. Harris v. Siegelman, 695 F. Supp. 517 (M.D. Ala. 1988).

For discussion of the history of this section, see Harris v. Siegelman, 695 F. Supp. 517 (M.D. Ala. 1988).

Failure to take oath. — Failure of an elector to state under oath his disability as required by this section does not render the vote prepared by an official marker illegal. Patton v. Watkins, 131 Ala. 387, 31 So. 93 (1901).

Substitution of elector's choice. — A ballot marked by an official marker substituting his own choice of candidates for that of the elector is void. Patton v. Watkins, 131 Ala. 387, 31 So. 93 (1901).

Cited in Gray v. Main, 309 F. Supp. 207 (M.D. Ala. 1968); Harris v. Siegelman, 700 F. Supp. 1083 (M.D. Ala. 1988).

Collateral references. — 29 C.J.S., Elections, §§ 208, 327.

§ 17-8-30. Making false declaration as to inability to prepare ballot.

Repealed by Acts 1977, No. 607, p. 812, § 9901, effective January 1, 1980.

§ 17-8-31. Deceiving elector in preparation of ballot.

Any inspector, marker, helper or assistant who wilfully deceives any elector in preparing his ballot, must, on conviction, be imprisoned in the penitentiary not less than one nor more than five years. (Code 1896, § 4680; Code 1907, § 6779; Code 1923, § 3897; Code 1940, T. 17, § 293.)

§ 17-8-32. Inspector refusing to appoint markers, etc.

Any inspector of election who wilfully fails or refuses to advise any elector, entitled thereto, that he is entitled to an assistant, or refuses to let him select an assistant as required by law, must, on conviction, be fined not less than $100.00 nor more than $500.00. (Code 1896, § 4684; Code 1907, § 6781; Code 1923, § 3899; Code 1940, T. 17, § 295.)

§ 17-8-33. Spoiled ballot.

Any elector who shall by accident or mistake spoil a ballot so that he cannot conveniently or safely vote the same may return it to the inspectors and may receive another in lieu thereof, which ballot must be voted or returned to the inspectors by such elector. (Code 1896, § 1624; Code 1907, § 402; Code 1923, § 492; Code 1940, T. 17, § 178.)

Collateral references. — 29 C.J.S., Elections, § 204.

§ 17-8-34. Ballot to be folded after voting; name of voter to be called by inspector.

After preparing his ballot, the elector shall fold the same so as to conceal the face thereof and show the stub thereto attached with the name or the initial of the inspector and hand it to the receiving inspector. The inspector must receive the ballot folded and call the name of the elector audibly and distinctly, and the name of each elector whose ballot has been received must immediately be taken down by the clerks on separate lists, which shall be headed "names of voters" and called "poll lists," and the number of the order in which such elector votes must at the same time be entered by each clerk against his name, the first elector voting being numbered one, the second two and so on to the last elector voting. (Code 1876, § 275; Code 1886, § 371; Code 1896, § 1625; Code 1907, § 403; Code 1923, § 493; Code 1940, T. 17, § 179.)

Cross references. — As to provisions for the disposition of records and forms after elections, see § 17-4-230 et seq.

Absentee ballot numbering which failed to preserve secrecy subject to federal preclearance. — Introduction of absentee ballot numbering in Greene, Perry and Sumter counties by a system which failed to preserve ballot secrecy was clearly a change in a voting practice or procedure which was subject to preclearance under § 5 of the Federal Voting Rights Act. Turner v. Webster, 637 F. Supp. 1089 (N.D. Ala. 1986).

Cited in Harris v. Conradi, 675 F.2d 1212 (11th Cir. 1982).

§ 17-8-35. Numbering of ballots and placing seal thereon.

When a voter casts his ballot, it shall be numbered by the inspector receiving the ballot in the following manner: At the bottom of each ballot and at a point an equal distance from the sides thereof, there shall be printed a one inch square, and the number of the ballot shall be placed by the inspector inside this square and nowhere else upon the ballot. Immediately after the inspector places the number on the ballot in the square provided therefor, he shall forthwith and in the presence of the voter and before placing the ballot in the ballot box, place a seal over the square in such manner as to make it impossible to see the number placed therein without removing the seal, but in such manner as that the seal may be removed without obliterating the number placed in the square. The seals to be used for this purpose shall be black and shall be furnished as a part of the election supplies by the persons now authorized by law to furnish other election supplies, shall be two inches square, and around the outer edge thereof, one-fourth inch in width, there shall be a mucilaginous surface so that the seal may be securely placed over the square and may be later removed in the manner provided for herein without obliterating the number placed in the square. As many seals shall be furnished for each voting place as there are ballots furnished for that voting place. (Acts 1939, No. 209, p. 361; Code 1940, T. 17, § 180.)

Absentee ballot numbering which failed to preserve secrecy subject to federal preclearance. — Introduction of absentee ballot numbering in Greene, Perry and Sumter counties by a system which failed to preserve ballot secrecy was clearly a change in a voting practice or procedure which was subject to preclearance under § 5 of the Federal Voting Rights Act. Turner v. Webster, 637 F. Supp. 1089 (N.D. Ala. 1986).

Cited in Harris v. Conradi, 675 F.2d 1212 (11th Cir. 1982).

Collateral references. — 29 C.J.S., Elections, § 171.

§ 17-8-36. Removal or breaking of seals.

No seal placed upon a ballot as herein provided for shall be removed or broken except in the case of an election contest or grand jury investigation and then only upon the order of the officer in charge of the election contest or grand jury investigation as the case may be. (Acts 1939, No. 209, p. 361; Code 1940, T. 17, § 181.)

§ 17-8-37. Penalty for violation of Sections 17-8-35 and 17-8-36.

Any election official found guilty of violating the provisions of Sections 17-8-35 and 17-8-36 by failing to number a ballot or ballots and seal the same in the manner hereinabove provided for shall be guilty of a misdemeanor and upon conviction shall be fined not less than $10.00 nor more than $100.00. Any person found guilty of violating the provisions of Sections 17-8-35 and 17-8-36 by removing, breaking or tampering with a seal placed on a ballot in conformity with the provisions of Sections 17-8-35 and 17-8-36, except in the manner hereinabove provided, shall be guilty of a felony and upon conviction shall be punished by imprisonment in the penitentiary for a term of not less than one nor more than five years. (Acts 1939, No. 209, p. 361; Code 1940, T. 17, § 182.)

Absentee ballot numbering which failed to preserve secrecy subject to federal preclearance. — Introduction of absentee ballot numbering in Greene, Perry and Sumter counties by a system which failed to preserve ballot secrecy was clearly a change in a voting practice or procedure which was subject to preclearance under § 5 of the Federal Voting Rights Act. Turner v. Webster, 637 F. Supp. 1089 (N.D. Ala. 1986).

§ 17-8-38. Applicability of Sections 17-8-35 through 17-8-37.

The provisions of Sections 17-8-35 through 17-8-37 shall apply to all elections held in this state, general, special, primary and municipal. (Acts 1939, No. 209, p. 361; Code 1940, T. 17, § 183.)

§ 17-8-39. Deposit of ballot.

Having numbered the ballot, the inspector shall detach the stub and pass the ballot to each of the other inspectors, and it must then, without being opened or examined, be deposited in the proper ballot box. (Code 1876, § 276; Code 1886, § 372; Code 1896, § 1626; Code 1907, § 404; Code 1923, § 494; Code 1940, T. 17, § 184.)

Legal evidence of voting. — The act of voting is not completed until the vote is deposited in the box, and the entry of the name upon the list is not the vote, but only the legal evidence of the voting, to prove which the list must be produced, or by parol evidence, after showing its loss or destruction. Blackwell v. Thompson, 2 Stew. & Port. 348 (1832).

§ 17-8-40. Changing of ballot by inspector. Repealed by Acts 1977, No. 607, p. 812, § 9901, effective January 1, 1980.

§ 17-8-41. Disclosing or removing ballot; interfering with or influencing elector; remaining in booth, etc.

Any elector who takes or removes, or attempts to take or remove, any ballot from the polling place before the close of the polls; or any person who interferes with any elector when inside the polling place or when marking the ballot, or unduly influences, or attempts to unduly influence, any elector in the preparation of his ballot; or any elector who remains longer than the time allowed by law in the booth or compartment after being notified his time has expired, must, on conviction, be fined not less than $10.00 nor more than $100.00. (Code 1896, § 4682; Code 1907, § 6780; Code 1923, § 3898; Code 1940, T. 17, § 294.)

§ 17-8-42. Comparing ballot with poll list.

Any person who compares the number on the ballot with the poll list shall be guilty of a misdemeanor, and, on conviction, shall be fined not less than $100.00; but this shall not apply on the trial of any contested elections. (Code 1907, § 6815; Code 1923, § 3933; Code 1940, T. 17, § 328.)

§ 17-8-43. Instruction cards to voters.

The judge of probate shall cause to be printed in large type cards of instructions for the guidance of electors in preparing their ballots. He shall furnish to the sheriff three, or more if necessary, of such cards for each precinct, and the sheriff shall post one of such cards in each booth or compartment for the preparation of ballots, and not less than three in prominent places elsewhere about the outside of the polling place on the day of the election. Such cards shall be printed in large clear type and shall contain full instructions to electors as to what should be done; first, to obtain ballots for voting; second, to prepare the ballot for deposit in the ballot box; third, to obtain a new ballot in place of one accidentally spoiled; fourth, to instruct as to the right and manner of obtaining a watcher for each political party having candidates to be voted for. (Code 1896, § 1617; Code 1907, § 405; Code 1923, § 495; Code 1940, T. 17, § 185.)

Collateral references. — 29 C.J.S., Elections, § 196.

§ 17-8-44. Blank forms and stationery for election.

The judge of probate for each county shall have printed, at the expense of the county, ballots, blank poll lists, certificates of results, oaths and any other stationery or blank forms necessary in the conduct of an election. The judge of probate shall also superintend and insure the delivery by the sheriff to the inspectors of the election of the ballots, blank poll lists, certificates of results, oaths and other stationery or blank forms necessary in the conduct of the elections. (Code 1907, § 406; Code 1923, § 496; Code 1940, T. 17, § 186.)

§ 17-8-45. Examination of ballots, voting machines, etc., by persons involved in certain election contests.

In all election contests other than political party primaries or run-offs, any person or candidate involved in the contest is entitled to make an examination of the ballots cast, given, or rejected in the election, to make an examination of the voting machines used in the election, and to make an examination of voting machine computations or printouts. (Acts 1989, No. 89-877, p. 1757, § 1.)

CHAPTER 9.

VOTING MACHINES.

§ 17-9-1. Definitions.

For the purposes of this chapter, the following terms shall have the meanings respectively ascribed to them by this section:

(1) OFFICIAL BALLOT. The list of offices and candidates, and the statements of questions on the voting machine.

(2) BALLOT LABELS. The cards, paper or other material, containing the names of offices and candidates and statements of questions to be voted on.

(3) DIAGRAM. An illustration of the official ballot, when placed upon the machine, showing the names of the parties, offices and candidates, and statements of the questions, in their proper places, together with the voting devices therefor, and shall be considered a specimen ballot.

(4) QUESTION. A statement of such constitutional amendment or other proposition as shall be submitted to a popular vote at any election.

(5) IRREGULAR BALLOT. The paper or other material on which a vote is cast on a voting machine for persons whose names do not appear on the ballot label.

(6) CANDIDATE COUNTERS and QUESTION COUNTERS. The counters on which are registered numerically the votes cast for candidates, and on questions, respectively.

(7) PUBLIC COUNTER. A counter or other device which shall publicly indicate how many times the machine has been operated at an election.

(8) PROTECTIVE COUNTER. A counter or protective device or devices that will register each time the machine is operated, and shall be constructed and so connected that it cannot be reset, altered or operated, except by operating the machine.

(9) VOTING MACHINE BOOTH. The enclosure occupied by the voter when voting.

(10) MODEL. A mechanically operating model of a portion of the face of the machine, illustrating the manner of voting.

(11) CUSTODIAN. Person charged with the storing and caring for the voting machines when not in use in elections.

(12) ELECTION and ELECTIONS. Such term shall include and mean all general, municipal, primary, bond, tax rate, school and special elections of any kind.

(13) SEAL. Such term, and other words of the singular number relative thereto, shall include the plural number as applied to a voting machine, designed to be made secure with two or more seals.

(14) CITY COMMISSIONER. Any municipal authority by whatever name called that is legally constituted to supervise and manage the affairs of the town or city or other like political subdivision of the state.

(15) COUNTY COMMISSION. The governing body of each county of this state.

(16) COUNTY, CITY or MUNICIPALITY. The use of such terms shall not be interpreted to exclude from the use of voting machines any other political subdivision of the state, but the same laws, rules and regulations that apply to the use of voting machines in counties, cities or municipalities shall apply to other political subdivisions of the state insofar as they are applicable and pertinent. (Acts 1939, No. 292, p. 443; Code 1940, T. 17, § 91.)

Discussions of chapter. — This chapter known as the voting machine law is discussed in Kendrick v. State ex rel. Shoemaker, 256 Ala. 206, 54 So. 2d 442 (1951).

As to proceedings to require county commission to furnish voting machines, see Kendrick v. State ex rel. Shoemaker, 256 Ala. 206, 54 So. 2d 442 (1951).

Authority to use machines. — The legislature may authorize the use in municipal elections of voting machines procured by the county where the use of such machines has been approved only in a county-wide election. Kendrick v. State ex rel. Shoemaker, 256 Ala. 206, 54 So. 2d 442 (1951).

§ 17-9-2. Authorization.

The governing body of any county or municipality or other political subdivision of the state may, in its discretion, by adoption of an appropriate resolution, authorize, adopt and direct the use of voting machines for registering or recording and computing the vote at all elections held in such county or municipality or other political subdivision or portion of any thereof without the requirement of submitting the question of the authorization and installation of voting machines to a vote of the qualified electors of such county, municipality or other political subdivision or portion of any thereof. (Acts 1939, No. 292, p. 443; Code 1940, T. 17, § 92; Acts 1959, No. 604, p. 1494, § 1.)

County may impose use of machines by city. — Under this section the power and duty to use voting machines in a city may be imposed by vote of the entire county in an election held at the instance of the county commission without a separate election in the city, and in such a case, a discontinuance of voting machines by vote of entire county will be operative in such city. Abrasley v. Jefferson County, 241 Ala. 660, 4 So. 2d 153 (1941).

Cited in Kendrick v. State ex rel. Shoemaker, 256 Ala. 206, 54 So. 2d 442 (1951).

Collateral references. — 29 C.J.S., Elections, § 203.

26 Am. Jur. 2d, Elections, §§ 232, 253.

§ 17-9-3. Referendum on adoption of voting machines.

The county commission of any county, may, upon their own motion, submit to the qualified electors of the county, at any general, special or primary election, the question, "Shall voting machines be used in the County of . . . . .?" The city commission may, upon their own motion, submit to the qualified electors of the city, at any general, special, primary or municipal election, the question, "Shall voting machines be used in the City of . . . . .?" The county commission, upon the filing of a petition with them signed by qualified voters of the county equal in number to at least five percent of the total number of electors who voted in said county at the last preceding general, special or primary election, but in no case less than 50, unless the total number of electors who voted therein at the last preceding general, special or primary election was less than 100, in which case one half of the number voting shall be sufficient, shall, at the next general, special or primary election occurring at least 30 days thereafter, submit to the qualified electors of such county, the question, "Shall voting machines be used in the County of . . . . .?" The city commission, upon the filing of a petition with them signed by qualified electors of the city equal in number to at least five percent of the total number of electors who voted in said city at the last preceding general, special, primary or municipal election, but in no case less than 50, unless the total number of electors who voted therein at the last preceding general, special, primary or municipal election was less than 100, in which case one half of the number so voting shall be sufficient, shall, at the next general, special, primary or municipal election, occurring at least 30 days thereafter, submit to the qualified electors of such city, the question, "Shall voting machines be used in the City of . . . . .?" The county commission or the city commission shall cause the said question to be printed upon the ballots to be used at the election, in the form and manner provided by the laws governing general, special, primary and municipal elections. The election on said question shall be held at the places, during the hours, and under the regulations provided by law for holding general, special, primary and municipal elections, and shall be conducted by the election officers provided by law to conduct such elections. The election officers shall count the votes cast at the election on said question, and shall make return thereof in county elections to the county commission, as required by law, and, in municipal elections, to the city commission, as required by law. Said returns shall be computed by the clerk of the county commission or by the city clerk, as the case may be, and, when so computed, a certificate of the total number of electors voting "yes" and of the total number of electors voting "no" on such question shall be filed in the office of the county commission in county elections, and in the office of the city commission in municipal elections; and copies of said certificates, certified by the respective governing bodies, shall forthwith be furnished to the Secretary of State. If a majority of the electors of any county, city or other political subdivision of the state, voting on such question, shall vote against the adoption of voting machines, no officers of said county, city or other political subdivision of the state shall authorize the use of voting machines nor shall the question again be submitted to the voters of such political subdivision within a period of two years. In the event a county, municipality or other political subdivision of the state shall vote in the majority, authorizing and directing the use of voting machines at elections as provided in the preceding sections, or in the event the county, municipality or other political subdivision of the state, through its proper officers, in pursuance of appropriate legislation, shall authorize and direct the use of voting machines at elections as herein otherwise provided, the county commission or city commission shall either purchase the necessary number of voting machines for said county, municipality or other political subdivision of the state under the conditions and requirements set out herein, or shall rent or lease the necessary number of voting machines for said county, municipality or other political subdivision of the state, with or without option to purchase said machines, at fair and reasonable rental or lease prices which shall not exceed 10 percent of the purchase price of said machines; or such county, municipality or other political subdivision may request the Department of Finance to acquire the requisite number of voting machines for it under the existing provisions of law; or such county, municipality or other political subdivision may make such request from any board, commission or authority of the state which may now or hereafter be provided by law. (Acts 1939, No. 292, p. 443; Code 1940, T. 17, § 93.)

Cited in Kendrick v. State ex rel. Shoemaker, 256 Ala. 206, 54 So. 2d 442 (1951).

§ 17-9-4. Installation.

Where voting machines have been adopted for a county, municipality, or other political subdivision of the state, or for a portion of the county, municipality, or other political subdivision, the county commission or the municipal governing body shall, as soon as practicable and in no case later than six months after the adoption thereof, provide for each voting ward, precinct, or beat designated, one or more approved voting machines, in complete working order, and shall thereafter preserve and keep them in repair. In each voting place in which voting machines are used, the county commission or municipal governing body shall provide by rental, lease, or purchase, at least one mechanical voting machine for each 600 registered voters or fraction thereof, or at least one electronic voting machine for each 1,200 registered voters or fraction thereof. The county commission or municipal governing body may, at its discretion, elect not to install voting machines in a ward, precinct, or beat having less than 100 registered voters. The adoption of the use of voting machines by a county or municipality, upon a petition signed by a majority of the registered voters in the ward, precinct, or beat, the county commission or municipal governing body may be required to install voting machines in the ward or precinct or beat for use in an election held after 90 days from the filing of the petition. Upon the installation of voting machines in a voting place, the use of paper ballots shall be discontinued, except as otherwise provided. Wherever, by reason of a constitutional or other legal debt limitation, it shall be impossible for a county or municipality to provide voting machines by either rental, lease, or purchase for each election district, then it shall provide as many machines as it shall be possible to procure, and, as soon thereafter as possible, shall provide the remainder of the machines required hereunder. The machines provided shall be first installed in wards, precincts, or beats having the largest number of registered voters. (Acts 1939, No. 292, p. 443; Code 1940, T. 17, § 94; Acts 1993, No. 93-760, p. 1514, § 4.)

The 1993 amendment, effective May 25, 1993, substituted "municipal governing body" for "city commission" throughout this section, in the first sentence, substituted "a county" for "any county," substituted "a portion" for "any portion," and substituted "the county" for "such county," in the second sentence, inserted "mechanical," and substituted "or at least one electronic voting machine for each 1,200 registered voters or fraction thereof" for "therein," divided the former third sentence into the present fourth and fifth sentences, and in the present third sentence, substituted "a ward" for "any ward," deleted "or" preceding "precinct," and deleted "provided, that after the" following "voters," in the present fourth sentence, added "The," substituted "a county" for "any county," substituted "the ward" for "any such ward," deleted "or" preceding "precinct," substituted "the ward" for "such ward," substituted "an election" for "any election," and substituted "the petition" for "such petition," in the present fifth sentence, substituted "a voting place," deleted "therein" following "ballots," and deleted "herein" following "provided," in the present next-to-last sentence, substi-

tuted "a constitutional" for "any constitutional," substituted "a county" for "any county," deleted "as provided therein," following "district," and substituted "the machines" for "such machines," and in the last sentence, deleted "so" preceding "provided," and deleted "or" preceding "precincts."

Use of voting machines in all elections not mandatory. — This section, providing for the optional use of paper ballots in precincts having less than 100 registered voters, was a clear legislative interpretation of amendment 41 that the use of voting machines in all elections is not mandatory. Jansen v. State ex rel. Downing, 273 Ala. 166, 137 So. 2d 47 (1962).

Where county was indebted to constitutional debt limit, it could not, after referendum under this chapter, enter into any contract for purchase, rent or lease of voting machines and create obligation against the county to be paid out of the funds of the county for future fiscal years. Wharton v. Knight, 241 Ala. 218, 2 So. 2d 310 (1941).

Cited in Kendrick v. State ex rel. Shoemaker, 256 Ala. 206, 54 So. 2d 442 (1951).

§ 17-9-5. Discontinuance of use.

Any county or city may, by a majority vote of its qualified electors voting thereon at any election held not earlier than six years after the adoption and installation of such machines, direct the discontinuance of the use of voting machines at elections held in such county or city. The question of the discontinuance of the use of such voting machines shall be submitted to the voters, subject to the same requirements as to resolution or petition and signatures thereon as is required for the submission of the question on the authorization of the use of such voting machines. Where the qualified electors of any city and the qualified electors of the entire county containing therein such city, both have voted by separate questions in favor of the adoption of the use of voting machines, or where any county and any city within any such county, through its proper officers, in pursuance of appropriate legislation, shall have separately authorized and directed the use of voting machines, a subsequent vote by the qualified electors of the entire county in favor of discontinuance will not be considered as a vote to discontinue the use of voting machines in such city. Such question as to the discontinuance of the use of voting machines shall be submitted in the following form: "Shall the use of voting machines be continued in the (City or County) of . . . . .?" (Acts 1939, No. 292, p. 443; Code 1940, T. 17, § 95.)

Cited in Kendrick v. State ex rel. Shoemaker, 256 Ala. 206, 54 So. 2d 442 (1951).

§ 17-9-6. Use in all elections.

When the use of voting machines is adopted in and for any voting precinct within any county or municipality, then voting machines must be used in all general, primary, municipal and special elections held thereafter in any such voting precinct. (Acts 1939, No. 292, p. 443; Code 1940, T. 17, § 96.)

Use of machines in state, county and municipal elections. — If in any city, voting must be by machines in state and county elections under a county-wide referendum, they must be also used there in municipal elections. And if in such city, voting must be by machines in municipal elections under a city referendum, they must be also used there in state and county elections, though there has been no county referendum. Abrasley v. Jefferson County, 241 Ala. 666, 4 So. 2d 153 (1941).

Cited in Kendrick v. State ex rel. Shoemaker, 256 Ala. 206, 54 So. 2d 442 (1951).

§ 17-9-7. Requirements and specifications.

No voting machine shall be installed for use in any election in this state unless it shall satisfy the following requirements:

(1) It shall provide facilities for voting for such candidates as may be nominated, and upon such questions as may be submitted.

(2) It shall permit each voter, at other than primary elections, to vote a straight political party ticket in one operation, and, in one operation, to vote for all the candidates of one political party for presidential electors, and, in one operation, to vote for all the candidates of one political party for every office to be voted for; except those offices as to which he votes for individual candidates.

(3) It shall permit each voter, at other than primary elections, to vote a ticket selected from the nominees of any and all political parties, from the nominees of any and all political bodies, and from persons not in nomination.

(4) It shall permit each voter to vote, at any election, for any person and for any office for whom and for which he is lawfully entitled to vote, whether or not the name of such person appears upon a ballot, at other than primary elections, as a candidate for nomination or election, as many persons for an office as he is entitled to vote for, and to vote for or against any question upon which he is entitled to vote.

(5) It shall preclude each voter from voting for any candidate or upon any question for whom or upon which he is not entitled to vote, and from voting for more persons or any office than he is entitled to vote for, and from voting for any candidate for the same office or upon any question more than once.

(6) It shall permit each voter to deposit, write in or affix upon receptacles or devices provided for the purpose, ballots containing the names of persons for whom he desires to vote, whose names do not appear upon the machine except in primary elections.

(7) It shall permit each voter to change his vote for any candidate, or upon any question appearing upon the ballot labels, up to the time he begins the final operation to register his vote.

(8) It shall permit and require voting in absolute secrecy and shall be so constructed that no person can see or know for whom any other elector has voted or is voting, save a voter whom he has assisted or is assisting in voting, as prescribed by law.

(9) It shall have voting devices for separate candidates and questions, which shall be arranged in separate parallel rows or columns, so that, at any primary election, one or more adjacent rows or columns may be assigned to the candidates of a party, and shall have parallel office columns or rows transverse thereto.

(10) It shall have a counter or other device which shall show during any period of voting the total number of voters who have operated the machine during said period of voting.

(11) It shall have a protective counter, or other device, the register of which cannot be reset, which shall record the cumulative total number of movements of the operating mechanism.

(12) It shall be provided with a lock or locks, by the use of which, immediately after the polls are closed, or the operation of the machine for an election is completed, all movement of the registering mechanism is absolutely prevented.

(13) It shall be provided with a screen, hood, or curtain, which shall conceal the actions of the voter while voting.

(14) It shall, when properly operated, register or record correctly and accurately every vote cast.

(15) It shall be constructed of material of good quality, in a neat and workmanlike manner.

(16) It shall be so constructed that a voter may readily learn the method of operating it.

(17) It shall be safely transportable.

(18) It shall be so constructed and controlled that, during the progress of voting, it shall preclude every person from seeing or knowing the number of

votes registered for any candidate, and from tampering with any of the registering mechanism.

(19) It shall be so constructed and equipped with devices or attachments as to comply with the "single short" provisions of the Alabama election laws, whenever and wherever such provisions are applicable at elections in said state.

(20) It shall be so constructed as to permit the casting and recording of challenged votes by means of the "irregular ballot" method or shall be equipped with such devices and attachments as to allow the casting and recording of challenged votes, as provided by law.

Before any voting machine is purchased, rented or leased, the person or corporation owning or manufacturing such machine must give an adequate guarantee, in writing, securing that such machines comply fully with the above requirements and will correctly, accurately and continuously register and record every vote cast. (Acts 1939, No. 292, p. 443; Code 1940, T. 17, § 97.)

Cited in Kendrick v. State ex rel. Shoemaker, 256 Ala. 206, 54 So. 2d 442 (1951).

§ 17-9-8. Payment for machines.

The county commission or city commission or such other authority as levies the taxes for county or city purposes of any county or city which adopts the use of voting machines, shall, upon the purchase, rental or lease thereof, provide for payment therefor by the county or city; provided, that bonds or other evidences of indebtedness, payable not later than 15 years from their dates of issuance, may be issued in accordance with the provisions of law relating to the increase of indebtedness of counties or cities, to meet all or any part of the cost of the voting machines. (Acts 1939, No. 292, p. 443; Code 1940, T. 17, § 98.)

County to furnish machines when so authorized. — Where the use of voting machines was authorized and directed by majority vote in county-wide election held at the instance of county commission and no separate referendum election on such proposition was held in a city within the county, the county and not the city was required to supply voting machines for the city for both general and municipal elections, and city was not required to share in acquisition of the machines or to pay for the use thereof in city election, notwithstanding statutory requirement that city bear the expense of city elections. Abrasley v. Jefferson County, 241 Ala. 660, 4 So. 2d 153 (1941).

But city may help where separate referendum elections held. — Voting machines must be provided by the county board for all precincts in county including municipalities within the county, if the use of voting machines was authorized by county-wide vote, and by the city, if approved in city election only, and if both county and city have separate referendum elections in each of which the use of voting machines is approved, county and city may jointly and equally provide voting machines. Abrasley v. Jefferson County, 241 Ala. 660, 4 So. 2d 153 (1941).

And where debt limitation prohibited county from buying or leasing machines. — The constitutional limitation on county indebtedness was effective to prohibit county from incurring any debt beyond such limitation for the purchase or lease of voting machines, notwithstanding the use of such machines was authorized and directed by majority vote in county-wide election. Abrasley v. Jefferson County, 241 Ala. 660, 4 So. 2d 153 (1941).

Such can be rented. — A county which owed debts equal to the limit prescribed by Constitution could rent voting machines for use in any election in the county or in any precinct or municipality thereof in which their use was required by law, and bind itself to pay for such use only out of current annual county revenue in preference to other claims not preferred by law over such an obligation, but an unconditional obligation to pay for such use, such that obligation might be extended to subsequent years for payment in event of an insufficiency of current revenue, would be invalid. Abrasley v. Jefferson County, 241 Ala. 660, 4 So. 2d 153 (1941).

Cited in Kendrick v. State ex rel. Shoemaker, 256 Ala. 206, 54 So. 2d 442 (1951).

§ 17-9-9. Warrants or certificates for purchase — Issuance; form; interest.

Each county in which voting machines may now or hereafter be authorized or required to be used in the conduct of elections in such county shall have the power from time to time to sell and issue interest-bearing warrants of such county or interest-bearing certificates of indebtedness of such county for the purpose of paying the cost of acquiring or providing voting machines for the conduct of elections in such county, or for providing a voter reidentification program, providing equipment for the county board of registrars or paying for construction for compliance with handicap regulations for accessibility to polling places. Such warrants and certificates may be in such denomination or denominations, may have such maturity or maturities not exceeding 15 years from their date, may bear interest from their date at an annual rate or rates not exceeding the prevailing rate, payable semiannually, may be payable at such place or places within or without this state, may be sold at such time or times and in such manner, may be executed in such manner, and may contain such terms not in conflict with the provisions of Sections 17-9-9 through 17-9-14, all as the county commission of such county may provide in the proceedings wherein the warrants or certificates are authorized to be issued. (Acts 1959, No. 603, p. 1492, § 2; Acts 1990, No. 90-559. p. 951.)

Collateral references. — 29 C.J.S., Elections, § 203.

§ 17-9-10. Warrants or certificates for purchase — Obligation of county; disposition of proceeds.

All such warrants and certificates shall evidence general obligation indebtedness of the county by which they are issued, and the full faith and credit of the county shall be irrevocably pledged for the payment of the principal thereof and interest thereon. The proceeds derived from the sale of any such warrants and certificates shall be used solely for the purpose for which they are authorized to be issued, including the payment of any expenses incurred in connection with the issuance thereof. (Acts 1959, No. 603, p. 1492, § 2.)

§ 17-9-11. Warrants or certificates for purchase — Pledge of general ad valorem tax for payment.

The county commission of the county issuing any such warrants or certificates may, in its discretion, pledge and use or cause to be used, for the payment of the principal of and interest on such warrants and certificates, so much as may be necessary for such purpose of the general annual ad valorem tax of one half of one percent which the county is authorized to levy without reference to the purpose thereof under the provisions of Section 215 of the Constitution of Alabama of 1901. If more than one such pledge shall be made of the said tax, then such pledges shall take precedence in the order in which they are made unless the proceedings making such pledge shall expressly provide that such pledge shall be on a parity with or subordinate to a subsequent pledge of the said tax. All warrants and certificates for which the pledge authorized in this section may be made shall constitute preferred claims against the said tax, and shall have preference over claims incurred in carrying on the governmental function of the county. (Acts 1959, No. 603, p. 1492, § 3.)

§ 17-9-12. Warrants or certificates for purchase — Refunding authorized.

Each such county may in like manner from time to time issue refunding warrants and certificates, either by sale or by exchange, for the purpose of refunding a like or greater principal amount of warrants and certificates then outstanding which were issued under the provisions of Sections 17-9-9 through 17-9-14 and the interest thereon and paying any premium necessary to be paid to retire the outstanding warrants and certificates refunded thereby. The provisions of Sections 17-9-9 through 17-9-14 applicable to the warrants and certificates so refunded shall likewise be applicable to such refunding warrants and certificates. (Acts 1959, No. 603, p. 1492, § 4.)

§ 17-9-13. Warrants or certificates for purchase — Sections 17-9-9 through 17-9-14 control inconsistent laws.

Insofar as the provisions of Sections 17-9-9 through 17-9-14 may be inconsistent with the provisions of any other law, the provisions of Sections 17-9-9 through 17-9-14 shall control, it being hereby specifically declared that the provisions of Section 11-8-10 shall not be applicable to the warrants and certificates issued under the provisions of Sections 17-9-9 through 17-9-14. (Acts 1959, No. 603, p. 1492, § 5.)

§ 17-9-14. Warrants or certificates for purchase — Applicability of Sections 17-9-9 through 17-9-14.

The provisions of Sections 17-9-9 through 17-9-14 shall apply to each county in this state in which voting machines may now or hereafter be authorized or required to be used in the conduct of elections in such county. (Acts 1959, No. 603, p. 1492, § 1.)

§ 17-9-15. Demonstration of machines.

Whenever a referendum is about to be held upon the adoption of the use of voting machines in any county or city, the county commission or city commission may lease or borrow a reasonable number of voting machines for demonstration purposes in such county or city, prior to such referendum. (Acts 1939, No. 292, p. 443; Code 1940, T. 17, § 99.)

Cited in Kendrick v. State ex rel. Shoemaker,
256 Ala. 206, 54 So. 2d 442 (1951).

§ 17-9-16. Election supplies.

Ballot labels, diagrams, seals and all other necessary election supplies for use on voting machines in general, special, primary or municipal elections shall be prepared and printed by the same authorities now charged by law with the duty of preparing, printing and furnishing the same. (Acts 1939, No. 292, p. 443; Code 1940, T. 17, § 100.)

§ 17-9-17. Preparation of voting machines.

It shall be the duty of the judge of probate of each county where voting machines are used in county elections, and of the city clerk in each municipality where voting machines are used in municipal elections, to cause the proper ballot labels to be placed on voting machines; to cause the machines to be placed in proper order for voting; to examine all voting machines in the presence of authorized watchers for any interested persons, before they are sent out to the polling places; to see that all the registering counters are set at zero; to lock, in the presence of authorized watchers, all voting machines so that the counting machinery cannot be operated and to seal each one with a numbered seal, a list of which numbered seals and the number on the protective counters, together with the number of the precinct to which it was sent, in all elections shall be kept as a permanent record open to any citizen, in the records of the probate judge. Such inspection and sealing of voting machines shall begin not later than 9:00 A.M. of the Saturday before any election at which such machines are to be used, and continue until all such machines are sealed. When all machines are locked and sealed, the key to each machine shall be placed in an envelope and sealed, the signature of the judge of probate or of the city clerk, as the case may be, and the signature of two watchers of opposed interest (if such there be) placed across the seal, and on the envelope shall be written the number then on the protective counter and the number on the seal of the voting machine, such envelope to be delivered to the inspector of each election district. It shall be the duty of the sheriff in all elections which the county is charged with the expense of, the duty of the city clerk in a city election, the duty of the president of a school board in school elections, and the duty of the authority holding other elections of any character, to have delivered a voting machine, or machines, together with an instruction model for each machine, showing a portion of the face of such machine in use at such election, to each and every polling place where same is required by law to be used, at least one hour before the time set for the opening of the polls in such voting precinct. After the machine has been delivered, the same authority shall cause such machine to be set up in the proper manner and cause protection to be given so such machine shall be free from molestation and injury. The protective curtains shall be examined to see that they conceal the actions of the voter properly, while such voter is operating the machine. All poll lists and necessary supplies shall be delivered to the inspector at the same time the key or keys to the machine are delivered. (Acts 1939, No. 292, p. 443; Code 1940, T. 17, § 101.)

§ 17-9-18. Preliminaries of opening polls.

The key or keys to the voting machine or machines shall be delivered to the inspector of each poll at least 30 minutes before the time for opening of the polls, the seal of the envelope containing the same to be unbroken. The seal shall be broken by the inspector only in the presence of at least two authorized watchers for opposing interests (if such there be), and shall only be broken after comparison shows that the number written on the envelope and the number shown in the protective counter are identical. If these numbers are found not to be the same, the seal shall not be broken until the judge of probate or the city clerk, as the case may be, or their representative, shall arrive and deliver the correct keys or until another and properly sealed machine is delivered. If the numbers written on the envelope and the respective numbers on the seal and on the protective counter are found to be the same, the inspector shall open the doors concealing the counters. And, before the polls are declared open, the election officials and each authorized watcher, or any person interested, shall carefully examine each and every counter and see that it registers zero. All of those last enumerated then shall examine the ballots and satisfy themselves they are in their proper places on the machine. The election officials shall cause to be conspicuously placed the sample ballots and model for the guidance of the voters. All of the persons authorized to be in the polls shall satisfy themselves that the voting machine is properly placed, and that the face of the machine is turned toward where the election officials and the public may obtain a clear and unobstructed view of the same at all times, except when the curtain on the machine is closed for the casting of the ballot. The election officials and at least two watchers of opposing interests (if any there be) shall then sign a certificate setting out that the keys were delivered intact, that the numbers on the protective counter and the seal correspond with that on the envelope, that all the counters were set at zero, and that the ballot labels were in their proper places. If any counter, however, shall be found not to register zero, the inspector shall summon the custodian of the machine, who shall set the counter back to zero. The machine shall then be opened for voting and the polls formally declared open. (Acts 1939, No. 292, p. 443; Code 1940, T. 17, § 102; Acts 1949, No. 681, p. 1051.)

Collateral references. — 29 C.J.S., Elections, §§ 192, 198.

§ 17-9-19. Instruction of election officials.

(a) Not less than five days before an election or primary election, the authority charged with holding the same shall cause to be held a school of instruction for those who will actually conduct the election or primary election at the polling places. The sheriff shall notify such election officials of the time and place of the holding of such school of instruction, and shall also publish notice at least 48 hours before the same is to be held.

(b) No election official shall serve in any election district in which a voting machine is used, unless he shall have received such instruction and is fully qualified to perform the duties in connection with the machine, and has received a certificate from the authorized instructor to that effect; provided, that this shall not prevent the appointment of an uninstructed person as an election official to fill a vacancy among the election officials. (Acts 1939, No. 292, p. 443; Code 1940, T. 17, § 103.)

§ 17-9-20. Compensation of election officials.

In all counties and municipalities of this state in which elections are conducted in whole or in part by voting machines, all election officials shall be entitled to $3.00 which shall be in addition to the compensation now provided by law for election officials. When the election is a municipal election, said compensation shall be paid out of the general fund of the municipality, and in all other elections, it shall be paid out of the county treasury, on proper proof of the service rendered. (Acts 1943, No. 409, p. 375; Acts 1945, No. 240, p. 359.)

Collateral references. — 29 C.J.S., Elections, §§ 63, 116.

§ 17-9-21. Failure of election officials to serve; record of persons excused; filling vacancy when person excused.

This section shall apply only in counties in which voting machines are used.

Any election or primary election official who fails to serve at the polls, unless previously excused by the appointing board, is guilty of a misdemeanor and upon conviction shall be fined not less than $50.00 and not more than $1,000.00. The names of all persons excused from serving and the reasons for which they were excused shall be entered upon the records of the appointing board, which records shall be kept in the office of the probate judge for the length of the contest period after any election or primary election and shall be open to public inspection at all reasonable times.

In the event a person appointed as an election or primary election official is excused from serving or otherwise disqualifies himself, the vacancy created thereby shall be filled by the appointing board in the same manner that original appointments are made. However, if the vacancy occurs after the school of instruction for election officials has been held, the appointing board shall appoint a person who has received a certificate from a previous school of instruction. (Acts 1949, No. 587, p. 913, §§ 1-3.)

§ 17-9-22. Delivery of voting machine supplies to election officers.

The authority designated in Section 17-9-18 shall furnish and deliver with each voting machine:

(1) Lighting facilities which shall give sufficient light to enable voters, while in the voting machine booth, to read the ballot labels, and suitable for

the use of election officers in examining the counters. The lantern, or proper substitute therefor, shall be prepared and in good order for use before the opening of the polls.

(2) A model and two diagrams or sample ballots, of suitable size, representing such part of the face of such voting machine as will be in use in the election, and accompanied by directions for voting on the machine. Such diagrams shall be posted prominently outside, for the instruction of electors. Such model shall be placed in the polling place and at or outside of the guard-rail or barrier.

(3) A seal, or seals, for sealing the machine after the polls are closed.

(4) An envelope for the return of the keys, if the construction of the voting machine shall permit their separate return.

(5) Such other election materials and supplies as may be necessary, or as may be required by law. (Acts 1939, No. 292, p. 443; Code 1940, T. 17, § 104.)

Collateral references. — 29 C.J.S., Elections, § 155.

§ 17-9-23. Enumeration and duties of election officers; length of time elector may remain in booth; challenging of voters.

The election officers for each voting machine shall consist of an inspector, a chief clerk and a first and second assistant clerk. The inspector shall be in general charge of the poll and shall see that the chief clerk properly marks off from the poll list, and that the first assistant clerk properly records, the name of each voter before such voter casts his ballot, and shall keep such other records as are required by law. It shall be the duty of the second assistant clerk to attend the voting machine at all times and to see that it is not tampered with. The second assistant clerk shall also inspect the ballot labels at frequent intervals to see that none have been tampered with and to see that the machine has not been injured. The inspector shall see that the counter compartments of the machine are never unlocked or opened so that the counters are exposed during voting. The election officers shall ascertain, as required by law, whether each applicant to vote is entitled to vote. If he is found to be entitled to vote, he shall be admitted within the voting machine booth, and shall be permitted to vote.

No voter shall remain within the voting machine booth an unreasonable length of time, and in no event longer than three minutes, and, if he shall refuse to leave after a reasonable period, he shall be removed by the election officers; provided, that they may grant him a longer time if other voters are not waiting to vote.

All laws now existing or as hereafter amended relating to the challenging of voters shall, insofar as practicable, relate to elections held with voting machines. Wherever in any election held under the provisions of this chapter, the right of any voter to cast his ballot shall have been challenged under the provisions of law referred to in this section, such challenged voter, after having first complied with provisions of the laws referred to in this section, shall be permitted to cast his ballot on the voting machine by means of the "irregular ballot" or by means of the device or devices specifically provided for the casting of challenged votes. (Acts 1939, No. 292, p. 443; Code 1940, T. 17, § 105.)

Cited in Vintson v. Anton, 786 F.2d 1023 (11th Cir. 1986); Harris v. Siegelman, 700 F. Supp. 1083 (M.D. Ala. 1988).

§ 17-9-24. Instruction of voters before election.

During the 30 days next preceding an election, the city commission in municipal elections, and the county commission in all other elections, shall place on public exhibition, in such public places and at such times as it may deem most suitable for the information and instruction of the voters, one or more voting machines, containing the ballot labels, and showing the offices and questions to be voted upon, the names and arrangements of parties, and, so far as practicable, the names and arrangements of the candidates to be voted for. Such machine or machines shall be under the charge and care of a person competent as custodian and instructor. No voting machine which is to be assigned for use in an election shall be used for such public exhibition and instruction after having been prepared and sealed for the election. Prior to any election, the county commission or city commission, as the case may be, may cause copies of any diagram or diagrams, required to be furnished with voting machines at polling places, to be made, either in full size or in reduced size, and to be posted, published, advertised or distributed among the electors in such manner as they may deem desirable. (Acts 1939, No. 292, p. 443; Code 1940, T. 17, § 106.)

§ 17-9-25. Instruction and assistance for voters at polls.

(a) The election officers shall, with the aid of the diagrams herein authorized, and the mechanically operated model, instruct each voter before he enters the voting machine booth, regarding the operation of the machine, and shall give the voter opportunity personally to operate the model. No voter shall be permitted to receive any assistance in voting at any election, unless he shall first state in writing upon printed forms supplied for that purpose and under oath or affirmation, which shall be administered to him by the inspector, that he is blind or that he cannot read the names on the voting machines, or that, by reason of physical disability, he is unable to see the machine or prepare it for voting, or to enter the voting machine booth without assistance. The voter shall state the specific physical disability which requires him to receive assistance. Thereupon the voter may request assistance of two inspectors of his choice or some other person of his own choice, and he shall be assisted by the two election officials of his choice or by such other person, who shall aid him in voting, and the inspector shall forthwith enter in writing on the record of assisted voters: the voter's name; the fact that the voter cannot read the names on the voting machine, if that be the reason for requiring assistance and, otherwise, the specific physical disability which requires him to receive assistance; and the name of the election officials or such other person furnishing the assistance; but if any voter, after entering the voting machine booth, and before the closing of such booth, shall ask for further instructions concerning the manner of voting, he may choose an election officer, who shall give him such instructions, but no official giving a voter such instructions shall, in any manner, request, suggest or seek to persuade or induce any such voter to vote any particular ticket, or for any particular candidate, or for or against any particular question. After giving such instructions, and before the elector closes the booth or votes, the election officer shall retire, and the voter shall forthwith vote.

(b) It shall be unlawful for any official to assist a voter who has not made the oath required herein, or for an official or any other person to do anything to enable himself to see how any voter votes other than in the course of assisting a voter as provided herein. (Acts 1949, No. 584, p. 911; Acts 1959, No. 406, p. 1038.)

Presence of federal observer when voter receives assistance. — See United States v. Executive Comm. of Democratic Party, 254 F. Supp. 543 (N.D. Ala. 1966).

Cited in Gray v. Main, 309 F. Supp. 207 (M.D. Ala. 1968).

Collateral references. — 29 C.J.S., Elections, § 208.

§ 17-9-26. Voting by irregular ballot.

Ballots, other than challenged ballots, voted for any persons whose name does not appear on the ballot shall be designated "irregular ballots." In the event a voter desires to vote an "irregular ballot," such person shall write the name of the person whom he desires to vote for on the roll of paper or other device designated on the voting machine for that purpose, and such "irregular ballot" shall be counted and included in the canvass officially made, but no "irregular ballot" shall be cast or counted for any person whose name shall appear on the ballot label, excepting challenged ballots cast under the provisions of this chapter. "Irregular ballots" shall not apply to nor be cast in primary elections. (Acts 1939, No. 292, p. 443; Code 1940, T. 17, § 108.)

Collateral references. — 29 C.J.S., Elections, § 156.

§ 17-9-27. Absentee ballots.

Absentee ballots, if any, shall be cast in the usual manner and under the laws and regulations as now provided or as hereafter amended, and voting machines shall not be required for the casting of absentee ballots. (Acts 1939, No. 292, p. 443; Code 1940, T. 17, § 109.)

Collateral references. — 29 C.J.S., Elections, §§ 151, 210, 224, 226, 239.

§ 17-9-28. Repair or substitution of machine; use of paper ballots instead or to avoid congestion.

If any voting machine being used in any election shall become out of order during such election, it shall, if possible, be repaired or another machine substituted by the authority holding such election, as promptly as possible, for which purpose the county commission or city commission may purchase, rent or lease as many extra voting machines as they may deem necessary; but in case such repair or substitution cannot be made, paper ballots, printed or written, and of any suitable form, may be used for the taking of votes.

In the event the use of paper ballots becomes necessary, as set out in this section, the authority holding such election shall provide a ballot box or similar appropriate receptacle for the deposit of the ballots, and such supplies and election officers as may be necessarily incident to voting by paper ballot. In the event the use of paper ballots becomes necessary as hereinabove provided, such use of paper ballots shall be in all respects as required by law. (Acts 1939, No. 292, p. 443; Code 1940, T. 17, § 110; Acts 1961, Ex. Sess., No. 228, p. 2240.)

Collateral references. — 29 C.J.S., Elections, §§ 203, 227.

§ 17-9-29. Watchers.

At all elections in which voting machines are used, duly appointed watchers shall have the right to see all oaths administered and signed, the record of assisted voters, the list of qualified voters, the poll lists and any and all records made in connection with the election. Watchers shall have the right to observe the preliminaries of opening the polls, as provided in Section 17-9-18, and the right to remain in the polling place throughout the election and until the results of the election shall have been posted, and the machines sealed, as provided by law. Watchers shall have the right generally to observe the conduct of the election. An official who refuses to allow any watchers to exercise such rights shall be guilty of a misdemeanor, and, upon conviction, shall be punished as prescribed by law. (Acts 1953, No. 867, p. 1165.)

Cited in Harris v. Conradi, 675 F.2d 1212 (11th Cir. 1982).

Collateral references. — 29 C.J.S., Elections, §§ 200, 209, 216(2), 323.

§ 17-9-30. Hours polls open. Repealed by Acts 1979, No. 79-616, p. 1086, § 13, effective July 30, 1979.

Cross references. — As to hours polls open, see §§ 17-7-5.1.

§ 17-9-31. Breaking seal of voting machine.

It shall be unlawful and constitute a misdemeanor for members of the county executive committee of any political party holding a primary election, or for any board of canvass, to break the seal of a voting machine for any purpose other than the following:

(1) For obtaining the results of an election when the election officials have failed to make a return, but only after the fact of failure to make a return has been certified to the circuit court having jurisdiction in that county and an order to break the seals to obtain the results of an election has been issued by that court;

(2) For the hearing of a contest conducted in accordance with law;

(3) For the purpose of a grand jury investigation, upon the order of a court having jurisdiction in the county in which the machines are used.

In the event that the seal of a machine is broken to obtain the results of an election, the chairman of the county executive committee of the political party holding the election, or the members of the board of canvass, and at least two other witnesses, shall sign a record of the action of breaking the seal, which record must show the date and time of opening the machine and the number of the seal broken. When the results have been obtained, the persons opening the machine shall reseal the machine with a metal seal, and shall make a record of the resealing of the machine, which record must show the number of the seal used to reseal the machine. The persons opening the machine, and at least two other witnesses, shall sign the record of the action of resealing the machine. When it becomes necessary to break the seal of a machine in order to obtain the results of an election, the persons breaking the seal shall report to the next grand jury sitting in that county the failure of the election officials to return the results of the election. (Acts 1953, No. 865, p. 1164.)

§ 17-9-32. Delivery of keys to authorities after closing of polls.

Upon the occasion of an election in which voting machines are used, all keys to voting machines, other than those in the possession of the election officials, must be delivered to the authority having jurisdiction over the election by not later than one hour after the official closing of the polls of the day on which the election is held, and shall remain in the possession of such authority for the time provided by law for the filing of contest. (Acts 1953, No. 866, p. 1165.)

Collateral references. — 29 C.J.S., Elections, § 203.

§ 17-9-33. Canvass of vote and proclamation of result.

When the time arrives for closing the polls, all qualified voters, who are then waiting within the voting room to vote, shall be permitted by the election officers to do so. As soon as the last voter has voted and the poll closed, the election officials shall immediately lock the machines against voting. They shall then sign a certificate stating that the machine was locked and sealed, giving the exact time; such certificate also stating the number of voters shown on the public counters, which shall be the total number of votes cast on such machine in that precinct; the number on the seal; and the number registered on the protective counter. They shall then open the counting compartment in the presence of the watchers and of at least one representative of any newspaper or press association which cares to be represented, giving full view of all the counter numbers. The inspector shall, under the scrutiny of the watchers, in the order of the officers, as their titles are arranged on the machines, read and announce in distinct tones the designating number and letter on each counter for each candidate's name, if the construction of the voting machine is such as to require a designating number and letter; the result as shown by the counter numbers; and shall then read the votes recorded for each office on the "irregular ballots"; and shall also read and the clerk shall tally the totals of all challenged ballots cast under the provisions of this chapter. He shall also in the same manner announce the result on each constitutional amendment, bond proposition or any other question voted on. The vote as registered shall be entered on the statements of canvass in ink by the clerks, such entries to be made in the same order on the space which has the same designating number and letter, if the construction of the voting machine is such as to require a designating number and letter, after which the figures shall again be verified by being called off in the same manner from the counters of the machines. The returns of the canvass as required by law shall then be filled out, verified and shall show the number of votes cast for each candidate, the number of votes cast for and against any proposition submitted and shall be signed by the election officials. The counter compartments of the voting machine shall remain open throughout the time of the making of all statements and certificates, and the official returns, and until such have been fully verified; and during such time the watchers of any candidate or any representative of any newspaper shall be admitted. The proclamation of the result of the votes cast shall be deliberately announced in a distinct voice by the inspector, who shall read the names of each candidate, with the designating number and letter, if the construction of the voting machine is such as to require a designating number and letter; of his counter and the vote registered on such counter; also the vote cast for and against each proposition submitted. During such proclamation ample opportunity shall be given to any person lawfully entitled to be in the polls to compare the results announced with the counter dials of the machine and any necessary corrections shall then and there be made, after which the doors of the voting machine shall be locked and sealed with the seal provided, so sealing the operating lever or electrical control, if an electrically operated machine, so that the voting and counting mechanism will be prevented from operation. Irregular and challenged ballots, properly sealed and signed, shall be filed with the original statement of canvass, which canvass shall be delivered in the same manner and to the same authorities as now provided by law. The inspector shall deliver to the chairman of the county executive committee in all primary elections, the city clerk in all municipal elections, and the county commission in all other elections, the keys of the machine, enclosed in a sealed envelope, across the seal of which shall be written his own name, together with that of the other election officials, and on this envelope shall be recorded the date of the election, the number of the voting district, the number of the seal with which the machine was sealed, the number of the public counter and the number on the protective counter. (Acts 1939, No. 292, p. 443; Code 1940, T. 17, § 112.)

Cross references. — As to provisions for the disposition of records and forms after elections, see § 17-4-230 et seq.

Collateral references. — 29 C.J.S., Elections, §§ 71, 72, 75, 117, 221-240.

§ 17-9-34. Statements of canvass.

The authority charged with the holding of an election or primary election where voting machines shall be used shall cause to be prepared a statement of canvass of a form to be approved by the judge of probate, in the necessary number as now required to be used by law, such statement of canvass to conform with the type of voting machine to be used, and the designating number and letter, if the construction of the voting machine is such as to require a designating number and letter, of each candidate (or proposition) shall be printed next to the candidate's name on the statement of canvass. Said statements of canvass shall be permanently preserved by the probate judge for use in the event of contests. In the event the construction and design of the voting machine is such as to permit photographing the name of the candidate or the question, together with the total vote cast on their respective counters, said photograph may be taken and kept as a permanent record for use in event of a contest. (Acts 1939, No. 292, p. 443; Code 1940, T. 17, § 113.)

§ 17-9-35. Preservation of ballots and records of voting machines.

The voting machines shall remain locked against voting for the time provided by law for the filing of contests and then shall have the seal broken only on the order of that body which, under the general provisions of law, now has charge of and control over ballot boxes in that county, municipality or other political subdivision, and if, in the opinion of such body, the contest has developed or is likely to develop, shall remain locked until such time as ordered opened by the court hearing the contest, or until a final determination thereof; provided, that on the order of any court of competent jurisdiction or on the order of any legislative body or governing body having jurisdiction over such election, the seal may be broken for the purpose of proper investigation and when such investigation is completed, the machine shall again be sealed and across the envelope containing the keys shall be written the signature of the person or persons having broken same; and provided further, that in the event another election is held during the time for which the machines are required by this section to be locked and the machines are needed at such election, the board charged with canvassing the returns of the election at which the machines were last used shall be authorized to break the seal and make a record of the numbers on all counters on each machine and to remove all of the election records from the machine. The canvassing board shall securely seal all records taken from a machine in an envelope or package and on the outside thereof label the package in such manner as to indicate plainly the machine from which they were removed and the month, day and the year of the election of which they are records. Each member of the canvassing board shall certify to the accuracy of the record of the numbers on the counters and shall sign the envelope or package across the seal. This certificate and all other records removed from the voting machines shall be delivered to the officer to whom paper ballots are delivered after an election and preserved by him for the same length of time and then destroyed in the same manner that paper ballots are handled. (Acts 1939, No. 292, p. 443; Code 1940, T. 17, § 114; Acts 1956, 1st Ex. Sess., No. 143, p. 207.)

Collateral references. — 29 C.J.S., Elections, § 277.

§ 17-9-36. Custody of voting machines and keys.

The governing body of any county, municipality or other political subdivision of the state procuring voting machines shall designate a person or persons who shall have the custody of the voting machines and the keys therefor, when the machines are not in use at an election; and shall provide for his compensation and for the safe storage and care of the machines and keys. All voting machines, when not in use, shall be properly boxed or covered, and stored in a suitable place or places, by said custodian. The same authority that caused the delivery of the voting machines shall be charged with the transporting of such machines back to the said custodian, and shall furnish all necessary protection to see that such machines are not molested nor injured from the time such machines leave the place where they are regularly stored until they are turned into the custody of the officials of a voting district and from the time that custody ceases on the part of the voting district officials and the machines are returned to the place of regular storage. (Acts 1939, No. 292, p. 443; Code 1940, T. 17, § 115.)

Collateral references. — 29 C.J.S., Elections, §§ 155, 203.

§ 17-9-37. Compensation and expenses of custodians of voting machines; expenses of transportation and operation.

(a) *Counties.* — All counties are hereby authorized and directed to pay to the custodian of voting machines, provided for by Section 17-9-36, reasonable compensation for his services, all necessary expenses incurred in transporting said machines to and from the polls, and all necessary expenses incurred in the operation of said machines during all elections held other than municipal elections, regardless of whether or not said counties have adopted the use of voting machines.

(b) *Municipalities.* — All municipalities are hereby authorized and directed to pay to the custodian of voting machines, provided for by Section 17-9-36, reasonable compensation for his services, all necessary expenses incurred in transporting said machines to and from the polls, and all necessary expenses incurred in the operation of said machines during all municipal elections, regardless of whether or not said municipalities have adopted the use of voting machines. (Acts 1945, No. 451, p. 688.)

Cited in Kendrick v. State ex rel. Shoemaker, 256 Ala. 206, 54 So. 2d 442 (1951).

§ 17-9-38. Provisions for recanvass of votes.

Any person now authorized by law may apply to the body which, under the general provisions of law, now have charge of and control over ballot boxes, for an order to break the seals of a voting machine for the purpose of recanvassing the vote should same become necessary, whereupon all the other provisions of this title shall be followed in making such recanvass and the machine shall be resealed as herein provided. (Acts 1939, No. 292, p. 443; Code 1940, T. 17, § 116.)

§ 17-9-39. Applicability of laws to use of voting machines in municipalities or other political subdivisions.

In the event a municipality or other political subdivision of the state within any county adopts the use of voting machines, whether such adoption be by resolution of the governing body thereof or by an election held therein as provided in this chapter, the pertinent and necessary laws and requirements pertaining to the use of voting machines in counties shall apply to the use of voting machines in said municipalities or other political subdivisions of the state insofar as said laws and requirements are pertinent and necessary to legalize the use of voting machines in such municipalities or other political subdivisions of the state. (Acts 1939, No. 292, p. 443; Code 1940, T. 17, § 117; Acts 1959, No. 604, p. 1494, § 2.)

§ 17-9-40. Violations of chapter; tampering with, injuring, etc., machines; misuse; unauthorized possession of keys.

Any election officer, or other person, who shall violate any of the provisions of this chapter, or who shall tamper with, injure or attempt to injure any voting machine to be used or being used in an election, or who shall wilfully misuse any such machine, or who shall prevent or attempt to prevent the correct operation of such machine, or any unauthorized person who shall make or have in his possession a key to a voting machine to be used or being used in an election, shall be guilty of a misdemeanor, and, upon conviction thereof, shall be sentenced to undergo imprisonment for not more than one year, or to pay a fine not exceeding $1,000.00, or both, in the discretion of the court. (Acts 1939, No. 292, p. 443; Code 1940, T. 17, § 118.)

Collateral references. — 29 C.J.S., Elections, §§ 7(3), 216(5), 355(1), 355(2).

§ 17-9-41. Applicability of other laws.

The provisions of all other laws relating to the conduct of elections shall, so far as practicable, apply to the conduct of elections where voting machines are used, unless herein otherwise provided. (Acts 1939, No. 292, p. 443; Code 1940, T. 17, § 119.)

Cited in Vintson v. Anton, 786 F.2d 1023 (11th Cir. 1986).

ELECTIONS

CHAPTER 10.

ABSENTEE VOTING.

Cross references. — As to registration of absentee electors, see § 17-4-134.

State must follow procedures in 1970 Amendments to Voting Rights Act. — Since the 1970 Amendments to the Voting Rights Act have been held to be constitutional and enforceable insofar as they pertain to federal elections, the state of Alabama must comply with the federal statute and follow the procedures outlined therein. Prigmore v. Renfro, 356 F. Supp. 427 (N.D. Ala. 1972), aff'd, 410 U.S. 919, 93 S. Ct. 1369, 35 L. Ed. 2d 582 (1973), decided under former Tit. 17, §§ 64(15) through 64(34), 1940 Code, which also pertained to absentee voting.

State statutes tested by the traditional equal protection standard are constitutional and may stand, but they must yield, under the supremacy clause of the United States Constitution, to the federal statute in the presidential and vice-presidential elections. Prigmore v. Renfro, 356 F. Supp. 427 (N.D. Ala. 1972), aff'd, 410 U.S. 919, 93 S. Ct. 1369, 35 L. Ed. 2d 582 (1973), decided under former Tit. 17, §§ 64(15) through 64(34), 1940 Code, which also pertained to absentee voting.

All absentee voters who apply must be provided with absentee ballots for the presidential and vice-presidential elections. Prigmore v. Renfro, 356 F. Supp. 427 (N.D. Ala. 1972), aff'd, 410 U.S. 919, 93 S. Ct. 1369, 35 L. Ed. 2d 582 (1973), decided under former Tit. 17, §§ 64(15) through 64(34), 1940 Code, which also pertained to absentee voting.

Cited in Carter v. Wiley, 406 So. 2d 340 (Ala. 1981).

Collateral references. — 29 C.J.S., Elections, §§ 210(1), 210(2).

Validity, construction and effect of absentee voters' laws. 97 ALR2d 218, 257.

§ 17-10-1. "Register" and "register in chancery" defined.

The words "register" or "register in chancery," as used in this chapter, shall also include any successor in function to such register. (Acts 1975, No. 1147, p. 2251, § 16.)

Substantial compliance required. — Absentee ballots, absence the presence of fraud, gross negligence or intentional wrongdoing will not be set aside if they are in substantial compliance with the requirements of voting statutes. Wells v. Ellis, 551 So. 2d 382 (Ala. 1989).

§ 17-10-2. Register or clerk designated absentee election manager; appointment, qualifications, duties, term and compensation of manager if register and clerk decline duties.

In each county there shall be an "absentee election manager," who shall fulfill the duties assigned by this chapter. The register of the county shall, at his option, be the absentee election manager. If the register declines such duties, the circuit clerk of the county, at his option, shall be the absentee election manager. If neither the register nor the circuit clerk of the county assumes the duties of absentee election manager, the presiding circuit judge shall thereupon appoint an absentee election manager, who shall be a person qualified by training and experience, who is a qualified elector of the county and who is not a candidate in the election to perform the duties assigned by this chapter. The presiding circuit judge shall designate the place or office where such duties shall be performed. Such place or office shall be open on the days and during the hours as that of the register prior to each election. Any person so appointed shall have all the powers, duties and responsibilities of the clerk or register for the purposes of this chapter, including the power to administer oaths. Such powers, duties and responsibilities shall terminate at the end of the day of the election. The absentee election manager, clerk, register or register in chancery shall be entitled to the same compensation for the performance of his duties as is provided in Section 17-10-14. (Acts 1978, No. 616, p. 873, § 1.)

§ 17-10-3. Persons eligible to vote absentee ballot; time for filing application; postcard application for certain military personnel and wives.

(a) Any qualified elector of this state and any person who, but for having moved from the state within the 30 days immediately preceding the election, is a qualified elector of this state who will be unable to vote at his or her regular polling place because of his or her absence from the county of his or her residence on the day of any primary, general, special, or municipal election, or who because of any physical illness or infirmity which prevents his or her attendance at the polls, whether he or she is within or without the county on the day of the election, or who works on a shift which has at least ten hours which coincide with the hours the polls are open at his or her regular polling place, may vote an absentee ballot, provided he or she makes application in writing therefor not less than five days prior to the election in which he or she desires to vote as authorized in this chapter.

(b) An applicant for an absentee ballot who is a member of the armed forces of the United States, including the Alabama National Guard, the United States Naval Reserves, the United States Air Force Reserves and the United States Military Reserves on active duty training or an applicant who is the spouse of any member of the armed forces may make application for an absentee ballot by filling out the federal postcard application form, authorized and provided for under the provisions of "The Federal Voting Assistance Act of 1955," Public Law 296, Chapter 656, H. R. 4048, approved August 9, 1955, 84th Congress 1st Session. (Acts 1975, No. 1147, p. 2251, § 1; Acts 1986, No. 86-428, p. 791, § 1; Acts 1994, No. 94-320, p. 553, § 1.)

The **1994 amendment,** effective January 1, 1995, in subsection (a), inserted "or who works on a shift which has at least ten hours which coincide with the hours the polls are open at his or her regular polling place," and made nonsubstantive changes.

Collateral references. — 29 C.J.S., Elections, §§ 210(3), 210(4).

§ 17-10-4. Form and contents of application; signature of applicant; filing of application.

The application shall be filed with the person designated to serve as the absentee election manager. The application shall be in a form prescribed and designed by the Secretary of State and shall be used throughout the state. Notwithstanding the foregoing, handwritten applications can also be accepted at any time prior to the five day deadline date to receive absentee ballot applications as provided in Section 17-10-3. The application shall contain sufficient information to identify the applicant and shall include the applicant's name, residence address, or such other information necessary to verify that the applicant is a registered voter. Any applicant may receive assistance in filling out the application as he or she desires, but each application shall be manually signed by the applicant and, if he or she signs by mark, the name of the witness to his or her signature shall be signed thereon. The application may be handed by the applicant to the absentee election manager or forwarded to him or her by United States mail. An application for an emergency absentee ballot pursuant to Section 17-10-12 may be forwarded to the absentee election manager by the applicant or his or her designee. Application forms which are printed and made available to any applicant by the absentee election manager shall have printed thereon all penalties provided for any violation of this chapter. (Acts 1975, No. 1147, p. 2251, § 2; Acts 1978, No. 616, p. 873, § 2; Acts 1980, No. 80-732, p. 1478, § 1; Acts 1994, No. 94-320, p. 553, § 1.)

The **1994 amendment,** effective January 1, 1995, created the first three sentences from the former first sentence which read "Such application which shall be filed with the person designated to serve as the absentee election manager, need not be in any particular form, but it shall contain sufficient information to identify the applicant and it shall include the applicant's name, residence address, or such other information necessary to verify that such applicant is a registered voter, and the address to which he desires the ballot to be mailed"; substituted "receive" for "have such" in the present fifth sentence; in the present sixth sentence, substituted "absentee election manager" for "register"; added the present seventh sentence; deleted "as are herein" following "penalties" in

the last sentence; and made nonsubstantive changes.

Substantial compliance required. — Absentee ballots, absence the presence of fraud, gross negligence or intentional wrongdoing will not be set aside if they are in substantial compliance with the requirements of voting statutes. Wells v. Ellis, 551 So. 2d 382 (Ala. 1989).

Collateral references. — 29 C.J.S., Elections, § 210.

25 Am. Jur. 2d, Elections, §§ 243-252.

§ 17-10-5. Delivering ballot to absentee voter; furnishing list of qualified voters to absentee election manager; procedure if suspicion of fraudulent address on application present; notation of absentee voters on list; filing of list after election; persons obtaining absentee ballots not to vote at polling place; necessity for separate applications.

Upon receipt of the application for an absentee ballot, if the applicant's name appears on the list of qualified voters in the election to be held or, if the voter makes an affidavit for a challenged vote, the absentee election manager shall furnish the absentee ballot to the applicant by (1) forwarding it by United States mail to the applicant's or voter's residence address or the address where the voter regularly receives mail or (2) by handing the absentee ballot to the voter or, in the case of emergency voting, his or her designee in person. If the absentee election manager has reasonable cause to believe that the applicant has given a fraudulent address on the application for the absentee ballot, the election manager shall turn over the ballot application to the district attorney for any action which may be necessary under Acts 1994, No. 94-320 or other acts. The absentee election manager further may require additional proof of a voter's eligibility to vote absentee when there is evidence of continuous absentee voting. The absentee election manager shall mail any absentee ballot requested to be mailed no later than the next business day after an application has been received unless the absentee ballots have not been delivered to the absentee election manager. If the absentee ballots have not been so delivered, the absentee election manager shall hold all requests until the ballots are delivered and shall then respond by placing ballots in the mail no later than the next business day.

The official list of qualified voters shall be furnished to the absentee election manager by the judge of probate or other person preparing the list at least 45 days before the election. Any supplemental list of qualified electors shall also be provided to the absentee election manager as soon as the list becomes available. The absentee election manager shall underscore on the list the name of the voter and shall write immediately beside his or her name the word "absentee." The absentee election manager shall enroll the name, residence, and polling place of the applicant, and the date the application was received on a list of absentee voters. Each day the absentee election manager shall enter on the list the names, addresses, and polling places of each voter who has that day applied for an absentee ballot and shall post a copy of the list of applications received each day on the regular bulletin board or other public place in the county courthouse. The list shall be maintained in the office of the clerk or register for 60 days after the election, at which time it shall be filed with the judge of probate. Before the polls open at any election, the absentee election manager shall effectuate the delivery to the election officers of each polling place a list showing the name and address of every person whose name appears on the official list of qualified electors for the polling place who applied for an absentee ballot in the election. The name of the person who applied for an absentee ballot shall be stricken from the list of qualified electors kept at the polling place, and the person shall not vote again. Separate applications for absentee ballots are required for elections which are more than 30 days apart. (Acts 1975, No. 1147, p. 2251, § 3; Acts 1978, No. 616, p. 873, § 3; Acts 1980, No. 80-732, p. 1478, § 2; Acts 1986, No. 86-428, p. 791, § 2; Acts 1994, No. 94-320, p. 553, § 1.)

The 1994 amendment, effective January 1, 1995, in the first paragraph, in the first sentence, substituted "the absentee election manager" for "he," substituted "the applicant's or voter's residence address or the address where the voter regularly receives mail" for "such person," and inserted "or his or her designee"; inserted the second sentence; and created two sentences out of the former second sentence by substituting "If the absentee ballots have not been so delivered, the absentee election manager" for "in which case he or she"; and in the second paragraph, in the fourth sentence, substituted "The absentee election manager" for "He"; in the seventh sentence, substituted "Before the polls open at any election, the absentee election manager shall deliver" for "The absentee election manager shall also, before the polls open at any election, cause to be delivered"; in the eighth sentence, substituted "the person who applied for an absentee ballot" for "every such person"; and substituted the present last sentence for the former which read "A prospective absentee voter who makes application for a primary ballot may at the same time apply for an absentee ballot for any subsequent run-off primary and/or general election."

Collateral references. — 29 C.J.S., Elections, § 210.

25 Am. Jur. 2d, Elections, §§ 243-252.

§ 17-10-6. Form of absentee ballots.

The official ballots for any election to which this chapter pertains shall be in the same form as the official regular ballots for the election, except that they shall have printed thereon the words, "Official Absentee Ballot." (Acts 1975, No. 1147, p. 2251, § 4; Acts 1980, No. 80-732, p. 1478, § 3.)

Absentee ballot numbering which failed to preserve secrecy subject to federal preclearance. — Introduction of absentee ballot numbering in Greene, Perry and Sumter counties by a system which failed to preserve ballot secrecy was clearly a change in a voting practice or procedure which was subject to preclearance under § 5 of the Federal Voting Rights Act. Turner v. Webster, 637 F. Supp. 1089 (N.D. Ala. 1986).

Collateral references. — 29 C.J.S., Elections, § 210.

25 Am. Jur. 2d, Elections, §§ 243-252.

§ 17-10-7. Form of affidavit to be printed on envelope — General, special or municipal elections.

Each absentee ballot shall be accompanied by an envelope upon which shall be printed an affidavit. This affidavit which shall be used in general, special or municipal elections shall be substantially as follows:

"State of Alabama

County of ....

I, the undersigned, do swear (or affirm) that:

(1) I am a resident of .... County in the State of Alabama.

(2) My place of residence in Alabama is:

....

(street)

...., Alabama

(city or town)   (zip code)

(3) My voting precinct (or place where I vote) is:..............................

....

(4) My date of birth is:...

                             month   day   year

(5) I am entitled to vote an absentee ballot because:

Check only one:

_____ I have moved from Alabama less than thirty days prior to the election.

_____ I will be out of the county or the state on election day.

_____ I am physically incapacitated and will not be able to vote in person on election day.

_____ I work a required workplace shift that conflicts with polling hours.

I further swear (or affirm) that I have not voted nor will I vote in person in the election to which this ballot pertains.

I have marked the enclosed absentee ballot voluntarily and that I have read or had read to me and understand the instructions accompanying this ballot and that I have carefully complied with such instructions.

Moreover, I further swear (or affirm) that all of the information given above is true and correct to the best of my knowledge and that I understand that by knowingly giving false information so as to vote illegally by absentee ballot that I shall be guilty of a misdemeanor which is punishable by a fine not to exceed $1,000.00 and/or confinement in the county jail for not more than six months.

....

(Signature or mark of voter.)

....

(Printed name of voter.)

Note: Your signature must be witnessed by either: A notary public or other officer authorized to acknowledge oaths or two witnesses 18 years of age or older.

Sworn to and subscribed before me this . . . . day of . . . .,
19. . . . . . I certify that the affiant is known (or made known) to me to be the
identical party he or she claims to be.

. . . . (Signature of official)

(Title of official)

. . . .

(Address of official)

OR

1st Witness . . . .

Signature

. . . .

Print name

. . . .

Address

. . . .

City   Zip Code

2nd Witness . . . .

Signature

. . . .

Print name

. . . .

Address

. . . .

City   Zip Code"

(Acts 1975, No. 1147, p. 2251, § 5; Acts 1980, No. 80-732, p. 1478, § 4; Acts
1994, No. 94-320, p. 553, § 1.)

The 1994 amendment, effective January 1, 1995, in the affidavit form, inserted "I work a required workplace shift that conflicts with polling hours" and added a line for the printed name of the voter following the line for the voter's signature or mark.

An absentee voter's affidavit need not be identical to the form contained in this section, the affidavit must comply substantially with this section and its irregularities must not "adversely affect the sanctity of the ballot and the integrity of the election." To fulfill these requirements, the trial court properly admitted into evidence only those absentee ballots that were accompanied by an affidavit containing the voter's (1) place of residence, (2) reason for voting absentee, and (3) signature. Williams v. Lide, 628 So. 2d 531 (Ala. 1993).

Testifying to supply missing information. — If an absentee voter's affidavit lacked information regarding voter's (1) place of residence, (2) reason for voting absentee, and (3) signature, the trial court may permit the voter to testify at trial to supply the missing elements. Williams v. Lide, 628 So. 2d 531 (Ala. 1993).

Collateral references. — 29 C.J.S., Elections, § 210.

25 Am. Jur. 2d, Elections, §§ 243-252.

§ 17-10-8. Form of affidavit to be printed on envelope — Primary elections.

The form of the affidavit which shall be printed on the envelope used in primary elections shall be the same as that used in general, special and municipal elections; except, that the following sentence shall be added and inserted therein immediately above the signature of the voter:

"I am a member of the . . . . Party and subscribe to all conditions and qualifications laid down by that party's committee as a requisite for participation in the election . . . . (Signature of Voter)."

Such affidavit shall be sworn to in the same manner and form as in general, special and municipal elections. (Acts 1975, No. 1147, p. 2251, § 6; Acts 1980, No. 80-732, p. 1478, § 4.)

Collateral references. — 29 C.J.S., Elections, § 210.   25 Am. Jur. 2d, Elections, §§ 243-252.

§ 17-10-9. Two envelopes to be furnished with ballot; form thereof; delivery of ballot to absentee election manager.

Each prospective absentee voter who meets the requirements of this chapter shall be furnished with the absentee ballot herein provided for, together with two envelopes for returning his marked ballot. One envelope shall be a plain envelope in which the ballot shall be sealed by the voter after he has marked it.

The second envelope shall have the voter's affidavit printed on the back and shall be large enough to seal the plain ballot envelope inside. The second envelope shall also be a return mail envelope.

Such return mail envelope shall be addressed on the front to the absentee election manager and shall be endorsed on the left-hand upper corner thereof substantially as follows:

"Absent Voter's Ballot. State, County, Municipal, General, Primary or Special Election (as the case may be) to be held on the . . . . day of . . . ., 19. . . . From . . . . (name of voter), precinct or districts . . . ., County of . . . ., Alabama."

After marking the ballot and subscribing the oath herein required, the voter shall seal his ballot in the plain envelope, place that plain envelope inside the affidavit envelope, complete the affidavit, and shall forward it by United States mail to the addressee or shall hand it to him in person. (Acts 1975, No. 1147, p. 2251, § 7; Acts 1978, No. 616, p. 873, § 4; Acts 1980, No. 80-732, p. 1478, § 5.)

Collateral references. — 29 C.J.S., Elections, § 210.   25 Am. Jur. 2d, Elections, §§ 243-252.

§ 17-10-10. Procedure upon receipt of ballot by absentee election manager; counting of ballots.

Upon receipt of the absentee ballot, the absentee election manager shall record its receipt thereof on the absentee list as provided in Section 17-10-5 and shall safely keep the ballot without breaking the seal of the affidavit envelope. On the day of the election, beginning at 12:00 noon, the absentee election manager shall deliver the sealed affidavit envelopes containing absentee ballots to the election officials provided for in Section 17-10-11, and such election officials shall call the name of each voter casting an absentee ballot with poll watchers present as may be provided under the laws of Alabama and shall open each affidavit envelope, review the affidavit to certify that such voter is entitled to vote and deposit the plain envelope containing the absentee ballot into a sealed ballot box. The absentee ballots shall upon the closing of the polls be counted and otherwise handled in all respects as if the said absentee voter were present and voting in person. As regards municipalities with populations of less than 10,000, in the case of municipal elections held at a time different from a primary or general election, such return mail envelopes containing the ballots shall be delivered to the election official of the precinct of the respective voters. (Acts 1975, No. 1147, p. 2251, § 8; Acts 1978, No. 616, p. 873, § 5; Acts 1980, No. 80-732, p. 1478, § 6.)

Collateral references. — 29 C.J.S., Elections, §§ 210, 227.   25 Am. Jur. 2d, Elections, §§ 250, 251, 291-303.

§ 17-10-11. Officials for counting of absentee ballots; poll watchers.

(a) For every primary, general, special or municipal election, there shall be appointed three managers, two clerks and a returning officer, named and notified as are other election officials under the general laws of the state, who shall meet, at the regular time of closing of the election on that day, in the office of the clerk or register for the purpose of receiving, counting and returning the ballots cast by absent voters. The returns from the absent box shall be made as required by law for all other boxes. It shall be unlawful for any election official or other person to publish or make known to anyone the results of the count of absentee votes before the polls close.

(b) Notwithstanding the provisions of subsection (a) of this section, in counties with populations of 50,000 or more, there shall be appointed three managers, two clerks and one returning officer for each 200 absentee ballots, or fraction thereof, cast at the election. In those counties, the appointing board for the election shall meet at least four days before the election, determine the number of officials to be appointed and appoint and notify them as other election officials are appointed and notified.

(c) Any person or organization authorized to appoint poll watchers under Section 17-6-8 or 17-16-26 may have a single watcher present at the counting of absentee ballots, with the rights as are conferred by the aforesaid sections and by any other provisions of state law.

(d) This section shall not apply to municipal elections in cities and towns of less than 10,000 inhabitants which are held at a time different from a primary or general election.

(e) Notwithstanding the provisions of subsections (a) and (b), in those counties using an optical scanning system to count absentee ballots, the election appointment board may appoint managers, clerks, and returning officers as are necessary to process and canvas absentee ballots. (Acts 1975, No. 1147, p. 2251, § 9; Acts 1980, No. 80-732, p. 1478, § 7; Acts 1994, No. 94-692, p. 1332, § 1.)

The 1994 amendment, effective May 3, 1994, added subsection (e), and made nonsubstantive changes.

Collateral references. — 29 C.J.S., Elections, §§ 210, 227.

25 Am. Jur. 2d, Elections, §§ 250, 251, 291-303.

§ 17-10-12. When ballots, envelopes, etc., to be delivered to absentee election manager; procedure when manager is candidate with opposition in election; eligibility for use of emergency absentee ballot.

(a) Not less than 40 days prior to the holding of any election, except a municipal election, to which this chapter pertains, or in the case of a run-off primary election, not more than seven days after the first primary election, the officer charged with the printing and distribution of the official ballots and election supplies shall deliver to the absentee election manager of each county in which the election is held or to the person designated to serve in his or her place a sufficient number of absentee ballots, envelopes, and other necessary supplies. Not more than seven days after the last day to qualify as a candidate in a municipal election, or in the case of a run-off municipal election, not more than seven days after the first election, or in the case of a municipal election held for a purpose other than the election of municipal officers, not more than seven days after the giving of notice of the election, the officer charged with the printing and distribution of the official ballots and election supplies shall deliver to the absentee election manager of the municipality in which the election is held, or to the person designated to serve in his or her place, a sufficient number of absentee ballots, envelopes, and other necessary supplies. If the absentee election manager is a candidate with opposition in the election, he or she shall immediately, upon receipt of the ballots, envelopes, and supplies, deliver them to the person authorized to act in his or her place, as provided in Section 17-10-13.

(b) Any registered elector who requires emergency treatment of a licensed physician within five days of an election may apply for an emergency absentee ballot for the election and may vote by returning the absentee ballot no later than 5:00 p.m. on the day before the election is held. The attendant physician shall describe and certify the circumstances as constituting an emergency on a special form designed by the Secretary of State and provided by his or her office to local absentee election managers. The special form shall be attached to the application.

(c) Any registered elector whose name appears on the poll list of qualified voters may vote by an emergency absentee ballot if he or she is required by his or her employer under unforeseen circumstances to be out of the county on an emergency business trip on election day. Under such circumstances, the applicant shall apply for an emergency absentee ballot at the office of the absentee election manager no later than the close of the business day one day prior to the election. The applicant shall complete and file an application form designed by the Secretary of State for emergency absentee voters. The form shall contain an affidavit which the applicant shall sign or swear acknowledging that he or she was not aware of the out of county business requirement prior to five days before the election. An applicant who meets the requirements of this subsection may vote by an emergency absentee ballot. After voting the ballot, the voter shall hand the ballot to the absentee election manager. (Acts 1975, No. 1147, p. 2251, § 10; Acts 1978, No. 616, p. 873, § 6; Acts 1980, No. 80-732, p. 1478, § 8; Acts 1986, No. 86-428, p. 791, § 3; Acts 1992, No. 92-152, p. 262, § 1; Acts 1994, No. 94-320, p. 553, § 1.)

The **1994 amendment,** effective January 1, 1995, designated the first paragraph as subsection (a); in the first sentence of subdivision (a), deleted "and not less than 15 days for the 1992 election cycle only" following "pertains," and deleted "to which this chapter pertains" following "election"; and added subsections (b) and (c).

Code Commissioner's note. — In 1994, the Code Commissioner deleted the phrase "Not more other necessary supplies" preceding "Not more than seven days" in the second sentence of subsection (a) to correct a typographical error in Acts 1944, 94-320, which amended this section.

Collateral references. — 29 C.J.S., Elections, §§ 210, 227.

25 Am. Jur. 2d, Elections, §§ 250, 251, 291-303.

§ 17-10-13. Circuit clerk, register and register in chancery disqualified from serving as absentee election manager when candidate for any office with opposition.

When the circuit clerk, register or register in chancery is a candidate for any office and has opposition, he shall be disqualified from performing any of the duties imposed by this chapter with reference to the handling of absentee ballots. At least 55 days prior to the election, the circuit clerk, register or register in chancery shall certify to the presiding circuit judge of the county his candidacy with opposition and that he is disqualified to serve or otherwise prevented from serving. The presiding circuit judge shall thereupon appoint a person to serve as absentee election manager in the manner provided for in Section 17-10-2. (Acts 1975, No. 1147, p. 2251, § 11, 16; Acts 1978, No. 616, p. 873, § 7; Acts 1986, No. 86-428, p. 791, § 4; Acts 1988, No. 88-88, p. 114, § 1.)

Appointee not to be another county official who is also a candidate. — In any election to which former Tit. 17, §§ 64(15) through 64(34), 1940 Code pertained, when the register was a candidate for any office he was disqualified from performing any duties imposed upon him by the terms of those sections, and the person to perform such duties was not another county official who was not a candidate for office, but an individual to be appointed by the presiding circuit judge of the county. Kendrick v. Boyd, 255 Ala. 422, 51 So. 2d 701 (1932), decided under former Tit. 17, § 64(18), 1940 Code which contained provisions similar to those in this section.

§ 17-10-14. Compensation of absentee election manager.

The county commission shall determine the amount of compensation to be paid to the absentee election manager or other absentee election manager for the performance of his duties with respect to the absentee ballots during the 45 day period prior to and on the day of the election for which his services are required, but such compensation shall not be less than $15.00 nor more than $25.00 per day. Such an amount shall be the total compensation allowed the absentee election manager for duties relating to absentee ballots in all elections held on the same day and shall be paid from the county treasury, except in case of a municipal election held at a time different from a primary or general election, in which event payment shall be made from the city or town treasury. However, no municipal employee shall be compensated for his services in this regard. (Acts 1975, No. 1147, p. 2251, § 12; Acts 1978, No. 616, p. 873, § 8; Acts 1986, No. 86-428, p. 791, § 5; Acts 1988, No. 88-88, p. 114, § 2.)

Register on salary basis entitled to compensation. — Former Tit. 17, §§ 64(15) through 64(34), 1940 Code could not be said to show a legislative intent to deprive the register of Jefferson county of compensation for the performance of the duties therein imposed because of statutory provisions theretofore enacted placing the register on a salary basis. Kendrick v. Boyd, 255 Ala. 422, 51 So. 2d 701 (1932), decided under former Tit. 17, § 64(31),

1940 Code, which contained provisions similar to those in this section.

A writ of mandamus was the appropriate remedy to direct the county commission to authorize the compensation provided in this section. 35 Ala. App. 592, 51 So. 2d 697, cert. denied, 255 Ala. 422, 51 So. 2d 701 (1951), decided under former Tit. 17, § 64(31), 1940 Code, which contained provisions similar to those in this section.

§ 17-10-15. Designation of person to perform duties of clerk or register in municipal elections held at time different from primary or general election.

In any municipal election that is held at a time different from a primary or general election, the duties with reference to the handling of absentee ballots which are required of the clerk or register shall be performed by the town clerk, city clerk or other officer performing the duties of the clerk. If such clerk or other officer is also a candidate in such election, the governing body of the city or town shall appoint a qualified elector of the city or town to perform the duties. Such person so appointed shall have all the powers, duties and responsibilities of the clerk or register under this chapter and shall be entitled to the compensation provided by Section 17-10-14. (Acts 1975, No. 1147, p. 2251, § 13.)

§ 17-10-16. Costs and expenses generally.

All necessary and proper expenses and costs incurred in the carrying out of the provisions of this chapter for which no special provision is made in this chapter shall be paid for in the same manner as are necessary costs and expenses incurred in the several classes of elections enumerated under this chapter. (Acts 1975, No. 1147, p. 2251, § 14.)

§ 17-10-17. Changing ballots, unauthorized assistance to voter, unlawful use of absentee ballot, etc.; Attorney General to provide assistance in investigating violations; provisions not to be construed as discouraging or inhibiting voter participation or use of absentee ballots.

(a) Any person who willfully changes an absentee voter's ballot to the extent that it does not reflect the voter's true ballot, any person who willfully votes more than once by absentee in the same election, any person who willfully votes for another voter or falsifies absentee ballot applications or verification documents so as to vote absentee, or any person who solicits, encourages, urges, or otherwise promotes illegal absentee voting, upon conviction, shall be punished by imprisonment in the penitentiary for not less than one nor more than two years, or by a fine of not less than $500.00 nor more than $2,000.00, or by being both fined and imprisoned. Any person who willfully aids any person unlawfully to vote an absentee ballot, any person who knowingly and unlawfully votes an absentee ballot, and any voter who votes both an absentee and a regular ballot at any election shall be similarly punished.

(b) Upon request by the local district attorney or the Secretary of State, the Attorney General shall provide investigating assistance in instances of absentee ballot or voting violations.

(c) Nothing in this section shall be construed to impede or inhibit organized legal efforts to encourage voter participation in the election process or to discourage a candidate from encouraging electors to lawfully vote by absentee ballot. (Acts 1975, No. 1147, p. 2251, § 15; Acts 1980, No. 80-732, p. 1478, § 9; Acts 1994, No. 94-320, p. 553, § 1.)

The 1994 amendment, effective January 1, 1995, designated the first paragraph as subsection (a); in subsection (a), in the first sentence, deleted "or" following "ballot" and "election," and substituted the language following "vote absentee" for "in violation of this chapter, upon conviction, shall be punished by imprisonment in the penitentiary for not less than one nor more than two years, or by a fine of not less than $500.00 nor more than $2,000.00, or by being both fined and imprisoned," and rewrote the second sentence; added subsections (b) and (c); and made nonsubstantive changes.

Collateral references. — 29 C.J.S., Elections, §§ 210, 214-220, 238, 334(2).

25 Am. Jur. 2d, Elections, §§ 251, 252, 277-290.

§ 17-10-18. Willfully refusing to perform duties as to absentee voters.

Any person who shall willfully fail or refuse to perform or discharge any duty required of him in this chapter shall be guilty of a misdemeanor, and, on conviction, shall be fined not more than $100.00. (Acts 1919, No. 75, p. 70; Acts 1919, No. 620, p. 862; Code 1923, § 3938; Code 1940, T. 17, § 333.)

§ 17-10-19. Voter making false oath. Repealed by Acts 1977, No. 607, p. 812, § 9901, effective January 1, 1980.

§ 17-10-20. Probate judges volunteering suggestions as to ballots for absent voters.

Any probate judge who sends any ballots or makes any suggestions in reference to furnishing ballots for absentee voters, except upon the application or request of the absent voter himself, shall be guilty of a misdemeanor. (Acts 1919, No. 75, p. 70; Acts 1919, No. 620, p. 862; Code 1923, § 3940; Code 1940, T. 17, § 335.)

CHAPTER 11.

IDENTIFICATION OF VOTERS.

§ 17-11-1. County commission authorized to require identification of voters; marking and examination of voter's hand; invisible marking substance.

The county commission of every county in this state is hereby authorized, by resolution or ordinance, to provide for and require the identification of persons who vote at general, primary, special or municipal elections in the county. The resolution or ordinance shall require all persons offering to vote to pass their hands under a light or some other device specially designed to make the voter's stamp or mark, hereinafter provided for, visible before a ballot is delivered to him or he is permitted to enter the voting machine, as the case may be, and to submit to the stamping or marking of one of his hands, as hereinafter provided upon placing his ballot in the box or other receptacle provided for paper ballots or upon leaving the voting machine. It shall also direct the election officials conducting the election before permitting a person to vote at the election to examine the voter's hands to be sure that he has not previously voted at such election and, upon a voter's casting his ballot, to mark or stamp one of his hands in the manner hereinafter prescribed. Marking or stamping of a voter's hand shall be done by a stamp or mark thereon made with a powder, liquid or other substance which is not visible on human skin to the naked eye under normal lighting conditions, whether natural daylight or customary electric lighting, but which shows up or is clearly visible on human skin when a special or certain type of light ray is projected thereon. The powder, liquid or other substance shall also be of a type which cannot be rubbed off, erased, washed off or removed and will not disappear from normal human skin for at least 12 hours. (Acts 1965, 2nd Ex. Sess., No. 105, p. 142, § 1.)

§ 17-11-2. Procurement of marking substances, applicators and inspection devices; supplying of marking substances to election officials; cost.

Every county commission in this state which enacts an ordinance or adopts a resolution requiring the identification of voters shall procure an adequate amount of the powder, liquid or other substance to be used to mark voters, proper equipment for applying the substance to the skin of one of the voter's

125

hands and an adequate number of lights or other devices for projecting the special rays which make such powder, liquid or other substance visible and shall supply such powder, liquid or other substance to the election officials at each polling place at the same time that other election materials are supplied. The cost of all such powder, liquid or other marking substance, the equipment necessary to apply it and the lamps or other devices for making it visible shall be paid out of the county treasury. (Acts 1965, 2nd Ex. Sess., No. 105, p. 142, § 1.)

§ 17-11-3. Person refusing to have hand examined or marked not permitted to vote.

No person who refuses to have his hand examined by an election official under the special light ray and no person who refuses to permit one of his hands to be marked, so as to identify him as a person who has voted, shall be permitted to vote in any election, general, special, primary or municipal in a county after the county commission of the county has adopted an ordinance or a resolution requiring such identification of voters. (Acts 1965, 2nd Ex. Sess., No. 105, p. 142, § 3.)

§ 17-11-4. Penalty for election officer failing to perform duty under chapter or guilty of corrupt conduct; when person deemed an officer.

Any inspector, clerk or other election officer who wilfully neglects or fails to perform a duty placed on him by this chapter or is guilty of any corrupt conduct in the performance of such duty must, on conviction, be fined not less than $100.00 nor more than $1,000.00; but no person shall be deemed an inspector, clerk or officer within the meaning of this section until he first shall have taken an oath to discharge well and truly the duties of such office to the best of his ability or until he shall have performed some of the duties pertaining to such office. (Acts 1965, 2nd Ex. Sess., No. 105, p. 142, § 4.)

CHAPTER 12.

CHALLENGE OF VOTERS.

§ 17-12-1. Right to challenge; communicating challenge to inspectors; timing of challenge.

(a) Any qualified elector of the precinct in which any person proposes to vote may challenge the person so offering to vote whom he or she may know or suspect is not entitled or duly qualified as an elector to vote at the precinct where he or she offers to vote.

(b) The challenge shall be communicated to the inspectors before the person is permitted to vote by the sheriff or some other person in attendance and in charge of admission to the polling place where his or her right to vote shall be determined as provided by Sections 17-12-3 and 17-12-4.

(c) The challenge to an absentee ballot shall be communicated to an absentee election officer before the absentee ballot is tabulated and certified by the absentee election officers. (Code 1876, § 277; Code 1886, § 373; Code 1896, § 1629; Code 1907, § 370; Code 1923, § 460; Code 1940, T. 17, § 143; Acts 1994, No. 94-320, p. 553, § 1.)

The 1994 amendment, effective January 1, 1995, in subsection (a), substituted "may" for "shall have the right to"; added subsection (c); and made nonsubstantive changes.

Cited in Harris v. Conradi, 675 F.2d 1212 (11th Cir. 1982).

Collateral references. — 29 C.J.S., Elections, §§ 118(1), 144, 200, 209, 210(3).

§ 17-12-2. Selection and duties of challenger.

(a) The inspectors shall select one of their number, on opening the polls, to act as challenger, and the challenger shall ascertain if each person presenting himself or herself to vote has registered. The finding of the challenger shall be from an examination of the official list of the voters furnished by the judge of probate. If the name of the person does not appear on the list, the challenger shall challenge the voter.

(b) The absentee election officers shall select jointly one official who shall ascertain if each challenged absentee ballot is a legitimate ballot as required by law. (Code 1907, § 407; Acts 1915, No. 56, p. 214; Code 1923, § 497; Code 1940, T. 17, § 187; Acts 1994, No. 94-320, p. 553, § 1.)

The 1994 amendment, effective January 1, 1995, in subsection (a), created two sentences from the former first sentence by substituting "registered. The finding of the challenger shall" for "registered, such finding to"; and added subsection (b); and made nonsubstantive changes.

Collateral references. — 29 C.J.S., Elections, § 200.

§ 17-12-3. Oath of challenged voter.

When any person offering to vote at the polls is challenged by an inspector or by any qualified elector, before the person shall be allowed to vote, he or she shall take and subscribe an oath which one of the inspectors shall tender, read, and administer to him or her, and which shall be in the following form:

"State of Alabama, County of . . . . I do solemnly swear (or affirm) that: 1. I am a duly qualified elector under the constitution and laws of the State of Alabama. 2. That I am 18 years of age or upwards. 3. That I have not been convicted of any crime which disfranchises me. 4. That I have been duly registered. 5. I know of no reason why I am not entitled to vote. 6. I am generally known by the name under which I now desire to vote, which is . . . . 7. I have not voted and will not vote in any other precinct (or if the precinct has been divided into districts, in any other voting district) in this election. 8. My occupation is . . . ., the name of my employer is . . . . 9. My residence is . . . . (if in a city or town give street number). 10. That . . . . and . . . . have personal knowledge of my residence in the State of Alabama. 11. This affidavit has been read to me. So help me God . . . . Signature. Subscribed and sworn to before me this . . . . day . . . . . ., 19. . . ."

(Code 1876, § 278; Code 1886, § 374; Code 1896, § 1630; Code 1907, § 408; Acts 1915, No. 56, p. 214; Code 1923, § 498; Code 1940, T. 17, § 188; Acts 1994, No. 94-320, p. 553, § 1.)

The 1994 amendment, effective January 1, 1995, inserted "at the polls" in the introductory clause, and made nonsubstantive changes.

Code Commissioner's note. — In 1995, the Code Commissioner added ": 1." near the beginning of the form to denote the first item in a sequence of numbered items.

Cited in Harris v. Conradi, 675 F.2d 1212 (11th Cir. 1982).

§ 17-12-4. Oath to establish identity of voter.

In addition to the oath provided for in Section 17-12-3, the person so challenged shall be required by the inspectors before he shall be allowed to vote to prove his identity, residence in the state, county and precinct in which he offers to vote by the oath of some elector personally known to some one of the inspectors to be a qualified elector and a freeholder and householder, which oath shall be administered by one of the inspectors, and be in the following form:

"State of Alabama, County of . . . . I, ... do solemnly swear (or affirm) that I have known . . . . (here insert the name of the person offering to vote) preceding this election, and that he has been a resident of this state, in this county, and he actually resides in this precinct or district at the time of this election. I do solemnly swear (or affirm) that I am a qualified elector of this precinct; that I have been a freeholder and householder in this precinct for one year next preceding this election; that my occupation is . . . .; my residence is . . . .; my business address is . . . .; Subscribed and sworn to before me this . . . . day of . . . ., 19. . . .";

and, upon such oath being duly taken and subscribed, the ballot of the person offering to vote must be received and deposited as other ballots of qualified electors, and the inspectors shall require the persons making said affidavits to swear to and subscribe to an original and a carbon, the carbon to be treated as an original, one set of said affidavits, when so taken and subscribed when the election is closed, shall be sealed by the inspectors in a sealed package and forwarded to the district attorney for the county, who shall lay them before the next grand jury sitting for the county. The other set of said affidavits shall be sealed and deposited in the ballot box. (Code 1876, § 278; Code 1886, § 374; Code 1896, § 1630; Code 1907, § 409; Acts 1915, No. 56, p. 214; Code 1923, § 499; Code 1940, T. 17, § 189.)

Cross references. — As to provisions for the disposition of records and forms after elections, see § 17-4-230 et seq.

§ 17-12-5. Vote rejected if voter refuses to take oath.

If the person challenged refuses to take the oath or if he fails to prove his identity and residence by the oath of the freeholder and householder, as above required, his vote shall be rejected and his ballot, marked with his name, shall be laid aside by the inspectors. (Code 1876, § 280; Code 1886, § 376; Code 1896, § 1632; Code 1907, § 410; Acts 1915, No. 56, p. 214; Code 1923, § 500; Code 1940, T. 17, § 190.)

§ 17-12-6. False oath.

When any person offering to vote at any election in this state has been challenged, before administering the oath prescribed, one of the inspectors shall inform such person that if he takes the oath wilfully and falsely he is guilty of perjury and, on conviction, may be imprisoned in the penitentiary for not less than two years. One of the inspectors shall also inform any person making the affidavit of identity that if he makes such oath wilfully and falsely he is guilty of perjury and, on conviction, may be imprisoned in the penitentiary for not less than two years. (Code 1876, § 279; Code 1886, § 375; Code 1896, § 1631; Code 1907, § 411; Acts 1915, No. 56, p. 214; Code 1923, § 501; Code 1940, T. 17, § 191.)

§ 17-12-7. Excluding or receiving votes unlawfully.

Any inspector of election or absentee election officer who wilfully excludes any ballot duly cast, knowing that the person offering the ballot is lawfully entitled to vote at the election, or who wilfully receives a ballot from any person who has been duly challenged in relation to his or her right to vote at the election, without exacting from the person an oath or other proof of qualification as required by law, shall be guilty of a misdemeanor, and, upon conviction, shall be fined not less than one hundred dollars ($100), and may also be sentenced to hard labor for the county for not more than six months. (Code 1907, § 6802; Code 1923, § 3920; Code 1940, T. 17, § 315; Acts 1994, No. 94-320, p. 553, § 1.)

The 1994 amendment, effective January 1, 1995, inserted "or absentee election officer"; substituted "ballot duly cast" for "vote duly tendered and unchallenged"; substituted "ballot" for "same" following "offering the"; substi-tuted "receives a ballot" for "receive a vote"; and made nonsubstantive changes.

Collateral references. — 29 C.J.S., Elections, § 340.

§ 17-12-8. Penalty for permitting unqualified person to vote.

Any inspector of election or absentee election officer who, without challenging a person, permits the person to vote, knowing that he or she is not a qualified elector, shall be fined not less than one hundred dollars ($100). (Code 1907, § 6803; Code 1923, § 3921; Code 1940, T. 17, § 316; Acts 1994, No. 94-320, p. 553, § 1.)

The 1994 amendment, effective January 1, 1995, inserted "or absentee election officer," deleted "shall" following "who" and substituted "a person" for "him"; and made nonsubstantive changes.

Collateral references. — 29 C.J.S., Elections, § 341.

CHAPTER 13.

COUNTING OF VOTES.

§ 17-13-1. Counting upon close of polls.

All inspectors of elections in the election precincts shall, immediately on the closing of the polls, count the votes polled, and no votes shall be counted until the polls are closed. (Code 1876, § 285; Code 1886, § 381; Code 1896, § 1637; Code 1907, § 413; Code 1923, § 503; Code 1940, T. 17, § 192.)

Collateral references. — 26 Am. Jur. 2d, Elections, § 291 et seq.

§ 17-13-2. Procedure; improperly marked ballots.

In counting, the returning officer or one of the inspectors must take the ballots, one by one, from the box in which they have been deposited, at the same time reading aloud the names of the persons voted for and the office for which such persons are voted for; they must separately keep a calculation of the number of votes each person receives and for what office he receives them; if the elector has marked more names than there are persons to be elected to an office, or if for any reason it is impossible to determine the elector's choice for any office to be filled, his ballot shall not be counted for such office, but this shall not vitiate the ballot so far as properly marked, nor shall any ballot be rejected for any technical error which does not make it impossible to determine the elector's choice, and nothing in the election law shall be construed so as to prevent any elector from voting for any qualified person other than those whose names are printed on the ballot. (Code 1852, § 222; Code 1867, § 264; Code 1876, § 286; Code 1886, § 382; Code 1896, § 1638; Code 1907, § 414; Code 1923, § 504; Code 1940, T. 17, § 193.)

In general. — The elector is authorized by statute to write the name of a person for whom he desired to vote in the proper place on the ballot and indicate his choice as required by law. And under the law a vote so cast must be counted, tabulated and reported to the board of supervisors, unless "it is impossible to determine the elector's choice for any office to be filled." Reed v. State ex rel. Davis, 234 Ala. 306, 174 So. 498 (1937); State ex rel. Smith v. Deason, 264 Ala. 596, 88 So. 2d 674 (1956).

Substantial compliance with law is sufficient. — A voter should not be disfranchised by rejection of his ballot in whole or in part when he has made an honest effort to comply with law and has substantially complied with its mandatory requirements. Garrett v. Cuninghame, 211 Ala. 430, 100 So. 845 (1924).

Cited in Black v. Pate, 130 Ala. 514, 30 So. 434 (1901); Wilkerson v. Cantelou, 165 Ala. 619, 51 So. 799 (1910); United States v. Executive Comm. of Democratic Party, 254 F. Supp. 537 (S.D. Ala. 1966).

Collateral references. — 29 C.J.S., Elections, §§ 221-240.

§ 17-13-3. Paper showing total votes received by each candidate to be attached to ballot box.

In every general, special, primary and municipal election hereafter held in this state, it shall be the duty of the election officials conducting such election, after the closing of the polls and after such officials have completed the count of ballots cast in said election, to attach to the outside of each ballot box used in such election a slip of paper, or other device, showing the total votes received by each candidate voted for in such election.

The provisions of this section shall have no application in those counties or municipalities in which voting machines are used. (Acts 1951, No. 800, p. 1399.)

§ 17-13-4. Ballots to be counted, labeled, sealed and delivered to returning officer.

The inspectors must count the ballots deposited in the box, and as soon as all the ballots contained in the box are counted, the inspectors shall roll up the ballots so counted and label the same so as to show for what officer or officers the ballots contained therein were received, and, when so rolled up and labeled, shall be securely sealed; the rejected ballots, if any, shall also be rolled up and labeled as rejected ballots and sealed up as the other parcels; and the packages so sealed up and labeled, together with one poll list, shall also be securely sealed up, shall be returned to and securely fastened up in the box from which such ballots were taken and counted and which shall also be securely sealed and labeled so as to show the nature of its contents and shall be delivered to the returning officer, who shall deliver them to the sheriff. (Code 1876, § 288; Code 1886, § 384; Code 1896, § 1640; Code 1907, § 416; Code 1923, § 506; Code 1940, T. 17, § 195.)

§ 17-13-5. Ballots kept by sheriff six months after election.

The sheriff shall keep the ballots six months, and then the packages shall be taken out of the box, without opening or unsealing the packages, and destroyed unless within six months the sheriff having them in custody is notified that the election of some officer for which the election was held will be contested, in which case he must preserve the box containing the ballots cast for such contestant until such contest is finally determined or until such box is demanded by some legally constituted custodian during such contest. (Code 1907, § 417; Code 1923, § 507; Code 1940, T. 17, § 196.)

Cited in Sartain v. Shepherd, 173 Ala. 474, 55 So. 919 (1911).

Collateral references. — 29 C.J.S., Elections, § 234.

§ 17-13-6. Count of votes to be sealed, certified and delivered to sheriff.

As soon as the ballots are all counted, the inspectors must ascertain the number of votes received for each person and for what office and must make a statement of the same in writing, which statement must be signed by them; they must also certify in writing on one of the poll lists, that such poll list is the poll list of the election precinct at which they were inspectors, the day and year on which such election was held and for what offices, which certificates must be signed by them; and such statement of the poll lists and votes, thus certified, must be sealed up, together with a list of the registered voters in such precinct at such election on such day, in a box to be furnished by the sheriff of the county, one or more for each precinct, and to consist of wood, tin or sheet iron, and securely fastened by locks, directed to the sheriff of the county, if there be one, and if none, then to the person discharging the duties of such office, and immediately deliver the same to the returning officer of the precinct.

The statement of votes and the poll list delivered to the returning officer of the precinct must be delivered to the returning officer of the county within 48 hours after the election.

Any returning officer of the precinct who fails to deliver the statement of votes and poll list to the returning officer of the county, within the time required by law, must, on conviction, be fined not less than $100.00 nor more than $500.00, and must also be imprisoned in the county jail for not more than six months. (Code 1876, §§ 287, 289, 4283; Code 1886, §§ 383, 385, 4182; Code 1896, §§ 1639, 1641, 4689; Code 1907, §§ 415, 418, 6786; Code 1923, §§ 505, 508, 3904; Code 1940, T. 17, §§ 194, 197, 300.)

Cross references. — As to provisions for the disposition of records and forms after elections, see § 17-4-230 et seq.

Probate judge is custodian of lists. — Votes prepared by election inspectors should be transmitted to probate judge, who shall be the legal custodian of the lists. Sartain v. Shepherd, 173 Ala. 474, 55 So. 919 (1911).

And lists are filed with him for public inspection. — After the votes are counted and the results declared by the inspectors the poll lists are filed with the probate judge for public inspection. Sartain v. Shepherd, 173 Ala. 474, 55 So. 919 (1911).

Cited in Leigh v. State, 69 Ala. 261 (1881); Ex parte Shepherd, 172 Ala. 205, 55 So. 627 (1911).

§ 17-13-7. Certificate of votes delivered to probate judge of each county to be forwarded.

The board of supervisors must, as soon as they have ascertained the result of an election, make on blanks furnished by the Secretary of State certificates stating the exact number of votes cast in the county by precincts for each person voted for and the office for which such person was voted for, and file the certificates with the judge of probate who must immediately forward such certificate as to all members of the Legislature and to all civil officers who are to be commissioned by the Governor, except the Attorney General, Auditor, Secretary of State, Treasurer and Commissioner of Agriculture and Industries, to the Secretary of State. (Code 1876, § 292; Code 1886, § 389; Code 1896,

§ 1646; Code 1907, § 435; Code 1923, § 525; Code 1949, T. 17, § 209; Acts 1988, 1st Ex. Sess., No. 88-908, p. 482, § 1.)

Determination of right to public office. — The right to a public office dependent on an election by the people is determined by the number of legal votes received at the election and not by the certificate of election.

McGallagher v. Bosarge, 273 Ala. 133, 136 So. 2d 181 (1961).

Collateral references. — 29 C.J.S., Elections, §§ 221-240.

26 Am. Jur. 2d, Elections, §§ 304, 305.

§ 17-13-8. Posting of certificate of result.

Immediately after the election the inspectors shall post in front of the polling place a copy of their certificate of the result of the election. (Code 1907, § 355; Code 1923, § 445; Code 1940, T. 17, § 128.)

Collateral references. — 29 C.J.S., Elections, §§ 221-240.

§ 17-13-9. Making false certificate of result. Repealed by Acts 1977, No. 607, p. 812, § 9901, effective January 1, 1980.

§ 17-13-10. Returns of election — How made; duty of probate judge.

One copy of the certificate of the result of the election shall be signed by the inspectors and enclosed in an envelope, which shall then be securely sealed, and each of the inspectors shall write his name across every fold at which the envelope, if unfastened, could be opened. Said envelope, with certificate enclosed, shall be at once delivered to the returning officer of the precinct, who shall deliver the same in the condition received to the judge of probate. The judge of probate shall keep and preserve the same unopened until the board of supervisors meets to ascertain the result of the election. In case of loss, mutilation or absence of the original certificate of the result of the election by the inspectors of any voting place, the envelope shall be opened, and the copy therein shall be accepted as a certificate of the result of the election for that voting place. (Code 1907, § 366; Code 1923, § 456; Code 1940, T. 17, § 139.)

Collateral references. — 29 C.J.S., Elections, §§ 221-240.

§ 17-13-11. Returns of election — Additional copy to be delivered to probate judge.

(a) The election officials whose duty it is to make election returns for each polling place in any state, county, municipal or local election shall make an additional carbon or duplicate copy thereof at the same time they make the original and shall deliver said additional copy within 24 hours after it is made to the judge of probate, whose duty it shall be to preserve said returns as a public record at least one year from the date of the election.

(b) Any person violating any provision of this section shall be deemed guilty of a misdemeanor. (Acts 1971, No. 1725, p. 2887, §§ 1, 2.)

CHAPTER 14.

CANVASSING RETURNS; DECLARATION OF RESULTS.

ARTICLE 1.

COUNTY ELECTIONS.

§ 17-14-1. Time and manner of canvassing.

Friday next after the election, at the hour of 12:00 noon, the returning officer of the county, in person or by deputy, and the judge of probate and the clerk of the circuit court shall assemble at the courthouse; and if there is no such judge or clerk, or if either of them fails to attend, or if either of them is interested by reason of having been a candidate at such election, his place must be supplied by a respectable freeholder or householder of the county, appointed by the board hereinbefore provided for the appointing of the inspectors in the various precincts for said election, at the time of appointing the election inspectors, and if said appointing board fails to provide for such member or members, or if any member or members as herein provided should fail to attend at the time and place herein mentioned, the returning officer shall supply such deficiency by a respectable freeholder or householder of the county who is a qualified elector; and if all such officers are of the same political party, then the returning officer of the county must summon three reputable persons resident householders or freeholders of the county, members of the opposite political party who are qualified electors, to attend at such time and place; and, in the presence of such other persons as choose to attend, the board shall make a correct statement from the returns of the votes from the several precincts of the county of the whole number of votes given therein for each officer, and the person to whom such votes were given. (Code 1876, § 291; Code 1886, § 387; Code 1896, § 1644; Code 1907, § 420; Code 1923, § 510; Code 1940, T. 17, § 199.)

Cited in Leigh v. State, 69 Ala. 261 (1881); Sartain v. Shepherd, 173 Ala. 474, 55 So. 919 (1911); Smothers v. State, 38 Ala. App. 553, 89 So. 2d 277 (1956).

Collateral references. — 26 Am. Jur. 2d, Elections, § 296 et seq.

§ 17-14-2. Declaration of election results.

Immediately after ascertaining the results of an election for county officers, including members of the House of Representatives of the Legislature, the board of supervisors must make in writing a public declaration of the result, stating the name of each officer elected and the office to which he was elected. The declaration must be signed by at least two of the supervisors and must be published by filing the original in the office of the judge of probate and by posting a copy thereof at the courthouse door. Said original certificate shall be recorded by the probate judge in a book to be provided for the purpose; and said record, or a duly certified copy thereof, shall constitute prima facie evidence of the result of said election and the declaration thereof as provided by law. (Code 1876, § 292; Code 1886, § 388; Code 1896, § 1645; Code 1907, § 421; Code 1923, § 511; Acts 1931, No. 334, p. 392; Code 1940, T. 17, § 200.)

Declaration conclusive evidence of election. — Declaration by two or three members of the board of supervisors, under this section and § 17-14-1, and commission of election based thereon, are conclusive evidence of result of election and right to hold office, except in election contest or in quo warranto proceedings, in which declaration is only prima facie evidence. Carnley v. Moore, 214 Ala. 114, 106 So. 604 (1925).

Cited in Prestwood v. Borland, 92 Ala. 599, 9 So. 223 (1891); Smothers v. State, 38 Ala. App. 553, 89 So. 2d 277 (1956).

ARTICLE 2.

STATE ELECTIONS.

§ 17-14-20. Canvass of election returns by state officials.

All returns of elections required by law to be sent to the Secretary of State must, within 15 days after an election, be opened and counted in the presence of the Governor, Secretary of State and Attorney General, or two of them. (Code 1886, § 390; Code 1896, § 1647; Code 1907, § 422; Code 1923, § 512; Code 1940, T. 17, § 201.)

Cited in Board of Registrars v. Mathews, 274 Ala. 73, 145 So. 2d 799 (1962).

Collateral references. — 29 C.J.S., Elections, §§ 221-240.

26 Am. Jur. 2d, Elections, § 296 et seq.

§ 17-14-21. Governor proclaims result of certain elections.

The Governor must give notice by proclamation published in some newspaper at the seat of government of the result of the election as ascertained in Section 17-14-20, except as to officers provided for in Sections 17-14-2 and 17-14-22. (Code 1886, § 390; Code 1896, § 1647; Code 1907, § 423; Code 1923, § 513; Code 1940, T. 17, § 202.)

§ 17-14-22. Returns of election of state officers.

The certificates of the board of supervisors as to the election of Governor, Lieutenant Governor, Attorney General, Auditor, Secretary of State, Treasurer and Commissioner of Agriculture and Industries must be by the judge of probate forwarded to the Governor for the Speaker of the House at least 10 days before the time fixed for the next meeting of the Legislature and must be by the Governor delivered unopened to the speaker on his election. (Code 1876, § 292; Code 1886, § 391; Code 1896, § 1648; Code 1907, § 424; Code 1923, § 514; Code 1940, T. 17, § 203.)

§ 17-14-23. List of registered voters open to inspection.

After having ascertained the result of an election, made declarations thereof and made the certificates provided for in Sections 17-13-7 and 17-14-22, the board of supervisors must file the lists of the registered voters in the office of the judge of probate, which shall be open to the inspection of any elector of the county. (Code 1876, § 293; Code 1886, § 392; Code 1896, § 1649; Code 1907, § 425; Code 1923, § 515; Code 1940, T. 17, § 204.)

Cited in Sartain v. Shepherd, 173 Ala. 474, 55 So. 919 (1911).

§ 17-14-24. Certificates of election to members of Congress and legislators.

The Secretary of State shall, within 10 days after receiving the returns of election from the judge of probate of each county, furnish, from a count of the actual vote cast, as the same appears by the returns certified to him, certificates of election to members of the Legislature and to members of Congress. (Code 1876, § 294; Code 1886, § 393; Code 1896, § 1650; Code 1907, § 426; Code 1923, § 516; Code 1940, T. 17, § 205.)

§ 17-14-25. Results of election of state officers; resolution of tie votes.

The Speaker of the House of Representatives shall, within the first five days of the session of the Legislature, in the presence of a majority of the members of the Legislature, open the returns furnished him under Section 17-14-22, ascertain and proclaim the result of such election, after which such returns shall be filed and kept in the office of the Secretary of State, subject to the inspection of any elector of the state. The person having the highest number of votes for either of said offices shall be declared duly elected; but if two or more shall have an equal and the highest number of votes for the same office, the Legislature, by joint vote, without delay, shall choose one of said persons for said office. The duty of the speaker and of the joint conventions, under this section, shall be purely ministerial. (Code 1876, § 295; Code 1886, § 394; Code 1896, § 1651; Code 1907, § 427; Code 1923, § 517; Code 1940, T. 17, § 206.)

§ 17-14-26. Penalty for failure to make returns.

If any officer required to make returns of any election to the Secretary of State or to the Speaker of the House of Representatives fails to make such returns within the time prescribed, he forfeits to the state $500.00, recoverable by motion to be made by the district attorney of the proper circuit, in the name of the state in the circuit court of the county of such returning officer, upon three days' notice of such motion; and the certificate of the Secretary of State or of the Speaker of the House of Representatives, as the case may be, setting forth that such return has not been received is presumptive evidence of the failure of such officer to make such return. (Code 1852, § 357; Code 1867, § 406; Code 1876, § 3372; Code 1886, § 448; Code 1896, § 1665; Code 1907, § 433; Code 1923, § 523; Code 1940, T. 17, § 207.)

§ 17-14-27. Notice of failure to make return.

Whenever the return of any officer, required to be made to the Secretary of State or to the Speaker of the House of Representatives, is not received within the time prescribed, the Secretary of State or Speaker of the House of Representatives must give notice thereof to the district attorney of the proper circuit and furnish him with the certificate specified in Section 17-14-26. (Code 1852, § 358; Code 1867, § 407; Code 1876, § 3373; Code 1886, § 449; Code 1896, § 1666; Code 1907, § 434; Code 1923, § 524; Code 1940, T. 17, § 208.)

CHAPTER 15.

CONTESTING ELECTIONS.

Election contests are not of common-law origin, but are creatures of statutes which prescribe the terms and conditions of their exercise. Parker v. Mount Olive Fire & Rescue Dist., 420 So. 2d 31 (Ala. 1982).

Strict construction. — Statutes providing for election contests are to be strictly construed. Parker v. Mount Olive Fire & Rescue Dist., 420 So. 2d 31 (Ala. 1982).

ARTICLE 1.

GENERAL PROVISIONS.

Cross references. — As to contesting primary elections, see § 17-16-70 et seq.

Cited in Turner v. Cooper, 347 So. 2d 1339 (Ala. 1977).

§ 17-15-1. Grounds of contest.

The election of any person declared elected to the office of Governor, Secretary of State, Auditor, Treasurer, Attorney General, Commissioner of Agriculture and Industries, Public Service Commissioner, senator or representative in the Legislature, justices of the Supreme Court, judges of the courts of appeals, judge of the circuit court or district court or to any office which is filled by the vote of a single county, or to the office of constable may be contested by any person who was at the time of either of the said elections a qualified elector for any of the following causes:

(1) Malconduct, fraud or corruption on the part of any inspector, clerk, marker, returning officer, board of supervisors or other person.

(2) When the person whose election to office is contested was not eligible thereto at the time of such election.

(3) On account of illegal votes.

(4) On account of the rejection of legal votes.

(5) Offers to bribe, bribery, intimidation or other malconduct calculated to prevent a fair, free and full exercise of the elective franchise. (Code 1896, § 1667; Code 1907, § 455; Code 1923, § 545; Code 1940, T. 17, § 231.)

Statutes must be strictly construed. — Statutes for the contest of political elections are summary in character and, so far as concerns the jurisdiction of the court to determine the issue, must be strictly construed, and the determination of an election contest under it is judicial only when and to the extent as therein authorized. Walker v. Junior, 247 Ala. 342, 24 So. 2d 431 (1945).

The contest of an election is strictly statutory, and the statute must be strictly observed and construed. Watters v. Lyons, 188 Ala. 525, 66 So. 436 (1914); Groom v. Taylor, 235 Ala. 247, 178 So. 33 (1937).

The right to contest an election being statutory, it must be instituted and prosecuted within the "jurisdiction," etc., and as prescribed by law and by person so authorized. Garrett v. Cuninghame, 211 Ala. 430, 100 So. 845 (1924).

Although the broad scope of this section permits a challenge of fraud in the tabulation of the vote totals, as well as other instances of official malconduct, a contestant's attempt to follow the statutory mandates of § 17-15-21 could put him at variance with his allegations of fraud on the part of officials. Where a contestant draws his fraud allegations as charging a particular species of fraud and contends that such allegations are authorized under the statute, he is left with no choice but to conform his formal notice of the nature of evidence to his charging averments or suffer defeat in his effort to discover evidentiary support for such allegations. Carter v. Wiley, 406 So. 2d 340 (Ala. 1981).

Alabama law provides adequate procedure for addressing election irregularities. Curry v. Baker, 802 F.2d 1302 (11th Cir. 1986), cert. dismissed, 479 U.S. 1023, 107 S. Ct. 1262, 93 L. Ed. 2d 819 (1987).

Section is inapplicable where property rights are involved. — Court held to have jurisdiction of bill to enjoin sale of waterworks and electric lighting plant of town pursuant to an election, under § 11-50-141 et seq., where fraud and illegality were charged; it being immaterial that legality of election is involved; this section being inapplicable as not providing for contesting elections involving property rights. Wakefield v. Town of Carbon Hill, 215 Ala. 22, 108 So. 855 (1926).

A valid election with some legal votes cast is presupposed as predicate for a contest thereunder. Section 17-15-2 is illustrative, where the setting aside of the election is specifically inhibited, "unless it appears that the number of illegal votes given to such (elected) person, if taken from him, would reduce the number of votes given to him below the number of legal votes given to some other person for the same office." Walker v. Junior, 247 Ala. 342, 24 So. 2d 431 (1945).

And in only one instance is authority conferred upon the court to declare an election void in a statutory contest, and that is in the third alternative of § 17-15-34. Walker v. Junior, 247 Ala. 342, 24 So. 2d 431 (1945).

"County office." — Office of county commissioner of subdivision of Coffee county held "county office" within this section and may be contested. Ammons v. Moore, 213 Ala. 201, 104 So. 432 (1925).

The election contest proceeding is one in which the public is interested as it is for the public good. Ex parte Hartwell, 238 Ala. 62, 188 So. 891 (1939); McGallagher v. Bosarge, 273 Ala. 133, 136 So. 2d 181 (1961).

An election contest may be instituted only by a qualified elector. Ex parte Hartwell, 238 Ala. 62, 188 So. 891 (1939).

To whom relief granted. — The relief is in favor only of the candidate receiving the highest number of legal votes. Ex parte Hartwell, 238 Ala. 62, 188 So. 891 (1939).

Relief is granted in an election contest only in favor of the candidate receiving the highest vote. McGallagher v. Bosarge, 273 Ala. 133, 136 So. 2d 181 (1961).

Eligibility as ground for contest. — Subdivision (2) of this section means when person was incompetent or disqualified at time of election, and not when he becomes disqualified because of illegal or improper conduct in and about election. Beatty v. Hartwell, 217 Ala. 239, 115 So. 164 (1927).

Specification, alleging that H., at time of holding election, was disqualified for office of commissioner of city of Mobile because he expended in election a sum greatly in excess of $1200.00, did not set up ground for contest, as provided by this section. Beatty v. Hartwell, 217 Ala. 239, 115 So. 164 (1927).

Specification that contestee was not eligible to office of commissioner of city of Mobile at time of election, while setting up ground of contest of election, under this section, was insufficient, because not stating grounds or facts showing that he was not eligible, since contestee should be informed of grounds or reasons for his noneligibility. Beatty v. Hartwell, 217 Ala. 239, 115 So. 164 (1927).

Mandamus is appropriate writ to compel election inspectors to perform their duties to count and tabulate votes and certify result of election in their respective precincts; such duties being purely ministerial. Reed v. State ex rel. Davis, 234 Ala. 306, 174 So. 498 (1937).

Mandamus, not election contest or quo warranto, is appropriate remedy of one not questioning validity of election or right of person declared elected to hold office, but seeking enforcement of relator's legal right to have votes cast for him for second of two offices to be filled, counted, tabulated and reported to board of election inspectors. Reed v. State ex rel. Davis, 234 Ala. 306, 174 So. 498 (1937).

And quo warranto is improper. — Election of relators to office could not be inquired into in quo warranto. Baker v. State ex rel. Green, 222 Ala. 467, 133 So. 291 (1931).

But mandamus will not lie to compel trial judge hearing election contest to grant contestee's motion to strike certain grounds of contest added by way of amendment to the statement of contest filed by contestant against contestee. Ex parte Taylor, 236 Ala. 219, 181 So. 760 (1938).

Jurisdiction of circuit court. — Statement of contest alleging that through manipulation of election officers first and second choice votes not legally cast were counted for one candidate for city commissioner, and that of remaining legal first and second choice votes cast another candidate received majority and was therefore elected, was sufficient to confer jurisdiction on circuit court, as against contention that court had no jurisdiction because no one was declared elected in first election. Groom v. Taylor, 235 Ala. 247, 178 So. 33 (1937).

Allowance of amendment. — Amendment of statement of election contest which alleged no new ground of contest, but merely clarified original statement and made certain the persons who had been declared elected to office, was authorized, as against contention that statement could not be amended after expiration of limit for filing contest. Groom v. Taylor, 235 Ala. 247, 178 So. 33 (1937).

Necessary allegations of petition. — To confer jurisdiction to hear an election contest under the first paragraph of this section petition must show intentional wrongdoing as distinguished from negligence or mere inefficient performance of an official duty. Ex parte Shepherd, 172 Ala. 205, 55 So. 627 (1911).

In view of § 17-15-2, in order for rejected legal votes to be sufficient ground of contest under the fourth paragraph of this section, contestant must allege that if the rejected votes had been counted contestant would have had a majority of the "legal" votes cast, an averment merely of a majority of the votes cast not being sufficient, despite the rule that if the votes are unchallenged and received and counted by the managers they are prima facie legal. Brunson v. Dobbs, 202 Ala. 603, 81 So. 545 (1919).

Allegations that the malconduct of the election officers consisted of the fact that they unlawfully failed or refused to record the vote cast for the candidates, and they wrongfully and unlawfully recorded votes for candidates which were not cast for them, invokes the jurisdiction of the court to hear the contest under this section and the holding in Ex parte Shepherd, 172 Ala. 205, 55 So. 627 (1911); McGallagher v. Bosarge, 273 Ala. 133, 136 So. 2d 181 (1961).

Evidence. — As to admissibility of evidence concerning contestee's domicile in contest of election, see Mitchell v. Kinney, 242 Ala. 196, 5 So. 2d 788 (1942).

Unchallenged votes are prima facie legal. — If votes were unchallenged and received and counted by the managers, they are prima facie legal in a proceeding to contest the election. Brunson v. Dobbs, 202 Ala. 603, 81 So. 545 (1919).

When election not annulled. — Under subdivision (4) of this section and § 17-15-2, if, after counting the legal rejected votes, there were cast for contestant enough illegal votes to let the result stand, an election will not be annulled. Brunson v. Dobbs, 202 Ala. 603, 81 So. 545 (1919).

The trial court's dismissal of the plaintiff's election contest was affirmed where the plaintiffs' complaint failed to state that the election would have been different but for the alleged irregularities. Pitman v. Macon County, 595 So. 2d 1333 (Ala. 1992).

Cited in Sigsbee v. City of Birmingham, 157 Ala. 418, 47 So. 1036 (1908); Finklea v. Farish, 160 Ala. 230, 49 So. 366 (1909); Dennis v. Chilton County, 192 Ala. 146, 68 So. 889 (1915); Ex parte Darnell, 262 Ala. 71, 76 So. 2d 770 (1954); Reed v. City of Montgomery, 376 So. 2d 708 (Ala. 1979); Parker v. Mount Olive Fire & Rescue Dist., 420 So. 2d 31 (Ala. 1982); Thomas v. Kellett, 489 So. 2d 554 (Ala. 1986).

Collateral references. — 29 C.J.S., Elections, §§ 249, 268(2), 274.

26 Am. Jur. 2d, Elections, § 321.

§ 17-15-2. When election not annulled.

No malconduct, fraud or corruption on the part of the inspector, clerk, marker, returning officer, board of supervisors or other person, nor any offers to bribe, bribery, intimidation or other malconduct which prevented a fair, free and full exercise of the elective franchise can annul or set aside any election unless thereby the person declared elected and whose election is contested is shown not to have received the highest number of legal votes, nor must any election contested under the provisions of this title be annulled or set aside because of illegal votes given to the person whose election is contested, unless it appears that the number of illegal votes given to such person, if taken from him, would reduce the number of votes given to him below the number of legal votes given to some other person for the same office. No election shall be annulled or set aside because of the rejection of legal votes unless it appears that such legal votes, if given to the person intended, would increase the number of his legal votes to or above the number of legal votes received by any other person for the same office. (Code 1896, § 1668; Code 1907, § 456; Code 1923, § 546; Code 1940, T. 17, § 232.)

Cross references. — See notes to § 17-15-1.

Malconduct must change result. — Under this section, malconduct of canvassing board, to vitiate elections, must change result, and declaring result which was true result is not ground for contest because contrary to certificate of inspectors. City of Florence v. State ex rel. Burtwell, 211 Ala. 617, 101 So. 462 (1924).

Such provision applies to stock law election. — The provision of this section that election is not to be annulled for matter which it does not appear would change the result applies to a stock law election. Campbell v. Jefferson County, 216 Ala. 251, 113 So. 230 (1927).

Case held properly dismissed for failure to comply with § 17-15-21. — Where plaintiffs in their notice of evidence made only one statement, that being that 55 votes rather than 35 votes should have been credited to plaintiff candidate and he trailed defendant candidate by approximately 700 votes, so that this 20-vote change in the vote total would not have placed defendant's vote at or below that of plaintiff, which is required ground for a contest under § 17-15-20, or for an annulment under this section, and where the notice of evidence was filed less than 10 days prior to the date set for the hearing, in contravention of § 17-15-21, the trial court's dismissal of the case on the grounds that the plaintiffs did not comply with § 17-15-21 was not error. Thomas v. Kellett, 489 So. 2d 554 (Ala. 1986).

Cited in Wade v. Oates, 112 Ala. 325, 20 So. 495 (1896); Garrett v. Cuninghame, 211 Ala. 430, 100 So. 845 (1924).

Collateral references. — 29 C.J.S., Elections, §§ 281, 283.

§ 17-15-3. Voter must answer as to his qualifications.

Any person examined as a witness may be required to answer if he voted at the election contested and to answer touching his qualifications; and if he was not at such election a qualified voter, he may be required to answer for whom he voted. If he makes full, true answers which may tend to incriminate him, he shall not be prosecuted for voting at such election. (Code 1896, § 1669; Code 1907, § 457; Code 1923, § 547; Code 1940, T. 17, § 233.)

Cross references. — For this section being commented on by new Rule 506, Alabama Rules of Evidence, effective January 1, 1996, see the Advisory Committee's Notes to new Rule 506 in the 1995 Cumulative Supplement to Volume 23.

Witness immune from prosecution. — A voter who was called, sworn and examined as a witness in election contest is immune from prosecution for illegal voting under this section and Constitution 1901, § 189. Ex parte Bullen, 236 Ala. 56, 181 So. 498 (1938).

Collateral references. — 29 C.J.S., Elections, § 281.

§ 17-15-4. Either party may have copy of registration and poll lists.

It shall be the duty of the judge of probate of any county, upon the application of either party to any contest, or his agent or attorney, to deliver to the party, his agent or attorney, a certified copy of the registration lists and poll lists (one or both) of his county, or of any election precinct therein, upon the payment of his fees for certifying and copying the same at the rate of $.15 per 100 words written by him in making such copy; and such copies, duly certified, shall be received as presumptive evidence of the facts therein stated; the registration lists that the persons therein named were duly registered, and the poll lists that the persons therein named voted at the election and precinct therein named. (Code 1896, § 1670; Code 1907, § 458; Code 1923, § 548; Code 1940, T. 17, § 234.)

Contestant for office of mayor of municipality held not entitled to mandamus to require judge of probate of county to furnish him with certified copy of poll and registration lists used in connection with municipal election, since this section relative to custody of lists by probate judge does not extend to embrace municipal elections, notwithstanding former Tit. 17, § 56, 1940 Code. Stiles v. Endsley, 219 Ala. 350, 122 So. 458 (1929); Endsley v. Culpepper, 219 Ala. 349, 122 So. 457 (1929).

Cited in Sartain v. Shepherd, 173 Ala. 474, 55 So. 919 (1911); Carter v. Wiley, 406 So. 2d 340 (Ala. 1981).

Collateral references. — 29 C.J.S., Elections, §§ 276, 284.

§ 17-15-5. Failure of officer to serve notices in contests of elections.

Any sheriff or constable who fails to give the notices necessary to be served in cases of contested elections, within the time and in the mode prescribed, if practicable for him to do so, must, on conviction, be fined not less than $100.00 nor more than $500.00. (Code 1876, § 4280; Code 1886, § 4179; Code 1896, § 4686; Code 1907, § 6783; Code 1923, § 3901; Code 1940, T. 17, § 297.)

§ 17-15-6. Jurisdiction denied judges or courts exercising chancery powers in election contests; appeal.

No jurisdiction exists in or shall be exercised by any judge, court or officer exercising chancery powers to entertain any proceeding for ascertaining the legality, conduct or results of any election, except so far as authority to do so shall be specially and specifically enumerated and set down by statute; and any injunction, process or order from any judge, court or officer in the exercise of chancery powers, whereby the results of any election are sought to be inquired into, questioned or affected, or whereby any certificate of election is sought to be inquired into or questioned, save as may be specially and specifically enumerated and set down by statute, shall be null and void and shall not be enforced by any officer or obeyed by any person; and should any judge or other officer hereafter undertake to fine or in any wise deal with any person for disobeying any such prohibited injunction, process or order, such attempt shall be null and void, and an appeal shall lie forthwith therefrom to the supreme court then sitting, or next to sit, without bond, and such proceedings shall be suspended by force of such appeal; and the notice to be given of such appeal shall be 14 days. (Code 1876, § 314; Code 1886, § 407; Code 1896, § 1671; Code 1907, § 459; Code 1923, § 549; Code 1940, T. 17, § 235.)

Election challenges are strictly statutory proceedings, and courts are expressly limited in the relief to be awarded in election contests. Yeargan v. Allen, 456 So. 2d 26 (Ala. 1984).

Section does not preclude court from exercising jurisdiction. — Where on the day following election, town council failed to count votes and declare a winner in accordance with § 11-46-55 but instead, several days later disallowed the results and declared candidate the winner, the court was not precluded from exercising jurisdiction over the case; if this section was allowed to stand between the judiciary and such acts, any canvassing board would be provided a license to change the results of an election by cabal and the purpose and intent of this section was not to undermine the sanctity of the individual vote. Sears v. Carson, 551 So. 2d 1054 (Ala. 1989).

The provisions of this section are confined to election of persons to office. Clarke v. Jack, 60 Ala. 271 (1877); Leigh v. State, 69 Ala. 261 (1881).

It is not applicable in action by members of board of education appointed by town council to enjoin adverse claimants from exercising duties as members of board. Wright v. Cook, 216 Ala. 270, 113 So. 252 (1927).

Question of court's jurisdiction over subject matter is always fundamental, and lack of jurisdiction cannot be waived or supplied by consent. Wilkinson v. Henry, 221 Ala.

254, 128 So. 362 (1930); also Malone v. Kellett, 229 Ala. 648, 159 So. 95 (1935); State v. Albritton, 251 Ala. 422, 37 So. 2d 640 (1948).

Injunction will not issue to control election. — Injunction will not issue, as a general rule, for the purpose of restraining holding of election, or of directing or controlling the mode in which, or determining the rules in pursuance of which, election shall be held. State ex rel. Tucker, 236 Ala. 284, 181 So. 761 (1938).

This section does not prevent enjoining of election. City of Adamsville v. City of Birmingham, 495 So. 2d 642 (Ala. 1986).

Prohibition will lie to restrain circuit judge from exercising jurisdiction of action to enjoin election officers from acting as officials in holding of primary election, and from interfering with holding of such elections by other officers. Ex parte State ex rel. Tucker, 236 Ala. 284, 181 So. 761 (1938).

Primary elections. — The substance of this section is applicable to primary elections. Boyd v. Garrison, 246 Ala. 122, 19 So. 2d 385 (1944).

In matters of contest of primary elections, the legislature had deemed it wise to commit the same to party tribunals. Ex parte Pollard, 251 Ala. 309, 37 So. 2d 178 (1948).

Referendum election concerning city ordinance. — This section has no application to a proceeding to enjoin the holding of a referendum election concerning a city ordinance under § 11-44-34. Birmingham Gas Co. v. City of Bessemer, 250 Ala. 137, 33 So. 2d 475 (1947).

Certificate of election. — A court can prevent the issuance of a certificate of election to a municipal office, but once the certificate is issued, the court is without authority to revoke it. City of Talladega v. Pettus, 602 So. 2d 357 (Ala. 1992).

Cited in Garrett v. Cuninghame, 211 Ala.

430, 100 So. 845 (1924); Wilson v. Duncan, 114 Ala. 659, 21 So. 1017 (1897); Perloff v. Edington, 293 Ala. 277, 302 So. 2d 92 (1974); Turner v. Cooper, 347 So. 2d 1339 (Ala. 1977); Graddick v. Baker, 496 So. 2d 688 (Ala. 1986).

Collateral references. — 29 C.J.S., Elections, §§ 122, 247, 248, 252, 308.

§ 17-15-7. Procedure for examination of ballots, voting machines, etc.; bond.

In all election contests involving elections other than party primaries or run-offs:

(1) The examining person or candidate seeking to examine the ballots, voting machines, or voting machine computations or printouts must move, within 10 days of the filing of the contest, the court before whom the election contest is pending for an examination. The court shall set a hearing on the motion for examination which must take place within 10 days after service of the motion on the parties and candidates involved in the election contest. The hearing shall be held to determine the procedures to be used for the examination and the court shall, within five days after the hearing, set forth the procedures for the examination. Absent a subsequent court order extending the time for reasonable cause shown, the examination must be finished within 15 days of the court order which sets forth the examination procedures.

(2) Examination procedures shall be within the discretion of the court. The court shall consider, in determining appropriate procedures, the need to preserve the integrity of the ballots, voting machines, and voting machine computations and printouts; the need to ensure that votes were accurately cast and counted; the need to ensure that all persons and candidates involved in the election have the opportunity to observe the examination and ensure that an examination does not wrongfully alter the election results; the need to expeditiously conclude the election contest; and any other factor which is relevant to the integrity of the election process. The court must, when so requested by any party or candidate involved in the contest, allow such party or candidate, and his agents, to observe all of the examination proceedings.

(3) The court shall require the examining party or candidate to make a deposit with the court or post a bond in a sum adequate to ensure prompt payment of all reasonable, necessary and actual expenses incurred by any governmental entity during and as a result of the examination. If the examining person or candidate prevails in the election contest as a result of information obtained from the examination of the ballots, voting machines, or voting machine computations or printouts, he shall not be responsible for any expenses or costs incurred by any governmental entity during and as a result of the examination. (Acts 1989, No. 89-877, p. 1757, § 2; Code 1975 § 17-8-46.)

Code Commissioner's note. — This section was formerly codified as § 17-8-46.

ARTICLE 2.

LEGISLATURE, JUDICIAL OR COUNTY OFFICES.

Cited in Turner v. Cooper, 347 So. 2d 1339 (Ala. 1977).

Collateral references. — 26 Am. Jur. 2d, Elections, § 316 et seq.

§ 17-15-20. Statement of grounds of contest.

When any elector chooses to contest the election of any person declared to be elected to the office of senator, representative in the Legislature, judge of the circuit court or district court, any office which is filled by the vote of a single county or constable, he must make a statement in writing setting forth specifically:

(1) The name of the party contesting and that he was a qualified voter when the election was held;

(2) The office which said election was held to fill and the time of holding the same; and

(3) The particular grounds of said contest.

This statement must be verified by the affidavit of such contesting party to the effect that the same is believed to be true. If the reception of illegal votes is alleged as a cause of contest, it is a sufficient statement of said cause to allege that illegal votes were given to the person whose election is contested, which, if taken from him, will reduce the number of legal votes given to him to or below the number of legal votes given to some other person for the same office. (Code 1896, § 1686; Code 1907, § 460; Code 1923, § 550; Code 1940, T. 17, § 236.)

Provisions strictly construed. — Election contests are special statutory proceedings, and, according to the best authorities, which have been followed by the supreme court, are to be strictly construed as to those provisions for inaugurating the contest, and which are necessary to jurisdiction. Pearson v. Alverson, 160 Ala. 265, 49 So. 756 (1909).

Statement must comply with section. — When the contest is of the general election to the legislature the statement of contest must be as provided in this section. Ex parte Brassell, 261 Ala. 265, 73 So. 2d 907 (1954).

Right to amend petition. — If the petition is defective as to any of the statutory requirements, it cannot be amended after the expiration of the time limited for commencing the contest as provided by § 17-15-22. Pearson v. Alverson, 160 Ala. 265, 49 So. 756 (1909).

Parol evidence is admissible to identify contestant. — In election contest in which it was claimed that contestant was not a qualified elector at time of election, as required by this section, parol evidence held admissible to identify contestant named "DeWitte T." with name "Duette T." appearing on official register of qualified voters. Davis v. Teague, 220 Ala. 309, 125 So. 51 (1929).

Case held properly dismissed for failure to comply with § 17-15-21. — Where plaintiffs in their notice of evidence made only one statement, that being that 55 votes rather than 35 votes should have been credited to plaintiff candidate and he trailed defendant candidate by approximately 700 votes, so that this 20-vote change in the vote total would not have placed defendant's vote at or below that of plaintiff, which is required ground for a contest under this section, or for an annulment under § 17-15-2, and where the notice of evidence was filed less than 10 days prior to the date set for the hearing, in contravention of § 17-15-21, the trial court's dismissal of the case on the grounds that the plaintiffs did not comply with § 17-15-21 was not error. Thomas v. Kellett, 489 So. 2d 554 (Ala. 1986).

Collateral references. — 29 C.J.S., Elections, §§ 249, 268(2), 274.

§ 17-15-21. Notice of nature of evidence.

No testimony must be received of any illegal votes or of the rejection of any legal votes in any contested election commenced under the provisions of this article unless the party complaining thereof has given to the adverse party notice in writing of the number of illegal votes and by whom given and for whom given, and at what precinct or voting place cast, or the number of legal votes rejected, and by whom offered, and at what precinct or voting place cast, which he expects to prove on the trial. Such notice must be served personally or left at the residence or usual place of business of the adverse party at least 10 days before the taking of testimony in reference to such votes. (Code 1896, § 1687; Code 1907, § 461; Code 1923, § 551; Code 1940, T. 17, § 237.)

This section applies to all illegal votes, whether by reason of residence or precinct, disqualification or illegal conduct or act of the elector. Campbell v. Jefferson County, 216 Ala. 251, 113 So. 230 (1927).

And to city elections. — The provisions of this section and § 17-15-31 are confined to contests of the official therein indicated, or any office filled by the vote of a single county, and apply to contests of city elections. Pope v. Howle, 227 Ala. 154, 149 So. 222 (1933).

Section is a constituent part of procedure for engaging in an election contest involving illegal votes or rejection of legal votes. — The legislature has made this section a constituent part of the procedure for engaging in an election contest when either illegal votes or the rejection of legal votes is in issue. Turner v. Cooper, 347 So. 2d 1339 (Ala. 1977).

Sections 11-46-71 and 11-46-69 subsume this section. — Sections 11-46-71 and 11-46-69 are in pari materia and establish that election contests which turn upon the number of legal or illegal votes cast or rejected, subsume this section, which requires the notice of the nature of the evidence. Turner v. Cooper, 347 So. 2d 1339 (Ala. 1977).

Court may recognize in advance of statutory deadline inability or unwillingness of complaining party to comply. — Although this section does place a deadline of 10 days prior to the taking of testimony for the service of the notice, it cannot have been intended to prevent a trial court from recognizing in advance of the statutory deadline the inability or unwillingness of the complaining party to comply. Turner v. Cooper, 347 So. 2d 1339 (Ala. 1977).

Giving of notice is mandatory. — When it is not shown that notice was given as required by this section it is not error to exclude evidence of the rejection of legal votes, contests of elections being statutory and strictly construed. Dobbs v. Brunson, 17 Ala. App. 318, 85 So. 38 (1920).

The only requirement of this section is that the notice therein defined shall be given the opposing party at least 10 days before the taking of testimony in reference to such votes. After a trial is entered upon, the court may exercise a discretion as to prolonging the hearing or adjourning over; but, when this is done, it is contemplated the parties may produce evidence touching any voter whose name is furnished the opposing party 10 days or more before such evidence is offered. Wilkerson v. Lee, 236 Ala. 104, 181 So. 296 (1938).

Method of giving notice. — While the language of this section does not explicitly mandate a method by which notice of the nature of the evidence in a contest based on malconduct of the election officials must be given to the contestee, the statute implicitly contemplates that notice of a sort applicable to the grounds asserted be required. If this were not true, a statute permitting malconduct as grounds for a contest would be useless absent a means to proceed under the notice requirements. Moreover, the lack of a remedy to enforce the statutory right of contest would be an obvious violation of a contestant's due process rights. Carter v. Wiley, 406 So. 2d 340 (Ala. 1981).

Admissibility of evidence as to supplemental list. — In election contest, where parties furnished their respective lists of alleged illegal votes received and legal votes rejected, trial was entered upon, and hearing was adjourned for over four weeks, and in the interim and more than 10 days before the day set, contestant gave notice of a supplemental list, court properly admitted evidence touching the supplemental list of voters. Wilkerson v. Lee, 236 Ala. 104, 181 So. 296 (1938).

Allegations of fraud. — Although the broad scope of § 17-15-1 permits a challenge of fraud in the tabulation of the vote totals, as well as other instances of official malconduct, a contestant's attempt to follow the statutory mandates of this section could put him at variance with his allegations of fraud on the part of officials. Where a contestant draws his fraud allegations as charging a particular species of fraud and contends that such allegations are authorized under the statute, he is left with no choice but to conform his formal notice of the nature of evidence to his charging averments or suffer defeat in his effort to discover evidentiary support for such allegations. Carter v. Wiley, 406 So. 2d 340 (Ala. 1981).

The provisions of this section, requiring a contestant to supply the contestee with the number of legal votes rejected or illegal votes counted which contestant expects to prove on the trial, cannot be read so literally as to exclude the right of a contestant to charge and prove fraud on the part of election officials. In establishing that proof, however, a contestant, via his notice of the nature of evidence, must reconcile his allegations of malconduct with his notice pleading in such a manner that the contestee is put on notice that those allegations of malconduct are matters which contestant seeks to prove. Carter v. Wiley, 406 So. 2d 340 (Ala. 1981).

Case held properly dismissed for failure to comply with this section. — Where plaintiffs in their notice of evidence made only one statement, that being that 55 votes rather than 35 votes should have been credited to plaintiff candidate and he trailed defendant candidate by approximately 700 votes, so that this 20-vote change in the vote total would not have placed defendant's vote at or below that of plaintiff, which is required ground for a contest under § 17-15-20, or for an annulment under § 17-15-2, and where the notice of evidence was filed less than 10 days prior to the date set for the hearing, in contravention of this section, the trial court's dismissal of the case on the grounds that the plaintiffs did not comply with this section was not error. Thomas v. Kellett, 489 So. 2d 554 (Ala. 1986).

Collateral references. — 29 C.J.S., Elections, §§ 273-288.

26 Am. Jur. 2d, Elections, §§ 332, 333.

Admissibility of parol evidence of election officials to impeach election returns. 46 ALR2d 1385.

§ 17-15-22. When contest commenced; security for costs.

All contests of elections provided for in this article must be commenced within 20 days after the result of the election is declared, except as in this article otherwise provided; and at the time of commencing such contest and of the filing the statement in writing, the party contesting must give security for the cost of such contest, to be filed and approved as in this article provided. (Code 1896, § 1688; Code 1907, § 462; Code 1923, § 552; Code 1940, T. 17, § 238.)

This section applies to all contests covered by this article. Robinson v. Winston County, 203 Ala. 671, 85 So. 22 (1920).

Applicability of statute of limitations. — The 20-day statute of limitations of this section applies to actions under the Fair Campaign Practices Act. Davis v. Reynolds, 592 So. 2d 546 (Ala. 1991).

Security is jurisdictional requirement. — The giving of security according to this section is a jurisdictional requirement. Pearson v. Alverson, 160 Ala. 265, 49 So. 756 (1909); Ex parte Shepherd, 172 Ala. 205, 55 So. 627 (1911); Groom v. Taylor, 235 Ala. 247, 178 So. 33 (1937); Cosby v. Taylor, 259 Ala. 41, 65 So. 2d 178 (1953).

As is commencement of contest within 20 days. — Statutory provision that contest must be commenced within 20 days after result of election has been declared is jurisdictional. Ex parte Hartwell, 238 Ala. 62, 188 So. 891 (1939).

But deposit of money is not sufficient. — By this section contestant must give security for the costs of such contest. That requirement is not complied with by the deposit of a sum of money. Ex parte Brassell, 261 Ala. 265, 73 So. 2d 907 (1954).

There is no requirement as to the form of the security, provided it secures all the costs without limit in amount. And it is not necessary to have a formal bond signed by a principal and sureties. Cosby v. Moore, 259 Ala. 41, 65 So. 2d 178 (1953).

When and where security filed. — Although it is preferable that security for cost be filed contemporaneously with the filing of the statement, this is not necessary under this section and if security for cost is filed within the prescribed time it will suffice. Ex parte Shepherd, 172 Ala. 205, 55 So. 627 (1911).

While this section does not expressly provide that the bond or security upon contests shall be filed with any particular officer it was evidently contemplated that, as the written security or bond and the declaration of contest are both jurisdictional, they shall be filed together and in the court with jurisdiction to hear and determine the contest within 20 days after the declaration of the result of the election. Robinson v. Winston County, 203 Ala. 671, 85 So. 22 (1920).

Right to amend petition. — See same catchline under § 17-15-20.

To amend bond. — A defect in bond given as security for costs in election contest is amendable. Groom v. Taylor, 235 Ala. 247, 178 So. 33 (1937).

Mandamus will not lie to compel trial court to dismiss election contest without ruling on the merits, where adequate remedy by appeal when case was finally decided on merits could be had and contestant was not prejudiced, in that dismissal would have deprived him of right to further contest election under this section requiring commencement of contest within 20 days after results of election are declared. Ex parte Hartwell, 238 Ala. 62, 188 So. 891 (1939).

Appeal. — Where no objection to form or sufficiency of bond given as security for costs in election contest was raised in lower court, court's action in dismissing contest could not be justified on ground that security for costs had not been given in form contemplated by statute. Groom v. Taylor, 235 Ala. 247, 179 So. 33 (1937).

Cited in State ex rel. Radcliff v. Lauten, 256 Ala. 559, 56 So. 2d 106 (1952).

Collateral references. — 29 C.J.S., Elections, § 321.

Exclusion or inclusion of terminal Sunday or holiday in computing time for taking or perfecting appeal from decision of election board. 61 ALR2d 482.

§ 17-15-23. Contest of senator or representative in Legislature — Filing.

If the contest is of the election of a senator or representative in the Legislature, the elector contesting must file in the office of the clerk of the circuit court of any county of the senatorial district, if such contest is of the election of a senator, or in the office of the clerk of the circuit court of the county in which the election was held, if the contest is of the election of a representative in the Legislature, a statement in writing of the grounds of contest, as provided in this article, and must give good and sufficient security for the costs of such contest, to be taken and approved by the clerk. Of the statement in writing the person whose election is contested must have 10 days' notice before the taking of testimony by the service on him of a certified copy of such statement by the sheriff or a constable of the county, and such sheriff or constable must indorse on the original the fact of such service and such indorsement is presumptive evidence of the fact. (Code 1896, § 1689; Code 1907, § 463; Code 1923, § 553; Code 1940, T. 17, § 239.)

§ 17-15-24. Contest of senator or representative in Legislature — Testimony.

The testimony in the case of a contest provided for in Section 17-15-23 must be taken by deposition under commission issued by the clerk of the court where the statement of contest is filed, which commission must issue upon the party applying for the same making and filing an affidavit stating the name of the witnesses, the place of residence of such witnesses, and that the testimony sought and expected is material. The depositions must be taken on interrogatories filed in the office of the clerk after making and filing the affidavit and of the interrogatories and affidavit and the names and residence of the commissioner or commissioners proposed to be appointed, 10 days' notice must be given the adverse party by service on him personally or by leaving at his usual place of residence or business a copy of the interrogatories and affidavit, to which must be appended notice of the name and residence of the commissioner proposed to be appointed. Such service must be made by the sheriff or a constable of the county, and within 10 days thereafter such adverse party may file cross-interrogatories, to which the party filing the interrogatories may file rebutting interrogatories, and thereafter commission may issue. Of the time and place of taking the depositions, the commissioner must give each party five days' notice in writing, which notice may be served by the sheriff or a constable of the county. If the witnesses reside or are to be examined within the county, the adverse party is entitled to demand that they be examined orally, separate and apart from each other, on giving notice within the 10 days allowed him to file cross-interrogatories that such examination is required; and if such notice be given, the commission issued must not be accompanied by the interrogatories filed, and must authorize and direct the commissioner to examine the said witnesses orally, separate and apart from each other, after giving each party five days' notice of the time and place of the examination. In the execution of all commissions to take testimony under this section, the commissioner must conform to and observe the requirements of the statutes and rules concerning the taking of depositions in civil actions and has and may exercise all the power and authority by the statute conferred on commissioners; and against defaulting witnesses all such proceedings may be had and taken as are authorized by said statutes and rules. (Code 1896, § 1690; Code 1907, § 464; Code 1923, § 554; Code 1940, T. 17, § 240.)

§ 17-15-25. Contest of senator or representative in Legislature — Depositions returned.

The commissioner must carefully envelop the depositions taken, with the commission attached, writing his name across the sealing of the envelope and indorsing thereon the names of the witnesses and the title and subject matter of the contest, and direct the envelope to the clerk issuing the commission, and must, within five days after taking the deposition, file the same with the said clerk, or transmit the same by mail through the nearest post office. The clerk must, within five days after the taking of testimony has been finished and the depositions received in his office, make and certify under the seal of the court a true and correct copy of the statement of the grounds of contest and of return of service thereon, and must inclose the same with the depositions so taken and filed in his office, and must securely envelop the same, indorsing thereon the title and subject matter of the contest, and direct the package to the presiding officer of that branch of the Legislature before which the contest is to be tried, at the seat of government and deposit the same, postage paid, in the nearest post office. (Code 1896, § 1691; Code 1907, § 465; Code 1923, § 555; Code 1940, T. 17, § 241.)

§ 17-15-26. Contest of senator or representative in Legislature — Costs taxed; execution issued.

The package mailed by the clerk must be opened by the presiding officer and presented to the house over which he presides for such action as such house may deem proper. On the determination of the contest, the Secretary of the Senate or the Clerk of the House, as the case may be, must certify the result thereof to the clerk of the court in which the statement of contest was filed. The certificate must be filed in the office of the clerk and shall have the force and effect of a judgment against the unsuccessful party for the costs of the contest. And the clerk having taxed the costs, allowing the fees and costs allowed for similar services in civil cases at law, must issue execution for the amount thereof in the name of the successful party. If the party contesting is the unsuccessful party, execution must issue against him and his sureties for the costs. (Code 1896, § 1692; Code 1907, § 466; Code 1923, § 556; Code 1940, T. 17, § 242.)

Cited in Cosby v. Moore, 259 Ala. 41, 65 So. 2d 178 (1953).

§ 17-15-27. Contest of election of judge of circuit or district court — Procedure generally.

If the contest is of an election to the office of judge of the circuit court or of the district court, the party contesting must file in the office of the probate judge of the county of the residence of the person declared elected, a statement in writing of the grounds of contest, verified by affidavit, as prescribed in this article, and must give good and sufficient security for the costs of the contest, to be approved by the judge of probate. On the filing of the statement and the giving of the security, the judge of probate must indorse thereon an order appointing a day for the trial of the contest, not less than 30 nor more than 50 days from the day of the reception of the certified statement and fixing the place of trial, which must be at some place in the circuit or district in which the election was held, and where a circuit or district court is required to be held, and must issue a summons directed to the person whose election is contested, accompanied with a certified copy of the statement requiring him to appear within 10 days after the service of the summons and make answer to the statement, which summons shall be served by the sheriff or a constable at least 20 days before the day appointed for the trial. The testimony must be taken by deposition, as is prescribed in Section 17-15-28. (Code 1896, § 1695; Code 1907, § 469; Code 1923, § 557; Code 1940, T. 17, § 243.)

Cited in Banks v. Zippert, 470 So. 2d 1147 (Ala. 1985).

§ 17-15-28. Contest of election of judge of circuit or district court — Testimony; heard without jury.

The testimony on the contest must be taken by deposition as in civil cases at common law, but no affidavit, other than that of the materiality of the testimony of the witnesses proposed to be examined, shall be required. Either party may, on giving five days' notice, require the examination before the commissioner to be oral and that the witnesses be examined separate and apart from each other. The party against whom the depositions are to be taken must have at least five days' notice of the time and place of taking such depositions and of the name and residence of the commissioner or commissioners proposed. The contest must be heard and determined by the court without the intervention of a jury. (Code 1896, § 1694; Code 1907, § 468; Code 1923, § 558; Code 1940, T. 17, § 244.)

Collateral references. — 29 C.J.S., Elections, §§ 245, 247, 291, 310.

§ 17-15-29. Contest of election of judge of probate court and other county and municipal officers — Generally.

If the contest is of an election to the office of judge of the probate court, sheriff, tax assessor, tax collector, county treasurer, clerk of the circuit court or any other office filled by the vote of a single county or any subdivision thereof, or any office of a city or town not in this article otherwise provided for, the party contesting must file in the office of the clerk of the circuit court of the county in which the election was held, a statement in writing, verified by affidavit, of the grounds of the contest as provided in this article and must give good and sufficient security for the costs of the contest, to be approved by the clerk. On the filing of the statement and the giving of the security, the clerk must enter the contest on the trial docket as a civil action pending in said court for trial, and, after having made such entry, the clerk must issue a summons, accompanied by a copy of the statement directed to the party whose election is contested, requiring him, within five days after the service of the summons, to appear and make answer to the statement, which summons must be served by the sheriff or by a constable, if the contest is with respect to the office of sheriff. The contest is triable by the court without the intervention of a jury and must be heard and tried in precedence of all other cases, civil or criminal, standing for trial in the court. Either party is entitled to the writ of subpoena to compel the personal attendance of witnesses on the trial of the contest, and against defaulting witnesses such proceedings may be had as against other defaulting witnesses in civil cases pending in the court. Testimony may also be taken by depositions in the case, and in like manner as depositions are taken in other civil cases. (Code 1896, § 1696; Code 1907, § 470; Acts 1911, No. 202, p. 195; Code 1923, § 559; Code 1940, T. 17, § 245.)

History. — See Ammons v. Moore, 213 Ala. 201, 104 So. 432 (1925).

Section is constitutional. — This section is not made contrary to Constitution 1901, § 45 by Acts 1911, No. 202, p. 195, which broadened its scope from probate judges only to all county officers. Dunning v. Holcombe, 203 Ala. 546, 84 So. 740 (1919).

A contest of election must be filed in the proper jurisdiction by a person so authorized as provided in this section. Garrett v. Cuninghame, 211 Ala. 430, 100 So. 845 (1924).

Officers elected by subdivisions of county. — When a county is divided into commissioner's districts and county commissioners elected from these districts, in view of the provisions of this section in treating the jurisdiction of the circuit court in which this language is used, "or any office filled by the vote of a single county, or any subdivision thereof," it would seem to be the legislative intent to bring such office of county commissioner within the provision of § 17-15-1 so that the election may be contested. Ammons v. Moore, 213 Ala. 201, 104 So. 432 (1925).

Security is jurisdictional requirement. — The exaction of security for costs of contest set down in this section is a jurisdictional requirement that, if wholly absent, will not allow the court to proceed a "single step." Bowen v. Holcombe, 204 Ala. 549, 87 So. 87 (1920). See same catchline under § 17-15-22.

Giving of good and sufficient security for the costs of an election contest is a jurisdictional requirement, and that security must be given within the time limits prescribed for the filing of an election contest. Ex parte Williams, 613 So. 2d 1266 (Ala. 1993).

This section requires the filing of the statement and the giving of a security for costs by the contestant of an election. The filing of the security for costs is a jurisdictional prerequisite to the court's going forward at all with the election contest; without some type of security for costs being filed the court has no jurisdiction in the matter, and the election contest must be dismissed. Dobbins v. City of Anniston, 469 So. 2d 583 (Ala. 1985).

Where a contestant has complied with the requirements of posting sufficient security "in form at least," the court should allow the bond to be amended; however, where the contestant failed to file any bond within the five day limit required by § 11-46-69 in challenging municipal elections despite his claim that he attempted to timely file a security for costs with the register his contest must fail. Dobbins v. City of Anniston, 469 So. 2d 583 (Ala. 1985).

Effect of insufficient bond. — Although a bond was insufficient under this section and the petition was properly dismissed therefor, it was error to refuse to set aside such order where the petitioner immediately offered to perfect the security. Lowery v. Petree, 175 Ala. 559, 57 So. 818 (1912).

Payment of required filing fee for election contest was not sufficient to constitute giving good and sufficient security for the costs, for jurisdictional purposes. Ex parte Williams, 613 So. 2d 1266 (Ala. 1993).

Section 17-15-22 applies to contests under this section. Robinson v. Winston County, 203 Ala. 671, 85 So. 22 (1920).

Cited in Davis v. Jones, 123 Ala. 647, 26 So. 321 (1899); Dobbs v. Brunson, 17 Ala. App. 318, 85 So. 38 (1920); May v. Head, 210 Ala. 112, 96 So. 869 (1923); Cosby v. Moore, 259 Ala. 41, 65 So. 2d 178 (1953); Carter v. Wiley, 406 So. 2d 340 (Ala. 1981); Thomas v. Kellett, 489 So. 2d 554 (Ala. 1986).

§ 17-15-30. Contest of election of judge of probate court and other county and municipal officers — Court open at all times.

For the purpose of hearing and determining any contest instituted under the provisions of Section 17-15-29, the circuit court shall at all times be open. (Acts 1911, No. 202, p. 195; Code 1923, § 560; Code 1940, T. 17, § 246.)

§ 17-15-31. Ballots may be examined.

In all contests of elections before the judge of probate or the circuit court, the judge presiding is authorized to make an examination of the ballots given or rejected in the election so far as he may deem it necessary to arrive at a correct judgment, and may make and enforce by attachment all necessary orders to obtain possession of the same, and must make all proper orders necessary for the return of the ballots to the proper custody after same have been examined by him. (Code 1896, § 1699; Code 1907, § 473; Code 1923, § 563; Code 1940, T. 17, § 249.)

This section does not require the judge to wait until the evidence is all in, nor indeed to assume that there will be any evidence offered to overcome prima facie illegality. Shepherd v. Sartain, 185 Ala. 439, 64 So. 57 (1913).

§ 17-15-32. Judgment of court.

If, on the trial of the contest of any election, either before the judge of probate or the circuit court, it shall appear that any person other than the one whose election is contested, received or would have received, had the ballots intended for him and illegally rejected been received, the highest number of legal votes, judgment must be given declaring such person duly elected, and such judgment shall have the force and effect of investing the person thereby declared elected, with full right and title to have and to hold the office to which he is declared elected. If it appears that two or more persons have, or would have had, if the ballots intended for them and illegally rejected had been received, the highest and equal number of votes for such office, judgment must be entered declaring the fact, and such fact must be certified to the officer having authority to fill vacancies in the office the election to which was contested. If the person whose election is contested is found to be ineligible to the office, judgment must be entered declaring the election void and the fact certified to the appointing power. If the party whose election is contested is found to have been duly and legally elected, judgment must be entered declaring him entitled to have and to hold the office to which he was so elected. (Code 1896, § 1700; Code 1907, § 474; Code 1923, § 564; Code 1940, T. 17, § 250.)

Proper judgment. — Where election officers stamped candidate's name at bottom of part of election ballots, there being no room to write name in where it belonged, and required electors before voting to declare which ballot they wanted, held not to vitiate result of election, and judgment under this section to that effect was proper. Garrett v. Cuninghame, 211 Ala. 430, 100 So. 845 (1924).

Erroneous judgment. — So much of a judgment for one contesting election of mayor of town on ground of latter's ineligibility for such office as declared contestant elected and entitled to office was erroneous. Huey v. Etheridge, 234 Ala. 264, 175 So. 268 (1937).

Evidence amply supported findings of trial judge. McGallagher v. Bosarge, 273 Ala. 133, 136 So. 2d 181 (1961).

Determining "correct" person duly elected. — This section applies to offer the remedy of declaring the correct person duly elected: (1) Where the contestant successfully demonstrates that, ignoring (or "subtracting") illegal votes, he or she actually received the majority of the votes cast, i.e., where "it shall appear that any person other than the one whose election is contested, received ... the highest number of legal votes," and (2) where the contestant successfully demonstrates that adding all of the legal votes cast (where some of those legal votes had been wrongly "rejected" previously) he or she is the true victor. Nunley v. Abernathy, 622 So. 2d 922 (Ala. 1993).

Application where election was not contested. — Where there is a contested election in Alabama, this section provides that if the person who received the highest number of legal votes be ineligible or disqualified, the election must be declared void. Reasoning by analogy, it should follow that where there is not a contested election, but there does arise the same question of what votes to count this statutory policy should be given effect. State ex rel. Cleveland v. Stacy, 263 Ala. 185, 82 So. 2d 264 (1955).

Cited in Walker v. Junior, 247 Ala. 342, 24 So. 2d 431 (1945); Banks v. Zippert, 470 So. 2d 1147 (Ala. 1985).

§ 17-15-33. Contest not abated by death of contestant.

In all contests of elections, such contests are not abated by the death of the party commencing them before final judgment, if any qualified elector appears in court and substitutes himself as a contestant and gives good and sufficient security for the costs which have accrued or may accrue on the contest. But if no qualified elector appears and proposes to substitute himself as the party contesting, the contest abates on the death of the contesting party, and judgment must be rendered against his sureties for the costs of the contest, which must be collected by execution in the name of the party whose election was contested. In all cases the person whose election is contested, if he is the successful party in such contest, is entitled to judgment for the cost thereof against the party contesting and his sureties, for which execution may issue returnable to the court of probate or to the circuit court, as the case may be. (Code 1896, § 1701; Code 1907, § 475; Code 1923, § 565; Code 1940, T. 17, § 251.)

Prerequisites to section becoming effective. — The latter part of this section authorizes judgment in favor of a successful contestee against the contestant and his sureties for the cost and for which execution may issue. Therefore, in order for this provision to be effectual, the bond or security must be on file in the court in which the contest was instituted and tried as provided in §§ 17-15-22, 17-15-29 and 17-15-31. Robinson v. Winston County, 203 Ala. 671, 85 So. 22 (1920).

Cited in Broadfoot v. City of Florence, 253 Ala. 455, 45 So. 2d 311 (1950); Cosby v. Moore, 259 Ala. 41, 65 So. 2d 178 (1953).

§ 17-15-34. Appeals — Generally.

In all contested elections before the judge of probate court, an appeal lies to the Supreme Court within 14 days after the rendition of the judgment. From the judgment of the circuit court on the contest of an election of a judge of probate or sheriff or any other officer mentioned in Section 17-15-29, an appeal lies to the Supreme Court within 14 days after the rendition of the judgment. (Code 1896, § 1702; Code 1907, § 476; Code 1923, § 566; Code 1940, T. 17, § 252.)

Cited in Wilkerson v. Lee, 236 Ala. 104, 181 So. 296 (1938); Thomas v. Kellett, 489 So. 2d 554 (Ala. 1986).

Collateral references. — 29 C.J.S., Elections, §§ 308-318.

26 Am. Jur. 2d, Elections, §§ 358-362.

§ 17-15-35. Appeals — Costs.

On the taking of an appeal as provided in Section 17-15-34, the appellant must give bond and security for the costs thereof to be approved by the judge of probate or clerk of the circuit court, as the appeal may be taken from the judgment of the judge of probate or circuit court, and the appeal bond must be certified with the record to the appellate court, and if judgment is entered confirming the judgment of the judge of probate or of the circuit court, the Supreme Court must render judgment against the appellant and his sureties for the costs. An appeal in any and all cases suspends the execution of the judgment or decree of the judge of probate or of the circuit court. (Code 1896, § 1703; Code 1907, § 477; Code 1923, § 567; Code 1940, T. 17, § 253.)

This section is sufficiently complied with by the filing and approval of the usual security for costs, with sureties, to be certified with the record that judgment for costs may be rendered thereon in the appellate court if the appeal fails. The appeal suspends the execution of the judgment. The only condition specified is payment of costs. No other supersedeas bond is contemplated. Wilkerson v. Lee, 236 Ala. 104, 181 So. 296 (1938).

Cited in Thomas v. Kellett, 489 So. 2d 554 (Ala. 1986).

Collateral references. — 29 C.J.S., Elections, § 319.

26 Am. Jur. 2d, Elections, §§ 363, 364.

ARTICLE 3.

STATE OFFICERS.

Collateral references. — 26 Am. Jur. 2d, Elections, § 316 et seq.

§ 17-15-50. Statement — Filing; bond.

When any elector shall choose to contest any election for the office of Governor, Secretary of State, Auditor, Treasurer, Attorney General, Commissioner of Agriculture and Industries, justices of the Supreme Court or judges of the courts of appeals, he must, within 10 days after the Speaker of the House of Representatives shall have opened the returns and proclaimed the result of the election for Governor, Secretary of State, Auditor, Treasurer and Attorney General, as provided in this chapter, file with the Speaker of the House of Representatives a written statement of the grounds of such contest and a bond with good and sufficient sureties payable to the State of Alabama and conditioned for the payment of such costs as may accrue upon such contest in the event such contest shall result in favor of the contestee. Such bond must be in the sum of $5,000.00 and must be subject to the approval of the Speaker of the House, and such bond, when it shall be approved, shall be filed and recorded in the office of the Secretary of State. (Code 1896, § 1672; Code 1907, § 478; Code 1923, § 568; Code 1940, T. 17, § 254.)

Collateral references. — 29 C.J.S., Elections, §§ 249, 268(2), 274.

§ 17-15-51. Statement — Contents of statement; verification; service; amendments.

The written statement of the grounds of contest must set forth specifically:

(1) The name of the person contesting and that he was a qualified voter when the election was held;

(2) The office which said election was held to fill, and the time of holding the same;

(3) The particular grounds of contest;

(4) The name of the counties in which any of the alleged grounds of the contest may have occurred, and shall state with particularity the names of the election precinct in each of such counties in which the grounds of contest may be alleged to have occurred; and

(5) The grounds on which the declared voter of each of the named election precincts in each county is contested.

Such statement of the grounds of contest must be sworn to by the elector making the contest before some officer authorized to administer oaths in the State of Alabama, and may be amended from time to time as may be determined by the two houses of the Legislature in joint convention assembled. The Speaker of the House shall cause the Clerk of the House forthwith to serve a copy of the statement on the person who may have been declared to have been elected to the contested office. (Code 1896, § 1673; Code 1907, § 479; Code 1923, § 569; Code 1940, T. 17, § 255.)

Collateral references. — 29 C.J.S., Elections, §§ 256, 268(5), 269, 270.

§ 17-15-52. Tried by joint convention of House and Senate.

The two houses of the Legislature, in joint convention assembled, and presided over by the Speaker of the House of Representatives, shall constitute the tribunal for the trial of all contests for the office of Governor, Secretary of State, Auditor, Treasurer, Attorney General or Commissioner of Agriculture and Industries, justices of the Supreme Court, judges of the courts of appeals and such joint convention shall fix a day for the trial, which may be adjourned from day to day, and from time to time, as may be determined by the joint convention. A majority of the joint convention shall be competent to try all issues involved in the contest and render judgment on all questions arising during the progress of the trial, including a final judgment on the contest. The proceedings of the joint convention, as well as all judgments rendered, shall be entered upon the journals of the Senate and the House of Representatives, and the final judgment of the joint convention upon the contest shall thereupon become effective as a judgment and shall have the force and effect of vesting the title to the office, which may be the subject of contest in the person in whose favor the judgment may be rendered. (Code 1896, § 1674; Code 1907, § 480; Code 1923, § 570; Code 1940, T. 17, § 256.)

Cited in Sellers v. State, 507 So. 2d 544 (Ala. 1986).

§ 17-15-53. Commission elected to take testimony.

When any contest shall have been commenced under the provisions of this article for any of the officers mentioned in Section 17-15-52, it shall be the duty of the Legislature, in joint convention, to elect by ballot three senators and five representatives, who shall act as a commission to take the testimony to be submitted on the contest. Every member of the joint convention, at such time, as may be fixed by resolution of the two houses, shall vote for two senators and three representatives as members of the commission, and the three senators and five representatives who receive the highest number of votes shall be declared elected commissioners. (Code 1896, § 1675; Code 1907, § 481; Code 1923, § 571; Code 1940, T. 17, § 257.)

Collateral references. — 29 C.J.S., Elections, §§ 55-59.

§ 17-15-54. Sitting of commission.

The commission provided for in Section 17-15-53 shall sit at such times and places as may be directed by the joint convention, and shall be presided over by a chairman of its own selection, and each member of the commission shall receive $4.00 per diem during the time of actual sitting when the Legislature is not in session, and necessary expenses, to be paid by the Comptroller's warrant drawn upon the Treasurer, when the chairman of the commission shall certify the same to the Comptroller. (Code 1896, § 1676; Code 1907, § 482; Code 1923, § 572; Code 1940, T. 17, § 258.)

§ 17-15-55. Commission to take testimony.

The commission shall take testimony on the part of the contestant, and also on the part of the contestee, and shall have power to send for witnesses, books and papers anywhere in the State of Alabama; shall have power to issue warrants, under the hand of the chairman, to any judge, or clerk of any court of record or such other competent and discreet person as the commission may appoint, to take the deposition of witnesses at such time and place as the warrant shall direct, and the points as to which the testimony is to be taken shall be set forth in such warrant. The evidence taken in the case of a contest of the election of one officer may be used in the contest of the election of any other officer voted for at the same election and contested before the Legislature; provided, that notice that such evidence will be used, or offered, shall be given to the party or parties interested in such other office, so that all parties interested may be present and participate in the taking of such testimony, and provided the party instituting the contest does not object by filing his written objection with the commission. (Code 1896, § 1677; Code 1907, § 483; Code 1923, § 573; Code 1940, T. 17, § 259.)

§ 17-15-56. Notice to adverse party.

Whenever either party shall apply to the commission to examine witnesses, either before the commission or by warrant issued from the commission, the adverse party shall have five days' notice of said application and of the time and place of taking such depositions. (Code 1896, § 1678; Code 1907, § 484; Code 1923, § 574; Code 1940, T. 17, § 260.)

§ 17-15-57. Commission has power to punish for contempt.

If any witness, being summoned, fails to attend, or being summoned with a subpoena duces tecum, fails and refuses to produce the paper or document required to be produced by the subpoena, the commission shall have the right and authority to punish said witness for contempt by a fine not exceeding $500.00, or by imprisonment in any county jail in the state for a period not to exceed 30 days, one or both, and in case any witness shall fail to appear or produce any book or document before any judge, clerk of court or other person having a warrant from the commission, the judge, clerk of court or other person, must certify the fact to the commission, which may thereupon punish such witness for contempt, as provided in this section. (Code 1896, § 1679; Code 1907, § 485; Code 1923, § 575; Code 1940, T. 17, § 261.)

§ 17-15-58. Evidence confined to allegations; exceptions.

No evidence shall be taken on the part of the contestant unless to sustain some one of the specific allegations of the original or amended statement of grounds of contest. Nor shall any evidence be taken on the part of the contestee except in rebuttal of the specific allegations of the original or amended statement of the grounds of contest. But upon five days' notice the contestee shall have the right to take evidence of any malconduct, fraud or corruption on the part of any inspector, clerk, marker, returning officer, board of supervisors or other person; of illegal votes cast for some person other than the contestee; of the rejection of legal votes cast for the contestee; of offers to bribe, bribery, intimidation or other malconduct which prevented a fair, free and full exercise of the elective franchise in any election precinct in the State of Alabama, the election in which is not put in issue by the original or amended statement of the grounds of contest; and when the contestee shall take evidence as herein provided, the contestant shall be permitted to take evidence in rebuttal. (Code 1896, § 1680; Code 1907, § 486; Code 1923, § 576; Code 1940, T. 17, § 262.)

Collateral references. — Admissibility of parol evidence of election officials to impeach election returns. 46 ALR2d 1385.

§ 17-15-59. Each party entitled to be present.

Each party shall have the right to be present at the taking of any evidence, in person or by agent or attorney. (Code 1896, § 1681; Code 1907, § 487; Code 1923, § 577; Code 1940, T. 17, § 263.)

§ 17-15-60. Commission to report conclusions and evidence.

It shall be the duty of the commission to examine the evidence adduced upon the contest, and shall report its conclusions to the joint convention of the two houses, and all evidence taken under the provisions of this article shall be returned by the commission to the Speaker of the House at such time as the joint convention may direct. (Code 1896, § 1682; Code 1907, § 488; Code 1923, § 578; Code 1940, T. 17, § 264.)

§ 17-15-61. Compensation of witnesses.

The witnesses shall be allowed for their attendance $1.00 a day and $.03 a mile coming and going by the route most usually traveled, from their place of residence to where such depositions are taken. (Code 1896, § 1683; Code 1907, § 489; Code 1923, § 579; Code 1940, T. 17, § 265.)

§ 17-15-62. Sheriffs to serve commission's writs.

The sheriffs of Alabama in their respective counties are required to serve subpoenas and such other writs as the commission may have authority to issue, and shall be allowed the same compensation as is now allowed by law for similar services performed at the command of the courts. (Code 1896, § 1684; Code 1907, § 490; Code 1923, § 580; Code 1940, T. 17, § 266.)

§ 17-15-63. Execution for costs.

After the determination of the contest, the Clerk of the House of Representatives must tax the costs accrued and certify the amount of each separate item, the name of the person entitled thereto, and the result of such contest and the names of the sureties on the bond for contest, to the clerk of the circuit court of Montgomery County, and said clerk must thereupon issue execution against the unsuccessful party, which execution must be made returnable in 30 days after its issue; and alias and pluries executions may be issued as often as may be necessary. And if it be certified that the determination of the contest was against the contestant, the execution must issue against the sureties on the bond for the contest as well as against the contestant. (Code 1896, § 1685; Code 1907, § 491; Code 1923, § 581; Code 1940, T. 17, § 267.)

CHAPTER 16.

PRIMARY ELECTIONS.

Article 2.

Contest of Elections.

Collateral references. — 29 C.J.S., Elections, § 111(4).

ARTICLE 1.

GENERAL PROVISIONS.

§ 17-16-1. "Primary election" defined.

A primary election, within the meaning of this chapter, is an election held by the qualified voters, who are members of any political party, for the purpose of nominating a candidate or candidates for public or party office. (Acts 1975, No. 1196, p. 2349, § 1.)

Cited in Crespi v. Carl, 494 So. 2d 30 (Ala. 1986).

Collateral references. — 29 C.J.S., Elections, § 1(4).
26 Am. Jur. 2d, Elections, § 147 et seq.

§ 17-16-2. "Political party" defined.

An assemblage or organization of electors which, at the general election for state and county officers then next preceding the primary, casts more than 20 percent of the entire vote cast in any county is hereby declared to be a political party within the meaning of this chapter within such county; and an assemblage or organization of electors which, at the general election for state officers then next preceding the primary, casts more than 20 percent of the entire vote cast in the state is hereby declared to be a political party within the meaning of this chapter for such state. (Acts 1975, No. 1196, p. 2349, § 2.)

Constitutionality. — The levels of support required by § 17-8-2.1, in conjunction with this section and § 17-16-3, are constitutional. Libertarian Party v. Wallace, 586 F. Supp. 399 (M.D. Ala. 1984).

Section 17-8-2.1, in conjunction with this section and § 17-16-3 provides a two-track system by which a political party may have its name placed on a ballot for statewide and local elections: (1) a candidate of the party must have garnered at least 20 percent of votes cast in the last general election; or (2) the party must gather one percent of the signatures of qualified electors who cast ballots for governor in the last general election. If the office sought requires a statewide vote, the percentage requirements apply statewide; but if the party is seeking only a local office, the percentage requirements apply to the local political unit only. The secretary of state, who is responsible for monitoring and implementing the level of support requirements, has also adopted the policy that if a party is qualified statewide it is also qualified, without further filings, for all local offices throughout the state. Libertarian Party v. Wallace, 586 F. Supp. 399 (M.D. Ala. 1984).

States have an important interest in protecting their electoral processes through restrictions that eliminate fraudulent or frivolous candidacies, ensure efficient election procedures, and minimize voter confusion as the result of overcrowded ballots. States may therefore require that a political party demonstrate a certain level of support among the electorate before it may obtain a place on the ballot. Such restrictions, however, substantially implicate constitutionally protected liberties under the first amendment and the equal protection clause of the fourteenth amendment. Therefore, states must adopt the least drastic means to achieve their ends. Libertarian Party v. Wallace, 586 F. Supp. 399 (M.D. Ala. 1984).

Alabama does not substantially restrict who may sign the access ballot petitions. There are no political affiliation restrictions for those who sign the petitions; there are no time limits on when the petition drive may begin; and there are no geographic restrictions on where the signatures may come from. Furthermore, if a party qualifies for the ballot statewide, it automatically qualifies for all local offices. Libertarian Party v. Wallace, 586 F. Supp. 399 (M.D. Ala. 1984).

Collateral references. — 25 Am. Jur. 2d, Elections, § 162.

Validity of percentage of vote or similar requirements for participation by political parties in primary elections. 70 ALR2d 1162.

§ 17-16-3. Determination of total vote of political party.

In determining the total vote of a political party whenever required by this chapter, the test shall be the total vote received by a candidate of that party who received the highest vote total of any of the candidates of that party. (Acts 1975, No. 1196, p. 2349, § 3.)

Constitutionality. — The levels of support required by § 17-8-2.1, in conjunction with this section and § 17-16-2, are constitutional. Libertarian Party v. Wallace, 586 F. Supp. 399 (M.D. Ala. 1984).

Section 17-8-2.1, in conjunction with this section and § 17-16-2 provides a two-track system by which a political party may have its name placed on a ballot for statewide and local elections; (1) a candidate of the party must have garnered at least 20 percent of votes cast in the last general election; or (2) the party must gather one percent of the signatures of qualified electors who cast ballots for governor in the last general election. If the office sought requires a statewide vote, the percentage requirements apply statewide; but if the party is seeking only a local office, the percentage requirements apply to the local political unit only. The secretary of state, who is responsible for monitoring and implementing the level of support requirements, has also adopted the policy that if a party is qualified statewide it is also qualified, without further filings, for all local offices throughout the state. Libertarian Party v. Wallace, 586 F. Supp. 399 (M.D. Ala. 1984).

Cited in Vintson v. Anton, 786 F.2d 1023 (11th Cir. 1986).

Collateral references. — 29 C.J.S., Elections, § 111(1).

§ 17-16-4. Applicability of chapter; applicability of general election laws to primary elections.

All primary elections held by any political party in this state for the nomination of any state, national, district, circuit, county or municipal officers shall be held and conducted under the provisions of this chapter and, except as herein modified, shall be held and conducted in the same manner and form, under the same requirements and subject to the same forfeitures, penalties and punishments as are now or shall hereafter be provided by law for the holding of regular state elections, but nothing herein contained shall make it obligatory upon any political party or parties to hold a primary election. (Acts 1975, No. 1196, p. 2349, § 4.)

Former section 17-22-5 was made applicable to primary elections by this section. Kirksey v. Democratic Party, 495 So. 2d 638 (Ala. 1986).

§ 17-16-5. Primary elections not compulsory; election by political party whether to come under provisions of chapter; presumption of acceptance of chapter.

Primary elections are not compulsory. A political party may, by its state executive committee, elect whether it will come under the primary election law. All political parties are presumed to have accepted and come under the provisions of the primary election law, but any political party may signify its election not to accept and come under the primary election law by filing with the Secretary of State, at least 60 days before the date herein fixed for the holding of any general primary election, a statement of the action of its state executive committee, certified by its chairman and secretary, which statement shall contain a copy of the resolution or motion adopted declining to accept and come under the primary election law. If a political party declines to accept and come under the primary election law, it shall not change its action and accept and come under the primary election law until after the next general election held thereafter. The governing body of a political party may determine from time to time what party officers shall be elected in the primary; provided, that candidates for all party offices shall be elected under the provisions of this chapter unless the method of their election is otherwise directed by the governing body of the party involved. (Acts 1975, No. 1196, p. 2349, § 1.)

Editor's note. — The cases cited below were decided under former Tit. 17, § 336, 1940 Code, which contained provisions similar to those in this section.

Provisions of chapter appear to be legitimate exercise of state's right. — The provisions governing primary elections are found in this chapter and, on their face, appear to be legitimate exercises of the state's right to lay down rules for the protection of the public in the conduct of an election. United States v. Executive Comm. of Democratic Party, 254 F. Supp. 537 (S.D. Ala. 1966).

And will be enforced with due protection for all county citizens. — The procedural regulations for Alabama elections found in the Alabama Code can and will be enforced with due protection for all the citizens of a county, white as well as negro. The object of judicial intervention of this nature is to insure, as far as possible, the effective administration of the Alabama election statutes without abridgment of the right of any citizen to vote and have the vote counted. United States v. Executive Comm. of Democratic Party, 254 F. Supp. 537 (S.D. Ala. 1966).

Primary elections may not be made compulsory. — Under Constitution 1901, § 190, and former Tit. 17, § 336, 1940 Code, containing provisions similar to this section, primary elections may not be made the compulsory method of selecting candidates for any political party. Moody v. Gallion, 286 F. Supp. 653 (M.D. Ala. 1968).

Discretion of state executive committee. — Constitution 1901, § 190 expressly provides against any compulsory primary, and former Tit. 17, § 336, 1940 Code, containing provisions similar to this section, represented a response to such mandate, granting to the state executive committee wide discretion. Smith v. McQueen, 232 Ala. 90, 166 So. 788 (1936), wherein the court said: "We interpret the concluding sentence of this section to mean simply this and nothing more — that party officers are to be elected in the primary, unless the state executive committee directs their selection otherwise."

Where mandamus does not lie to require committee to certify names. — Candidates for positions of delegates to national convention of political party were held not entitled to mandamus to require state executive committee to certify their names for election in primary, where delegates had been appointed by state executive committee. Smith v. McQueen, 232 Ala. 90, 166 So. 788 (1936).

A candidate seeking nomination of a party to run for a state or county office is a candidate for a party office and, when nominated, has a status as a quasi officer. Bridges v. McCorvey, 254 Ala. 677, 49 So. 2d 546 (1950).

Cited in Bogard v. Hobbie, 569 F. Supp. 477 (M.D. Ala. 1983); Crespi v. Carl, 494 So. 2d 30 (Ala. 1986).

Collateral references. — 29 C.J.S., Elections, § 111(3).

§ 17-16-6. Time and place for holding elections.

Presidential preference primaries and primary elections, except special primary elections, held at the expense of the state or counties, shall be held on the first Tuesday in June. When necessary, as provided in this chapter, a second or runoff primary election shall be held on the last Tuesday in June following said primary election. Any second primary shall be held by the same election officers who held the first primary, and be held at the same places as the first primary election. No primary shall be held by any political party except as herein provided. Primary elections herein provided for shall be held at the regular polling places established for the purpose of holding general elections. (Acts 1975, No. 1196, p. 2349, § 5; Acts 1977, 1st Ex. Sess., No. 69, p. 1493, § 1; Acts 1978, No. 691, p. 994, § 16; Acts 1979, No. 79-800, p. 1463, § 1; Acts 1985, No. 85-389, p. 344; Acts 1990, No. 90-699, p. 1359, § 1.)

Certain time provisions not consistent with change to September primaries. — The time provisions in certain statutory provisions authorizing election contests within the state political parties and requiring the prompt determination of such contests with certain time periods before the next ensuing election cause difficulties because of the more recent statutes, such as this section, changing the time for holding primary elections of political parties to the month of September. Most of the statutes governing the contest of elections were enacted at a time when the primary elections were held in May rather than in September. Thus, the time provisions contained in the statutes no longer fit the realities of the state election procedure. Godfrey v. Oswalt, 428 So. 2d 40 (Ala. 1983).

Cited in White v. Knight, 424 So. 2d 566 (Ala. 1982).

Collateral references. — 29 C.J.S., Elections, § 117.

§ 17-16-7. Selection of delegates to national conventions by political parties.

Political parties may provide for the selection of delegates to national conventions by the holding of a presidential preference primary or by popular election of the delegates or otherwise. In the event a presidential preference primary is called by the governing body of any party, notice of such action shall be given to the Secretary of State as part of the notice required by Section 17-16-13. Said notice shall prescribe the procedure for the listing of the names of presidential candidates on the primary ballot and for the selection of delegates pledged under party rules to vote for the respective presidential candidates. A presidential preference primary, when called, will appear in the first or top position on the primary ballot. When no presidential preference primary is to be utilized, delegates may be elected in the primary election in the same manner as other party officers; except, that subject to such rules and procedures as the respective political parties may adopt, any delegate candidate may be permitted to list opposite his or her name on the primary ballot the surname of the presidential candidate to whom he or she is pledged or the word "uncommitted." When delegates are to be so elected, the candidates for such position or positions shall appear in the first or top position on the primary ballot. (Acts 1975, No. 1196, p. 2349, § 6.)

§ 17-16-8. Party committees for state and political subdivisions; state executive committees vested with party powers when local committees not established.

There may be provided a committee of each party for the state and each political subdivision of the state, including counties, said committees to be selected in such manner as may be provided for by the governing authority of each party, but if there shall not be elected or chosen any committee for any county or other political subdivision, then all the powers which could be exercised by any such committee shall be vested in the state executive committee, under such rules and regulations as the governing body of the party may designate, or the state committee or the chairman thereof may appoint a county committee to act until such a committee is elected or chosen as provided by law or party rule. When a state executive committee of a party is provided, said state executive committee shall be the governing body of the party within the meaning of this chapter; except, that it shall have the authority to delegate to county executive committees authority over the conduct of party affairs within the respective counties, including authority over the conduct of primary elections within the respective counties. (Acts 1975, No. 1196, p. 2349, § 7.)

Executive committeemen of a party are party officers when elected as such in the primary. Bridges v. McCorvey, 254 Ala. 677, 49 So. 2d 546 (1950), decided under former Tit. 17, § 341, 1940 Code, which contained provisions similar to those in this section.

Election of county democratic executive committee members is within purview by law of state committee. Clark v. Marengo County, 469 F. Supp. 1150 (S.D. Ala. 1979), rev'd on other grounds, 731 F.2d 1546 (11th Cir. 1984).

Collateral references. — 29 C.J.S., Elections, § 86(1).

25 Am. Jur. 2d, Elections, § 153.

§ 17-16-9. Provision for election of members of state executive committees.

The state or county executive committee of any political party may, by a majority vote of said committee, require that members of said committee be elected by the qualified electors of such political party. If such committee adopts an appropriate resolution requiring that such members be so elected, such election shall be held on the same ballot as the gubernatorial primary election. When members of county or state executive committees are to be elected in a primary, their declarations of candidacy shall be filed in the same manner and within the same time as candidates for nomination for public office. (Acts 1975, No. 1196, p. 2349, § 8.)

There appears to be no law prescribing the terms of office of committee members. Smith v. Paris, 386 F.2d 979 (5th Cir. 1967), decided under former Tit. 17, § 342, 1940 Code, which contained provisions similar to those in this section.

Change in method of electing members held unconstitutional. — A resolution changing the method of electing committee members so that the members previously elected by beats (or districts) were elected on an at-large basis, although each candidate was required to reside within a particular beat and, after election, represent the beat in which he resides, was racially motivated and as a result, was unconstitutional. Smith v. Paris, 257 F. Supp. 901 (M.D. Ala. 1966) (denying request for new election in view of failure to explain delay in filing suit), modified and aff'd, 386 F.2d 979 (5th Cir. 1967), decided under former Tit. 17, § 342, 1940 Code, which contained provisions similar to those in this section.

Collateral references. — 29 C.J.S., Elections, § 86(1).

§ 17-16-10. Payment of compensation of officers and other expenses of elections.

The compensation of officers and other expenses of any and all primary elections, general or special, held under the provisions of this chapter, shall be paid in the same manner and to the same extent as is or may be provided by law for the payment of the expenses and officers of general elections held under

the general election laws of Alabama and shall be paid out of the county
treasury in same manner. (Acts 1975, No. 1196, p. 2349, § 9.)

Collateral references. — 29 C.J.S., Elections, § 116.

§ 17-16-11. Filing of declarations of candidacy by candidates; certification of names of candidates to Secretary of State and probate judges; preparation of ballots; unopposed candidates not listed on ballots.

(a)(1) Except as provided in subdivision (2), all candidates for nomination to
public office or for election to party office in the primary election provided for
in this chapter shall file their declaration of candidacy with the state party
chair if they seek any federal, state, circuit, or district office, or the state
Senate, House of Representatives, or any other office that is not a county
office not later than 5:00 P.M. 60 days before the date of the primary election.
All candidates for nomination or election to a county office shall file their
declaration with the county party chair not later than 5:00 P.M. 60 days
before the date of the primary election.

(2) With regard to the 1992 election cycle for candidates for the United
States House of Representatives only, and only if the Legislature adopts an
approved congressional reapportionment plan in the 1992 Regular Session,
candidates shall file their declaration not later than 29 days before the
primary election.

(b)(1) Except as provided in subdivision (2) the state party chair shall, no
later than 5:00 P.M. 55 days before the primary election, certify the names
of all primary election candidates, except candidates for county offices, to the
Secretary of State. The county party chair shall, not later than 5:00 P.M. 55
days prior to the date of the primary election, certify to the probate judge the
names of all candidates for nomination to county offices or election to county
party offices. The Secretary of State shall, not less than 50 days prior to the
date of the primary election, and not less than 25 days prior to the primary
election in the 1992 election cycle only, certify to the probate judge of every
county in which the election is to be held the names of the opposed
candidates for nomination to federal, state, circuit, or district offices, the
state Senate, House of Representatives, and all other opposed candidates to
public or party office, except candidates for county offices.

(2) With regard to the 1992 election cycle for candidates for the United
States House of Representatives only, and only if the Legislature adopts an
approved congressional reapportionment plan in the 1992 Regular Session:

a. The state party chair shall certify the candidates to the Secretary of
State not later than 5:00 P.M. 27 days before the primary election.

b. The Secretary of State shall certify the candidates to the probate
judge not later than 5:00 P.M. 25 days before the primary election.

(c) The probate judge of each county shall have the ballots prepared for the
primary election. If a legally qualified candidate for nomination to an office is

unopposed when the last date for filing declarations of candidacy has passed, his or her name shall not appear on the ballots to be used in the primary election, and he or she shall be the nominee of the party with which he or she has qualified for the office. If a legally qualified candidate for election to a party office is unopposed when the last date for filing declarations of candidacy has passed, his or her name shall not appear on the ballots to be used in the primary election, and he or she shall be declared elected to the party office for which he or she qualified. (Acts 1975, No. 1196, p. 2349, § 10; Acts 1977, 1st Ex. Sess., No. 69, p. 1493, § 1; Acts 1986, No. 86-428, p. 791, § 6; Acts 1992, No. 92-152, p. 262, § 1.)

As to unconstitutionality of former filing fee system, see Harper v. Vance, 342 F. Supp. 136 (N.D. Ala. 1972), decided under former Tit. 17, § 348, 1940 Code, which contained provisions similar to those in subsection (a) of this section.

This statute is mandatory and political parties have no power to alter the time fixed by the legislature. Bostwick v. Harris, 421 So. 2d 492 (Ala. 1982).

State party chairman may not designate third party to receive declaration. — That part of subsection (a), which provides that all candidates for nomination to public office file their declaration of candidacy with the state party chairman is not directory and the state party chairman cannot legally, pursuant to subsection (a), designate a third-party as his agent or designee to receive the declaration of candidacy from a person seeking nomination to public office. Harris v. Weatherford, 459 So. 2d 876 (Ala. 1984).

Deadline provisions placed unconstitutional burden on parties. — Deadline provisions having the effect of requiring a minor party to submit its qualifying petitions and nominate its candidates seven months prior to the election placed an unconstitutional burden on such a party and its candidates in attempting to access the Alabama ballot. New Alliance Party v. Hand, 933 F.2d 1568 (11th Cir. 1991).

Applicability of ethics law. — Filing of a declaration of candidacy under this section triggers the necessity for compliance with the Alabama Ethics Law, and in particular § 36-25-15(a). Muncaster v. Alabama State Ethics Comm'n, 372 So. 2d 853 (Ala. 1979).

Collateral references. — 29 C.J.S., Elections, §§ 113, 114, 135.

§ 17-16-12. Only qualified candidates to be listed on ballots.

The name of no candidate shall be printed upon any official ballot used at any primary election unless such person is legally qualified to hold the office for which he is a candidate and unless he is eligible to vote in the primary election in which he seeks to be a candidate and possesses the political qualifications prescribed by the governing body of his political party. (Acts 1975, No. 1196, p. 2349, § 11.)

The democratic party has authority to hear pre-primary challenges to the political or legal qualifications of its candidates. Knight v. Gray, 420 So. 2d 247 (Ala. 1982).

The state democratic executive committee may prescribe political qualifications of candidates in a democratic primary election. Ray v. Blair, 257 Ala. 151, 57 So. 2d 395, rev'd on other grounds, 343 U.S. 214, 72 S. Ct. 654, 96 L. Ed. 894 (1952), decided under former Tit. 17, § 345, 1940 Code, which contained provisions identical to those in this section.

The state executive committee of a political party has full right, power and authority to fix and prescribe the political and other qualifications of its own members and to determine who shall be entitled and qualified to vote in primary elections or be candidates or otherwise participate therein just so such committee action does not run afoul of some statutory or constitutional provision. Knight v. Gray, 420 So. 2d 247 (Ala. 1982).

Cited in Kirksey v. Democratic Party, 495 So. 2d 638 (Ala. 1986).

Collateral references. — 29 C.J.S., Elections, § 114.

§ 17-16-13. Notice by governing body of political party of desire to enter primary.

When it shall be desired by the governing body of any political party to enter the primary election ordered to be held under the provisions of this chapter, said governing body for the state shall give public notice thereof by filing a copy of the resolution of such governing body with the Secretary of State of Alabama. Such notice may be given to the Secretary of State by the chairman of the county executive committee where the primary election affects only one county, and a copy of such notice shall be filed with the probate judge of such county. (Acts 1975, No. 1196, p. 2349, § 12.)

No federal jurisdiction over action as to inclusion on primary ballot for county democratic committee. — Federal district court lacked jurisdiction over an action under 42 U.S.C. § 1983 brought by individual seeking to be included on the democratic primary ballot as a candidate for the Madison county democratic committee, for want of a justiciable controversy. Thompson v. Woodall, 637 F. Supp. 944 (N.D. Ala. 1986), aff'd, 819 F.2d 1052 (11th Cir. 1987).

§ 17-16-14. Persons eligible to vote in primary elections; establishment of qualifications for voters; voters to sign pledge of party support in general election on poll lists.

(a) All persons who are qualified electors under the general laws of the State of Alabama and who are also members of a political party and entitled to participate in such primary election under the rules of said party shall be entitled to vote therein and shall receive the official primary ballot of that political party, and no other; but every governing body of a party shall have the right, power and authority to fix and prescribe the political or other qualifications of its own members and shall, in its own way, declare and determine who shall be entitled and qualified to vote in such primary election or to be candidates therein or to otherwise participate in such political parties and primaries. The qualifications of electors entitled to vote in such primary election shall not necessarily be the same as the qualifications for electors entitled to become candidates therein. Nothing herein contained shall be so construed as to prohibit any state executive committee of a party from fixing such qualifications as it may deem necessary for persons desiring to become candidates for nomination to offices at a primary election.

(b) All poll lists for primary elections shall state at the top thereof that by participating in said primary election a voter shall indicate his preference for the party holding said primary, and will support the nominees of that party in the general election, and that he is qualified under the rules of such party to vote in its primary election. No person shall be eligible to participate in said primary unless he signs said poll list and thereby certifies to the truth of said statement. (Acts 1975, No. 1196, p. 2349, § 13.)

The state executive committee of a political party has full right, power and authority to fix qualifications of its own members and to determine who shall be entitled and qualified to vote in primary elections or be candidates or otherwise participate therein just so such committee action does not run afoul of some statutory or constitutional provision.

Knight v. Gray, 420 So. 2d 247 (Ala. 1982).

The democratic party has authority to hear preprimary challenges to the political or legal qualifications of its candidates. Knight v. Gray, 420 So. 2d 247 (Ala. 1982).

As to right of political party to require primary candidate for presidential elector to pledge support of nominees of national convention, see Ray v. Blair, 343 U.S. 214, 72 S. Ct. 654, 96 L. Ed. 894 (1952), decided under former Tit. 17, § 347, 1940 Code, which contained provisions similar to those in this section.

Rule against crossover voting in primary elections is a proper response to the Alabama state democratic executive committee's responsibility under Alabama law. It is clear and unambiguous. It is manifestly reasonable. It has the force and effect of state law. Curry v. Baker, 802 F.2d 1302 (11th Cir. 1986), cert. dismissed, 479 U.S. 1023, 107 S. Ct. 1262, 93 L. Ed. 2d 819 (1987).

Advising voters to vote in democratic runoff after republican primary and allowing "crossover" voting violated federal law. — Attorney general of Alabama, a candidate for the democratic party's nomination for governor, violated § 5 of the Voting Rights Act of 1965 by using his office to advise voters that they could vote in the democratic runoff in violation of democratic party rules even though they had voted in the republican primary, and by preventing the democratic party from enforcing its rule prohibiting such "crossover" voting, which rule had been precleared by the U.S. attorney general, by threatening election officials with civil and criminal penalties if they attempted to prohibit crossover voting. Henderson v. Graddick, 641 F. Supp. 1192 (M.D. Ala.), appeal dismissed, 479 U.S. 1023, 107 S. Ct. 681, 93 L. Ed. 2d 819 (1986).

As to unconstitutionality of former filing fee system, see Harper v. Vance, 342 F. Supp. 136 (N.D. Ala. 1972), decided under former Tit. 17, § 347, 1940 Code, which contained provisions similar to those in this section.

Cited in Curry v. Baker, 802 F.2d 1302 (11th Cir. 1986).

Collateral references. — 29 C.J.S., Elections, §§ 115(1)-115(7).

25 Am. Jur. 2d, Elections, §§ 158-161.

§ 17-16-15. Assessments and other qualifications for candidates for nomination.

The governing body of a party may fix assessments upon those able to pay, or other qualifications as it may deem necessary, for persons desiring to become candidates for nomination to offices at a primary election, but such assessments shall not exceed two percent of one year's salary of the office sought and, for an unremunerative or party county office or an unremunerative or party office to be filled by a vote of a subdivision greater than one county, it shall not exceed $50.00 or $150.00 for an unrenumerative or party office to be filled by a vote of the entire state. (Acts 1975, No. 1196, p. 2349, § 14; Acts 1981, 2nd Ex. Sess., No. 81-1071, p. 318, § 1.)

As to unconstitutionality of former filing fee system, see Harper v. Vance, 342 F. Supp. 136 (N.D. Ala. 1972), decided under former Tit. 17, §§ 347 and 348, 1940 Code, which contained provisions relating to assessments.

§ 17-16-16. Assessment of unauthorized fees against candidates.

Any person who shall, as a condition for standing for nomination to any office in a primary election, assess or cause to be assessed a fee by any committee or other governing body of any political party in this state in excess of that allowed by law shall be guilty of a misdemeanor and, on conviction, shall be fined not less than $25.00 nor more than $100.00. (Acts 1919, No. 669, p. 969; Code 1923, § 3955; Code 1940, T. 17, § 408.)

Collateral references. — 29 C.J.S., Elections, § 114.

§ 17-16-17. Selection and appointment of officers to conduct elections.

Each candidate for nomination may, at least 25 days before the primary, present to the county executive committee of his party a list of election officers desired by him for any one or more of the districts, wards or precincts, and his county committee shall, so far as practicable, make up, from the list so presented to it, a list of names of election officers, six in number, for each district, ward or precinct, which it will nominate to the appointing board of the county for appointment as officers to conduct the primary election. The county committee shall present the list so made up by it to the appointing board of the county which appoints the election officers to conduct elections for state and county officers in November, or at any other lawful time, which appointing board, from the list so presented to it by the county committee, shall, if there be on said list the names of sufficient persons who are legally eligible, select and appoint the officers to conduct the primary election, observing the above rule as to representation wherever more than one party enters the primary; and, in the latter case, if a county committee has not given a sufficient number of names for a box, then the appointing board shall supply the deficiency from electors of that party. In the event the persons selected as officers fail to appear at the polling place on the day of the primary election at least one hour before the polls are scheduled to open, then their places shall be filled by such of those who have been named by such appointing board as do appear; and, in the event none so named appear by then, the voters present and qualified to participate in such primary election may, from among themselves, select officers to conduct such election in such district or precinct, and such substituted persons shall have the authority to conduct such elections and to be paid for their service in the same manner as if they had been originally appointed. All officers serving in such primary elections shall take the same oath required to be taken by officers of regular state elections and shall be subject to the same restrictions, limitations, penalties and conditions. (Acts 1975, No. 1196, p. 2349, § 15.)

Interpretation of section 17-6-1. — Section 17-6-1 provides that the appointing board shall make the appointment not more than 20 nor less than 15 days before the holding of any election. Former Tit. 17, § 349, 1940 Code, meant that the executive committee must act, if they do so at all, before the appointing board shall act in said intervening period. And if within such period the board makes the selection before the committee acts under former Tit. 17, § 349, 1940 Code, such selection and appointment is not void and the board could not then make a selection from the list so furnished by the committee. Ex parte Register, 257 Ala. 408, 60 So. 2d 41 (1952), decided under former Tit. 17, § 349, 1940 Code, which contained provisions substantially similar to those in this section.

This section provides that, for primary elections, the county committee of the political party conducting the election may certify to the county appointing authority six persons to act as poll officials in each precinct. This list is presented to the county appointing authority which then appoints the poll officials usually going by the supplied lists. Clark v. Marengo County, 469 F. Supp. 1150 (S.D. Ala. 1979), rev'd on other grounds, 731 F.2d 1546 (11th Cir. 1984).

Board may not disregard lists of suggested election officers. — In appointing officers to conduct primary elections, the appointing board may not disregard lists of suggested election officers submitted by political party county executive committees, but, so long as it does not abuse its discretion in selecting the election officers from among the candidate's nominations, it is in compliance with statute governing the selection and appointment of officers to conduct primary elections. Mobile County Republican Executive Comm. v. Mandeville, 363 So. 2d 754 (Ala. 1978).

Cited in Harris v. Graddick, 593 F. Supp. 128 (M.D. Ala. 1984).

Collateral references. — 29 C.J.S., Elections, § 61.

§ 17-16-18. Ballots, stationery and supplies; effect of change, mutilation, etc., by voter of pledge on ballot.

Separate official ballots and other election stationery and supplies for each political party shall be printed and furnished for use at each election district or precinct and shall be of a different color for each of the political parties participating in such primary election. All ballots for the same political party shall be alike, except as herein otherwise provided, printed in plain type and upon paper so thick that the printing cannot be distinguished from the back. Across the top of the ballot shall be printed the party's emblem, if any, and the words, "Official Primary Election Ballot." Beneath this heading shall be printed the year in which said election is held and the words "Democratic Party" or "Republican Party" or other proper party designation. Each group of candidates to be voted on shall be preceded by the designation of the office for which the candidates seek nomination, and in the proper place shall be printed the words "Vote for one" or "Vote for two" (or more) according to the number to be elected to such office at the ensuing election. At the bottom of the ballot and after the name of the last candidate shall be printed the following: "By casting this ballot I do pledge myself to abide by the result of this primary election and to aid and support all the nominees thereof in the ensuing general election." Should any voter scratch out, deface or in any way mutilate or change the pledge printed on the ballot, he shall not be considered or held to have repudiated or to have refused to take the pledge, but shall, conclusively, be presumed and held to have scratched out, defaced or mutilated or changed the same for the sole purpose of identifying his ballot; and, accordingly, such ballot shall be marked "spoiled ballot" and shall not be counted. (Acts 1975, No. 1196, p. 2349, § 16.)

The probate judge cannot be required to have printed on the ballot full text of the voter pledge as prescribed by the state democratic executive committee. Ray v. Garner, 257 Ala. 168, 57 So. 2d 824 (1952), decided under former Tit. 17, § 350, 1940 Code, which contained provisions virtually identical to those in this section.

The statute specifying what shall be printed on the ballot does not prohibit other words being printed which would convey full information to the elector as to the nature and effect of his voting. Ray v. Garner, 257 Ala. 168, 57 So. 2d 824 (1952), decided under former Tit. 17, § 350, 1940 Code, which contained provisions virtually identical to those in this section.

Collateral references. — 29 C.J.S., Elections, §§ 118(1)-118(7), 227.

§ 17-16-19. Ballot boxes or voting machines; disposition of returns, certificates and lists of voters after canvass of votes.

Where more than one political party has entered such primary, it shall be the duty of the county governing body to furnish to the election officers of each voting place separate ballot boxes or, where voting machines are used, separate rows or columns on such machines for each party participating in such primary. Ballot boxes shall be distinctly marked, and the ballots of electors of each party shall be deposited in the box assigned to and designated for that party. The returns, certificates and official list of voters, after the canvass of the votes, shall be deposited in the ballot box of the party to which they relate. (Acts 1975, No. 1196, p. 2349, § 17.)

§ 17-16-20. Order of listing of candidates on ballots.

The names of candidates for each office shall be listed on the ballot in alphabetical order by surname, and the offices shall be listed in the following order:

(1) President (if preference primary);

(2) Delegate to national convention;

(3) Governor;

(4) Lieutenant Governor;

(5) United States senator;

(6) United States representative;

(7) Attorney General;

(8) State senator;

(9) State representative;

(10) Supreme Court justice;

(11) Court of Civil Appeals judge;

(12) Court of Criminal Appeals judge;

(13) Secretary of State;

(14) State Treasurer;

(15) State Auditor;

(16) Commissioner of Agriculture and Industries;

(17) Public Service Commissioner;

(18) State Board of Education member;

(19) Circuit court judge;

(20) District attorney;

(21) District court judge;

(22) Circuit clerk;

(23) Other public officers (to be listed in the order prescribed by the probate judge); and

(24) Other party officers (to be listed in the order prescribed by the probate judge). (Acts 1975, No. 1196, p. 2349, § 18.)

§ 17-16-21. Numbering of places when candidates for two or more state offices of same classification to be nominated.

Whenever and wherever candidates for two or more state offices of the same classification are to be nominated in said primary, each of said places to be filled shall be numbered, and each candidate for such offices, in the announcement of his candidacy, shall designate the number of the office for which he is a candidate. The same person shall not be a candidate or be permitted to file his declaration for more than one of such places. No ballot shall be counted for any candidate except for the place and number for which he announced in his declaration filed with the legally constituted authorities to receive and file declaration of candidacy. (Acts 1975, No. 1196, p. 2349, § 19.)

Cited in Bostwick v. Harris, 421 So. 2d 492
(Ala. 1982).

§ 17-16-22. Duty of probate judge to furnish election supplies; delivery of election supplies.

The judge of probate of each county is hereby required to furnish to the officers of the primary election a copy of the official list of voters of each precinct or district in his county, of the same kind and in the same manner as he is required by law to furnish such list to the officers at any general state election. The probate judge shall also furnish all necessary election supplies, including stamped addressed envelopes in which to mail certificates of results and other papers herein required to be forwarded. The probate judge shall deliver such election supplies and lists to the sheriff of the county not less than three days before the day of the election, and it shall be the duty of the sheriff to deliver the same, together with ballot boxes, to the officers of said election, at the place provided by law for holding said election and not later than one hour before the polls are scheduled to open on said election day. (Acts 1975, No. 1196, p. 2349, § 20.)

Collateral references. — 29 C.J.S., Elections, §§ 47-50.

§ 17-16-23. Challenge of voters — Duty of inspectors when voter's name not on official list of voters; affidavit by voter; certificate from probate judge entitles voter to vote without challenge.

If the name of a person desiring to vote in the primary of a party does not appear on the official list of voters for said district, ward or precinct, as furnished by the judge of probate, it shall be the duty of the inspectors to challenge such vote in the same manner as they are required to challenge voters in the general elections whose names do not appear on the official list of voters; and, when challenged, such voter, before his ballot shall be received, shall be required to swear and subscribe to the same affidavit of qualification which is required of a voter challenged at a general election and shall be required to swear and subscribe to an affidavit that he is a member of the party in whose primary he is attempting to vote and shall also be required to produce the same kind of affidavit of identification as is required of a voter challenged at a general election, and the affidavit of identification must be sworn to and subscribed in like manner as required at general elections; provided, that wherever a person duly qualified in a district, ward or precinct presents to the inspectors a certificate (dated subsequent to the date of publication by the probate judge of the list of qualified voters), signed by the probate judge and under his seal or that of his court, that such person's name appears upon the lists of qualified voters entitled to vote in that primary on file or record in his office, then such applicant may be allowed to vote without any challenge made upon the above ground. (Acts 1975, No. 1196, p. 2349, § 21.)

Collateral references. — 29 C.J.S., Elections, § 118(1).

§ 17-16-24. Challenge of voters — Marking of challenged ballots; disposition of affidavits of challenged voters.

All challenged votes shall be marked "challenged" on the back thereof by one of the inspectors and with a number corresponding to the number opposite the name of the challenged voter as it appears on the official list of the qualified voters for such election. If the name of such challenged voter does not appear on the official list of qualified voters, one of the inspectors shall add such name to the official list of qualified voters and assign it its proper number on the list. All affidavits of challenged voters shall be taken in duplicate in the same manner as affidavits are taken of challenged voters in the general elections. One copy of such affidavits in reference to such challenged voters shall be returned with the votes in the ballot box of the party to which they pertain, and the other copy shall be mailed to the district attorney to be presented by him to the next grand jury meeting in said county. (Acts 1975, No. 1196, p. 2349, § 22.)

Collateral references. — 29 C.J.S., Elections, § 209.

§ 17-16-25. Ballots to be kept secret and inviolate; procedure for handling ballots by inspectors; delivery of sealed records to chairman of county executive committee; restrictions on opening of sealed records; when sealed records to be destroyed.

The ballot of every voter shall be kept secret and inviolate. As the inspectors deposit the ballot, the name of the voter shall be checked off the official voting lists. One of the inspectors, as he hands out the ballot to the voter, shall initial the same on its back and, before depositing it in the ballot box, shall examine said ballot and see that it contains the identical initials aforesaid, and said ballot shall be numbered by one of the inspectors before being deposited in the ballot box and a corresponding number placed by the clerks on a record to be kept for that purpose by them, which records shall be enclosed in a separate envelope and sealed and directed to the chairman of the county executive committee, shall be delivered to him by the returning officer and shall be kept by such chairman and opened only as herein provided. In the event of a contest, such sealed record of only the counties, districts, precincts or wards concerned in the contest shall be open and, when opened, may be used in evidence so far as necessary. Such chairman shall not open such sealed records except on proper demand, as provided for in this chapter, or as permitted by law, or to make certified copies on such demand; and he shall not open them except in the presence of the trial committee. The seal of the ballots shall be removed or broken only as provided for in the provisions of law applicable to general elections. After the time allowed by law for filing contests, if no contest is filed, the chairman of the county executive committee shall destroy the sealed records. (Acts 1975, No. 1196, 2349, § 23.)

Color coding poll list. — A plan, calling for color coding of the official voting list to indicate in which party's primary those voting participated does not violate § 17-7-17. Haughton v. McCollum, 530 So. 2d 758 (Ala. 1988).

Collateral references. — 29 C.J.S., Elections, § 118(4).

§ 17-16-26. Watchers at polls.

A candidate who has qualified may have a single watcher in the polling place, to be appointed by him in writing over his own signature, and the appointment shall be presented to and filed with the inspectors. A returning officer shall not be a watcher. A watcher shall not act as or be an election officer and shall not render assistance to anyone in preparing a ballot. The watcher may remain in the voting place from the opening of the polls until the box is sealed and delivered to the returning officer and shall have the right to see and inspect the ballots as they are called off and to see the tally as it is being made and generally to watch the conduct of the election. Any watcher who shall violate any of the provisions of this chapter, any person who shall pretend to be a watcher when he has not been appointed, any person who shall impersonate a watcher and any watcher who shall on election day, either directly or indirectly, electioneer or campaign with any of the electors or suggest how he shall vote shall be guilty of a misdemeanor and, on conviction, shall be fined not less than $100.00 nor more than $1,000.00. (Acts 1975, No. 1196, p. 2349, § 24.)

Collateral references. — 29 C.J.S., Elections, §§ 200, 209, 216(2).

§ 17-16-27. Assistance to illiterate or disabled voters.

If a qualified elector is unable to read the English language or is so physically disabled that he cannot cast his ballot and requests assistance in preparing his ballot, the inspector shall swear him as to such disability, and thereupon said voter may have the assistance of any person he may select. Each elector, in preparing his ballot, shall prepare the same in the room or place where such election is being held, and not elsewhere. (Acts 1975, No. 1196, p. 2349, § 25.)

Editor's note. — The cases cited below were decided under former Tit. 17, § 359, 1940 Code, which contained provisions similar to those in this section.

Effect of federal Voting Rights Act of 1965. — It is true that former Tit. 17, § 359, 1940 Code, stated that no more than two people can be present during this voting procedure. However, certain state regulatory authority has been supplanted by the fifteenth amendment. The supremacy clause of the United States Constitution requires that this procedure of Alabama law give way to enforcement of the Voting Rights Act of 1965. United States v. Executive Comm. of Democratic Party, 254 F. Supp. 543 (N.D. Ala. 1966).

Presence of federal observer when voter receives assistance. United States v. Executive Comm. of Democratic Party, 254 F. Supp. 543 (N.D. Ala. 1966).

Voter may take memorandum of names into polling place. — There is nothing in the Alabama law which forbids a voter, whether literate or illiterate, to take a memorandum of names with him into the polling place to assist him in the marking of his ballot. Gilmore v. Greene County Democratic Party Executive Comm., 435 F.2d 487 (5th Cir. 1970).

Illiterate voter has right to direct inspectors to cast ballot as listed in memo-

randum. — Former Tit. 17, § 359, 1940 Code, was clearly susceptible of the construction that the illiterate voter has the affirmative right to direct the "inspectors" to cast his ballot in the same manner as listed on a sheet of paper which he hands them. Gilmore v. Greene County Democratic Party Executive Comm., 435 F.2d 487 (5th Cir. 1970).

Cited in Clark v. Marengo County, 469 F. Supp. 1150 (S.D. Ala. 1979).

Collateral references. — 29 C.J.S., Elections, § 208.

§ 17-16-28. Unauthorized assistance to voter in preparation of ballot.

Any person who assists a voter in preparing his ballot to be voted at a primary election, except as he is authorized to assist such voter under this chapter, shall be guilty of a misdemeanor, and on conviction shall be fined not less than $100.00 nor more than $1,000.00. (Acts 1919, No. 669, p. 969; Code 1923, § 3950; Code 1940, T. 17, § 404.)

Collateral references. — 29 C.J.S., Elections, §§ 208, 340.

§ 17-16-29. Elector receiving unauthorized assistance, divulging vote, etc.

Any elector who receives assistance other than that provided or authorized by this chapter, or who prepares his ballot in the presence of any person contrary to this chapter, or who divulges to another how he voted otherwise than as authorized by this chapter, shall be guilty of a misdemeanor. (Acts 1915, No. 78, p. 218; Code 1923, § 3952; Code 1940, T. 17, § 406.)

Collateral references. — 29 C.J.S., Elections, § 206.

§ 17-16-30. Returning officers.

The sheriff shall perform the duty of returning officer as in general elections, unless someone else has been named and designated as authorized by law. It shall be his duty or the duty of such returning officer as may be otherwise legally named and designated, as the case may be, to return and deliver to the chairman of the county executive committee of each of the political parties participating in the primary election, at the office of the judge of probate at the county seat, the ballot boxes and returns which have been delivered to him by the officers of said election, and such ballot boxes and returns shall not be allowed to leave his possession and must be returned by him to such chairman not later than 10:00 A.M. on Wednesday following said primary election. Each and all persons failing to perform any of the duties herein required shall be guilty of a misdemeanor. (Acts 1975, No. 1196, p. 2349, § 26.)

§ 17-16-31. Votes to be counted at close of election at each polling place.

At the close of the primary election at each polling place, and nowhere else, the inspectors and clerks shall proceed forthwith, without adjournment, in the manner provided by law in the case of general elections, to count the votes. (Acts 1975, No. 1196, p. 2349, § 27.)

Collateral references. — 29 C.J.S., Elections, § 119(3).

§ 17-16-32. Procedure for counting of ballots and returning results of election; posting of certificate of results at polling place.

(a) No ballot shall be counted until the polls are closed; and, before counting any ballot or examining the same, one of the official lists of voters for each party participating in the primary which was furnished by the probate judge and the numbered poll list signed by the voters participating in the primary election shall be securely sealed in separate envelopes and each of the inspectors shall write his name across every fold at which the envelope, if fastened, could be opened. After the counting of the votes is finished and certificates of the result have been prepared and signed, the inspectors shall seal up in a separate envelope all the ballots cast at such election and shall put such ballots so sealed into the proper party ballot box and shall also put into the ballot box one tally sheet and one certificate of the results, and the ballot box with those contents in it shall be securely locked and sealed. The inspectors shall also, in an envelope addressed to the chairman of the county executive committee or other governing body of each political party participating, seal up one certificate of the results and one tally sheet, and such envelope, with those contents in it, together with the proper party ballot box, shall thereupon be immediately delivered to the returning officer, who shall keep the same securely in his possession and, by 10:00 A.M. on Wednesday following the primary, shall carry and deliver the box and envelope separately to the proper chairmen of the county executive committees of the political parties participating in such primary, at the office of the probate judge of the county.

(b) The inspectors shall also post in a conspicuous place at the polling place, for public inspection there, a copy of the certificate of the result. (Acts 1975, No. 1196, p. 2349, § 28.)

Cross references. — As to provisions for the disposition of records and forms after elections, see § 17-4-230 et seq.

Former Title 17, section 363, 1940 Code, outlined procedure. — Former Tit. 17, § 363, 1940 Code, containing provisions virtually identical to those of this section and § 17-16-33 outlined the procedure to be used at the polls when the polls have closed and it is time to count the vote. United States v. Executive Comm. of Democratic Party, 254 F. Supp. 537 (S.D. Ala. 1966), decided under former Tit. 17, § 363, 1940 Code.

The function of the executive committee at this stage is purely ministerial, and this is not the appropriate forum to challenge the inclusion of any ballot or box, unless said ballot does not appear genuine and regular on its face. United States v. Executive Comm. of Democratic Party, 254 F. Supp. 537 (S.D. Ala. 1966), decided under former Tit. 17, § 363, 1940 Code.

The committee cannot exclude a box on

the basis of the bare allegation that it was unattended, especially when the evidence contradicts that contention. United States v. Executive Comm. of Democratic Party, 254 F.

Supp. 537 (S.D. Ala. 1966), decided under former Tit. 17, § 363, 1940 Code.

Collateral references. — 29 C.J.S., Elections, §§ 119(1)-119(15), 194.

§ 17-16-33. Disposition of ballot box after canvass of result; when ballot box may be opened by chairman of county executive committee.

After the result has been canvassed and declared by the county executive committee, the chairman of such county committee shall securely keep the ballot box, until it is known that there will be no contest but, in any event, not less than 30 days; and, if in that time no contest has been properly instituted, such chairman shall then destroy the contents of such box without examining the same. Such ballot box shall not be opened except in one or the other of the following events:

(1) In the event of a contest, where the opening of the box has been authorized under authority of the chairman of the executive committee trying the contest; and

(2) Where a box has been returned but no certificate of the result of the election has been sent the chairman outside of the box, the box may be opened by the chairman of the county committee, under the direction and in the presence of the committee, and the committee, for canvassing purposes, may obtain the result at any particular district, ward or precinct from the contents of the box, using the certificate of result contained therein, if any, or otherwise, so far as necessary in order to obtain it from the box; after which the papers shall be returned into the box, and the box shall be resealed by the chairman in the presence of the committee. (Acts 1975, No. 1196, p. 2349, § 29.)

Former Title 17, section 363, 1940 Code, outlined procedure. — Former Tit. 17, § 363, 1940 Code, containing provisions virtually identical to those of this section and § 17-16-32, outlined the procedure to be used at the polls when the polls have closed and it is time to count the vote. United States v. Executive Comm. of Democratic Party, 254 F. Supp. 537 (S.D. Ala. 1966), decided under former Tit. 17, § 363, 1940 Code.

The function of the executive committee at this stage is purely ministerial, and this is not the appropriate forum to challenge the inclusion of any ballot or box, unless said ballot does not appear genuine and regular on its face. United States v. Executive Comm. of Democratic Party, 254 F. Supp. 537 (S.D. Ala. 1966), decided under former Tit. 17, § 363, 1940 Code.

The committee cannot exclude a box on the basis of the bare allegation that it was unattended, especially when the evidence

contradicts that contention. United States v. Executive Comm. of Democratic Party, 254 F. Supp. 537 (S.D. Ala. 1966), decided under former Tit. 17, § 363, 1940 Code.

Tabulation by county committee as legal and binding as tabulation at polls. — When the certificate of result was not in its proper form and the committee tabulated pursuant to former Tit. 17, § 363, 1940 Code, it exercised a function of counting similar to that which should have been exercised at the polls had not difficulties been encountered, and the result thereby achieved was just as legal and binding as one obtained by tabulation at the polling place. United States v. Executive Comm. of Democratic Party, 254 F. Supp. 537 (S.D. Ala. 1966), decided under former Tit. 17, § 363, 1940 Code.

Collateral references. — 29 C.J.S., Elections, §§ 194, 234.

§ 17-16-34. Public proclamation of results of election; distribution of certificates of results.

The counting of the ballots having been completed, the results shall be publicly proclaimed. Separate certificates for each of the political parties entering said primary and the results of said election shall be drawn up by said inspectors and clerks at each and every election district or precinct, which shall contain all matters and things provided for in the law regulating general elections. Said certificates shall be signed in triplicate by each of the inspectors; one copy of the same shall be forthwith posted in a conspicuous place at such polling place, one copy shall be deposited with or mailed to the chairman of the county executive committee of each of the political parties in the primary, at such place as the county executive committee of the county shall designate at which to receive such returns, and another copy shall be mailed to the chairmen of the state executive committees of the political parties participating in said primary. (Acts 1975, No. 1196, p. 2349, § 30.)

Collateral references. — 29 C.J.S., Elections, § 117.

§ 17-16-35. Canvass, tabulation and declaration of results by county executive committees; certification and return of results to chairman of state executive committee; canvass, tabulation and declaration of results by state executive committee; results final; provision of results to Secretary of State.

The county executive committee of the party or parties participating in said primary election shall meet at the courthouse of its county, not later than noon on Wednesday next following said primary election, and receive said returns, canvass and tabulate the same, by precincts, and publicly declare the results thereof. The chairman of each county executive committee shall forthwith, and not later than noon on the Friday next following said primary election, certify and return to the chairman of the state executive committee a statement and tabulation, by precincts, of the result of said primary election and of the number of votes received by each candidate therein for office, except candidates for county office. Not later than noon on the Monday next following such primary election, the state executive committee, or such subcommittee thereof as may have been appointed by the chairman thereof for such purpose, shall meet at the State Capitol in Montgomery and receive said returns, canvass and tabulate the same by counties and publicly declare on that day the results thereof as to all candidates for office therein, except candidates for county office, which results shall be final. The state executive committee or such subcommittee as provided in this section shall also provide the Secretary of State with the primary election returns by precincts according to county on a form authorized by the Secretary of State on the Monday next following the primary election, county and municipal returns excepted. (Acts 1975, No. 1196,

p. 2349, § 28; Acts 1979, No. 79-800, p. 1463, § 2; Acts 1988, 1st Ex. Sess., No. 88-908, p. 482, § 2.)

This section and § 17-16-70 must be read in pari materia. Doing so eliminates uncertainty which could result from statements made by the chairman of the party's state executive committee, and establishes a time certain for the commencement of the 24 hours in which to contest a primary election. Graddick v. Baker, 496 So. 2d 688 (Ala. 1986).

Duties purely ministerial. — The executive committee in canvassing and tabulating the returns and declaring the result thereof, and the chairman in certifying the name of the nominee to the probate judge under the provisions of this section exercise a purely ministerial duty. These duties are in no sense judicial. Ex parte Pollard, 251 Ala. 309, 37 So. 2d 178 (1948), decided under former Tit. 17, § 366, 1940 Code, which contained provisions substantially similar to those in this section.

Cited in Godfrey v. Oswalt, 428 So. 2d 40 (Ala. 1983).

Collateral references. — 29 C.J.S., Elections, § 226.

§ 17-16-36. Candidate receiving majority vote nominee of party; second primary to be held if no candidate receives majority vote; persons eligible for second primary; procedure for conducting and determining results of second primary; provision of results to Secretary of State.

(a) At the respective meetings of the respective executive committees, said county executive committee shall, as to candidates in said primary election for office, except candidates for county office, publicly ascertain, determine and declare whether any candidate for office in said primary election has received a majority of the votes cast for the office, and, if so, declare said candidate the nominee of the party for the office for which he was a candidate and for which he received a majority of the votes cast for that office in said primary election.

(b) If no candidate receives a majority of all of the votes cast in such primary election for any one office or offices for the nomination to which there were more than two candidates, then there shall be held a second primary election on the third Tuesday next thereafter following said primary election, and the chairman of the state executive committee shall certify to the Secretary of State, immediately upon the completion of such canvass as aforesaid, the names of the two candidates of his party to receive the highest number of votes in the first primary election for such office or offices, except county officers, and who are to be voted for in the second primary election. The chairman of each county executive committee shall, immediately upon the completion of such canvass, certify to the probate judge of the county the names of the two candidates who received the highest number of votes in the first primary for nomination to any county office. The Secretary of State shall, within not more than six days from the date said certificate is received from the chairman of the state executive committee, certify to the probate judge of any county where a second primary election is to be held the name or names of the candidates certified to him as herein provided by the chairman of the state executive committee. The probate judge of each county in Alabama shall in the manner and form as required by this chapter and the general laws of Alabama, have prepared and printed all election supplies and all ballots to be voted in the second primary election, which ballots shall contain, under appropriate headings or titles of the offices to be filled, the names of the two candidates for each office so certified to him by the Secretary of State and the chairman of the county executive committee, as herein required, as well as such other matters as are required by this chapter and the general laws of Alabama, on ballots for the first primary election.

(c) At the second primary election, no person can be a candidate except the two persons who receive the highest number of votes for the offices for which they were candidates in the first primary election.

(d) The returns from the second primary election shall be made and the votes canvassed, tabulated and certified and the results declared in the same manner provided in this chapter for making, canvassing, tabulating, certifying and declaring the results of the first primary election. The county executive committee of the parties participating in said primary election shall meet at the courthouse of their respective counties not later than Wednesday next following the second primary election and receive said returns, canvass and tabulate the same by precinct and publicly declare the results thereof. The chairman of each county executive committee shall forthwith, and not later than noon on the Friday next following said primary election, certify and return to the chairman of the state executive committee a statement and tabulation by precincts of the results of the second primary election and of the number of votes received by each candidate for office therein voted for except candidates for county office. Not later than noon on the Monday next following the second primary election, the state executive committee, or such subcommittee thereof as may have been appointed by the chairman thereof for such purpose, shall meet at the State Capitol in Montgomery and receive said returns and canvass and tabulate the same by counties, and publicly declare on that day the result thereof as to all candidates voted for, except as to candidates for county office which results shall be final. At said respective meetings of said respective executive committees, said county executive committee shall, as to candidates for county office voted for in the second primary election, and said state executive committee shall, as to candidates for office in the second primary election voted for therein, except candidates for county office, publicly ascertain and determine the candidates receiving a majority of all of the votes cast in such second primary election for any one office, and the candidates so ascertained and determined to have received a majority of all of the votes cast in such second primary election for said office shall be declared the nominee of the party for such office by said respective county and state executive committees. Thereupon and immediately upon the completion of such canvass as aforesaid, the chairman thereof shall certify to and file with the probate judge of his county the names of those who have been nominated in the first or the second primary election or as otherwise authorized or provided by this chapter, as candidates of his party for county offices; and in like manner, and immediately upon the completion of such canvass, as aforesaid by the state executive committee, or subcommittee thereof, the chairman of the state executive committee shall certify to and file with the Secretary of State the names of those who have been nominated in the first or second primary election or as otherwise authorized or provided by this chapter as candidates of his party for office, except candidates for county office, and the names of the persons so certified shall be placed upon the official ballot of the general election to be held in November next thereafter as the candidates of the party for the offices for which they, respectively, have been so nominated.

(e) The state executive committee or such subcommittee as provided in this section shall also provide the Secretary of State with the second primary election returns by precincts according to county on a form authorized by the Secretary of State on the Monday next following the secondary primary, county and municipal returns excepted. (Acts 1975, No. 1196, p. 2349, § 32; Acts 1977, 1st Ex. Sess., No. 69, p. 1493, § 1; Acts 1979, No. 79-800, p. 1463, § 3; Acts 1988, 1st Ex. Sess., No. 88-908, p. 482, § 3.)

Duties purely ministerial. — The executive committee in canvassing and tabulating the returns and declaring the result thereof, and the chairman in certifying the name of the nominee to the probate judge under the provisions of this section exercise a purely ministerial duty. These duties are in no sense judicial. Ex parte Pollard, 251 Ala. 309, 37 So. 2d 178 (1948), decided under former Tit. 17, § 366, 1940 Code, which contained provisions substantially similar to those in this section.

Mandamus is the proper remedy to compel the committee chairman to perform the ministerial duty imposed by former Tit. 17, § 366, 1940 Code. Ex parte Pollard, 251 Ala. 309, 37 So. 2d 178 (1948), decided under former Tit. 17, § 366, 1940 Code, which contained provisions substantially similar to those in this section.

§ 17-16-37. Procedure when one candidate declines to enter second primary.

In the event either of the two candidates receiving the highest number of votes in the first primary election shall determine not to enter the second primary election provided for in this chapter, he shall, as soon as possible and not more than three days after holding of the first primary election, certify his declination to enter such second primary election to the chairman of the state executive committee of his party, if the office is an office other than a county office, or to the chairman of the county executive committee of his party if the office is a county office. Upon the receipt of such notification, the chairman of such committee shall declare the other candidate the nominee of the party for such office and certify his name as such nominee to the Secretary of State or the probate judge, as the case may require, and a second primary election for the nomination of a candidate for that particular office shall not be held. (Acts 1975, No. 1196, p. 2349, § 33; Acts 1977, 1st Ex. Sess., No. 69, p. 1493, § 1.)

Duties purely ministerial. — The executive committee in canvassing and tabulating the returns and declaring the result thereof, and the chairman in certifying the name of the nominee to the probate judge under the provisions of this section exercise a purely ministerial duty. These duties are in no sense judicial. Ex parte Pollard, 251 Ala. 309, 37 So. 2d 178 (1948), decided under former Tit. 17, § 366, 1940 Code, which contained provisions similar to those in this section.

Mandamus is the proper remedy to compel the committee chairman to perform the ministerial duty imposed by former Tit. 17, § 366, 1940 Code. Ex parte Pollard, 251 Ala. 309, 37 So. 2d 178 (1948), decided under former Tit. 17, § 366, 1940 Code, which contained provisions substantially similar to those in this section.

§ 17-16-38. Determination of "majority" of votes cast.

If a nominee for a single office is to be selected, with more than one candidate, then the majority of votes cast for said office in such election shall be ascertained by dividing the total votes cast for all candidates for said office by two, and any number of votes in excess of one half of such total votes cast for all candidates for such office shall be a majority within the meaning of this section. If nominees for two or more offices (constituting a group) are to be selected and there are more candidates for nomination than there are such offices, then the majority of votes cast for said office in such election shall be ascertained by dividing the total votes cast for all such candidates by the number of positions to be filled, and then dividing the result by two. Any number of votes in excess of the number ascertained by such last division shall be the majority herein provided for necessary for nomination. If, in ascertaining the result in this way, it appears that more candidates have obtained this majority than there are positions to be filled, then those having the highest vote, if beyond the majority just defined, shall be declared the nominees for the positions to be filled. (Acts 1975, No. 1196, p. 2349, § 34.)

Duties purely ministerial. — The executive committee in canvassing and tabulating the returns and declaring the result thereof, and the chairman in certifying the name of the nominee to the probate judge under the provisions of this section exercise a purely ministerial duty. These duties are in no sense judicial. Ex parte Pollard, 251 Ala. 309, 37 So. 2d 178 (1948), decided under former Tit. 17, § 366, 1940 Code, which contained provisions virtually identical to those in this section.

§ 17-16-39. Tie votes.

If, in any primary election held under the provisions of this chapter, there shall be a tie vote cast, then such tie shall be decided by the chairman of the state executive committee, if the office is an office other than a county office, and by the chairman of the county executive committee if the office is a county office. (Acts 1975, No. 1196, p. 2349, § 35.)

Collateral references. — 29 C.J.S., Elections, § 119(4).

§ 17-16-40. Certification of nominees by Secretary of State to probate judge after second primary.

The Secretary of State shall, within 45 days after the second primary election, certify to the probate judge of each county in the state a separate list of nominees of each party for office and for each candidate who has requested to be an independent candidate and has filed a written petition in accordance with Section 17-7-1(a) (3), except nominees for county offices, to be voted for by the voters of such county. (Acts 1975, No. 1196, p. 2349, § 36; Acts 1995, No. 95-786, § 1.)

The 1995 amendment, effective August 9, 1995, substituted "45 days" for "six days," and inserted the language beginning "and for each candidate" and ending "Section 17-7-1 (a)(3)."

§ 17-16-41. Filling of vacancies in nominations.

The state executive committee, in cases where the office to be filled is not a county office, and the county executive committee, in cases where the office to be filled is a county office, but subject to the approval of and in accordance with the method prescribed by the state executive committee, where a vacancy may occur in any nomination, either by death, resignation, revocation or otherwise, or in case of any special election, shall have the power and authority to fill such vacancy, either by action of the committee itself or by such other method as such committee may see fit to pursue. (Acts 1975, No. 1196, p. 2349, § 37.)

Construction of phrase "or otherwise." — The words, "or otherwise" in law when used as a general phrase following an enumeration of particulars are commonly interpreted in a restricted sense as referring to such other matters as are kindred to the classes before mentioned, receiving ejusdem generis interpretation. Foster v. Dickinson, 293 Ala. 298, 302 So. 2d 111 (1974), decided under former Tit. 17, § 371, 1940 Code.

Under the doctrine ejusdem generis the phrase "or otherwise" as used in this section cannot be construed to include the failure to nominate in the primary election when it is evident there is no legal impediment present to preclude the party from offering a candidate in the primary. Foster v. Dickinson, 293 Ala. 298, 302 So. 2d 111 (1974), decided under former Tit. 17, § 371, 1940 Code.

Removal of party's candidate for failure to timely file a statement naming his principal campaign committee created a vacancy, and the party's executive committee could exercise its prerogative to fill the vacancy by such a method as the committee saw fit to pursue. Megginson v. Turner, 565 So. 2d 247 (Ala. 1990), overruled on other grounds, 592 So. 2d 546 (Ala. 1991).

Cited in Harris v. Weatherford, 459 So. 2d 876 (Ala. 1984).

Collateral references. — 29 C.J.S., Elections, §§ 94, 130, 137.

§ 17-16-42. State and other conventions.

The state executive committee or other governing body of any political party may provide for state conventions or conventions of other subdivisions and may provide for the election of delegates to such convention or other party officers at the general primary herein provided for. (Acts 1975, No. 1196, p. 2349, § 38.)

Collateral references. — 29 C.J.S., Elections, §§ 84, 87, 88, 97-102.

§ 17-16-43. Mass meetings, beat meetings, etc., for purpose of nominating candidates or selecting delegates to conventions — Time, place and notice of holding; right of public to attend meetings.

(a) When any political party shall desire to hold any mass meeting, beat meeting or other meeting of the voters of such party for the purpose of nominating any candidate or candidates for public office, to be voted for in a general election in Alabama, or for the purpose of selecting delegates or other representatives to any convention which may select such candidates for public office, or when any such party shall desire to hold such mass meeting, beat meeting or other meeting of the voters of such party for the purpose of selecting committeemen, representatives or other party officers of such party, all of such meetings shall be held at the times and places set out in this section, and at no other times or places.

(b) All such meetings shall be held at least 60 days before the first primary election. The general public is privileged to attend such meetings, but not to participate. No less than five days prior to the date upon which any such mass meeting, beat meeting or other meeting is to be held, notice of such meeting, including the time and place of such meeting, shall be filed with the probate judge of the county in which any such meeting is to be held and shall be published in a newspaper of general circulation in said county at the expense of the political party holding such meeting. The probate judge shall immediately forward to the Secretary of State a certified copy of all notices filed under this section. (Acts 1975, No. 1196, p. 2349, §§ 39, 40; Acts 1977, 1st Ex. Sess., No. 69, p. 1493, § 1; Acts 1982, No. 82-611, p. 1109, § 2.)

Section mandatory. — Former Tit. 17, §§ 413 and 414, 1940 Code, fixing the time for holding a mass meeting for nominating candidates for public office, which sections contained provisions virtually identical to those contained in this section, were "mandatory." Kinney v. House, 243 Ala. 393, 10 So. 2d 167 (1942).

Former Tit. 17, § 413, 1940 Code, fixed the time for holding mass meetings and was mandatory. Herndon v. Lee, 281 Ala. 61, 199 So. 2d 74 (1967).

Candidates named at adjourned committee meeting. — Candidates for county office who were not nominated at a mass meeting at time for holding such meeting authorized by former Tit. 17, §§ 413 and 414, 1940 Code, but were named by a committee at an adjourned meeting 30 days later were not nominated in accordance with statute and were not entitled to have names placed on the ballot. Kinney v. House, 243 Ala. 393, 10 So. 2d 167 (1942), decided under former Tit. 17, § 413, 1940 Code.

Collateral references. — 29 C.J.S., Elections, §§ 97, 100.

§ 17-16-44. Mass meetings, beat meetings, etc., for purpose of nominating candidates or selecting delegates to conventions — Holding, participating in, etc., illegal meetings; other violations of chapter relative to meetings.

Any person or persons who shall hold, attend or participate in the holding of any meeting for the purpose of nominating a candidate or candidates for public office, to be voted for at any general election in Alabama, or for the purpose of electing delegates or other representatives to any convention which may select such candidates for public office, at any time or place other than as provided for in any provision of this chapter relating to mass meetings or beat meetings, or who shall otherwise violate the laws of this state regulating mass meetings or beat meetings, shall be guilty of a misdemeanor. (Acts 1975, No. 1196, p. 2349, § 42.)

§ 17-16-45. Mass meetings, beat meetings, etc., for purpose of nominating candidates or selecting delegates to conventions — Applicability of Sections 17-16-43 and 17-16-44.

Sections 17-16-43 and 17-16-44 shall not apply where a special election is called for the election of a public officer for which said party has no candidate or where, by death, resignation or otherwise, a vacancy has occurred in any nomination made by such party. Sections 17-16-43 and 17-16-44 shall not apply to municipal elections. (Acts 1975, No. 1196, p. 2349, § 41.)

§ 17-16-46. Certificate of nomination by convention, mass meeting, etc.

The certificate of nomination by any caucus, convention, mass meeting or other assembly of any political party or faction in this state not conducting a primary election at the expense of the state shall be filed on or before 5:00 P.M. of the day required for political parties holding primaries to certify their nominees with the probate judge, in the case of nominations for county office, and with the Secretary of State in the case of all other offices. Each such certificate must have attached thereto a separate sworn statement from the nominee, signed by him, stating that he accepts the nomination. (Acts 1975, No. 1196, p. 2349, § 43.)

§ 17-16-47. Intoxication at polling place.

Any person found drunk or intoxicated about any polling place during any primary election shall be deemed guilty of a misdemeanor and, upon conviction thereof, shall be fined not less than $10.00 nor more than $100.00, or sentenced to hard labor for not less than five nor more than 10 days. (Code 1907, § 6818; Code 1923, § 3941; Code 1940, T. 17, § 395.)

§ 17-16-48. False or fraudulent returns.

Any person who makes a false or fraudulent return of the result of any primary election, or who falsely or fraudulently changes the votes, ballots, figures or results of any election shall be deemed guilty of a misdemeanor, and on conviction thereof shall be fined not less than $50.00 and not more than $1,000.00, and may be sentenced to hard labor for a term not exceeding 12 months. (Code 1907, § 6820; Code 1923, § 3943; Code 1940, T. 17, § 397.)

Collateral references. — 29 C.J.S., Elections, § 327.

§ 17-16-49. Officers not to compare poll list with ballot.

Any manager, clerk, returning officer, watcher or chairman of an executive committee who compares the number on the poll list with the number of the ballot of any voter for the purpose of ascertaining how any voter voted, except in case of contest, shall be guilty of a misdemeanor, and, on conviction, shall be fined not less than $50.00. (Code 1907, § 6821; Code 1923, § 3944; Code 1940, T. 17, § 398.)

§ 17-16-50. Opening poll list.

Any person who opens any envelope containing the poll list of any voting place, except in case of a contest, shall be guilty of a misdemeanor, and, upon conviction, shall be fined not less than $50.00. (Code 1907, § 6822; Code 1923, § 3945; Code 1940, T. 17, § 399.)

§ 17-16-51. Voting more than once.

Any voter who shall vote more than once, or attempt to vote more than once, in any primary election held in this state, shall, on conviction be punished in the same manner as provided for voting or attempting to vote more than once in a general election. (Acts 1927, No. 130, p. 89; Code 1940, T. 17, § 410.)

Collateral references. — 29 C.J.S., Elections, § 341.

§ 17-16-52. Changing or altering returns of primary elections.

Any person who shall change or in any wise alter the returns of any primary election, or remove the copy of the returns posted at any polling place before the result of the election is announced by the committee or governing authority, shall be punished in the same form and manner as provided by the general law for the punishment of any person who changes or in any wise alters the returns of the regular state elections. (Code 1907, § 6824; Code 1923, § 3947; Code 1940, T. 17, § 401.)

Collateral references. — 29 C.J.S., Elections, § 233.

§ 17-16-53. Failure to place candidate's name, etc., on ballot.

Any officer of the state or of any county or municipality whose duty it is by law to prepare and have printed ballots for any election authorized by law to be held, and any executive officer or member of a political party charged with the duty of preparing and having printed ballots for any primary election authorized by the rules and regulations of said political party to be held, who shall wilfully or negligently fail to have printed on said ballots, as required by law or the rules and regulations of the political party holding the election, the names of all persons entitled to be printed thereon and all issues entitled to be printed thereon and entitled to be submitted to a vote, shall be guilty of a misdemeanor and, on conviction, shall be fined not more than $1,000.00, and may be sentenced to hard labor for the county for not more than one year. (Code 1907, § 6825; Code 1923, § 3948; Code 1940, T. 17, § 402.)

Collateral references. — 29 C.J.S., Elections, § 156.

§ 17-16-54. Failure of primary election officers to serve.

Any person appointed to serve as an election officer at any primary election who fails to serve as such officer at such primary election, except on account of illness, shall be guilty of a misdemeanor. (Acts 1919, No. 669, p. 969; Code 1923, § 3949; Code 1940, T. 17, § 403.)

Collateral references. — 29 C.J.S., Elections, § 403.

§ 17-16-55. Inspector marking ballot, electioneering with voter or divulging how elector voted.

Any person acting as an inspector at a primary election who shall mark the ballot of a voter contrary to the voter's direction or request, or who shall electioneer or attempt to electioneer with a voter or attempt to influence his vote by suggestion or otherwise, or who shall afterwards divulge how such elector voted in any race on the ballot, shall be guilty of a misdemeanor, and on conviction shall be fined not less than $100.00 nor more than $1,000.00. (Acts 1919, No. 669, p. 969; Code 1923, § 3951; Code 1940, T. 17, § 405.)

§ 17-16-56. Additional duties of sheriff, chief of police, etc.

The sheriff of each county on the day of such primary election shall be present in person or by deputy at each election precinct or voting district where such elections are held, and shall preserve good order. All duties imposed and powers conferred upon the sheriff in said county and district elections by this section are imposed and conferred on the marshal or chief of police in all municipal primary elections. Not more than one officer shall be allowed, however, to enter into the polling place. (Acts 1915, No. 78, p. 218; Code 1923, § 3953; Code 1940, T. 17, § 407.)

§ 17-16-57. Penalty for violation of chapter.

Any person who violates any of the provisions of this chapter for which a penalty is not otherwise provided shall be guilty of a misdemeanor and, upon conviction, shall be punished by a fine of not less than $50.00 and not more than $500.00, and may also be imprisoned in the county jail or sentenced to hard labor for the county for not more than six months, at the discretion of the court. (Acts 1931, No. 56, p. 73; Code 1940, T. 17, § 411.)

ARTICLE 2.

CONTEST OF ELECTIONS.

Cross references. — As to contesting elections generally, see § 17-15-1 et seq.

Right to contest election is not a common-law right. Godfrey v. Oswalt, 428 So. 2d 40 (Ala. 1983).

Contest provisions to be strictly construed. — Election contests exist only by virtue of statutory enactment and such statutes are to be strictly construed. Godfrey v. Oswalt, 428 So. 2d 40 (Ala. 1983).

Powers of political party committees. — This article provides for the contests of primary elections and confers on the committees of political parties powers such as those conferred on a court of special or limited jurisdiction. Crespi v. Carl, 494 So. 2d 30 (Ala. 1986).

§ 17-16-70. Time for contesting generally; hearing.

All nominations made by primary election may be contested within 24 hours after the results of the primary election have been declared, weekends excluded, under the same conditions and on the same grounds as provided in the laws of Alabama for general elections of state and county officers and as provided in this chapter. Such contest shall be heard and tried by the county executive committee as to candidates for county offices and by the state committee as to candidates for all other offices; and wherever there is no county executive committee consisting of enough members to obtain a quorum, then by the state executive committee. (Acts 1931, No. 56, p. 73; Code 1940, T. 17, § 373; Acts 1977, 1st Ex. Sess., No. 69, p. 1493, §§ 3, 4; Acts 1979, No. 79-800, p. 1463, § 4.)

Editor's note. — Many of the cases cited below were decided under former Tit. 17, § 373, 1940 Code, which contained provisions identical to those in this section.

Section 17-16-35 and this section must be read in pari materia. Doing so eliminates uncertainty which could result from statements made by the chairman of the party's state executive committee, and establishes a time certain for the commencement of the 24 hours in which to contest a primary election. Graddick v. Baker, 496 So. 2d 688 (Ala. 1986).

Powers of political party committees. — Alabama statutes commit to the state executive committees of the political parties the responsibility and authority to conduct primary election contests. In discharging that responsibility the party committee exercises powers such as those conferred on a court of special and limited jurisdiction. Curry v. Baker, 802 F.2d 1302 (11th Cir. 1986), cert. dismissed, 479 U.S. 1023, 107 S. Ct. 1262, 93 L. Ed. 2d 819 (1987).

Contests of primary elections have been committed to party tribunals by the legislature and the courts scrupulously avoid interfering with action of such tribunals. Ex parte State ex rel. Bragg, 240 Ala. 80, 197 So. 32 (1940).

And county executive committee has exclusive jurisdiction. — Where statement of ground of contest of primary election was sufficient to invoke jurisdiction of the county democratic executive committee to hear the contest, the committee acquired exclusive jurisdiction

to hear the contest and the circuit court was without power to invade or defeat such jurisdiction. Ex parte State ex rel. Bragg, 240 Ala. 80, 197 So. 32 (1940).

When a party committee's jurisdiction to hear a contest of a primary election has been invoked, the committee acquires exclusive jurisdiction to hear the contest, and the circuit court is without power to invade or defeat such jurisdiction. Ex parte Skidmore, 277 Ala. 221, 168 So. 2d 483 (1964).

State committee has right to hear contests regarding candidates for party office. — When this section confers on the state committee the right to hear and determine contests regarding candidates in primary elections for all offices voted for in that election, except candidates for county offices, it necessarily includes candidates for the party office of membership on the state committee voted for in the primary election, pursuant to the provisions of the resolution of the state committee calling the primary and specifying the offices to be filled. Bridges v. McCorvey, 254 Ala. 677, 49 So. 2d 546 (1950), cited in Prather v. Ray, 258 Ala. 106, 61 So. 2d 46 (1952).

This section discloses and was intended to make no distinction between contests of persons elected in a primary election as nominees of the party to run for office, and those named in the same primary to fill other party offices, such as that of executive committeemen. Bridges v. McCorvey, 254 Ala. 677, 49 So. 2d 546 (1950).

§ 17-16-71. Grounds.

The contests of nomination by a party for office, other than a county office, may be instituted by any qualified elector of the state, or of the political subdivision, as the case may be, who belongs to that party and who legally participated in such primary election, upon the following grounds, which may be used separately, or else be joined in the same contest:

(1) Malconduct, fraud or corruption on the part of any inspector, clerk, marker, returning officer, board of supervision or canvassers or other persons;

(2) When a person whose nomination is contested was not eligible to the office sought at the time of the declaration of nomination;

(3) On account of illegal votes given;

(4) On account of the rejection of legal votes;

(5) Offers to bribe, bribery, intimidation or other malconduct or misconduct calculated to prevent a fair, free and full exercise of the elective franchise;

(6) Miscalculation, mistake or misconduct in counting, tallying, certifying or canvassing which of itself alone or in conjunction with the giving of illegal votes or the rejection of legal votes, or any other ground, would, when everything is corrected, reduce the number of legal votes cast for the declared nominee down to or below those of some other candidate in that race. (Acts 1931, No. 56, p. 73; Code 1940, T. 17, § 374.)

Section applies to contest of nomination of candidate for legislature. — This section prescribes the grounds of contest of the nomination for an office other than a county office, and therefore it must be followed in the contest of the nomination of a candidate for the legislature. Ex parte Brassell, 261 Ala. 265, 73 So. 2d 907 (1954), decided under former Tit. 17, § 374, 1940 Code, which contained provisions identical to those in this section.

There is no statutory right of appeal from subcommittee of party's executive committee to the supreme court, regarding the subcommittee's finding as to the winner of a runoff election for the party nomination. Graddick v. Baker, 495 So. 2d 1367 (Ala. 1986).

Cited in Graddick v. Baker, 496 So. 2d 688 (Ala. 1986).

Collateral references. — 29 C.J.S., Elections, §§ 120-129.

§ 17-16-72. Effect of contest on declared nomination.

None of the grounds of contest enumerated in Section 17-16-71 shall serve to annul or set aside any declared nomination, unless such ground alone or in conjunction with other of such grounds alleged shall serve to show to the reasonable satisfaction of the committee trying the contest that the person who was declared nominated and whose nomination is contested did not receive at such primary the number of legal votes necessary under this chapter to nominate him. But upon such contest, the committee shall have power to declare who was legally nominated at such primary for such office. (Acts 1931, No. 56, p. 73; Code 1940, T. 17, § 375.)

Cited in Curry v. Baker, 802 F.2d 1302 (11th Cir. 1986).

§ 17-16-73. Certification of candidate in case of contest.

When a contest of a nomination is instituted or where a special primary to nominate is held, as provided for in this chapter, the declared nominee for such office shall not be certified until after termination of the contest filed in the time herein prescribed. (Acts 1931, No. 56, p. 73; Code 1940, T. 17, § 368.)

Section to be strictly construed. — Election contests exist only by virtue of statutory enactment and such statutes are to be strictly construed. Godfrey v. Oswalt, 428 So. 2d 40 (Ala. 1983).

Right to contest election is not a common-law right. Godfrey v. Oswalt, 428 So. 2d 40 (Ala. 1983).

Certification is only rendered ineffective during the initial contest before the

county committee and is not suspended or invalidated by any subsequent appeals to the state committee. Godfrey v. Oswalt, 428 So. 2d 40 (Ala. 1983).

This section cannot be held to mean that certification of a candidate is ineffective not only during the original contest heard by the county committee, but also during the appeal of the state committee. Such an approach would allow a contesting party to keep an individual off the general election ballot simply by filing a contest, presenting evidence at the county committee level and then pursuing an appeal until it became too late to get the contestee's name on the ballot. The clear intent of the legislature in § 17-16-86, is to get the nominee on the ballots for the general election. Godfrey v. Oswalt, 428 So. 2d 40 (Ala. 1983).

Inapplicable to appeal past county committee level. — This section clearly covers the "institution" of a contest at the county committee level. It arguably could be applied to a subsequent appeal; however, a strict construction approach mandates rejected of such an expansive reading of the statute. Godfrey v. Oswalt, 428 So. 2d 40 (Ala. 1983).

Collateral references. — 29 C.J.S., Elections, §§ 135-145.

§ 17-16-74. Summoning witnesses and production of documents.

In the hearing of any contest before any committee or subcommittee under the provisions of this article, such committee, through its chairman, or through such other authority as may be designated, shall have authority to summon witnesses to appear before it, or before any subcommittee appointed by it, in the hearing of any contest pending before such committee, and can require any witnesses by a subpoena duces tecum to produce any books, papers, poll lists, tally sheets, ballots, certificates or other documents which it may consider necessary to a rightful determination of the case. (Acts 1931, No. 56, p. 73; Code 1940, T. 17, § 392.)

Cited in Graddick v. Baker, 496 So. 2d 688 (Ala. 1986).

Collateral references. — 29 C.J.S., Elections, § 300.

§ 17-16-75. Witnesses — Testifying as to vote.

Any person examined as a witness on a contest of a nomination may be required to answer as to whether he voted at the primary and touching his qualification to vote thereat and to answer for whom he voted in the race concerned in the contest. If he swears falsely upon such contest to any material matter, he may be prosecuted for any perjury thereby committed, as defined by Section 13A-10-100; but if on such contest he makes full and true answers, any of which may incriminate or tend to incriminate him, he shall not be prosecuted in any court, either for voting in the primary or for any offense committed by him and disclosed by his answers. (Acts 1931, No. 56, p. 73; Code 1940, T. 17, § 376.)

Cross references. — For this section being commented on by new Rule 506, Alabama Rules of Evidence, effective January 1, 1996, see the Advisory Committee's Notes to new Rule 506 in the 1995 Cumulative Supplement to Volume 23, Code of Alabama.

Cited in Curry v. Baker, 802 F.2d 1302 (11th Cir. 1986).

Collateral references. — 29 C.J.S., Elections, § 127.

§ 17-16-76. Witnesses — Oaths; deposits by persons summoning witnesses; witness fees and mileage allowances.

The chairman of any committee or subcommittee before which may be pending any contest as herein provided shall have authority to administer oaths to witnesses in such contests and to summon persons and officers to be and appear before such committee or subcommittee. The person who desires the summoning of any witnesses, at the time he makes request of the chairman of such committee to summon any witness, shall deposit with the chairman of such committee, in cash, sufficient money to pay the cost of summoning any such witness and also to pay such witness the sum of $1.00 per day while attending upon such committee and the sum of $.03 per mile each way in coming and returning from attendance upon such committee. All witnesses summoned to testify in any contest pending before any committee shall be paid at the rate of $1.00 per day and $.03 per mile. Any party to the contest may file with the chairman an instrument in writing, signed by any such desired witness, waiving his right to claim such per diem and mileage, in which event the chairman shall not require a deposit for the payment of such witness fees, but only for the expense of summoning him. (Acts 1931, No. 56, p. 73; Code 1940, T. 17, § 390.)

Cited in Graddick v. Baker, 496 So. 2d 688 (Ala. 1986).

Collateral references. — 29 C.J.S., Elections, § 127.

§ 17-16-77. Registration lists to be furnished upon request.

It shall be the duty of the probate judge of any county, upon the application of either party to any contest, his agent or attorney, to deliver to the party, his agent or attorney a certified copy of the registration list of his county or for any election district, ward or precinct therein, upon payment of his fees for certifying and copying the same at the rate of $.15 per 100 words written by him in making such copy. Such copies, duly certified, shall be prima facie evidence of the facts stated therein; namely, copies of the registration lists that the persons named therein were duly registered. Any chairman of any committee or other authority or person in whose possession, control or custody there is any list of persons voting at the primary election or any other paper lawfully pertaining to the primary election, shall furnish a copy thereof for any state, county, district, ward or precinct, duly certified by him, whenever required in writing by either party to a contest or his agent or attorney, upon the applicant's paying in advance the reasonable cost of preparing such copy, and such duly certified copies shall be prima facie evidence of the truth of the matter indicated or recited therein. (Acts 1931, No. 56, p. 73; Code 1940, T. 17, § 377.)

§ 17-16-78. Statement by elector contesting election.

(a) Any elector of a party desiring to contest the nomination by his party of any candidate declared the nominee for any office shall make a statement in writing setting forth specifically:

(1) The name of the party contesting and that he was a qualified elector when the primary was held and he participated therein;

(2) The nomination which said election was held to fill;

(3) The time of holding the election;

(4) The name of the person declared nominated; and

(5) The particular grounds on which the nomination is contested.

(b) The contest is instituted by filing this statement and giving security as provided in this article, which said statement must be certified by the affidavit of such contesting party to the effect that he believes the same to be true.

(c) If the reception of illegal votes is alleged as a ground for contest, it is a sufficient statement of said ground to allege that illegal votes were given to the person whose nomination is contested, which, if taken from him will, of themselves alone or in conjunction with other alleged grounds of contest, if any, reduce the number of legal votes given to him down to or below the number of legal votes given to some other candidate for the same nomination; and if the rejection of legal votes is alleged as a ground, it is a sufficient statement of the ground to allege the legal votes were offered and rejected which, if cast and counted, would of themselves alone or in conjunction with other alleged grounds, if any, increase the number of legal votes cast for such candidate to a number equal to or greater than the number to which the contestee was legally entitled. (Acts 1931, No. 56, p. 73; Code 1940, T. 17, § 378.)

Editor's note. — The cases cited below were decided under former Tit. 17, § 378, 1940 Code, which contained provisions virtually identical to those in this section.

No denial of due process. — This section is not void on ground that it constitutes denial of "due process of law" for failure to require contestant to give contestee names of alleged illegal votes received and counted for contestee or names of alleged legal votes rejected, in view of § 17-16-79, which provides for furnishing to the parties all data essential to due process of law. Ex parte State ex rel. Bragg, 240 Ala. 80, 197 So. 32 (1940).

Whether averments sufficient to invoke jurisdiction of executive committee. — Statement instituting contest of primary election which literally followed this section was sufficient to invoke jurisdiction of the county democratic executive committee to hear and determine the contest. Ex parte State ex rel. Bragg, 240 Ala. 80, 197 So. 32 (1940).

In determining, on collateral attack, whether petition seeking to contest nomination of candidate contains sufficient averments to invoke jurisdiction of county executive committee, a construction must be adopted that will support the committee's order, guarding against supplying thereby of omitted essentials. Boyd v. Garrison, 246 Ala. 122, 19 So. 2d 385 (1944).

On collateral attack, in determining sufficiency of petition contesting nomination of candidate, if allegations of petition may be reasonably construed to mean to allege the necessary matter, though they may also be otherwise construed, the contest will not be declared void on that account for want of jurisdiction. Boyd v. Garrison, 246 Ala. 122, 19 So. 2d 385 (1944).

Sufficiency of other grounds not for court. — When statement of grounds of contest of election was sufficient to invoke jurisdiction of the county democratic executive committee, sufficiency of other grounds of contest alleged in the language of the statute was for the committee and not the court. Ex parte State ex rel. Bragg, 240 Ala. 80, 197 So. 32 (1940).

And grounds may be made more specific by amendment. — Although new grounds of contest of election of a candidate at primary election may not be added after the time for contest has expired, amendments making more specific, grounds expressed in too general terms in the statement of contest, may be allowed. Ex parte State ex rel. Bragg, 240 Ala. 80, 197 So. 32 (1940).

Records of committee must show jurisdiction. — Under statute conferring powers on county and state party committees such as those conferred on a court of special and limited jurisdiction, to support committees' proceedings, their records must affirmatively show jurisdiction. Boyd v. Garrison, 246 Ala. 122, 19 So. 2d 385 (1944).

The statute does not change rule of

pleading so as to make use of certain words necessary to describe a status otherwise clearly shown. Boyd v. Garrison, 246 Ala. 122, 19 So. 2d 385 (1944).

The Declaratory Judgment Act (§ 6-6-220 et seq.) is available insofar as a petition seeks to have a declaration regarding validity and legal effect of proceedings contesting right to certificate of nomination in primary. Boyd v. Garrison, 246 Ala. 122, 19 So. 2d 385 (1944).

Collateral references. — 29 C.J.S., Elections, § 120.

§ 17-16-79. Contestant to notify contestee of votes sought to be proved illegal.

No testimony shall be received of any illegal votes or of the rejection of any legal votes in any contest commenced under the provisions of this article unless the party complaining thereof has given to the adverse party notice in writing of the number of illegal votes and by whom given, for whom given and at what precinct or voting place cast, or the number of legal votes rejected, by whom offered and at what precinct or voting place they were not allowed to be cast, which he expects to prove on the trial. Such notice shall be served personally or left at the residence or usual place of business of the adverse party at least five days before the taking of the testimony in reference to such votes. (Acts 1931, No. 56, p. 73; Code 1940, T. 17, § 379.)

Collateral references. — 29 C.J.S., Elections, §§ 120, 325, 341.

§ 17-16-80. Contest of nomination to county office — Time and manner of commencement.

Any contest of a nomination to any county office must be commenced within five days after the result has been canvassed and the nomination declared by the county executive committee of the party holding the primary, by filing a statement of contest with the chairman of such county committee, in the same manner and form as is provided in this article for contest of other nominations, and depositing at the same time with such chairman the sum of $50.00 in cash to be used by the said county executive committee in paying the expenses of such contest from time to time as such expenses may be authorized or directed by said county executive committee. The person whose nomination is contested under this section shall have five days after notice of the filing of the contest within which to file with such chairman his objections and his answers to such contest. (Acts 1931, No. 56, p. 73; Code 1940, T. 17, § 380.)

Cross references. — See notes to §§ 17-16-78 and 17-16-83.

History of section. — See Ex parte Brassell, 261 Ala. 265, 73 So. 2d 907 (1954), decided under former Tit. 17, § 380, 1940 Code, which contained provisions virtually identical to those in this section.

§ 17-16-81. Contest of nomination to county office — Duty of chairman of county executive committee in case of contest.

The chairman of the county executive committee, upon the filing with him of any contest as provided in this article, shall, within five days, call said committee together at the county seat at a time not less than 10 days nor more than 20 days after the filing of such contest to hear and determine the same. (Acts 1931, No. 56, p. 73; Code 1940, T. 17, § 381.)

Recourse where committee or chairman disobeys statutory mandate. — If the committee or the chairman fail or refuse to follow the mandates of the statutes, the only recourse of either the contestant or the contestee is to the courts. In such cases, the courts are open. Godfrey v. Oswalt, 428 So. 2d 40 (Ala. 1983).

§ 17-16-82. Contest of nomination to county office — Appeals from decisions of county executive committee.

(a) Either party to a contest under this article shall have the right of an appeal to the state executive committee from the final decision of the county executive committee upon the same. Notice of such appeal shall be filed with the chairman of the state executive committee within 10 days after determination of such contest by the county executive committee. At the time of filing with the chairman of the state executive committee his notice of appeal, such appellant shall deposit with the chairman of the state executive committee the sum of $100.00 to cover such cost and expenses as may be incurred by the state executive committee to hear and determine said appeal. Upon the filing of any such appeal, the chairman of the county executive committee from whose decision the appeal is taken shall certify to the chairman of the state executive committee, forthwith upon receiving notice of such appeal, a transcript showing a complete record of the proceedings before the county executive committee in such contests, and also a statement of the substance of the testimony of each witness taken on the trial of the contest before the county committee. Such statement may be offered in evidence upon the hearing of the appeal by either party to the appeal.

(b) The chairman of the state executive committee shall call said committee to meet at a time not less than 10 days nor more than 20 days from the time of the filing of any such appeal for the purpose of hearing and determining the same. Upon a final determination of said appeal, the chairman of the state executive committee shall issue to the county executive committee from which the appeal was taken the order of judgment of such state executive committee upon the appeal, and said county executive committee shall immediately act thereon in accordance with the terms of such order of judgment. Upon the failure or refusal of such county executive committee to comply with the terms of such order or judgment within the time named in such order or judgment, such state executive committee, if it is then in session, otherwise, the chairman of such state executive committee, is hereby vested with full and complete authority to take such measures or adopt such steps as it may deem necessary to carry out such order or judgment, and is invested with all the powers of such county executive committee or its chairman insofar as such powers may be necessary or convenient in carrying out such order or judgment.

(c) The chairman of the state executive committee may appoint a subcommittee of not less than three to hear and decide any contest, and the subcommittee so appointed shall, if so authorized by the chairman of the state executive committee, have all of the power and authority given to or possessed by the state executive committee to hear such contest. The subcommittee may be appointed to hear evidence and report their recommendations to the full state executive committee. (Acts 1931, No. 56, p. 73; Code 1940, T. 17, §§ 382, 383.)

Collateral references. — 29 C.J.S., Elections, § 128.

§ 17-16-83. Manner of commencing contest of nomination to office other than county office.

Any qualified elector of a party participating in any primary election held under the provisions of this chapter may, if he participated in the primary, contest a nomination declared by his party to any office, other than a county office, by filing with the chairman of the state executive committee his statement of contest and grounds thereof, as required by this article, for contest before a committee, verified and with averments the same as therein provided and by giving security as provided in this article. The person whose nomination is contested shall at once be notified by such chairman in writing of such fact, and such contestee shall have 10 days after the receipt of such notice of such contest within which to file with the chairman of the state executive committee his objections and answers to the statement of contest. (Acts 1931, No. 56, p. 73; Code 1940, T. 17, § 384.)

Editor's note. — The cases cited below were decided under former Tit. 17, § 384, 1940 Code, which contained provisions virtually identical to those in this section.

History of section. — See Ex parte Brassell, 261 Ala. 265, 73 So. 2d 907 (1954).

Giving security is jurisdictional requirement. — This section requires a sufficient statement of the contest to be supported "by giving security as provided in this article." That clause must be given such interpretation as is consistent with its clearly expressed requirements. In the first place, "security" of some sort is expressly required. It does not take interpretation to reach that conclusion. There is no provision of law for the contest of an election either of a general or primary election without security for costs being given as a jurisdictional requirement. So there must be "security." It is further specified as to the security that it must be "as provided in this article." That is exclusive of any provision not in this article and relates exclusively to primary elections. Ex parte Brassell, 261 Ala. 265, 73 So. 2d 907 (1954).

And security must be as provided in section 17-16-80. — This section provides for security for costs in such a contest as provided in this chapter. In § 17-16-80 is found the only provision specifying the security to be given on filing a contest under this article. It specifies a deposit of $50.00 as such security and applies by its terms to contests of the nomination to a county office. By its terms it does not apply to members of the legislature. But since that is the only provision in the article specifying the security which shall be given on initiating a contest provided for in it, this section refers to it to specify the nature of the security to be given. Ex parte Brassell, 261 Ala. 265, 73 So. 2d 907 (1954).

Section applies to nomination of members of legislature. — This section has to do with contests for nomination to an office other than a county office, thus applying to the nomination of members of the legislature. Ex parte Brassell, 261 Ala. 265, 73 So. 2d 907 (1954).

Collateral references. — 29 C.J.S., Elections, § 121.

§ 17-16-84. Filing statements of contests; depositions; costs; service of process; contempt.

Upon the filing of any contest of nomination, the chairman of the executive committee with which the contest is filed shall file a statement in the office of the clerk of the circuit court of the county where the contestant resides of the fact that such a contest has been filed, giving the names of the parties thereto, the nomination contested and the day set for hearing. After such statement is filed, the clerk of the circuit court shall issue such subpoenas for witnesses and orders for production of documents and shall issue commissions for the taking of testimony by deposition as required by either party, each party to the contest being responsible for costs incurred by him for the summoning and attendance of witnesses on his behalf, and the clerk may issue execution for such costs the same as in civil cases. It shall be the duty of the sheriff to serve all process issued by the circuit clerk and execute all orders and processes of the executive committee or subcommittee trying the contest. Such executive committee or subcommittee shall have the same power and authority as the circuit judges of this state to enforce obedience to its orders and process and to punish disobedience to its orders by fine or imprisonment, as for contempt. Such executive committee or subcommittee shall, of its own motion or at the request of either party, have power to require any person to produce before it papers or documents pertinent to any inquiry before such executive committee or subcommittee. The chairman of the executive committee or subcommittee trying the contest may issue directly to the sheriff process for the attendance of witnesses or the production of documents or commissions for taking depositions without the intervention of the circuit clerk, as provided in this article. (Acts 1931, No. 56, p. 73; Code 1940, T. 17, § 385.)

Collateral references. — 29 C.J.S., Elections, §§ 123-129.

§ 17-16-85. Meeting of state executive committee.

The state executive committee shall, upon the filing of a contest with the chairman, be called by such chairman to meet at a time not less than 10 days nor more than 20 days from the time of filing such contest for the purpose of hearing and determining the same, or, without calling the committee to meet, the chairman may appoint a subcommittee as herein provided for. (Acts 1931, No. 56, p. 73; Code 1940, T. 17, § 386.)

Editor's note. — Many of the cases cited below were decided under former Tit. 17, § 386, 1940 Code, which contained provisions identical to those in this section.

Party committees sit as courts. — In hearing election contests, party committees sit as courts of special or limited jurisdiction. Perloff v. Edington, 293 Ala. 277, 302 So. 2d 92 (1974).

Time limit jurisdictional. — The time limit in this section is jurisdictional because there can be no contest until the hearings begin and the first hearing must be held within twenty days after the filing of the contest. To state it differently, the contest does not start until a date is set for the first hearing. Perloff v. Edington, 293 Ala. 277, 302 So. 2d 92 (1974).

And mandatory. — The public has an interest in the speedy determination of election contests, and provisions of the statute limiting the time within which steps may by taken are universally regarded as mandatory, and unless they are strictly complied with, the tribunal hearing the contest is without jurisdiction to proceed. Perloff v. Edington, 293 Ala. 277, 302 So. 2d 92 (1974).

Writ of prohibition. — If the subcommittee loses jurisdiction of the contest a writ of prohibition is proper. Perloff v. Edington, 293 Ala. 277, 302 So. 2d 92 (1974).

Legislature did not intend that contests be concluded in 20 days. — The legislature could not have intended to require that all primary election contests be concluded within 20 days of the filing of the contest. Graddick v. Baker, 496 So. 2d 688 (Ala. 1986).

Subcommittee to hear contest. — This section provides sufficient statutory authority for the appointment of a subcommittee to hear the contest. Graddick v. Baker, 496 So. 2d 688 (Ala. 1986).

Cited in Godfrey v. Oswalt, 428 So. 2d 40 (Ala. 1983).

§ 17-16-86. Declaration of result of contest.

Upon the hearing of any contest, if the state or county executive committee finally determines who is the legal nominee for any office, it shall make a declaration of its judgment upon the question, but a failure or refusal by the committee in which the contest is brought to hear and determine the same as much as 40 days before the general election in November shall be treated as a dismissal or the rendition of judgment against the contestant, and a certificate thereof shall be forwarded by the chairman to the proper destination: the county chairman to the probate judge within five days, the state chairman to the Secretary of State within 10 days and the Secretary of State to the probate judge within 12 days after the result, but all certificates shall be made so as to get the nominee on the ballots for the general election in November. (Acts 1931, No. 56, p. 73; Code 1940, T. 17, § 387.)

Time provisions are not consistent with change to September primaries. — The time provisions in certain statutory provisions authorizing election contests within the state political parties and requiring the prompt determination of such contests within certain time periods before the next ensuing election cause difficulties because of the more recent statutes, such as § 17-16-6, changing the time for holding primary elections of political parties to the month of September. Most of the statutes governing the contest of elections were enacted at a time when the primary elections were held in May rather than in September. Thus, the time provisions contained in the statutes no longer fit the realities of the state election procedures. Godfrey v. Oswalt, 428 So. 2d 40 (Ala. 1983).

Contest procedures still workable despite changing in primary election schedule. — The 40-day rule contained in this section no longer fits the state primary election schedule and such rule has been held to be directory rather than mandatory. However, the procedures for indicating that a contest has been terminated are still workable. The statute directs the county executive committee to forward a "declaration of its judgment" to the probate judge. Godfrey v. Oswalt, 428 So. 2d 40 (Ala. 1983).

Recourse where committee or chairman disobeys statutory mandate. — If the committee or the chairman fail or refuse to follow the mandates of the statutes, the only recourse of either the contestant or the contestee is to the courts. In such cases, the courts are open. Godfrey v. Oswalt, 428 So. 2d 40 (Ala. 1983).

Cited in White v. Knight, 424 So. 2d 566 (Ala. 1982); Henderson v. Harris, 804 F. Supp. 288 (M.D. Ala. 1992).

Collateral references. — 29 C.J.S., Elections, § 305.

§ 17-16-87. New primary in case contest cannot be decided.

If, upon the hearing of any contest for any office, as provided for in this article, the committee, after an investigation and hearing of the contest, shall determine that it is impossible from the evidence before it to decide who is the legally nominated candidate for the office contested, it shall have the right and authority to direct a new primary election for the nomination to any such office, but where any action is taken by any county executive committee, either person to the contest, in the same manner as herein provided for in the case of appeals from the action of any county committee, may take an appeal to the state executive committee, which shall be the court of final appeal in all party contests of nominations; provided that, upon hearing of any contest or appeal, as provided for in this chapter, which is not referred to and decided by a subcommittee, 15 members of any such state executive committee shall constitute a quorum for the hearing and determining of such contest or appeal; provided further, that the entire committee shall be notified of the meeting in the usual way. (Acts 1931, No. 56, p. 73; Code 1940, T. 17, § 388.)

There is no statutory right of appeal from subcommittee of party's executive committee to the supreme court, regarding the subcommittee's finding as to the winner of a runoff election for the party nomination. Graddick v. Baker, 495 So. 2d 1367 (Ala. 1986).

Preclearance requirement. — An action taken pursuant to a statute which does not require preclearance does not itself require preclearance. Henderson v. Harris, 804 F. Supp. 288 (M.D. Ala. 1992).

Cited in Graddick v. Baker, 496 So. 2d 688 (Ala. 1986); Curry v. Baker, 802 F.2d 1302 (11th Cir. 1986).

Collateral references. — 29 C.J.S., Elections, §§ 246-248.

§ 17-16-88. Power of state committee to provide rules of party procedure.

The state executive committee may prescribe such other additional rules governing contests and other matters of party procedure as it may deem necessary not in conflict with the provisions of this article. (Acts 1931, No. 56, p. 73; Code 1940, T. 17, § 389.)

There is no statutory right of appeal from subcommittee of party's executive committee to the supreme court, regarding the subcommittee's finding as to the winner of a runoff election for the party nomination. Graddick v. Baker, 495 So. 2d 1367 (Ala. 1986).

§ 17-16-89. Commissioners to take testimony.

Upon filing of any contest as herein provided, the executive committee before whom any such contest is pending, if in session, or the chairman of such committee, if it is not in session, may appoint a commissioner, upon the request of either party, for the purpose of taking testimony in such contest, and such commissioner shall take testimony in such contest as he may be directed to take by the chairman of such committee, and five days' notice of the time when and place where such commissioner expects to take such testimony and the names of the witnesses to be examined shall be given the opposite party to the contest. Each party to the contest may be represented before such commissioner, but before any such commissioner is appointed, the party desiring the appointment made shall deposit with the chairman of such committee sufficient funds to pay the expenses and fees of such commissioner and the fees and mileage of any witness which may be summoned before such commissioner. And such commissioner, when appointed, shall, for the purpose of the contest in which he is to take testimony, have authority to summon witnesses to appear before him in such contest and to administer oaths to such witnesses and shall have all the authority vested in a judge of a district court to punish for contempt. Such commissioner shall not be of kin to either party to the contest. (Acts 1931, No. 56, p. 73; Code 1940, T. 17, § 391.)

CHAPTER 16A.

PRESIDENTIAL PREFERENCE PRIMARY ELECTIONS.

§ 17-16A-1. When held.

(a) Primary elections for the purpose of determining the preferred candidates for President of the United States shall be held in conjunction with the primary elections on the first Tuesday in June of each year in which a President is to be elected.

(b) Subject to rules and procedures of the political party of any such presidential candidate, the names of any candidates for delegate to the national conventions pledged to a presidential candidate shall be placed under his name and such delegates shall be elected in the primary election on the first Tuesday in June of each year as provided herein. (Acts 1978, No. 691, p. 994, § 1; Acts 1979, No. 79-547, p. 994, § 1; Code 1975, § 17-18A-1; Acts 1990, No. 90-699, p. 1359, § 1.)

Code Commissioner's note. — This section was formerly codified as § 17-18A-1 of the 1975 Code.

§ 17-16A-2. Applicability of Section 17-7-1 and Chapter 16.

The provisions of Section 17-7-1 and Chapter 16 of this title shall apply to presidential preference primaries held under the provisions of this chapter unless clearly inconsistent herewith or inappropriate for the conduct of a presidential preference primary. Any political party holding a presidential preference primary may promulgate rules for the conduct of such primary not inconsistent with the provisions of this chapter. (Code 1975, § 17-18A-2; Acts 1978, No. 691, p. 994, § 2.)

Code Commissioner's note. — This section was formerly codified as § 17-18A-2 of the 1975 Code.

§ 17-16A-3. Filing of petitions; number of signatures required; form of petitions; decision of state party chairman as to regularity of petitions final.

In order to qualify the name of any person to appear on the ballot at a presidential preference primary, a petition or petitions in support of his candidacy must be filed with the state party chairman of the appropriate political party, hereinafter referred to as "chairman," after March 1 of the year in which the presidential preference primary is to be held and before March 15 of that same year. To comply with this section, a candidate may file a petition or petitions signed by a total of not less than 500 qualified electors of the state, or petitions signed by not less than 50 qualified electors of each congressional district of the state, in which case there shall be a separate petition for each congressional district. The petitions shall be in such form as the chairman may prescribe; provided, that there shall be a space for the county of residence of each signer next to the space provided for his signature. No signature may be counted as valid unless the county of residence of the signer is provided. Each petition shall contain an affirmation under the penalties of perjury that each signer is a qualified elector in his congressional district or in the state, as appropriate. The decision of the chairman as to the regularity of the petitions shall be final. (Code 1975, § 17-18A-3; Acts 1978, No. 691, p. 994, § 3; Acts 1979, No. 79-547, p. 994, § 1; Acts 1990, No. 90-699, p. 1359, § 1.)

Code Commissioner's note. — This section was formerly codified as § 17-18A-3 of the 1975 Code.

Collateral references. — 29 C.J.S., Elections, §§ 111-114.
25 Am. Jur. 2d, Elections, §§ 147-157.

§ 17-16A-4. Filing fee.

No candidate shall be allowed to have his name placed on the ballot at a presidential preference primary unless there shall be paid to the chairman, at the time of filing his qualifying petition, such fee as the party may prescribe. (Code 1975, § 17-18A-4; Acts 1978, No. 691, p. 994, § 4; Acts 1979, No. 79-547, p. 994, § 1.)

Code Commissioner's note. — This section was formerly codified as § 17-18A-4 of the 1975 Code.

Collateral references. — 29 C.J.S., Elections, § 114.
25 Am. Jur. 2d, Elections, § 155.

§ 17-16A-5. Notice to candidate of qualification; withdrawal by candidate.

Whenever the chairman shall receive petitions, timely filed, which appear to qualify the name of a candidate for President to be placed on the ballot, he shall forthwith notify the prospective candidate by the most expeditious means of communication and shall advise such prospective candidate that unless he withdraws his name from the ballot within 10 days after receipt of such notice, his name will appear on the ballot of his party at such presidential preference primary. If a candidate signifies his desire to withdraw his name within the above time limit, his name shall not be printed on the ballot. (Code 1975, § 17-18A-5; Acts 1978, No. 691, p. 994, § 5; Acts 1979, No. 79-547, p. 994, § 1.)

Code Commissioner's note. — This section was formerly codified as § 17-18A-5 of the 1975 Code.

Collateral references. — 29 C.J.S, Elections, § 118(3).

§ 17-16A-6. Political party to file resolution with Secretary of State.

Each political party authorized to hold a primary and wishing to hold such a presidential preference primary shall, not less than 60 days before such primary is to be held, adopt and file with the Secretary of State a resolution stating said intention, the method by which electors are to indicate one or more preferences, the method by which delegates are to be selected, elected, chosen and replaced, and the pledge, if any, by which delegates are to be bound. (Code 1975, § 17-18A-7; Acts 1978, No. 691, p. 994, § 7; Acts 1979, No. 79-547, p. 994, § 1; Acts 1990, No. 90-699, p. 1359, § 1.)

Code Commissioner's note. — This section was formerly codified as § 17-18A-7 of the 1975 Code.

Collateral references. — 29 C.J.S., Elections, § 118(2).

CHAPTER 17.

AMENDMENTS TO THE CONSTITUTION.

Cross references. — As to ballots for constitutional amendments, see § 17-8-22.

Cited in Gafford v. Pemberton, 409 So. 2d 1367 (Ala. 1982).

§ 17-17-1. Counting and returning vote on constitutional amendment.

The vote on an amendment proposed to the Constitution shall be counted and return made thereof as the vote for members of the Legislature is counted and returned, the amendments, if more than one, being designated by substantially the language used to designate them on the official ballot. (Code 1852, § 352; Code 1867, § 401; Code 1876, § 352; Code 1886, § 445; Code 1896, § 1662; Code 1907, § 436; Code 1923, § 526; Code 1940, T. 17, § 210.)

§ 17-17-2. Returns made to Secretary of State.

The board of supervisors shall ascertain the number of votes given in their respective counties for and against the proposed amendment when ascertaining the vote given for officers; the returning officers of such county shall thereupon make returns of such vote, by precincts, to the Secretary of State immediately, together with a certificate, prepared from the poll lists of the total number of qualified electors in said county who voted at such election. (Code 1852, § 354; Code 1867, § 403; Code 1876, § 354; Code 1886, § 446; Code 1896, § 1663; Code 1907, § 437; Code 1923, § 527; Code 1940, T. 17, § 211; Acts 1988, 1st Ex. Sess., No. 88-908, p. 482, § 4.)

Cited in Opinion of Justices, 447 So. 2d 1305 (Ala. 1984).

§ 17-17-3. Returns counted; result proclaimed.

The Secretary of State shall, in the presence of the Governor and Attorney General, or one of them, open such certificates and therefrom ascertain whether a majority of all the qualified electors of the state who voted at such election voted in favor of such amendment or amendments; and the result of said election shall be made known by proclamation of the Governor. (Code 1886, § 447; Code 1896, § 1664; Code 1907, § 438; Code 1923, § 528; Code 1940, T. 17, § 212.)

§ 17-17-4. Expense of publication of proclamation.

Whenever any proposed amendment to the Constitution of Alabama, regardless of the nature thereof, is submitted to the people for ratification or adoption, the expense of publication of the Governor's proclamation concerning such amendment shall be paid out of the General Fund of the State of Alabama. Payment of the expense of the publication of any such proclamation shall be made upon account stated, certified to be correct, approved by the Governor, upon warrant of the State Comptroller.

There is hereby appropriated out of the General Fund of the State of Alabama such sum or sums as may be necessary to pay the expense of the publication of any such proclamation. (Acts 1951, No. 980, p. 1654, §§ 1, 2.)

§ 17-17-5. Cost of elections on constitutional amendments.

Unless otherwise stated in the act or resolution calling such election, whenever any special election is ordered by the Legislature upon any proposed amendment or amendments to the Constitution of this state and said amendment affects only one municipality in this state, then if such municipality has as much or more than 68,000 and under 200,000 inhabitants according to the last or any subsequent federal census, and if no amendment or amendments other than those affecting said municipality are submitted to the voters of the state at said election, the expense of holding such election, including the cost of publishing the notices and proclamation required by the Constitution shall be paid by such municipality. (Acts 1931, No. 365, p. 430; Code 1940, T. 17, § 213.)

§ 17-17-6. Duty of State Comptroller to ascertain expenses and file same.

It shall be the duty of the Comptroller to ascertain the expense of such election and, within 30 days after the holding of the same, to present to and file with the clerk of such municipality a statement of said expense, duly certified by such officer, and the governing body of such municipality, by whatever name called, shall cause said expense to be paid out of the funds of the municipality to the Treasurer of the State of Alabama. Every such claim shall be a preferred claim against such municipality, and the courts may enforce by writ of mandamus performance of the duty herein entailed upon the Comptroller and the members of the governing body of such municipality. (Acts 1931, No. 365, p. 430; Code 1940, T. 17, § 214.)

CHAPTER 18.

SPECIAL ELECTIONS.

Cited in Carson v. Hornsby, 402 So. 2d 931 (Ala. 1981).

§ 17-18-1. When and for what offices held.

Special elections are to be held in the following cases:

(1) When a vacancy occurs in the office of senator or representative in the Legislature, when the Legislature will be in session prior to the next general election for that office;

(2) When a vacancy occurs in the office of representative in the Congress of the United States, by which the state may be deprived of its full representation at any time Congress will be in session prior to the next general election for that office;

(3) Whenever any general or special election for members of the Legislature or for representatives in Congress is not held;

(4) When any vacancy occurs in any state or county office filled by election of the people not otherwise provided for by the Constitution or laws of this state; and

(5) In such other cases as are or may be provided for by law. (Code 1876, § 249; Code 1886, § 359; Code 1896, § 1598; Code 1907, § 439; Code 1923, § 529; Code 1940, T. 17, § 215.)

The **primary purpose of this section** is to provide elections to fill vacancies in legislative bodies, in the state legislature or in congress, in keeping with the policy of not naming members of the legislative department by the executive.

State ex rel. Murphy v. Johnson, 243 Ala. 114, 8 So. 2d 890 (1942).

Collateral references. — 29 C.J.S., Elections, § 70.

§ 17-18-2. Day for holding special elections.

All special elections shall be held on such day as the governor may direct. (Code 1876, § 250; Code 1886, § 360; Code 1896, § 1599; Code 1907, § 440; Code 1923, § 530; Code 1940, T. 17, § 217.)

Collateral references. — 29 C.J.S., Elections, § 72.

§ 17-18-3. Special elections ordered by Governor.

All special elections provided for by this chapter are to be ordered by the Governor, who must issue writs of election, directed to the sheriffs of the counties in which such election is required to be held and must specify therein the district or county in which, and the day on which, such election is to be held; the cause and object of the same; the name of the person in whose office the vacancy has occurred and, in all cases in which a special election is directed in a district composed of more than one county, such election must be directed to be held on the same day in each county. (Code 1852, § 191; Code 1867, § 233; Code 1876, § 266; Code 1886, § 361; Code 1896, § 1600; Code 1907, § 441; Code 1923, § 531; Code 1940, T. 17, § 217.)

Collateral references. — 29 C.J.S., Elections, § 66.

§ 17-18-4. Proclamation of election for Congress or state officers.

The Governor must give notice of any special election for representatives in Congress, or state officers, by proclamation. (Code 1876, § 267; Code 1886, § 362; Code 1896, § 1601; Code 1907, § 442; Code 1923, § 532; Code 1940, T. 17, § 218.)

§ 17-18-5. Sheriff to give notice of elections in his county.

Whenever the sheriff of any county receives a writ of election directing a special election to be held or receives notice of a special election for representatives in congress or for any state or county officers, such sheriff must immediately give notice by proclamation of the time, place and object of such election as provided by law.

Any sheriff who fails to give notice of a special election ordered by the Governor, as required by law, is guilty of a misdemeanor. (Code 1876, §§ 268, 4279; Code 1886, §§ 363, 4178; Code 1896, §§ 1602, 4685; Code 1907, §§ 443, 6782; Code 1923, §§ 533, 3900; Code 1940, T. 17, §§ 219, 296.)

This section has no application to notice required for constitutional amendment. In re Opinions of Justices, 238 Ala. 150, 192 So. 905 (1939).

Cited in Ex parte Turner, 24 F. Cas. 334, (No. 14,246) (M.D. Ala. 1879).

Collateral references. — 29 C.J.S., Elections, §§ 72-74.

§ 17-18-6. Sheriff must notify probate judge and clerk.

When any special election is ordered by the Governor, the sheriffs of the counties in which such election is to be held must, within three days after receiving notice thereof, notify the probate judge and clerk of the circuit court of their respective counties of such special election.

Any sheriff who fails to notify the judge of probate and clerk of the circuit court that any special election is ordered by the Governor, as required by law, must, on conviction, be fined not less than $100.00 nor more than $500.00. (Code 1876, §§ 269, 4281; Code 1886, §§ 364, 4180; Code 1896, §§ 1603, 4687;

Code 1907, §§ 444, 6784; Code 1923, §§ 534, 3902; Code 1940, T. 17, §§ 220, 298.)

§ 17-18-7. How conducted and certificates given.

Special elections are to be held and conducted, the returns thereof made and certificates given and, unless otherwise expressly provided, regulated in all respects by the provisions in relation to general elections. (Code 1876, § 270; Code 1886, § 365; Code 1896, § 1604; Code 1907, § 445; Code 1923, § 535; Code 1940, T. 17, § 221.)

Cited in Opinion of Justices No. 305, 442 So. 2d 42 (Ala. 1983).

CHAPTER 18A.

PRESIDENTIAL PREFERENCE PRIMARY ELECTIONS.

§ 17-18A-1. Transferred.

Code Commissioner's note. — This section has been transferred and renumbered as § 17-16A-1.

§ 17-18A-2. Transferred.

Code Commissioner's note. — This section has been transferred and renumbered as § 17-16A-2.

§ 17-18A-3. Transferred.

Code Commissioner's note. — This section has been transferred and renumbered as § 17-16A-3.

§ 17-18A-4. Transferred.

Code Commissioner's note. — This section has been transferred and renumbered as § 17-16A-4.

§ 17-18A-5. Transferred.

Code Commissioner's note. — This section has been transferred and renumbered as § 17-16A-5.

§ 17-18A-6. Repealed by Acts 1979, No. 79-547, p. 994, § 2, effective July 30, 1979.

§ 17-18A-7. Transferred.

Code Commissioner's note. — This section has been transferred and renumbered as § 17-16A-6.

§§ 17-18A-8 through 17-18A-15. Repealed by Acts 1979, No. 79-547, p. 994, § 2, effective July 30, 1979.

CHAPTER 19.

PRESIDENTIAL AND VICE-PRESIDENTIAL ELECTORS.

Cross references. — As to when elections for presidential and vice-presidential electors to be held, see § 17-2-10.

§ 17-19-1. Number of presidential electors.

On the day prescribed by this code there are to be elected, in the manner provided in this chapter, a number of electors for President and Vice-President of the United States equal to the number of senators and representatives in Congress to which this state is entitled at the time of such election. (Code 1852, § 339; Code 1867, § 388; Code 1876, § 342; Code 1886, § 435; Code 1896, § 1653; Code 1907, § 446; Code 1923, § 536; Code 1940, T. 17, § 222.)

Electoral college is not unconstitutional. — While the "discrimination" of having one's vote "counted" more often in a large state than a small state may be considered by some to be unfair, election of the President of the United States by means of the electoral college is not unconstitutional. Hitson v. Baggett, 446 F. Supp. 674 (M.D. Ala.), aff'd, 580 F.2d 1051 (5th Cir. 1978), cert. denied, 439 U.S. 1129, 99 S. Ct. 1047, 59 L. Ed. 2d 90 (1979).

Electors not officers or agents of United States. — The sole function of the presidential electors is to cast, certify and transmit the vote of the state for president and vice-president of the nation. Although the electors are appointed and act under and pursuant to the Constitution of the United States, they are no more officers or agents of the United States than are the members of the state legislatures when acting as electors of federal senators, or the people of the states when acting as electors of representatives in congress. Opinion of Justices, 283 Ala. 341, 217 So. 2d 53 (1968).

A presidential elector does not hold an "office of profit" within the meaning of Constitution 1901, § 280. Opinion of Justices, 283 Ala. 341, 217 So. 2d 53 (1968).

Collateral references. — 29 C.J.S., Elections, §§ 91, 94, 97, 106.

§ 17-19-2. Certification of names of candidates for President and Vice-President; nominating petitions; names of electors; execution of statement by electors.

(a) When presidential electors are to be chosen, the Secretary of State of Alabama shall certify to the judges of probate of the several counties the names of all candidates for President and Vice-President who are nominated by any national convention or other like assembly of any political party or by written petition signed by at least 5,000 qualified voters of this state.

(b) The certificate of nomination by a political party convention must be signed by the presiding officer and secretary of the convention and by the chairman of the state executive or central committee of the political party making the nomination. Any nominating petition, to be valid, must contain the signatures as well as the addresses of the petitioners. Such certificates and petitions must be filed in the office of the Secretary of State no later than the last day of August next preceding the day fixed for the election.

(c) Each certificate of nomination and nominating petition must be accompanied by a list of the names and addresses of persons, who shall be qualified voters of this state, equal in number to the number of presidential electors to be chosen. Each person so listed shall execute the following statement which shall be attached to the certificate or petition when the same is filed with the Secretary of State: "I do hereby consent and do hereby agree to serve as elector for President and Vice-President of the United States, if elected to that position, and do hereby agree that, if so elected, I shall cast my ballot as such elector for .... for President and .... for Vice-President of the United States" (inserting in said blank spaces the respective names of the persons named as nominees for said respective offices in the certificate to which this statement is attached). (Acts 1975, 3rd Ex. Sess., No. 138, p. 370, § 2.)

At-large features of election for presidential electors does not discriminate against minority voters. — A claim that the statewide and at-large features of Alabama's election for presidential electors violate the rights of minority voters fails to state a good basis for relief. Hitson v. Baggett, 446 F. Supp. 674 (M.D. Ala.), aff'd, 580 F.2d 1051 (5th Cir. 1978), cert. denied, 439 U.S. 1129, 99 S. Ct. 1047, 59 L. Ed. 2d 90 (1979).

§ 17-19-3. Names on ballots; vote for candidate counted as vote for designated electors.

The names of all candidates for President and Vice-President who are nominated as provided in this chapter shall be printed on the official ballots under the emblem of their respective political parties, as filed in the office of the Secretary of State of Alabama. The names of the electors of the candidates for President and Vice-President shall not be printed upon the ballots. A vote for a candidate for President or Vice-President shall be counted as a vote for the electors of the political party or independent body by which such candidates were named, as listed on the certificate of nomination or nominating petition. (Acts 1975, 3rd Ex. Sess., No. 138, p. 370, § 3.)

Popular election of presidential electors is consistent with federal Constitution. — Consistent with the federal Constitution, a state may provide for the selection of presidential electors through popular election. Hitson v. Baggett, 446 F. Supp. 674 (M.D. Ala.), aff'd, 580 F.2d 1051 (5th Cir. 1978), cert. denied, 439 U.S. 1129, 99 S. Ct. 1047, 59 L. Ed. 2d 90 (1979).

§ 17-19-4. Making returns to Secretary of State.

In all elections for electors for President and Vice-President, the board of supervisors of each county must, within five days after making the statement of the county vote by precincts, return the result of the same to the Secretary of State. (Code 1876, § 343; Code 1886, § 436; Code 1896, § 1654; Code 1907, § 447; Code 1923, § 537; Code 1940, T. 17, § 223; Acts 1988, 1st Ex. Sess., No. 88-908, p. 482, § 5.)

§ 17-19-5. Governor to estimate returns and give notice of election.

Within 15 days after the time for making the returns, the Governor, in the presence of the Secretary of State and Attorney General, or either of them in the absence of the other, must estimate the returns, ascertain which electors are elected and notify them by proclamation. (Code 1876, § 344; Code 1886, § 437; Code 1896, § 1655; Code 1907, § 448; Code 1923, § 538; Code 1940, T. 17, § 224.)

§ 17-19-6. Tie vote.

If, on such estimate, it is found that an election of the number of electors to which the state is entitled is not made by reason of two or more candidates having received an equal number of votes, the Governor must forthwith decide between those having an equal number of votes. (Code 1852, § 342; Code 1867, § 391; Code 1876, § 345; Code 1886, § 438; Code 1896, § 1656; Code 1907, § 449; Code 1923, § 539; Code 1940, T. 17, § 225.)

§ 17-19-7. Electoral meeting; filling of vacancies.

The electors of President and Vice-President are to assemble at the office of the Secretary of State, at the seat of government at 12:00 noon on the second Tuesday in December next after their election, or at that hour on such other day as may be fixed by Congress, to elect such President and Vice-President, and those of them present at that hour must at once proceed by ballot and plurality of votes to supply the places of those who fail to attend on that day and hour. (Code 1852, § 345; Code 1867, § 394; Code 1876, § 346; Code 1886, § 439; Code 1896, § 1657; Code 1907, § 450; Code 1923, § 540; Acts 1935, No. 425, p. 895; Code 1940, T. 17, § 226; Acts 1945, No. 386, p. 605; Acts 1951, No. 557, p. 973.)

The electors meet only one day during the four years following their election. Opinion of Justices, 283 Ala. 341, 217 So. 2d 53 (1968).

§ 17-19-8. Compensation of electors.

Each elector for President and Vice-President shall receive $8.00 for each day he necessarily attends at the seat of government, and $.20 for every mile traveled to and from the same, to be estimated in the same manner as is provided by law in relation to members of the Legislature from his county, to be paid, on oath of such elector, by warrant on the Treasurer. (Code 1876, § 347; Code 1886, § 440; Code 1896, § 1658; Code 1907, § 451; Code 1923, § 541; Code 1940, T. 17, § 227.)

Travel allowance is reimbursement for travel expense. Opinion of Justices, 283 Ala. 341, 217 So. 2d 53 (1968).

The eight dollars and travel allowance is nothing more than provision for actual expenses alone. Opinion of Justices, 283 Ala. 341, 217 So. 2d 53 (1968).

CHAPTER 20.

CONGRESSIONAL DISTRICTS AND ELECTIONS.

Cross references. — As to when elections for United States senators to be held, see § 17-2-11. As to resignation of members of Congress, see § 36-9-12.

§ 17-20-1. State divided into congressional districts.

The state is hereby divided into seven congressional districts as follows:

District 1: Baldwin County, Clarke County, Escambia County, Mobile County, Monroe County: Tract 9857, Tract 9858: Block Group 1: Block 103, Block 104, Block 105, Block 106, Block 107, Block 116, Block 117, Block 118, Block 119, Block 120, Block 121, Block 122, Block 123, Block 124; Block Group 2: Block 246, Block 247, Block 248, Block 251, Block 252, Block 253, Block 254, Block 255; Tract 9859, Tract 9860, Tract 9861, Tract 9862; Washington County.

District 2: Barbour County, Butler County, Coffee County, Conecuh County, Covington County, Crenshaw County, Dale County, Geneva County, Henry County, Houston County, Lee County, Monroe County: Tract 9856, Tract 9858: Block Group 1: Block 101, Block 102, Block 108, Block 109, Block 110, Block 111, Block 112, Block 113, Block 114, Block 115, Block 125, Block 126, Block 127, Block 128, Block 129, Block 130, Block 131; Block Group 2: Block 201, Block 202, Block 203, Block 204, Block 205, Block 206, Block 207, Block 208, Block 209, Block 210, Block 211, Block 212, Block 213, Block 214, Block 215, Block 216, Block 217, Block 218, Block 219, Block 220, Block 221, Block 222, Block 223, Block 224, Block 225, Block 226, Block 227, Block 228, Block 229, Block 230, Block 231, Block 232, Block 233, Block 234, Block 235, Block 236, Block 237, Block 238, Block 239, Block 240, Block 241, Block 242, Block 243, Block 244, Block 245, Block 249, Block 250, Block 256, Block 257, Block 258, Block 259; Montgomery County: Tract 0001: Block Group 1: Block 129, Block 130, Block 131, Block 132, Block 133, Block 134, Block 140, Block 141, Block 152, Block 153, Block 154, Block 155, Block 156, Block 157, Block 158, Block 159, Block 160, Block 161, Block 162, Block 163, Block 164, Block 165, Block 166, Block 167, Block 168, Block 169, Block 170, Block 171, Block 172, Block 173, Block 174, Block 175, Block 176, Block 177, Block 178, Block 179, Block 180, Block 181, Block 182, Block 183, Block 184, Block 185, Block 186, Block 187, Block 191, Block 192; Block Group 2: Block 208; Tract 0002: Block Group 1: Block 101, Block 102, Block 103, Block 104, Block 105, Block 106, Block 107, Block 108, Block 109, Block 110, Block 111, Block 118, Block 119; Block Group 2: Block 201; Tract 0005: Block Group 1: Block 101, Block 102, Block 103, Block 104, Block 105, Block 106, Block 107, Block 108, Block 109, Block 110, Block 111, Block 112, Block 113, Block 114, Block 115, Block 116, Block 117, Block

118; Block Group 2: Block 201, Block 202, Block 203, Block 204, Block 205, Block 206, Block 207, Block 208, Block 209, Block 210, Block 211, Block 212, Block 213, Block 214, Block 215, Block 216, Block 217, Block 218; Block Group 3: Block 301, Block 302, Block 303, Block 304, Block 305, Block 306, Block 307, Block 308, Block 309, Block 310, Block 311, Block 312, Block 313, Block 314, Block 315; Block Group 4: Block 404, Block 405, Block 406, Block 407, Block 408, Block 409, Block 410, Block 411, Block 412, Block 413, Block 414, Block 415, Block 416, Block 417, Block 418, Block 419, Block 420, Block 421; Tract 0006: Block Group 1: Block 111, Block 118; Tract 0009.85, Tract 0010: Block Group 1: Block 101, Block 102, Block 103, Block 104, Block 105, Block 106, Block 107, Block 110, Block 111, Block 113, Block 114; Tract 0011: Block Group 1: Block 101; Tract 0013: Block Group 1: Block 101, Block 102, Block 103, Block 104, Block 105, Block 106, Block 107, Block 108, Block 109, Block 110, Block 111, Block 112, Block 113, Block 114; Block Group 2: Block 201, Block 202, Block 203, Block 204, Block 205, Block 206, Block 207, Block 208, Block 209, Block 210, Block 211, Block 212, Block 213, Block 214; Tract 0014: Block Group 1: Block 101, Block 102, Block 108, Block 109, Block 110, Block 111, Block 112, Block 113, Block 114, Block 115, Block 116, Block 117, Block 118, Block 119, Block 120, Block 121, Block 122; Block Group 2: Block 201, Block 202, Block 203, Block 204, Block 205, Block 206, Block 207, Block 208, Block 209, Block 210, Block 211, Block 212, Block 213, Block 214, Block 215, Block 216, Block 217, Block 218, Block 219, Block 220, Block 221; Block Group 3: Block 301, Block 302, Block 304, Block 305, Block 306, Block 307, Block 308, Block 309, Block 310, Block 311, Block 312, Block 313, Block 314, Block 315, Block 316, Block 317; Block Group 4: Block 401, Block 402, Block 403, Block 404, Block 405, Block 406, Block 407, Block 408, Block 409, Block 410, Block 411, Block 412; Block Group 5: Block 505, Block 508, Block 509, Block 510, Block 511, Block 512, Block 515, Block 517, Block 518, Block 519, Block 520; Tract 0015: Block Group 1: Block 101, Block 102, Block 103, Block 104, Block 105, Block 106, Block 107, Block 108, Block 109, Block 110, Block 111, Block 112, Block 113, Block 114, Block 115, Block 116, Block 117, Block 118, Block 119, Block 120; Block Group 2: Block 201, Block 202, Block 203, Block 205, Block 206, Block 207, Block 208, Block 209, Block 210, Block 215, Block 216, Block 217, Block 218, Block 219, Block 220, Block 224, Block 225, Block 226, Block 227, Block 228; Tract 0016, Tract 0017, Tract 0018, Tract 0019, Tract 0020: Block Group 1: Block 108, Block 109, Block 110, Block 111, Block 112, Block 113, Block 114, Block 115, Block 116, Block 117, Block 118, Block 119, Block 120, Block 121, Block 122, Block 123, Block 130; Block Group 2: Block 201, Block 202, Block 203, Block 204, Block 205, Block 206, Block 207, Block 208, Block 209, Block 210, Block 211, Block 212, Block 213, Block 214, Block 215, Block 216; Block Group 3: Block 309, Block 310, Block 311, Block 312, Block 313; Block Group 4: Block 401, Block 402, Block 403, Block 404, Block 405, Block 406, Block 407, Block 408, Block 409, Block 410, Block 411, Block 412, Block 413, Block 414, Block 415, Block 418; Block Group 5: Block 501, Block 502, Block 503, Block 504, Block 505, Block 506, Block 507, Block 508, Block 509, Block 510, Block 511; Tract 0021: Block Group 1: Block 101, Block 102, Block

217

103, Block 104, Block 105, Block 106, Block 107, Block 108, Block 109, Block 110, Block 111, Block 112, Block 113, Block 114, Block 115, Block 116, Block 117, Block 118, Block 119, Block 120; Block Group 4: Block 401, Block 402, Block 406, Block 407, Block 420, Block 421, Block 422; Tract 0026, Tract 0027, Tract 0028, Tract 0033.01, Tract 0033.02, Tract 0051.01: Block Group 1: Block 148A, Block 148B, Block 149; Block Group 2: Block 212; Tract 0053.01, Tract 0053.02, Tract 0054.01: Block Group 1: Block 108A, Block 108B, Block 109A, Block 109B, Block 110; Block Group 2: Block 204A, Block 204B, Block 204C, Block 204D, Block 205A, Block 205B, Block 206, Block 207, Block 208, Block 209, Block 210, Block 211A, Block 211B, Block 212, Block 213, Block 214, Block 215, Block 216, Block 217, Block 218, Block 219, Block 220, Block 221, Block 222, Block 223, Block 224, Block 225, Block 226, Block 227; Block Group 3: Block 301, Block 302A, Block 302B, Block 303, Block 304, Block 305, Block 306, Block 307A, Block 307B, Block 308A, Block 308B, Block 309A, Block 309B, Block 309C, Block 310A, Block 310B, Block 311A, Block 311B, Block 312; Block Group 4: Block 401A, Block 401B, Block 402, Block 403A, Block 403B, Block 404, Block 405; Tract 0054.02: Block Group 1: Block 101, Block 102, Block 103, Block 104, Block 105, Block 106, Block 107, Block 108, Block 109, Block 110, Block 113, Block 114, Block 115, Block 116, Block 117, Block 118, Block 119; Block Group 2: Block 201, Block 202, Block 203, Block 204, Block 205, Block 206, Block 207, Block 208, Block 209, Block 210, Block 211, Block 212, Block 213, Block 214, Block 230; Block Group 3: Block 301, Block 302; Block Group 4: Block 401, Block 402, Block 403, Block 404, Block 405, Block 406, Block 407, Block 408, Block 409, Block 410, Block 411, Block 412, Block 413, Block 414; Tract 0054.03, Tract 0054.05, Tract 0054.06, Tract 0055: Block Group 1: Block 102A, Block 102B, Block 102C, Block 103, Block 104, Block 105; Tract 0056.01: Block Group 3: Block 301, Block 302, Block 303, Block 304, Block 305, Block 306, Block 307, Block 308, Block 310, Block 311; Block Group 4: Block 401, Block 402, Block 403, Block 404, Block 405, Block 406A, Block 406B, Block 407A, Block 411, Block 412; Block Group 5: Block 501A, Block 501B, Block 501C, Block 502, Block 503, Block 504, Block 505, Block 506, Block 507; Tract 0056.02, Tract 0056.03: Block Group 6: Block 601; Tract 0056.04: Block Group 2: Block 211, Block 212, Block 213, Block 214, Block 215, Block 217, Block 218, Block 219, Block 220, Block 221; Block Group 3: Block 303, Block 304, Block 305, Block 306, Block 307, Block 309, Block 310, Block 313; Block Group 4: Block 406, Block 407, Block 408, Block 409, Block 410, Block 411, Block 412, Block 413, Block 414, Block 415, Block 416, Block 417, Block 418, Block 419, Block 420, Block 421, Block 422, Block 423, Block 424, Block 425, Block 426, Block 427, Block 428, Block 429, Block 430, Block 431, Block 432, Block 433, Block 434; Tract 0057: Block Group 1: Block 119, Block 120, Block 121, Block 122, Block 123, Block 127; Tract 0058: Block Group 1: Block 103, Block 104, Block 105, Block 106, Block 107, Block 109, Block 119, Block 120, Block 121, Block 122, Block 123, Block 152, Block 153, Block 154; Block Group 2: Block 201, Block 202, Block 203, Block 204, Block 206, Block 208, Block 209, Block 210, Block 211, Block 217, Block 218, Block 219, Block 220, Block 221, Block 222, Block 223, Block 224, Block 225; Block Group 3: Block 302, Block 303,

Block 304, Block 305, Block 306, Block 307, Block 308, Block 309, Block 310, Block 311, Block 312, Block 313, Block 314, Block 322, Block 323, Block 324, Block 325, Block 326, Block 327, Block 328, Block 329, Block 330, Block 331; Block Group 4: Block 401, Block 402; Tract 0059.01: Block Group 2: Block 207, Block 208, Block 209, Block 210, Block 211, Block 214, Block 215, Block 216, Block 217, Block 218, Block 219, Block 220, Block 221, Block 222, Block 224, Block 225, Block 226, Block 227, Block 228, Block 236, Block 237; Tract 0060.85: Block Group 1: Block 101A, Block 101B, Block 116A, Block 117, Block 118, Block 135; Block Group 5: Block 501B; Block Group 9: Block 901A, Block 901B; Pike County, Russell County.

District 3: Autauga County: Tract 0201, Tract 0202, Tract 0203, Tract 0204, Tract 0205, Tract 0206, Tract 0207, Tract 0208: Block Group 1: Block 101, Block 102, Block 103, Block 104, Block 105, Block 106, Block 109, Block 110A, Block 110B, Block 111, Block 112, Block 113, Block 114, Block 115, Block 116, Block 117, Block 118A, Block 118B, Block 119, Block 120, Block 121, Block 122, Block 123, Block 124, Block 125, Block 126, Block 127, Block 128, Block 129, Block 130A, Block 130B, Block 131, Block 132, Block 133, Block 134, Block 135, Block 136, Block 137A, Block 137B, Block 138, Block 139, Block 140, Block 141, Block 142, Block 143, Block 144, Block 145, Block 147, Block 148, Block 149, Block 150, Block 151, Block 152, Block 154, Block 155, Block 156, Block 157, Block 158, Block 159, Block 160, Block 161, Block 162, Block 163, Block 164, Block 165, Block 166; Block Group 2: Block 201, Block 202, Block 223, Block 224, Block 225, Block 226, Block 227, Block 228, Block 229, Block 230, Block 232, Block 242; Block Group 3: Block 306, Block 307, Block 308, Block 309, Block 310, Block 313, Block 314, Block 316, Block 317, Block 318, Block 319, Block 320, Block 321, Block 322; Block Group 4: Block 430, Block 432, Block 433, Block 434, Block 435, Block 437, Block 438, Block 439, Block 440, Block 441, Block 442, Block 443; Block Group 5: Block 501, Block 502, Block 503, Block 504A, Block 504B, Block 505A, Block 505B, Block 506, Block 507, Block 508, Block 509, Block 510, Block 511; Calhoun County, Chambers County, Chilton County, Clay County, Cleburne County, Coosa County, Elmore County, Randolph County, St. Clair County, Shelby County, Talladega County, Tallapoosa County.

District 4: Blount County, Cherokee County, Cullman County, DeKalb County, Etowah County, Fayette County, Franklin County, Jefferson County: Tract 0113: Block Group 1: Block 161E, Block 166A, Block 166B, Block 167; Block Group 2: Block 246B, Block 247B, Block 248B, Block 248C, Block 250, Block 252, Block 253, Block 254A, Block 254C, Block 254D, Block 255, Block 256B, Block 260A, Block 260B, Block 261, Block 263A, Block 263B, Block 263C, Block 264A, Block 264B, Block 264C, Block 264D, Block 265A, Block 265B, Block 266A, Block 266B, Block 267, Block 268, Block 269, Block 270A, Block 270B, Block 270C, Block 270D, Block 271, Block 272; Block Group 5: Block 502, Block 503, Block 504, Block 505A, Block 505B, Block 506, Block 507, Block 508, Block 509, Block 510, Block 511, Block 512, Block 513, Block 514, Block 515, Block 516, Block 517A, Block 517B, Block 518A, Block 518B, Block 519, Block 520, Block 521, Block 522, Block 523, Block 524, Block 525, Block

526, Block 527, Block 528A, Block 528B, Block 529, Block 530, Block 531, Block 532, Block 533A, Block 533B, Block 534, Block 535, Block 536, Block 537A, Block 537B, Block 538, Block 539, Block 540, Block 541A, Block 541B, Block 542A, Block 542B, Block 543, Block 544A, Block 544B; Tract 0114: Block Group 1: Block 119, Block 120; Block Group 2: Block 230, Block 231, Block 232A, Block 232B, Block 232C, Block 232D, Block 232E, Block 233, Block 257, Block 258, Block 259, Block 260A, Block 260B, Block 261; Block Group 3: Block 301A, Block 301B, Block 301C, Block 302, Block 303, Block 304, Block 305C, Block 305D, Block 305E, Block 305G, Block 305H, Block 307; Block Group 4: Block 401, Block 402, Block 403, Block 404, Block 405, Block 406, Block 407, Block 408, Block 409, Block 410, Block 414, Block 415, Block 416, Block 418, Block 419, Block 420, Block 421, Block 422, Block 423, Block 424, Block 425, Block 426, Block 427, Block 428, Block 429, Block 430, Block 431, Block 432, Block 433, Block 434, Block 435, Block 436, Block 437, Block 438, Block 439, Block 440; Tract 0116: Block Group 1: Block 101, Block 102, Block 103, Block 104, Block 105, Block 106, Block 107, Block 108, Block 109, Block 110, Block 111, Block 112, Block 126, Block 127, Block 129, Block 130, Block 131, Block 132, Block 140, Block 141, Block 142, Block 143, Block 153, Block 154, Block 155, Block 156, Block 157, Block 158, Block 159, Block 196; Tract 0117.03: Block Group 1: Block 101, Block 102, Block 103, Block 104A, Block 104B, Block 104C, Block 105A, Block 105B, Block 105C, Block 106, Block 107, Block 108, Block 109A, Block 109B, Block 109C, Block 110, Block 111, Block 114, Block 115, Block 116; Block Group 2: Block 201, Block 202, Block 203, Block 204, Block 206, Block 208, Block 209, Block 211; Block Group 3: Block 301, Block 302, Block 303, Block 304, Block 305A, Block 305B, Block 306A, Block 306B, Block 307, Block 308, Block 309, Block 310, Block 311, Block 312, Block 315, Block 316; Block Group 5: Block 501, Block 502, Block 503, Block 504, Block 505, Block 506, Block 507, Block 508, Block 509A, Block 509B, Block 509C, Block 510, Block 511, Block 512, Block 513; Block Group 7: Block 701A, Block 701B, Block 702B, Block 702C, Block 703C, Block 712, Block 713, Block 714, Block 716, Block 718, Block 719, Block 720, Block 726; Block Group 9: Block 901A, Block 901B, Block 902, Block 903, Block 904A, Block 904B, Block 904C, Block 904D, Block 904E, Block 905A, Block 905B, Block 905C, Block 905D, Block 905E, Block 906A, Block 906B, Block 906C, Block 907, Block 908, Block 909A, Block 909B, Block 909C, Block 909D, Block 910A, Block 910B, Block 911B, Block 911C, Block 911D, Block 912B, Block 915B; Tract 0117.04: Block Group 1: Block 101, Block 104, Block 105, Block 106, Block 108, Block 109, Block 110, Block 111, Block 112A, Block 112B, Block 112C, Block 112D, Block 112E, Block 112F, Block 112G, Block 113, Block 114, Block 115, Block 116, Block 117, Block 118, Block 119, Block 120, Block 121A, Block 121B, Block 121C, Block 121D, Block 121E, Block 122, Block 123, Block 124, Block 125, Block 126, Block 127, Block 128, Block 129, Block 130, Block 131, Block 132, Block 133, Block 134, Block 135, Block 136, Block 137, Block 138, Block 139, Block 140, Block 141, Block 142A, Block 142B, Block 142C, Block 143, Block 144A, Block 144B, Block 144C, Block 144D, Block 144E, Block 145A, Block 145B, Block 145C, Block 145D, Block 145E, Block 146A, Block 146B, Block 147, Block 148, Block 149,

Block 150, Block 151, Block 152, Block 153, Block 154, Block 155, Block 156, Block 157, Block 158, Block 159A, Block 159B, Block 160A, Block 160B; Tract 0117.05: Block Group 1: Block 101, Block 102A, Block 102B, Block 102C, Block 103, Block 104A, Block 104B, Block 105A, Block 105B, Block 105C, Block 105D, Block 105E, Block 105F, Block 105G, Block 106, Block 107, Block 108A, Block 108B, Block 109, Block 110, Block 111A, Block 111B, Block 113A, Block 113B, Block 114A, Block 114B, Block 114C, Block 115A, Block 115B, Block 118, Block 122A, Block 122C, Block 122D, Block 122E, Block 122F, Block 123, Block 124, Block 125, Block 126A, Block 126B, Block 127, Block 128, Block 129, Block 130, Block 131, Block 132, Block 133; Block Group 3: Block 301, Block 302A, Block 302B, Block 305, Block 306; Block Group 4: Block 401, Block 402, Block 403, Block 404, Block 405, Block 407; Block Group 6: Block 601, Block 602, Block 603, Block 604A, Block 604B, Block 604C, Block 605A, Block 605B, Block 606A, Block 606B, Block 607, Block 608, Block 609, Block 610, Block 611, Block 612, Block 613, Block 614, Block 615, Block 616, Block 617, Block 618A, Block 618B, Block 619A, Block 619B, Block 619C, Block 619E, Block 620A, Block 620B, Block 620E, Block 621C, Block 622A, Block 622B, Block 624, Block 625D, Block 625E, Block 628C, Block 629, Block 630, Block 632, Block 635, Block 637, Block 640, Block 641B; Tract 0119.01: Block Group 9: Block 911C, Block 911E, Block 912B, Block 912C, Block 912D, Block 913B; Lamar County, Lawrence County, Marion County, Marshall County: Tract 0301, Tract 0302, Tract 0303: Block Group 1: Block 129; Block Group 2: Block 259; Block Group 4: Block 463, Block 464, Block 465, Block 466A, Block 466B, Block 467, Block 473; Tract 0304: Block Group 1: Block 102, Block 103, Block 104, Block 109, Block 110, Block 112, Block 113, Block 114, Block 115, Block 116, Block 117, Block 121, Block 123, Block 124, Block 125, Block 126, Block 127A, Block 127B, Block 128, Block 129, Block 130, Block 131, Block 132, Block 133, Block 134, Block 135, Block 136, Block 137A, Block 137B, Block 138, Block 139, Block 140A, Block 140B, Block 141, Block 142, Block 143A, Block 143B, Block 144, Block 145, Block 146A, Block 146B, Block 147, Block 148, Block 149, Block 150, Block 151, Block 152, Block 153A, Block 153B, Block 154; Block Group 2: Block 201, Block 203, Block 204, Block 205, Block 206, Block 207, Block 208, Block 209, Block 210, Block 211, Block 212, Block 213, Block 214, Block 215, Block 216, Block 217, Block 218A, Block 218B, Block 219A, Block 219B, Block 219C, Block 219D, Block 219E, Block 220A, Block 220B, Block 220C, Block 221, Block 222, Block 223, Block 224, Block 225, Block 226, Block 227, Block 228, Block 229, Block 230, Block 231, Block 232A, Block 232B, Block 232C, Block 232D, Block 232E, Block 232F, Block 232G, Block 233, Block 234, Block 235A, Block 235B, Block 236A, Block 236B, Block 237, Block 238, Block 239, Block 240, Block 241A, Block 241B, Block 242A, Block 242B, Block 243, Block 244, Block 245, Block 246, Block 247, Block 248, Block 249, Block 250, Block 251, Block 252, Block 253A, Block 253B, Block 254, Block 255, Block 256, Block 257, Block 258, Block 259, Block 260, Block 261, Block 262, Block 263; Block Group 3: Block 301, Block 302, Block 303, Block 304A, Block 304B, Block 305, Block 306, Block 307, Block 308, Block 309, Block 310, Block 311, Block 312, Block 313, Block 314, Block 315, Block 316, Block 317, Block 318, Block 319, Block 320,

Block 321, Block 322, Block 323, Block 324, Block 325, Block 326, Block 327, Block 328, Block 329, Block 330, Block 331, Block 332, Block 333, Block 334, Block 335, Block 336, Block 337, Block 338, Block 339, Block 340, Block 341, Block 342, Block 343, Block 344, Block 345, Block 346, Block 347, Block 348, Block 349, Block 350; Block Group 4: Block 401A, Block 401B, Block 402, Block 403, Block 404A, Block 404B, Block 405A, Block 405B, Block 406A, Block 406B, Block 407A, Block 407B, Block 408, Block 409, Block 410, Block 411, Block 412, Block 413, Block 414, Block 415, Block 416, Block 417, Block 418, Block 419, Block 420, Block 421, Block 422, Block 423, Block 424, Block 425, Block 426, Block 427, Block 428, Block 429, Block 430, Block 431, Block 432, Block 433, Block 434; Block Group 5: Block 501, Block 502, Block 503, Block 504, Block 505, Block 506, Block 507, Block 508, Block 509, Block 510, Block 511, Block 512, Block 513, Block 514, Block 515, Block 516, Block 517, Block 518, Block 519, Block 520, Block 521, Block 522, Block 523, Block 524, Block 525, Block 526, Block 527, Block 528, Block 529, Block 530, Block 531, Block 532, Block 533, Block 534, Block 535, Block 536; Block Group 6: Block 601A, Block 601B, Block 601C, Block 601D, Block 602, Block 603A, Block 603B, Block 604A, Block 604B, Block 605, Block 606, Block 607A, Block 607B, Block 608, Block 609A, Block 609B, Block 610, Block 611, Block 612, Block 613, Block 614, Block 615, Block 616; Tract 0305, Tract 0306, Tract 0307, Tract 0308, Tract 0309.01, Tract 0309.02, Tract 0310, Tract 0311, Tract 0312; Pickens County: Tract 9878: Block Group 1: Block 107, Block 108A, Block 108B, Block 137, Block 138, Block 139, Block 140, Block 141, Block 142, Block 144, Block 145, Block 146, Block 161, Block 162, Block 163, Block 164, Block 165, Block 186, Block 187, Block 188, Block 189, Block 190, Block 191, Block 192, Block 193; Block Group 2: Block 239, Block 240, Block 241, Block 242, Block 244; Tract 9879: Block Group 4: Block 413, Block 414, Block 415, Block 416, Block 425, Block 426, Block 427, Block 428, Block 451, Block 452, Block 453, Block 480, Block 481, Block 482B, Block 483, Block 484, Block 485, Block 486, Block 487, Block 488, Block 489, Block 490, Block 491, Block 495; Walker County, Winston County.

District 5: Colbert County, Jackson County, Lauderdale County, Limestone County, Madison County, Marshall County: Tract 0303: Block Group 1: Block 101, Block 102, Block 103, Block 104, Block 105, Block 106, Block 107, Block 108, Block 109, Block 110, Block 111, Block 112, Block 113, Block 114, Block 115, Block 116, Block 117, Block 118, Block 119, Block 120, Block 121, Block 122, Block 123, Block 124, Block 125, Block 126, Block 127, Block 128, Block 130; Block Group 2: Block 201, Block 202, Block 203, Block 204, Block 205, Block 206, Block 207, Block 208, Block 209, Block 210, Block 211, Block 212, Block 213, Block 214, Block 215, Block 216, Block 217, Block 218, Block 219, Block 220, Block 221, Block 222, Block 223, Block 224, Block 225, Block 226, Block 227, Block 228, Block 229, Block 230, Block 231, Block 232, Block 233, Block 234, Block 235, Block 236, Block 237, Block 238, Block 239, Block 240, Block 241, Block 242, Block 243, Block 244, Block 245, Block 246, Block 247, Block 248, Block 249, Block 250, Block 251, Block 252, Block 253, Block 254, Block 255, Block 256, Block 257, Block 258, Block 260, Block 261, Block 262,

Block 263, Block 264, Block 265, Block 266, Block 267, Block 268, Block 269, Block 270, Block 271, Block 272, Block 273, Block 274, Block 275, Block 276, Block 277, Block 278, Block 279, Block 280; Block Group 3: Block 301, Block 302, Block 303, Block 304, Block 305, Block 306, Block 307, Block 308, Block 309, Block 310, Block 311, Block 312, Block 313, Block 314, Block 315, Block 316, Block 317, Block 318, Block 319, Block 320, Block 321, Block 322, Block 323A, Block 323B, Block 323C, Block 324, Block 325, Block 326, Block 327, Block 328, Block 329, Block 330, Block 331, Block 332, Block 333, Block 334A, Block 334B, Block 335A, Block 335B, Block 336, Block 337, Block 338, Block 339, Block 340, Block 341, Block 342, Block 343; Block Group 4: Block 401, Block 402, Block 403, Block 404, Block 405, Block 406, Block 407, Block 408, Block 409, Block 410, Block 411, Block 412, Block 413, Block 414, Block 415, Block 416, Block 417, Block 418, Block 419, Block 420, Block 421, Block 422, Block 423A, Block 423B, Block 424, Block 425, Block 426, Block 427, Block 428, Block 429, Block 430, Block 431, Block 432, Block 433, Block 434, Block 435, Block 436, Block 437, Block 438, Block 439, Block 440, Block 441, Block 442, Block 443, Block 444, Block 445, Block 446, Block 447, Block 448, Block 449, Block 450, Block 451, Block 452, Block 453, Block 454, Block 455, Block 456, Block 457, Block 458, Block 459, Block 460, Block 461, Block 462, Block 468, Block 469A, Block 469B, Block 470, Block 471A, Block 471B, Block 472A, Block 472B, Block 472C; Block Group 5: Block 501, Block 502, Block 503, Block 504, Block 505, Block 506, Block 507, Block 508, Block 509, Block 510, Block 511, Block 512A, Block 512B, Block 512C, Block 513A, Block 513B, Block 514A, Block 514B, Block 515, Block 516, Block 517, Block 518, Block 519, Block 520, Block 521, Block 522, Block 523, Block 524, Block 525, Block 526, Block 527, Block 528, Block 529; Tract 0304: Block Group 1: Block 101, Block 105, Block 106, Block 107, Block 108, Block 111, Block 118, Block 119, Block 120, Block 122; Block Group 2: Block 202; Morgan County.

District 6: Choctaw County, Hale County: Tract 9743: Block Group 1: Block 101, Block 102, Block 103, Block 104, Block 105, Block 106, Block 107A, Block 107B, Block 108A, Block 108B, Block 109, Block 110, Block 111, Block 112, Block 113, Block 114, Block 115, Block 116, Block 117, Block 118, Block 119, Block 120, Block 121, Block 122, Block 123, Block 124, Block 125, Block 126, Block 127, Block 128, Block 129, Block 130, Block 131, Block 132, Block 133, Block 134, Block 135, Block 136, Block 137, Block 138, Block 139, Block 140, Block 141A, Block 141B, Block 142, Block 143A, Block 143B, Block 144, Block 145, Block 146, Block 147, Block 148, Block 149A, Block 149B, Block 150, Block 151, Block 152, Block 153, Block 154, Block 155, Block 156, Block 157, Block 158, Block 159, Block 160, Block 161, Block 162, Block 163, Block 164, Block 165, Block 166, Block 167, Block 168, Block 169, Block 170, Block 171, Block 172, Block 173, Block 174, Block 175, Block 176, Block 177, Block 178, Block 179, Block 180, Block 181, Block 182; Block Group 2: Block 208, Block 209, Block 210A, Block 210B, Block 210C, Block 211A, Block 211B, Block 211C, Block 212, Block 213, Block 214, Block 215, Block 216, Block 217A, Block 217B, Block 217C, Block 218, Block 219A, Block 219B, Block 220, Block 221, Block 222, Block 223, Block 224, Block 227, Block 228A, Block 228B, Block 229, Block

230, Block 231, Block 232, Block 233, Block 234, Block 235, Block 236, Block 237, Block 264, Block 265, Block 266, Block 267, Block 268, Block 269, Block 270, Block 271, Block 272, Block 273, Block 274, Block 275, Block 276, Block 277, Block 278, Block 279, Block 280, Block 281, Block 282, Block 283, Block 284, Block 285, Block 286; Tract 9744: Block Group 1: Block 103, Block 104, Block 105, Block 106; Jefferson County: Tract 0001: Block Group 1: Block 101, Block 102, Block 103, Block 104; Block Group 2: Block 201, Block 202, Block 219, Block 220, Block 221, Block 222, Block 223, Block 224, Block 225, Block 226, Block 227; Block Group 3: Block 301, Block 302, Block 303, Block 304, Block 305, Block 306, Block 307, Block 308, Block 309, Block 310, Block 311, Block 312; Tract 0011: Block Group 2: Block 205B; Tract 0020: Block Group 1: Block 101A, Block 101B, Block 102, Block 106, Block 107, Block 108, Block 110; Block Group 2: Block 201, Block 202, Block 203, Block 208, Block 209, Block 211, Block 212, Block 213, Block 216, Block 217, Block 218, Block 219, Block 220, Block 221, Block 222, Block 223, Block 224, Block 226, Block 227, Block 228, Block 229, Block 230, Block 232; Block Group 3: Block 301, Block 302, Block 303, Block 304, Block 305, Block 306, Block 318, Block 319; Block Group 4: Block 407, Block 408, Block 411, Block 412, Block 413, Block 414, Block 415, Block 416; Tract 0021, Tract 0022: Block Group 1: Block 101, Block 102, Block 103, Block 104, Block 105, Block 106, Block 113, Block 116, Block 117, Block 118, Block 123; Block Group 2: Block 207, Block 219A, Block 219B, Block 219C, Block 220; Tract 0023.03: Block Group 3: Block 305, Block 308, Block 309, Block 310, Block 311, Block 344, Block 345, Block 347, Block 348, Block 349, Block 354, Block 356, Block 357; Tract 0023.04: Block Group 3: Block 301, Block 302, Block 303, Block 304, Block 312; Tract 0023.06, Tract 0035: Block Group 1: Block 101, Block 102, Block 103, Block 104, Block 105, Block 106, Block 107, Block 108, Block 109, Block 110, Block 111, Block 112, Block 113, Block 114, Block 115, Block 116A, Block 116B, Block 117, Block 118, Block 119A, Block 119B, Block 120, Block 121, Block 122, Block 123, Block 124A, Block 124B, Block 124C, Block 125, Block 126, Block 127, Block 128, Block 129, Block 130, Block 131, Block 132, Block 133, Block 134, Block 135, Block 136, Block 137, Block 138, Block 140, Block 141, Block 143, Block 144; Block Group 2: Block 201, Block 202, Block 203, Block 204, Block 205, Block 206, Block 207, Block 208, Block 209, Block 210, Block 211, Block 212, Block 213, Block 214, Block 215, Block 216, Block 217, Block 218, Block 219, Block 220, Block 221, Block 222, Block 223, Block 224, Block 225, Block 226, Block 227, Block 228, Block 229, Block 230, Block 231, Block 232, Block 233, Block 237, Block 241, Block 242, Block 243, Block 244, Block 246, Block 247, Block 248, Block 252; Block Group 3: Block 301, Block 302, Block 303A, Block 304, Block 305A, Block 305B, Block 306, Block 307, Block 308, Block 309, Block 310, Block 311, Block 312, Block 313, Block 314, Block 315, Block 316, Block 317, Block 320, Block 321, Block 322, Block 323, Block 324, Block 325, Block 326, Block 327, Block 328, Block 329, Block 330, Block 336, Block 338, Block 339, Block 340; Block Group 4: Block 401, Block 402, Block 403, Block 404, Block 405, Block 406, Block 407A, Block 408, Block 409, Block 410A, Block 410B, Block 410C, Block 411, Block 412A, Block 412B, Block 413A, Block 414, Block 415, Block 416,

Block 417, Block 418, Block 419, Block 423, Block 424, Block 425, Block 426, Block 429, Block 431, Block 433A, Block 433B, Block 433C, Block 434, Block 436, Block 438; Tract 0047.01: Block Group 6: Block 606, Block 608, Block 609, Block 610, Block 611, Block 625; Block Group 7: Block 707, Block 708, Block 711, Block 716, Block 718, Block 719, Block 720, Block 723, Block 727, Block 728; Block Group 8: Block 801, Block 802, Block 803, Block 805, Block 806; Tract 0047.02, Tract 0048, Tract 0049: Block Group 2: Block 207, Block 208, Block 209, Block 210, Block 232, Block 235, Block 236; Tract 0053.02, Tract 0055: Block Group 2: Block 202B; Block Group 3: Block 301A, Block 301B, Block 302B, Block 302C, Block 302D, Block 302E, Block 302F, Block 306, Block 307, Block 311B; Block Group 4: Block 403A, Block 403B, Block 403C, Block 404A, Block 404B, Block 441, Block 442; Tract 0056, Tract 0059.03, Tract 0059.05, Tract 0059.06, Tract 0059.07, Tract 0059.08, Tract 0100.01, Tract 0100.02: Block Group 2: Block 201, Block 202, Block 206A, Block 206B, Block 207A, Block 207B, Block 208A, Block 208B, Block 213, Block 214, Block 218, Block 219, Block 220, Block 222, Block 223A, Block 223B, Block 223C, Block 224A, Block 224B, Block 225, Block 226, Block 227, Block 228, Block 229; Block Group 3: Block 301, Block 302A, Block 302B, Block 302C, Block 302D, Block 302E, Block 302F, Block 303, Block 304, Block 305, Block 313, Block 314, Block 315, Block 316, Block 318, Block 319, Block 320, Block 321, Block 322, Block 337, Block 338, Block 339A, Block 339B, Block 340, Block 341; Block Group 5: Block 501A, Block 501B, Block 502, Block 503A, Block 503B, Block 504, Block 505, Block 506, Block 507B, Block 508, Block 509, Block 510, Block 511, Block 512, Block 513, Block 514, Block 515, Block 516, Block 517, Block 518, Block 519, Block 520B, Block 521, Block 522, Block 523, Block 524, Block 526, Block 531, Block 532, Block 533, Block 534; Block Group 6: Block 601, Block 602, Block 603, Block 604, Block 605, Block 606, Block 607, Block 609, Block 610, Block 611, Block 613, Block 614, Block 615, Block 617, Block 618, Block 621A, Block 621B, Block 622, Block 623, Block 624, Block 625, Block 626, Block 627, Block 630, Block 631, Block 632; Tract 0107.01, Tract 0107.02, Tract 0107.03, Tract 0107.04: Block Group 3: Block 301, Block 302, Block 303, Block 304, Block 305, Block 307, Block 308, Block 309, Block 310, Block 314, Block 315, Block 316, Block 331, Block 334, Block 338, Block 341, Block 342, Block 343, Block 344; Block Group 8: Block 817, Block 818; Tract 0107.05: Block Group 6: Block 601, Block 609, Block 610, Block 621, Block 626, Block 627, Block 628; Tract 0108.01, Tract 0108.02, Tract 0108.03, Tract 0108.04, Tract 0108.05, Tract 0110, Tract 0111.03, Tract 0111.04, Tract 0111.05, Tract 0111.06, Tract 0111.07, Tract 0111.08, Tract 0112.03, Tract 0112.04, Tract 0112.05, Tract 0112.06, Tract 0112.07, Tract 0112.08, Tract 0112.09, Tract 0112.10, Tract 0113: Block Group 1: Block 101A, Block 101B, Block 101C, Block 101D, Block 101E, Block 102A, Block 102B, Block 102C, Block 102D, Block 102E, Block 103, Block 104, Block 105, Block 106, Block 107, Block 108A, Block 108B, Block 109, Block 110, Block 111, Block 112, Block 113, Block 114A, Block 114B, Block 115A, Block 115B, Block 115C, Block 115D, Block 116, Block 117, Block 118, Block 119A, Block 119B, Block 120, Block 121A, Block 121B, Block 121C, Block 122, Block 123, Block 124, Block 125, Block 126, Block 127, Block 128, Block

129, Block 130, Block 131, Block 132, Block 133, Block 134, Block 135, Block 136A, Block 136B, Block 137A, Block 137B, Block 138, Block 139, Block 140, Block 141A, Block 141B, Block 142A, Block 142B, Block 143, Block 144, Block 145, Block 146, Block 147, Block 148, Block 149, Block 150, Block 151A, Block 151B, Block 151C, Block 151D, Block 151E, Block 152A, Block 152B, Block 153, Block 154, Block 155, Block 156, Block 157, Block 158, Block 159, Block 160A, Block 160B, Block 161A, Block 161B, Block 161C, Block 161D, Block 161F, Block 162A, Block 162B, Block 163, Block 164, Block 165A, Block 165B; Block Group 2: Block 201, Block 202, Block 203, Block 204, Block 205, Block 206, Block 207, Block 208, Block 209, Block 210, Block 211, Block 212, Block 213, Block 214, Block 215, Block 216, Block 217, Block 218, Block 219, Block 220, Block 221, Block 222, Block 223, Block 224, Block 225, Block 226, Block 227, Block 228, Block 229, Block 230, Block 231, Block 232, Block 233, Block 234, Block 235A, Block 235B, Block 236, Block 237A, Block 237B, Block 237C, Block 237D, Block 237E, Block 237F, Block 238, Block 239, Block 240, Block 241A, Block 241B, Block 242, Block 243, Block 244, Block 245, Block 246A, Block 247A, Block 248A, Block 249A, Block 249B, Block 251, Block 254B, Block 256A, Block 256C, Block 257, Block 258A, Block 258B, Block 259A, Block 259B, Block 262A, Block 262B, Block 262C, Block 273, Block 274, Block 275, Block 276, Block 277, Block 278, Block 279, Block 280, Block 281, Block 282, Block 283, Block 284, Block 285, Block 286, Block 287, Block 288, Block 289, Block 290, Block 291, Block 292, Block 293, Block 294, Block 295, Block 296, Block 297; Block Group 3: Block 301, Block 302, Block 303, Block 304, Block 305, Block 306, Block 307, Block 308, Block 309, Block 310, Block 311, Block 312, Block 313, Block 314, Block 315, Block 316, Block 317, Block 318, Block 319, Block 320, Block 321, Block 322, Block 323, Block 324, Block 325, Block 326, Block 327, Block 328, Block 329, Block 330, Block 331, Block 332, Block 333, Block 334, Block 335, Block 336, Block 337, Block 338, Block 339, Block 340, Block 341, Block 342, Block 343, Block 344, Block 345, Block 346; Block Group 4: Block 401, Block 402, Block 403, Block 404, Block 405, Block 406, Block 407, Block 408, Block 409, Block 410; Block Group 5: Block 501; Tract 0114: Block Group 1: Block 101A, Block 101B, Block 102A, Block 102B, Block 102C, Block 103A, Block 103B, Block 103C, Block 104, Block 105A, Block 105B, Block 106A, Block 106B, Block 107A, Block 107B, Block 108A, Block 108B, Block 109A, Block 109B, Block 110, Block 111, Block 112A, Block 112B, Block 113, Block 114, Block 115, Block 116, Block 117A, Block 117B, Block 118, Block 121, Block 122A, Block 122B, Block 123, Block 124, Block 125, Block 126, Block 127, Block 128, Block 129, Block 130, Block 131, Block 132A, Block 132B, Block 132C, Block 132D, Block 133, Block 134, Block 135, Block 136, Block 137, Block 138, Block 139, Block 140, Block 141, Block 142, Block 143, Block 144, Block 145, Block 146, Block 147, Block 148; Block Group 2: Block 201, Block 202, Block 203, Block 204, Block 205, Block 206, Block 207, Block 208, Block 209, Block 210, Block 211, Block 212, Block 213, Block 214, Block 215, Block 216, Block 217, Block 218, Block 219, Block 220, Block 221, Block 222, Block 223, Block 224, Block 225, Block 226, Block 227, Block 228, Block 229A, Block 229B, Block 234, Block 235, Block 236, Block 237, Block 238, Block 239, Block

240, Block 241, Block 242A, Block 242B, Block 243, Block 244, Block 245, Block 246, Block 247, Block 248, Block 249, Block 250, Block 251, Block 252, Block 253A, Block 253B, Block 254A, Block 254B, Block 254C, Block 255, Block 256; Block Group 3: Block 305A, Block 305B, Block 305F, Block 306A, Block 306B; Block Group 4: Block 411, Block 412, Block 413, Block 417, Block 441, Block 442, Block 443, Block 444, Block 445, Block 446, Block 447, Block 448, Block 449, Block 450, Block 451; Block Group 5: Block 501, Block 502, Block 503, Block 504, Block 505, Block 506, Block 507, Block 508, Block 509, Block 510, Block 511, Block 512, Block 513, Block 514, Block 515, Block 516, Block 517, Block 518, Block 519, Block 520, Block 521, Block 522, Block 523, Block 524; Block Group 6: Block 601, Block 602, Block 603, Block 604, Block 605A, Block 605B, Block 606, Block 607, Block 608; Tract 0115, Tract 0116: Block Group 1: Block 113, Block 114, Block 115, Block 116, Block 117, Block 118, Block 119, Block 120, Block 121, Block 122, Block 123, Block 124, Block 125, Block 128, Block 133, Block 134, Block 135, Block 136, Block 137, Block 138, Block 139, Block 144, Block 145, Block 146, Block 147, Block 148, Block 149, Block 150, Block 151, Block 152, Block 160A, Block 160B, Block 160C, Block 161, Block 162, Block 163A, Block 163B, Block 163C, Block 164A, Block 164B, Block 165, Block 166, Block 167, Block 168, Block 169, Block 170A, Block 170B, Block 171A, Block 171B, Block 171C, Block 172, Block 173A, Block 173B, Block 173C, Block 174A, Block 174B, Block 175, Block 176, Block 177, Block 178, Block 179, Block 180, Block 181, Block 182, Block 183, Block 184, Block 185A, Block 185B, Block 185C, Block 186, Block 187, Block 188, Block 189, Block 190A, Block 190B, Block 191A, Block 191B, Block 191C, Block 192A, Block 192B, Block 192C, Block 193A, Block 193B, Block 194, Block 195, Block 197; Tract 0117.03: Block Group 7: Block 702A, Block 703A, Block 703B, Block 703D, Block 704A, Block 704B, Block 705, Block 706, Block 707, Block 708, Block 709, Block 710, Block 711, Block 715, Block 717, Block 721, Block 722, Block 723, Block 724, Block 725; Block Group 9: Block 911A, Block 912A, Block 913, Block 914, Block 915A, Block 916A, Block 916B, Block 916C, Block 917A, Block 917B, Block 918; Tract 0117.04: Block Group 1: Block 102A, Block 102B, Block 103, Block 107; Tract 0117.05: Block Group 1: Block 112A, Block 112B, Block 112C, Block 112D, Block 116A, Block 116B, Block 116C, Block 116D, Block 116E, Block 116F, Block 116G, Block 116H, Block 116J, Block 116K, Block 116L, Block 116M, Block 116N, Block 116P, Block 116R, Block 117A, Block 117B, Block 117C, Block 117D, Block 119A, Block 119B, Block 120A, Block 120B, Block 120C, Block 120D, Block 120E, Block 121A, Block 121B, Block 121C, Block 122B; Block Group 6: Block 619D, Block 620C, Block 620D, Block 621A, Block 621B, Block 621D, Block 621E, Block 621F, Block 621G, Block 621H, Block 621J, Block 623, Block 625A, Block 625B, Block 625C, Block 625F, Block 625G, Block 626, Block 627, Block 628A, Block 628B, Block 628D, Block 631A, Block 631B, Block 633, Block 634, Block 636, Block 638, Block 639, Block 641A, Block 642, Block 643, Block 644, Block 645, Block 646, Block 647, Block 648, Block 649A, Block 649B, Block 649C, Block 649D, Block 649E, Block 650; Tract 0117.06, Tract 0118.01, Tract 0118.02, Tract 0118.03, Tract 0118.04, Tract 0119.01: Block Group 6: Block 601A, Block 601B, Block 602A, Block

602B, Block 603A, Block 603B, Block 604A, Block 604B, Block 605, Block 606, Block 607A, Block 607B, Block 608, Block 609, Block 610A, Block 610B, Block 611, Block 612, Block 613, Block 614, Block 615A, Block 615B, Block 616, Block 617, Block 618, Block 619, Block 620, Block 621, Block 622, Block 623, Block 624, Block 625, Block 626, Block 627, Block 628, Block 629, Block 630, Block 631, Block 632, Block 633, Block 634, Block 635A, Block 635B, Block 636, Block 637, Block 638A, Block 638B, Block 638C, Block 639, Block 640, Block 641, Block 642, Block 643, Block 644, Block 645, Block 647, Block 648, Block 649; Block Group 7: Block 701A, Block 701B, Block 701C, Block 701D, Block 701E, Block 701F, Block 702, Block 703, Block 704, Block 705A, Block 705B, Block 705C, Block 706A, Block 706B, Block 707A, Block 707B, Block 708A, Block 708B, Block 709A, Block 709B, Block 710, Block 719, Block 722, Block 725, Block 728, Block 738A, Block 738B, Block 738C, Block 749, Block 750, Block 751, Block 752A, Block 752B, Block 752C, Block 753A, Block 753B, Block 753C, Block 753D, Block 755, Block 756, Block 757A, Block 757B, Block 758, Block 759A, Block 759B, Block 759C, Block 759D; Block Group 8: Block 801A, Block 801B, Block 801C, Block 801D, Block 802A, Block 802B, Block 803, Block 804, Block 805, Block 806, Block 807, Block 808, Block 809, Block 810, Block 811, Block 812, Block 813, Block 814, Block 815, Block 816, Block 817, Block 818, Block 819, Block 820, Block 821, Block 822; Block Group 9: Block 901A, Block 901B, Block 901C, Block 901D, Block 901E, Block 901F, Block 901G, Block 901H, Block 901J, Block 902, Block 903, Block 904A, Block 904B, Block 905A, Block 905B, Block 906A, Block 906B, Block 907A, Block 907B, Block 907C, Block 907D, Block 908, Block 909A, Block 909B, Block 909C, Block 910, Block 911A, Block 911B, Block 911D, Block 912A, Block 913A, Block 913C, Block 913D, Block 914A, Block 914B, Block 915, Block 916, Block 917, Block 918, Block 919A, Block 919B, Block 919C, Block 919D, Block 919E, Block 919F, Block 920A, Block 920B, Block 920C, Block 921, Block 949; Tract 0119.02: Block Group 1: Block 105, Block 106, Block 107; Tract 0120.01, Tract 0120.02: Block Group 1: Block 101A, Block 101B, Block 102A, Block 102B, Block 103A, Block 103B, Block 103C, Block 103D, Block 103E, Block 104, Block 105, Block 106, Block 107, Block 108, Block 109, Block 110, Block 111A, Block 111B, Block 111C, Block 111D, Block 112, Block 113, Block 114A, Block 114B, Block 125, Block 128; Block Group 2: Block 201A, Block 201B, Block 202, Block 203A, Block 203B, Block 203C, Block 203D, Block 204, Block 209, Block 210, Block 211, Block 212, Block 213, Block 214, Block 215, Block 216, Block 217, Block 218, Block 219, Block 220, Block 221, Block 222, Block 223, Block 225, Block 226, Block 227, Block 228, Block 230, Block 231, Block 232, Block 233; Block Group 3: Block 301A, Block 301B, Block 302, Block 303, Block 304, Block 305, Block 306, Block 307, Block 308, Block 309, Block 310, Block 311, Block 312, Block 313, Block 314, Block 315, Block 316, Block 318; Block Group 4: Block 401, Block 402, Block 403, Block 404, Block 405, Block 406, Block 407, Block 408, Block 409, Block 410, Block 411, Block 412, Block 413; Block Group 8: Block 801, Block 802; Block Group 9: Block 901, Block 902A, Block 902B, Block 902C, Block 902D, Block 903A, Block 903B, Block 903C, Block 904A, Block 904B, Block 904C, Block 904D, Block 904E, Block 904F, Block 905A, Block

905B, Block 905C, Block 906A, Block 906B, Block 906C, Block 906D, Block 907A, Block 907B, Block 907C, Block 908A, Block 908B, Block 908C, Block 909A, Block 909B, Block 912, Block 913, Block 930, Block 932, Block 933, Block 939A, Block 939B, Block 939C, Block 939D, Block 940, Block 941, Block 942, Block 943, Block 944, Block 945, Block 946, Block 969, Block 970, Block 971; Tract 0121.03, Tract 0121.04, Tract 0122, Tract 0123.01, Tract 0123.02, Tract 0123.03, Tract 0123.04, Tract 0124.01: Block Group 1: Block 101, Block 102B, Block 105, Block 106, Block 107, Block 108, Block 109, Block 110, Block 121, Block 122, Block 123, Block 124, Block 125, Block 126, Block 128, Block 132, Block 133, Block 134, Block 136, Block 137, Block 138, Block 139, Block 140, Block 142, Block 143, Block 144, Block 145, Block 146, Block 147, Block 148, Block 152; Block Group 3: Block 301, Block 302, Block 303, Block 304, Block 305, Block 306, Block 307, Block 308, Block 311, Block 312, Block 313, Block 314, Block 316, Block 317; Tract 0124.02: Block Group 1: Block 107, Block 108, Block 109, Block 110, Block 114, Block 115, Block 116, Block 117, Block 118, Block 119, Block 122, Block 124, Block 125, Block 126, Block 127, Block 128; Block Group 2: Block 201B, Block 201C, Block 202, Block 203B, Block 207, Block 216, Block 221, Block 222, Block 223, Block 224, Block 225, Block 226, Block 227, Block 228; Block Group 4: Block 401, Block 402, Block 403, Block 404, Block 405, Block 406, Block 407, Block 408, Block 409, Block 410, Block 411, Block 412, Block 413, Block 414, Block 415, Block 416, Block 417, Block 418, Block 419, Block 420, Block 421A, Block 421B, Block 423, Block 424A, Block 424B, Block 425, Block 426A, Block 426B; Block Group 9: Block 901, Block 902, Block 903A, Block 903B, Block 904, Block 905, Block 906, Block 907, Block 908, Block 909, Block 910, Block 911, Block 912, Block 913, Block 914, Block 915, Block 916, Block 917, Block 918, Block 919, Block 920A, Block 920B, Block 921, Block 922, Block 923, Block 924A, Block 924B, Block 925; Tract 0124.03, Tract 0125: Block Group 1: Block 101, Block 102C, Block 103B, Block 103C, Block 104, Block 105, Block 106, Block 107, Block 108, Block 109, Block 110, Block 111, Block 112, Block 113, Block 114, Block 115, Block 116, Block 117, Block 118, Block 123, Block 124, Block 125; Block Group 2: Block 201B, Block 201C, Block 202, Block 203, Block 204, Block 205, Block 206, Block 207, Block 208C, Block 208D, Block 209, Block 210, Block 211, Block 212, Block 213, Block 214, Block 215, Block 216, Block 217, Block 218, Block 219, Block 220, Block 221, Block 222, Block 223, Block 224, Block 225, Block 226, Block 227, Block 228B, Block 229, Block 230, Block 231, Block 233, Block 234, Block 235, Block 236, Block 237, Block 240, Block 245, Block 246, Block 247, Block 248B, Block 249, Block 255; Block Group 4: Block 401A, Block 401B, Block 401C, Block 401D, Block 402, Block 403, Block 404, Block 405A, Block 405B, Block 405C, Block 406, Block 407, Block 408, Block 409A, Block 409B, Block 410, Block 411, Block 414, Block 416, Block 417, Block 418, Block 419, Block 421, Block 422, Block 423, Block 424, Block 425, Block 426, Block 427, Block 428, Block 438, Block 439, Block 440, Block 441, Block 442, Block 443, Block 445, Block 446, Block 447; Block Group 5: Block 501A, Block 501B, Block 502, Block 503, Block 504, Block 505, Block 506, Block 507, Block 508, Block 509, Block 510, Block 511, Block 512, Block 513, Block 514, Block 515, Block 516, Block

517, Block 518, Block 519, Block 520, Block 521A, Block 521B, Block 522A, Block 522B, Block 522C, Block 522D, Block 523, Block 524, Block 525, Block 526, Block 527, Block 528, Block 529, Block 530, Block 531, Block 532, Block 533, Block 534, Block 535, Block 536, Block 537, Block 538, Block 539, Block 540, Block 542A, Block 542B, Block 545; Block Group 6: Block 601, Block 602, Block 603, Block 604, Block 605, Block 606, Block 607, Block 608, Block 609, Block 610, Block 611, Block 612, Block 613, Block 614, Block 615, Block 616; Block Group 8: Block 801A, Block 801B, Block 801C, Block 801D, Block 801E, Block 802, Block 803, Block 804, Block 805A, Block 805B, Block 805C, Block 817, Block 818, Block 819, Block 820, Block 821, Block 822, Block 841, Block 843, Block 844, Block 845, Block 846, Block 847, Block 848, Block 849; Block Group 9: Block 901A, Block 901B, Block 901C, Block 901D, Block 902A, Block 902B, Block 903A, Block 903B, Block 903C, Block 903D, Block 904, Block 905, Block 906, Block 907, Block 908, Block 909, Block 910A, Block 910B, Block 910C; Tract 0126.02, Tract 0127.01, Tract 0127.02, Tract 0128.01, Tract 0129.01, Tract 0129.03, Tract 0129.05, Tract 0129.06, Tract 0129.07, Tract 0129.08, Tract 0129.09, Tract 0138.01: Block Group 1: Block 101A, Block 101B, Block 101C, Block 102, Block 103A, Block 103B, Block 104A, Block 104B, Block 104C, Block 104D, Block 104E, Block 105A, Block 105B, Block 106, Block 107, Block 108, Block 109; Tract 0139.01: Block Group 1: Block 101A, Block 101B, Block 102A, Block 102B, Block 102C, Block 103A, Block 103B, Block 104, Block 105A, Block 105B, Block 106, Block 107A, Block 107B, Block 108, Block 109, Block 110, Block 111, Block 112, Block 113, Block 114, Block 115, Block 116, Block 117, Block 118, Block 119A, Block 119B, Block 120, Block 121, Block 122, Block 123, Block 124, Block 125, Block 126, Block 127, Block 128, Block 129, Block 130, Block 131A, Block 131B, Block 132, Block 133A, Block 133B, Block 134, Block 135, Block 136, Block 137, Block 139, Block 141, Block 142, Block 143, Block 144, Block 145, Block 148, Block 149A, Block 149B, Block 149C, Block 149D, Block 150; Block Group 2: Block 201, Block 202A, Block 202B, Block 203, Block 204A, Block 204B, Block 205, Block 206A, Block 206B, Block 207A, Block 207B, Block 207C, Block 208, Block 209, Block 210, Block 216, Block 218; Block Group 4: Block 401A, Block 401B, Block 414, Block 415A, Block 415B, Block 416A, Block 416B, Block 417, Block 418, Block 419A, Block 419B, Block 423, Block 424, Block 425, Block 443, Block 444, Block 446A, Block 446B, Block 446C, Block 446D, Block 447A, Block 447B, Block 447C, Block 447D; Block Group 9: Block 902A; Tract 0139.02, Tract 0140, Tract 0141.02: Block Group 1: Block 102, Block 103, Block 105, Block 107, Block 108, Block 109, Block 111, Block 117, Block 118, Block 124, Block 125, Block 126, Block 127; Block Group 2: Block 201, Block 202, Block 203, Block 204, Block 205, Block 206, Block 207, Block 208, Block 209, Block 210, Block 211, Block 212, Block 213, Block 214, Block 215, Block 216, Block 217A, Block 217B, Block 218A, Block 218B, Block 219, Block 220, Block 221, Block 222A, Block 222B, Block 222C, Block 222D, Block 223A, Block 223B, Block 224, Block 225, Block 226A, Block 226B, Block 227, Block 228, Block 229, Block 230, Block 231, Block 232, Block 233, Block 234, Block 235, Block 236, Block 237, Block 238, Block 239, Block 240, Block 241, Block 242, Block 243, Block 244, Block 245, Block

246, Block 247, Block 248, Block 249, Block 250, Block 251, Block 252, Block 253, Block 254, Block 255, Block 256, Block 257, Block 258, Block 259, Block 260, Block 261, Block 262, Block 263, Block 264, Block 265, Block 266, Block 267, Block 268, Block 269, Block 270, Block 271, Block 272, Block 273, Block 274, Block 275, Block 276, Block 277A, Block 277B, Block 278, Block 279, Block 280, Block 281; Block Group 3: Block 301, Block 302, Block 303, Block 304, Block 305, Block 306, Block 307, Block 308, Block 309, Block 310, Block 311, Block 312, Block 313, Block 314, Block 315, Block 316, Block 317, Block 318, Block 319, Block 320, Block 321, Block 322, Block 323, Block 324, Block 325, Block 326, Block 327, Block 328, Block 329, Block 330, Block 331, Block 332, Block 333, Block 334, Block 335, Block 336, Block 337, Block 338, Block 339, Block 340, Block 341, Block 342, Block 343, Block 344, Block 345, Block 346, Block 347, Block 348, Block 349, Block 350, Block 351, Block 352, Block 353, Block 354, Block 355, Block 356, Block 357, Block 358, Block 359, Block 360, Block 361, Block 362, Block 363, Block 364, Block 365, Block 366, Block 367, Block 368, Block 369, Block 370, Block 371, Block 372, Block 373, Block 374, Block 375, Block 376, Block 377, Block 378; Block Group 4: Block 401, Block 402, Block 403, Block 404, Block 405, Block 406, Block 407, Block 408, Block 409, Block 410, Block 411, Block 412, Block 413, Block 414, Block 415, Block 416, Block 417, Block 418, Block 419, Block 420, Block 421, Block 422; Block Group 5: Block 501, Block 502, Block 503, Block 504, Block 505, Block 506, Block 507, Block 508, Block 509, Block 510, Block 511, Block 512, Block 513, Block 514, Block 515, Block 516, Block 517, Block 518, Block 519, Block 520, Block 521, Block 522, Block 523, Block 524, Block 525, Block 526, Block 527, Block 528, Block 529, Block 530, Block 531, Block 532, Block 533, Block 534, Block 535, Block 536, Block 537, Block 538, Block 539, Block 540, Block 541, Block 542, Block 543, Block 544, Block 545, Block 546, Block 547, Block 548, Block 549; Tract 0142.03: Block Group 2: Block 201, Block 202, Block 203, Block 204, Block 205, Block 206, Block 207, Block 208, Block 209, Block 210, Block 211, Block 212, Block 213, Block 214, Block 223, Block 224, Block 225, Block 226, Block 227, Block 228; Tract 0142.04, Tract 0143.02: Block Group 1: Block 103C, Block 105B, Block 106A, Block 106B, Block 106C, Block 107, Block 109, Block 110, Block 113, Block 115, Block 116, Block 117, Block 118, Block 119, Block 120, Block 121, Block 122, Block 123; Block Group 3: Block 301A, Block 301B, Block 302, Block 303, Block 304A, Block 304B, Block 304C, Block 304D, Block 304E, Block 305, Block 306, Block 339, Block 340, Block 341, Block 342, Block 344; Tract 0144.03: Block Group 1: Block 101A, Block 101C, Block 101D, Block 101E, Block 101G, Block 101H, Block 101J, Block 101K, Block 101L, Block 101M, Block 101N, Block 101P, Block 101R, Block 102A, Block 102D, Block 102E, Block 105, Block 106, Block 107A, Block 107B, Block 108A, Block 108B, Block 108C, Block 109, Block 110A, Block 110B, Block 111A, Block 111B; Block Group 2: Block 201A, Block 201B, Block 202, Block 203, Block 204, Block 205, Block 206A, Block 206B, Block 207, Block 208A, Block 208B, Block 209A, Block 209B, Block 210A, Block 210B, Block 211, Block 212, Block 213, Block 214, Block 215, Block 216, Block 217, Block 218, Block 219, Block 220A, Block 220B, Block 221, Block 222, Block 223, Block 224A, Block 224B, Block

224C, Block 225, Block 226, Block 227A, Block 227B, Block 228, Block 229, Block 230A, Block 230B, Block 230C, Block 230D, Block 230E, Block 231, Block 232A, Block 232B, Block 233, Block 234, Block 235, Block 236, Block 237, Block 238, Block 239, Block 240, Block 241, Block 242, Block 243; Block Group 3: Block 301A, Block 301B, Block 301C, Block 301D, Block 301E, Block 301F, Block 301G, Block 301H, Block 301J, Block 301K, Block 301L, Block 301M, Block 301N, Block 301P, Block 302, Block 303, Block 304, Block 305, Block 306, Block 307, Block 308, Block 309A, Block 309B, Block 309C, Block 309D, Block 310A, Block 310B, Block 311, Block 312, Block 313A, Block 313B, Block 314, Block 315, Block 316, Block 317, Block 318A, Block 318B, Block 319, Block 320, Block 321A, Block 321B, Block 321C, Block 322, Block 323, Block 324A, Block 324B, Block 324C, Block 325, Block 326, Block 327, Block 328, Block 329A, Block 329B; Block Group 4: Block 401A, Block 401B, Block 402, Block 403A, Block 403B, Block 403C, Block 403D, Block 403E, Block 404A, Block 404B, Block 404C, Block 404D, Block 405, Block 406A, Block 406B, Block 406C, Block 406D, Block 406E, Block 406F, Block 406G, Block 406H, Block 406J, Block 406K, Block 406L, Block 407, Block 408, Block 409, Block 410, Block 411, Block 412, Block 413, Block 414, Block 415, Block 416A, Block 416B, Block 416C, Block 416D, Block 416E, Block 416F, Block 416G, Block 416H, Block 417, Block 418, Block 419A, Block 419B, Block 419C, Block 420, Block 421, Block 422A, Block 422B, Block 423A, Block 423B, Block 423C, Block 423D, Block 424; Tract 0144.04: Block Group 1: Block 113, Block 114, Block 115, Block 116, Block 117, Block 118, Block 119, Block 120A, Block 120B, Block 121, Block 122A, Block 122B, Block 122C; Block Group 2: Block 201A, Block 201B, Block 201C, Block 201D, Block 202A, Block 202B, Block 203, Block 204, Block 205, Block 206, Block 207, Block 208, Block 209A, Block 209B, Block 210A, Block 210B, Block 210C, Block 210D, Block 210E, Block 210F, Block 210G, Block 211, Block 212, Block 213, Block 214, Block 215, Block 216, Block 217, Block 218, Block 219, Block 220, Block 221, Block 222, Block 223, Block 224, Block 225; Tract 0144.05, Tract 0144.06, Tract 0144.07; Marengo County, Pickens County: Tract 9876, Tract 9877, Tract 9878: Block Group 1: Block 101, Block 102, Block 103, Block 104, Block 105, Block 106, Block 109, Block 110, Block 111, Block 112, Block 113, Block 114, Block 115, Block 116, Block 117, Block 118, Block 119, Block 120, Block 121, Block 122, Block 123, Block 124, Block 125, Block 126, Block 127, Block 128, Block 129, Block 130, Block 131A, Block 131B, Block 132, Block 133, Block 134, Block 135, Block 136, Block 143, Block 147, Block 148, Block 149, Block 150, Block 151, Block 152A, Block 152B, Block 153, Block 154, Block 155, Block 156, Block 157, Block 158, Block 159, Block 160, Block 166, Block 167A, Block 167B, Block 168A, Block 168B, Block 169A, Block 169B, Block 170, Block 171A, Block 171B, Block 172, Block 173, Block 174, Block 175, Block 176, Block 177, Block 178, Block 179, Block 180, Block 181, Block 182A, Block 182B, Block 183, Block 184, Block 185; Block Group 2: Block 201, Block 202, Block 203, Block 204, Block 205, Block 206, Block 207, Block 208, Block 209, Block 210, Block 211, Block 212, Block 213, Block 214, Block 215, Block 216, Block 217, Block 218, Block 219, Block 220, Block 221, Block 222, Block 223, Block 224, Block 225, Block 226, Block 227, Block 228, Block 229, Block

230, Block 231A, Block 231B, Block 232A, Block 232B, Block 233, Block 234A, Block 234B, Block 235, Block 236A, Block 236B, Block 237, Block 238, Block 243, Block 245, Block 246, Block 247, Block 248, Block 249, Block 250, Block 251, Block 252, Block 253, Block 254, Block 255, Block 256; Tract 9879: Block Group 1: Block 101, Block 102, Block 103, Block 104, Block 105, Block 106, Block 107, Block 108A, Block 108B, Block 109, Block 110, Block 111, Block 112, Block 113, Block 114, Block 115, Block 116, Block 117, Block 118, Block 119, Block 120A, Block 120B, Block 121A, Block 121B, Block 122, Block 123, Block 124A, Block 124B, Block 125, Block 126, Block 127, Block 128A, Block 128B, Block 129, Block 130, Block 131, Block 132, Block 133, Block 134, Block 135, Block 136, Block 137, Block 138, Block 139, Block 140, Block 141, Block 142, Block 143, Block 144A, Block 144B, Block 145A, Block 145B, Block 145C, Block 146, Block 147, Block 148, Block 149, Block 150; Block Group 2: Block 201, Block 202, Block 203, Block 204, Block 205A, Block 205B, Block 206A, Block 206B, Block 207, Block 208, Block 209, Block 210, Block 211, Block 212, Block 213, Block 214, Block 215, Block 216, Block 217, Block 218, Block 219, Block 220, Block 221, Block 222, Block 223, Block 224, Block 225A, Block 225B, Block 226, Block 227A, Block 227B, Block 228, Block 229A, Block 229B, Block 230, Block 231, Block 232, Block 233A, Block 233B, Block 234A, Block 234B, Block 235, Block 236, Block 237, Block 238, Block 239, Block 240, Block 241, Block 242, Block 243, Block 244, Block 245, Block 246, Block 247, Block 248A, Block 248B, Block 249, Block 250, Block 251, Block 252, Block 253, Block 254, Block 255, Block 256, Block 257, Block 258; Block Group 3: Block 301A, Block 301B, Block 302A, Block 302B, Block 303, Block 304, Block 305, Block 306A, Block 306B, Block 307, Block 308, Block 309, Block 310, Block 311, Block 312, Block 313, Block 314, Block 315, Block 316, Block 317, Block 318, Block 319, Block 320, Block 321, Block 322, Block 323, Block 324, Block 325, Block 326A, Block 326B, Block 327, Block 328A, Block 328B, Block 329; Block Group 4: Block 401, Block 402, Block 403, Block 404, Block 405, Block 406, Block 407, Block 408, Block 409, Block 410, Block 411, Block 412, Block 417, Block 418, Block 419, Block 420, Block 421, Block 422, Block 423, Block 424, Block 429, Block 430, Block 431, Block 432, Block 433, Block 434, Block 435, Block 436, Block 437, Block 438, Block 439, Block 440, Block 441, Block 442, Block 443, Block 444, Block 445, Block 446, Block 447, Block 448, Block 449A, Block 449B, Block 450A, Block 450B, Block 450C, Block 454, Block 455, Block 456, Block 457A, Block 457B, Block 458, Block 459, Block 460A, Block 460B, Block 461, Block 462, Block 463A, Block 463B, Block 464, Block 465, Block 466, Block 467A, Block 467B, Block 468, Block 469, Block 470, Block 471, Block 472, Block 473, Block 474, Block 475, Block 476, Block 477A, Block 477B, Block 478A, Block 478B, Block 479A, Block 479B, Block 482A, Block 492, Block 493, Block 494; Tract 9880, Tract 9881; Sumter County, Tuscaloosa County.

District 7: Autauga County: Tract 0208: Block Group 1: Block 107, Block 108, Block 146, Block 153; Block Group 2: Block 203, Block 204, Block 205, Block 206, Block 207, Block 208, Block 209, Block 210, Block 211, Block 212, Block 213, Block 214, Block 215, Block 216, Block 217, Block 218, Block 219, Block 220, Block 221, Block 222, Block 231, Block 233, Block 234, Block 235, Block

236, Block 237, Block 238, Block 239, Block 240, Block 241, Block 243, Block 244, Block 245, Block 246; Block Group 3: Block 301, Block 302, Block 303, Block 304, Block 305, Block 311, Block 312, Block 315; Block Group 4: Block 401, Block 402, Block 403, Block 404, Block 405, Block 406, Block 407, Block 408, Block 409, Block 410, Block 411, Block 412, Block 413, Block 414, Block 415, Block 416, Block 417, Block 418, Block 419, Block 420, Block 421, Block 422, Block 423, Block 424, Block 425, Block 426, Block 427, Block 428, Block 429, Block 431, Block 436; Tract 0209, Tract 0210, Tract 0211; Bibb County, Bullock County, Dallas County, Greene County, Hale County: Tract 9743: Block Group 2: Block 201, Block 202, Block 203, Block 204, Block 205, Block 206, Block 207, Block 225, Block 226, Block 238, Block 239, Block 240, Block 241, Block 242, Block 243, Block 244, Block 245, Block 246, Block 247, Block 248, Block 249, Block 250, Block 251, Block 252, Block 253, Block 254, Block 255, Block 256, Block 257, Block 258, Block 259, Block 260, Block 261, Block 262, Block 263, Block 287, Block 288, Block 289, Block 290, Block 291, Block 292, Block 293, Block 294, Block 295, Block 296, Block 297; Tract 9744: Block Group 1: Block 101, Block 102, Block 107, Block 108, Block 109, Block 110, Block 111, Block 112, Block 113, Block 114, Block 115, Block 116, Block 117, Block 118, Block 119, Block 120, Block 121, Block 122, Block 123, Block 124, Block 125, Block 126, Block 127, Block 128, Block 129, Block 130, Block 131, Block 132, Block 133, Block 134, Block 135, Block 136, Block 137, Block 138, Block 139A, Block 139B, Block 140A, Block 140B, Block 141A, Block 141B, Block 142, Block 143, Block 144, Block 145, Block 146, Block 147, Block 148, Block 149, Block 150A, Block 150B, Block 151A, Block 151B, Block 152, Block 153, Block 154, Block 155A, Block 155B, Block 156, Block 157, Block 158, Block 159, Block 160, Block 161, Block 162, Block 163, Block 164, Block 165A, Block 165B, Block 166A, Block 166B, Block 167, Block 168, Block 169, Block 170, Block 171, Block 172, Block 173, Block 174, Block 175A, Block 175B, Block 176A, Block 176B, Block 177A, Block 177B, Block 178, Block 179, Block 180, Block 181, Block 182, Block 183, Block 184, Block 185, Block 186, Block 187, Block 188A, Block 188B, Block 189, Block 190, Block 191, Block 192, Block 193, Block 194, Block 195, Block 196, Block 197; Block Group 2: Block 201, Block 202, Block 203, Block 204, Block 205, Block 206, Block 207, Block 208, Block 209, Block 210, Block 211, Block 212, Block 213, Block 214, Block 215, Block 216, Block 217, Block 218, Block 219, Block 220, Block 221, Block 222, Block 223, Block 224, Block 225, Block 226, Block 227, Block 228, Block 229, Block 230, Block 231, Block 232, Block 233, Block 234, Block 235, Block 236, Block 237, Block 238, Block 239, Block 240, Block 241, Block 242, Block 243, Block 244, Block 245, Block 246, Block 247, Block 248, Block 249, Block 250, Block 251; Tract 9745, Tract 9746, Tract 9747, Tract 9748, Tract 9749; Jefferson County: Tract 0001: Block Group 1: Block 105, Block 106, Block 107, Block 108, Block 109, Block 110, Block 111, Block 112, Block 113; Block Group 2: Block 203, Block 204, Block 205, Block 206, Block 207, Block 208, Block 209, Block 210, Block 211, Block 212, Block 213, Block 214, Block 215, Block 216, Block 217, Block 218; Block Group 4: Block 401, Block 402, Block 403, Block 404, Block 405, Block 406, Block 407, Block 408, Block 409, Block 410, Block 411, Block 412, Block 413,

Block 414, Block 415; Block Group 5: Block 501, Block 502, Block 503, Block 504, Block 505, Block 506, Block 507, Block 508, Block 509, Block 510, Block 511, Block 512, Block 513, Block 514; Block Group 6: Block 601, Block 602, Block 603, Block 604, Block 605, Block 606, Block 607, Block 608, Block 609, Block 610, Block 611, Block 612, Block 613, Block 614, Block 615, Block 616; Block Group 7: Block 701, Block 702, Block 703, Block 704, Block 705, Block 706, Block 707, Block 708, Block 709, Block 710, Block 711, Block 712, Block 713, Block 714, Block 715, Block 716, Block 717, Block 718, Block 719, Block 720, Block 721, Block 722, Block 723, Block 724, Block 725, Block 726, Block 727, Block 728, Block 729, Block 730, Block 731, Block 732, Block 733; Block Group 8: Block 801, Block 802, Block 803, Block 804, Block 805, Block 806, Block 807, Block 808, Block 809, Block 810, Block 811, Block 812, Block 813, Block 814; Block Group 9: Block 901, Block 902, Block 903, Block 904, Block 905, Block 906, Block 907, Block 908; Tract 0003, Tract 0004, Tract 0005, Tract 0007, Tract 0008, Tract 0011: Block Group 1: Block 115, Block 116, Block 117, Block 118; Block Group 2: Block 201, Block 202, Block 203, Block 204, Block 205A, Block 206, Block 207, Block 208, Block 209, Block 210, Block 211, Block 212, Block 214, Block 219, Block 220, Block 223, Block 224; Block Group 3: Block 301, Block 302, Block 303, Block 304, Block 305, Block 306, Block 307, Block 308, Block 309, Block 312, Block 313, Block 322, Block 332, Block 333, Block 334, Block 335; Block Group 4: Block 401, Block 402, Block 403, Block 404, Block 405, Block 406, Block 407, Block 408, Block 409, Block 410, Block 411, Block 412, Block 413, Block 414, Block 415, Block 416, Block 417, Block 418, Block 419, Block 420, Block 421, Block 422, Block 423, Block 424, Block 425, Block 426, Block 427, Block 428, Block 429, Block 431, Block 432, Block 433, Block 434, Block 435; Block Group 5: Block 501, Block 502, Block 503, Block 504, Block 505, Block 506, Block 507, Block 508, Block 509, Block 510, Block 511, Block 517, Block 518, Block 519, Block 520, Block 521, Block 522, Block 523, Block 524, Block 525, Block 527, Block 529, Block 530, Block 531, Block 533, Block 534, Block 541, Block 544, Block 546, Block 547, Block 548, Block 549, Block 550, Block 551, Block 552, Block 555, Block 556, Block 557, Block 558, Block 561, Block 565, Block 568, Block 569, Block 570; Block Group 6: Block 601, Block 602A, Block 602B, Block 603A, Block 603B, Block 604, Block 605, Block 606, Block 607, Block 608, Block 609, Block 610, Block 611, Block 612, Block 613, Block 614, Block 615, Block 616A, Block 616B, Block 617, Block 626, Block 627, Block 628, Block 629, Block 631; Block Group 9: Block 901, Block 902, Block 903, Block 904, Block 905, Block 906, Block 907, Block 908, Block 909, Block 910, Block 911, Block 912, Block 913, Block 914, Block 915, Block 961, Block 963; Tract 0012, Tract 0014, Tract 0015, Tract 0016, Tract 0019.02, Tract 0020: Block Group 3: Block 309, Block 310, Block 311, Block 314, Block 315, Block 316, Block 320; Block Group 4: Block 401, Block 402, Block 403, Block 404, Block 405, Block 406; Tract 0022: Block Group 1: Block 112, Block 120, Block 121, Block 122; Block Group 2: Block 201, Block 202, Block 212, Block 216, Block 221, Block 222, Block 223, Block 225; Block Group 3: Block 301, Block 308, Block 309, Block 312, Block 313, Block 314, Block 315, Block 316, Block 318, Block 320, Block 321, Block 322, Block 323,

Block 324, Block 325, Block 326, Block 327, Block 328, Block 329, Block 330, Block 331, Block 332, Block 333, Block 335, Block 336, Block 337, Block 338, Block 339, Block 340, Block 341; Block Group 4: Block 401, Block 402, Block 403, Block 404, Block 412, Block 413, Block 414, Block 415, Block 416, Block 417, Block 418, Block 419, Block 420, Block 421; Tract 0023.03: Block Group 1: Block 101, Block 108, Block 109, Block 110, Block 114, Block 116, Block 117, Block 123, Block 126, Block 127, Block 128, Block 130, Block 131, Block 132, Block 133, Block 134, Block 135, Block 136, Block 137, Block 138, Block 139, Block 140; Block Group 2: Block 201, Block 202, Block 203, Block 204, Block 205, Block 206, Block 207, Block 212, Block 214, Block 216, Block 219; Block Group 3: Block 301, Block 302, Block 303, Block 304, Block 306, Block 307; Tract 0023.04: Block Group 3: Block 333, Block 337, Block 338, Block 339, Block 341, Block 342; Block Group 4: Block 401, Block 402, Block 403, Block 404, Block 405, Block 406, Block 407, Block 408, Block 409, Block 410, Block 411, Block 412, Block 413, Block 414, Block 415, Block 416, Block 417, Block 418, Block 419, Block 420, Block 421; Tract 0023.05, Tract 0024, Tract 0027, Tract 0029, Tract 0030.01, Tract 0030.02, Tract 0031, Tract 0032, Tract 0033, Tract 0034, Tract 0035: Block Group 3: Block 303B, Block 303C, Block 305C, Block 305D; Block Group 4: Block 407B, Block 413B, Block 413C; Tract 0036, Tract 0037, Tract 0038.02, Tract 0038.03, Tract 0039, Tract 0040, Tract 0042, Tract 0045, Tract 0047.01: Block Group 6: Block 601, Block 613, Block 614, Block 615, Block 616, Block 618, Block 621, Block 622, Block 623; Block Group 7: Block 701, Block 703, Block 704, Block 705, Block 706, Block 709, Block 710, Block 712, Block 713, Block 715, Block 725; Block Group 8: Block 808, Block 810, Block 812, Block 816, Block 819, Block 820, Block 822; Tract 0049: Block Group 1: Block 101, Block 102, Block 103, Block 104, Block 105, Block 106, Block 107, Block 108, Block 109, Block 110, Block 111, Block 112, Block 113, Block 114, Block 115, Block 116, Block 117, Block 118, Block 119; Block Group 2: Block 205; Block Group 4: Block 401, Block 402, Block 403, Block 404, Block 405, Block 406, Block 407, Block 408, Block 409, Block 410, Block 411, Block 412, Block 413; Block Group 7: Block 701, Block 702, Block 703, Block 704, Block 705, Block 706, Block 707, Block 708, Block 709, Block 710, Block 711, Block 712, Block 713, Block 714, Block 715, Block 716, Block 717, Block 718, Block 719; Block Group 8: Block 801, Block 802, Block 803, Block 804, Block 805, Block 806, Block 807, Block 808, Block 809, Block 810, Block 811, Block 812, Block 813, Block 814, Block 815, Block 816, Block 817, Block 818, Block 819, Block 820, Block 821; Tract 0050, Tract 0051.01, Tract 0051.02, Tract 0052, Tract 0055: Block Group 1: Block 101, Block 102, Block 103, Block 104, Block 105, Block 106, Block 107, Block 108, Block 109, Block 110, Block 111, Block 112, Block 120, Block 121, Block 122; Block Group 2: Block 201, Block 202A, Block 203, Block 204, Block 205, Block 206; Block Group 3: Block 302A, Block 302G, Block 303, Block 304, Block 305, Block 308, Block 309, Block 310, Block 311A, Block 312, Block 313, Block 314, Block 315, Block 316, Block 317, Block 318, Block 322, Block 323, Block 333; Block Group 4: Block 401, Block 402, Block 405, Block 406, Block 407A, Block 407B, Block 408, Block 409, Block 410, Block 411A, Block 411B, Block 414A, Block 414B, Block 416, Block 427,

Block 428, Block 432, Block 433, Block 434; Block Group 5: Block 501, Block 502A, Block 502B, Block 503, Block 504, Block 505, Block 506, Block 507, Block 508, Block 509, Block 510A, Block 510B, Block 510C, Block 511, Block 512, Block 513, Block 514A, Block 514B, Block 515, Block 516, Block 520, Block 523, Block 524, Block 525, Block 527, Block 529, Block 530, Block 531, Block 532, Block 555A, Block 555B, Block 555C, Block 556; Block Group 6: Block 602, Block 603, Block 605, Block 606, Block 607, Block 608, Block 609, Block 611, Block 614, Block 615, Block 616, Block 617, Block 623, Block 645, Block 646, Block 647, Block 648, Block 649; Tract 0057.01, Tract 0057.02, Tract 0058, Tract 0100.02: Block Group 5: Block 507A, Block 520A; Tract 0101, Tract 0102, Tract 0103.01, Tract 0103.02, Tract 0104.01, Tract 0104.02, Tract 0105, Tract 0106.02, Tract 0106.03, Tract 0107.04: Block Group 3: Block 306; Block Group 8: Block 801, Block 802, Block 809, Block 811, Block 812, Block 813, Block 819, Block 820, Block 821, Block 822, Block 823, Block 824, Block 825, Block 827, Block 828, Block 829, Block 843, Block 846A, Block 846B, Block 847; Tract 0107.05: Block Group 6: Block 602, Block 603, Block 604, Block 605, Block 606, Block 607, Block 608, Block 629, Block 630, Block 631, Block 632, Block 633, Block 634, Block 635, Block 636, Block 637, Block 638, Block 639, Block 640, Block 641, Block 642, Block 645, Block 646, Block 649; Block Group 7: Block 701, Block 751, Block 752, Block 753; Block Group 8: Block 801, Block 804, Block 807, Block 808; Tract 0107.06, Tract 0109, Tract 0119.02: Block Group 1: Block 101, Block 102, Block 103, Block 104, Block 108, Block 109, Block 110, Block 115, Block 116, Block 118, Block 119, Block 120, Block 121; Block Group 5: Block 501, Block 502A, Block 502B, Block 502C, Block 502D, Block 502E, Block 503, Block 504, Block 505, Block 506, Block 507, Block 508, Block 509, Block 510, Block 511, Block 512, Block 513, Block 514, Block 515A, Block 515B, Block 516A, Block 516B, Block 517, Block 518, Block 519A, Block 519B, Block 520A, Block 520B, Block 521A, Block 521B, Block 522; Tract 0119.03, Tract 0120.02: Block Group 5: Block 501A, Block 501B, Block 501C, Block 501D, Block 501E, Block 502A, Block 502B, Block 502C, Block 503, Block 504, Block 505, Block 506A, Block 506B, Block 506C, Block 507A, Block 507B, Block 508, Block 509A, Block 509B, Block 513, Block 530, Block 533, Block 534, Block 535, Block 536, Block 537, Block 539, Block 540, Block 550, Block 557, Block 558; Block Group 9: Block 910A, Block 910B, Block 910C, Block 910D, Block 910E, Block 911, Block 966A, Block 966B; Tract 0124.01: Block Group 1: Block 102A, Block 103, Block 104; Tract 0124.02: Block Group 2: Block 201A, Block 203A; Tract 0125: Block Group 1: Block 102A, Block 102B, Block 102D, Block 102E, Block 103A, Block 103D, Block 103E, Block 103F, Block 103G, Block 103H, Block 119, Block 120, Block 121A, Block 121B, Block 122A, Block 122B, Block 122C, Block 126A, Block 126B, Block 126C, Block 126D, Block 127, Block 128A, Block 128B, Block 128C, Block 128D, Block 128E, Block 128F, Block 128G; Block Group 2: Block 201A, Block 208A, Block 208B, Block 228A, Block 248A; Block Group 7: Block 701A, Block 701B, Block 701C, Block 702, Block 703, Block 704, Block 705, Block 706, Block 707, Block 708, Block 710, Block 711, Block 716, Block 717, Block 718, Block 722, Block 723, Block 725, Block 726, Block 727, Block 728, Block 729; Tract 0130.02, Tract 0131, Tract 0132,

Tract 0133, Tract 0134, Tract 0136.01, Tract 0138.01: Block Group 1: Block 110A, Block 110B, Block 110C, Block 110D, Block 111, Block 112A, Block 112B, Block 112C, Block 113A, Block 113B, Block 113C, Block 113D, Block 114, Block 115, Block 116A, Block 116B, Block 117, Block 118, Block 119, Block 120, Block 121, Block 122, Block 123, Block 124, Block 125, Block 126, Block 127, Block 128, Block 129, Block 130, Block 131, Block 132, Block 133, Block 134, Block 135, Block 136, Block 137, Block 138, Block 139, Block 140, Block 141, Block 142, Block 143, Block 144, Block 145, Block 146, Block 147; Block Group 2: Block 201, Block 202, Block 220, Block 221, Block 222, Block 223; Block Group 3: Block 301, Block 302, Block 303, Block 304, Block 305, Block 306, Block 307, Block 308, Block 309, Block 313, Block 317, Block 318, Block 319, Block 320, Block 321; Block Group 4: Block 401, Block 402, Block 403, Block 404, Block 405, Block 406, Block 407, Block 408; Block Group 5: Block 501, Block 502, Block 503, Block 504, Block 513, Block 514, Block 517, Block 518, Block 519, Block 520, Block 521, Block 522, Block 523, Block 524, Block 525, Block 526; Block Group 6: Block 601, Block 602, Block 605, Block 606, Block 607, Block 608, Block 612, Block 613, Block 614, Block 615, Block 616, Block 617, Block 618, Block 619, Block 620, Block 621, Block 622, Block 623, Block 624, Block 625, Block 626, Block 627, Block 628; Block Group 7: Block 721A, Block 721B, Block 721C, Block 722, Block 723, Block 724, Block 725; Tract 0139.01: Block Group 9: Block 901A, Block 901B, Block 902B, Block 902C, Block 903A, Block 903B, Block 903C, Block 904A, Block 904B, Block 905, Block 906A, Block 906B, Block 907A, Block 907B; Tract 0141.02: Block Group 1: Block 101A, Block 101B, Block 101C, Block 104, Block 106, Block 110, Block 112, Block 113, Block 114, Block 115, Block 116, Block 119, Block 120, Block 121, Block 122, Block 123; Tract 0141.03, Tract 0141.04, Tract 0141.05, Tract 0142.03: Block Group 1: Block 101, Block 102, Block 103, Block 104, Block 105, Block 106, Block 107, Block 108, Block 109, Block 110, Block 111, Block 112, Block 113, Block 114, Block 115, Block 116, Block 117, Block 118, Block 119, Block 120, Block 121, Block 122, Block 123, Block 124, Block 125, Block 126, Block 127, Block 128, Block 129, Block 130, Block 131, Block 132, Block 133, Block 134, Block 135, Block 136, Block 137, Block 138A, Block 138B, Block 138C, Block 138D, Block 139A, Block 139B, Block 140, Block 141, Block 142, Block 143, Block 144, Block 145, Block 146, Block 147, Block 148, Block 149, Block 150, Block 151, Block 152; Block Group 2: Block 215, Block 216, Block 217, Block 218, Block 219, Block 220, Block 221, Block 222; Block Group 3: Block 301, Block 302, Block 303, Block 304, Block 305, Block 306, Block 307, Block 308, Block 309, Block 310, Block 311, Block 312, Block 313, Block 314, Block 315, Block 316, Block 317, Block 318, Block 319, Block 320, Block 321, Block 322, Block 323, Block 324, Block 325, Block 326, Block 327, Block 328, Block 329, Block 330, Block 331, Block 332, Block 333; Block Group 9: Block 901A, Block 901B, Block 902, Block 903, Block 904, Block 905, Block 906, Block 907, Block 908, Block 909A, Block 909B, Block 910, Block 911, Block 912A, Block 912B, Block 913, Block 914A, Block 914B, Block 914C, Block 915A, Block 915B; Tract 0143.01, Tract 0143.02: Block Group 1: Block 101, Block 102, Block 103A, Block 103B, Block 104A, Block 104B, Block 104C, Block 105A, Block 108A,

Block 108B, Block 108C, Block 108D, Block 108E, Block 108F, Block 108G, Block 108H, Block 111A, Block 111B, Block 112A, Block 112B, Block 112C, Block 114; Block Group 2: Block 201, Block 202A, Block 202B, Block 202C, Block 203; Block Group 9: Block 901, Block 902, Block 903, Block 904, Block 905, Block 906, Block 907, Block 908; Tract 0144.03: Block Group 1: Block 101B, Block 101F, Block 102B, Block 102C, Block 103A, Block 103B, Block 104; Tract 0144.04: Block Group 1: Block 101, Block 102A, Block 102B, Block 102C, Block 102D, Block 102E, Block 102F, Block 103, Block 104A, Block 104B, Block 104C, Block 104D, Block 104E, Block 104F, Block 104G, Block 104H, Block 104J, Block 104K, Block 105, Block 106A, Block 106B, Block 107, Block 108A, Block 108B, Block 108C, Block 108D, Block 109A, Block 109B, Block 109C, Block 109D, Block 109E, Block 109F, Block 109G, Block 109H, Block 109J, Block 109K, Block 109L, Block 109M, Block 109N, Block 110A, Block 110B, Block 110C, Block 110D, Block 111A, Block 111B, Block 111C, Block 112A, Block 112B, Block 112C, Block 112D, Block 112E, Block 112F, Block 112G, Block 112H, Block 112J, Block 112K, Block 112L, Block 112M, Block 112N, Block 123, Block 124; Lowndes County, Macon County, Montgomery County: Tract 0001: Block Group 1: Block 101, Block 102, Block 103, Block 104, Block 105, Block 106, Block 107, Block 108, Block 109, Block 110, Block 111, Block 112, Block 113, Block 114, Block 115, Block 116, Block 117, Block 118, Block 119, Block 120, Block 121, Block 122, Block 123, Block 124, Block 125, Block 126, Block 127, Block 128, Block 135, Block 136, Block 137, Block 138, Block 139, Block 142, Block 143, Block 144, Block 145, Block 146, Block 147, Block 148, Block 149, Block 150, Block 151, Block 188, Block 189, Block 190; Block Group 2: Block 201, Block 202, Block 203, Block 204, Block 205, Block 206, Block 207, Block 209, Block 210, Block 211, Block 212, Block 213, Block 214, Block 215, Block 216, Block 217, Block 218, Block 219, Block 220; Tract 0002: Block Group 1: Block 112, Block 113, Block 114, Block 115, Block 116, Block 117, Block 120; Block Group 2: Block 202, Block 203, Block 204, Block 205, Block 206, Block 207, Block 208, Block 209, Block 210, Block 211, Block 212, Block 213, Block 214, Block 215, Block 216, Block 217, Block 218, Block 219, Block 220, Block 221, Block 222, Block 223, Block 224, Block 225, Block 226, Block 227, Block 228, Block 229, Block 230, Block 231, Block 232; Block Group 3: Block 301, Block 302, Block 303, Block 313, Block 314, Block 315, Block 319, Block 320, Block 331, Block 332; Block Group 4: Block 401, Block 402, Block 403, Block 404, Block 405, Block 406, Block 407, Block 408, Block 409, Block 410, Block 411, Block 416, Block 417, Block 418, Block 419, Block 426; Tract 0003.85, Tract 0004, Tract 0005: Block Group 3: Block 316, Block 317, Block 318; Block Group 4: Block 401, Block 402, Block 403; Tract 0006: Block Group 1: Block 101, Block 102, Block 103, Block 104, Block 105, Block 106, Block 107, Block 108, Block 109, Block 110, Block 112, Block 113, Block 114, Block 115, Block 117; Block Group 2: Block 201, Block 202, Block 203, Block 204, Block 205, Block 206, Block 207, Block 208, Block 209, Block 210, Block 211, Block 212, Block 213, Block 214, Block 215, Block 216, Block 217, Block 218, Block 219, Block 220, Block 221, Block 222, Block 223, Block 224, Block 225; Block Group 3: Block 301, Block 302, Block 303, Block 304, Block 305, Block 306,

Block 307, Block 308, Block 309, Block 310, Block 311, Block 312, Block 313, Block 314, Block 315, Block 316, Block 317, Block 318, Block 319, Block 320, Block 321, Block 322, Block 323, Block 324, Block 325, Block 326, Block 327, Block 328; Tract 0007, Tract 0010: Block Group 2: Block 201, Block 202, Block 203, Block 204, Block 205, Block 206, Block 207, Block 208, Block 209, Block 210, Block 211, Block 212, Block 213, Block 214, Block 215, Block 216, Block 217, Block 218, Block 219, Block 220, Block 221, Block 222, Block 223, Block 224, Block 225, Block 226, Block 227, Block 228, Block 229, Block 230, Block 231, Block 232, Block 233, Block 234, Block 235, Block 236, Block 237, Block 238, Block 239, Block 240, Block 241, Block 242, Block 243, Block 244, Block 245, Block 246, Block 247, Block 248, Block 249, Block 250, Block 251, Block 252, Block 253, Block 254, Block 255, Block 256; Block Group 3: Block 301, Block 302, Block 303, Block 304, Block 305, Block 306, Block 307, Block 308, Block 309, Block 310, Block 311, Block 312, Block 313, Block 314, Block 315; Block Group 4: Block 401, Block 402, Block 403, Block 404, Block 405, Block 406, Block 407, Block 408, Block 409, Block 410, Block 411, Block 412, Block 413, Block 414, Block 415, Block 416, Block 417; Block Group 5: Block 501; Tract 0011: Block Group 1: Block 102, Block 103, Block 104, Block 105, Block 106, Block 107, Block 108, Block 109, Block 110, Block 111, Block 112, Block 113, Block 114, Block 115, Block 116, Block 117, Block 118, Block 119, Block 120, Block 121, Block 122, Block 123, Block 124, Block 125, Block 126, Block 127, Block 130, Block 134, Block 135; Block Group 2: Block 203, Block 204, Block 205, Block 209, Block 210, Block 211, Block 212, Block 215, Block 222, Block 225; Block Group 3: Block 301, Block 302, Block 303, Block 304, Block 305, Block 306, Block 307, Block 308, Block 309, Block 310, Block 311, Block 312, Block 313, Block 314, Block 315, Block 316, Block 317, Block 318, Block 319, Block 320, Block 321, Block 322, Block 323, Block 324, Block 325; Block Group 4: Block 401, Block 402, Block 403, Block 404, Block 405, Block 406, Block 407, Block 408, Block 409, Block 410, Block 411, Block 412, Block 413, Block 414, Block 415, Block 416, Block 417; Block Group 5: Block 501, Block 502, Block 503, Block 504, Block 505, Block 506, Block 507, Block 508, Block 509, Block 510, Block 511, Block 512, Block 513, Block 514, Block 515, Block 516, Block 517, Block 518, Block 519; Block Group 6: Block 601, Block 602, Block 603, Block 604, Block 605, Block 606, Block 607, Block 608, Block 609; Block Group 7: Block 701, Block 702, Block 703, Block 704, Block 705, Block 706, Block 707, Block 708; Block Group 8: Block 801, Block 802, Block 803, Block 804, Block 805, Block 806, Block 807, Block 808; Tract 0012, Tract 0013: Block Group 3: Block 301, Block 302, Block 303, Block 304, Block 305, Block 306, Block 307, Block 308, Block 309, Block 310, Block 311, Block 312, Block 313, Block 314, Block 315, Block 316; Block Group 4: Block 401, Block 402, Block 403, Block 405, Block 406, Block 407, Block 408, Block 409, Block 410, Block 411, Block 415; Tract 0014: Block Group 1: Block 103, Block 104, Block 105, Block 106, Block 107; Block Group 4: Block 413, Block 414, Block 415, Block 416, Block 417, Block 418; Block Group 5: Block 501, Block 502, Block 503, Block 504, Block 506, Block 507, Block 513, Block 514; Tract 0015: Block Group 2: Block 204, Block 211, Block 212, Block 213, Block 214, Block 221,

Block 222, Block 223, Block 229; Block Group 3: Block 301, Block 302, Block 303, Block 304, Block 305, Block 306, Block 307, Block 308, Block 309, Block 310, Block 311, Block 312, Block 313, Block 314, Block 315, Block 316, Block 317, Block 318, Block 319, Block 320, Block 321, Block 322; Block Group 4: Block 401, Block 402, Block 403, Block 404, Block 405, Block 406, Block 407, Block 408, Block 409, Block 417; Tract 0020: Block Group 3: Block 301, Block 302, Block 303, Block 304, Block 305, Block 306, Block 307, Block 308, Block 314, Block 315; Tract 0021: Block Group 2: Block 201, Block 202, Block 203, Block 204, Block 205, Block 206, Block 207, Block 208, Block 209, Block 210, Block 211, Block 212, Block 213, Block 214, Block 215, Block 216; Block Group 3: Block 301, Block 302, Block 303, Block 308, Block 310, Block 311, Block 312, Block 313, Block 314, Block 315, Block 316, Block 317, Block 318, Block 319; Block Group 4: Block 403, Block 404, Block 405, Block 408, Block 409, Block 410, Block 411, Block 412, Block 413, Block 414, Block 415, Block 416, Block 417, Block 418, Block 419, Block 423, Block 424, Block 425, Block 426; Tract 0022, Tract 0023, Tract 0024, Tract 0025, Tract 0029, Tract 0030, Tract 0031, Tract 0032, Tract 0051.01: Block Group 1: Block 101, Block 102, Block 103, Block 104, Block 105, Block 106, Block 107A, Block 107B, Block 108, Block 109, Block 110, Block 111, Block 112, Block 113A, Block 113B, Block 114, Block 115A, Block 115B, Block 116, Block 117, Block 118, Block 119, Block 120, Block 121, Block 122, Block 123A, Block 123B, Block 124A, Block 124B, Block 125, Block 126, Block 127, Block 128A, Block 128B, Block 129, Block 130A, Block 130B, Block 131, Block 132, Block 133, Block 134, Block 135, Block 136, Block 137, Block 138, Block 139, Block 140, Block 141, Block 142, Block 143, Block 144, Block 145, Block 146, Block 147, Block 150, Block 151, Block 152, Block 153, Block 154, Block 155, Block 156, Block 157, Block 158, Block 159, Block 160, Block 161, Block 162, Block 163, Block 164, Block 165, Block 166, Block 167; Block Group 2: Block 201A, Block 201B, Block 202A, Block 202B, Block 203A, Block 203B, Block 204, Block 205A, Block 205B, Block 206, Block 207, Block 208, Block 209, Block 210, Block 211, Block 213, Block 214, Block 215, Block 216, Block 217, Block 218; Tract 0051.02, Tract 0054.01: Block Group 1: Block 101, Block 102, Block 103, Block 104, Block 105A, Block 105B, Block 105C, Block 106, Block 107, Block 111, Block 112; Block Group 2: Block 201, Block 202, Block 203; Tract 0054.02: Block Group 1: Block 111, Block 112; Tract 0055: Block Group 1: Block 101, Block 106, Block 107, Block 108, Block 109, Block 110, Block 111, Block 112, Block 113; Block Group 2: Block 201, Block 202, Block 203, Block 204, Block 205, Block 206, Block 207, Block 208, Block 209, Block 210A, Block 210B, Block 211, Block 212, Block 213, Block 214, Block 215, Block 216, Block 217, Block 218, Block 219, Block 220, Block 221, Block 222, Block 223, Block 224, Block 225, Block 226, Block 227, Block 228, Block 229, Block 230, Block 231, Block 232, Block 233, Block 234, Block 235, Block 236, Block 237, Block 238, Block 239, Block 240, Block 241, Block 242, Block 243, Block 244, Block 245, Block 246, Block 247, Block 248; Block Group 3: Block 301, Block 302, Block 303, Block 304, Block 305, Block 306, Block 307, Block 308, Block 309, Block 310, Block 311, Block 312, Block 313, Block 314, Block 315, Block 316, Block 317, Block 318, Block 319, Block 320, Block 321,

Block 322, Block 323, Block 324, Block 325, Block 326, Block 327, Block 328, Block 329, Block 330, Block 331, Block 332, Block 333, Block 334, Block 335, Block 336, Block 337, Block 338, Block 339, Block 340, Block 341, Block 342, Block 343; Block Group 4: Block 401, Block 402, Block 403, Block 404, Block 405, Block 406, Block 407, Block 408, Block 409, Block 410, Block 411, Block 412, Block 413, Block 414, Block 415, Block 416, Block 417, Block 418, Block 419, Block 420, Block 421, Block 422, Block 423, Block 424; Block Group 5: Block 501, Block 502, Block 503, Block 504, Block 505, Block 506, Block 507, Block 508, Block 509, Block 510, Block 511, Block 512, Block 513, Block 514, Block 515, Block 516, Block 517, Block 518, Block 519, Block 520, Block 521, Block 522, Block 523, Block 524, Block 525, Block 526, Block 527, Block 528, Block 529, Block 530, Block 531, Block 532, Block 533, Block 534, Block 535, Block 536, Block 537, Block 538, Block 539, Block 540, Block 541, Block 542, Block 543, Block 544, Block 545, Block 546, Block 547, Block 548, Block 549, Block 550, Block 551, Block 552, Block 553, Block 554, Block 555, Block 556, Block 557, Block 558, Block 559, Block 560, Block 561, Block 562, Block 563, Block 564, Block 565, Block 566, Block 567, Block 568, Block 569, Block 570, Block 571, Block 572, Block 573, Block 574, Block 575, Block 576, Block 577, Block 578, Block 579, Block 580, Block 581, Block 582, Block 583, Block 584, Block 585, Block 586, Block 587; Tract 0056.01: Block Group 1: Block 101A, Block 101B, Block 101C, Block 102, Block 103, Block 104A, Block 104B, Block 105A, Block 105B, Block 106, Block 107, Block 108, Block 109; Block Group 2: Block 201, Block 202A, Block 202B, Block 203A, Block 203B, Block 204, Block 205, Block 206; Block Group 3: Block 309; Block Group 4: Block 407B, Block 408, Block 409, Block 410; Block Group 6: Block 601, Block 602, Block 603, Block 604, Block 605, Block 606, Block 607, Block 608, Block 609; Block Group 7: Block 701, Block 702, Block 703, Block 704, Block 705, Block 706, Block 707, Block 708, Block 709; Tract 0056.03: Block Group 1: Block 101, Block 102, Block 103, Block 104; Block Group 2: Block 201, Block 202, Block 203, Block 204, Block 205, Block 206; Block Group 3: Block 301, Block 302; Block Group 4: Block 401, Block 402, Block 403, Block 404, Block 405; Block Group 5: Block 501, Block 502, Block 503, Block 504, Block 505, Block 506, Block 507, Block 508, Block 509, Block 510, Block 511, Block 512; Block Group 6: Block 602, Block 603, Block 604, Block 605, Block 606, Block 607, Block 608A, Block 608B, Block 609, Block 610, Block 611; Tract 0056.04: Block Group 1: Block 101, Block 102, Block 103, Block 104, Block 105, Block 106, Block 107, Block 108, Block 109, Block 110, Block 111, Block 112, Block 113, Block 114, Block 115, Block 116, Block 117, Block 118, Block 119, Block 120, Block 121, Block 122, Block 123, Block 124, Block 125, Block 126, Block 127, Block 128, Block 129, Block 130, Block 131, Block 132, Block 133, Block 134, Block 135, Block 136, Block 137, Block 138, Block 139, Block 140, Block 141, Block 142, Block 143, Block 144, Block 145, Block 146, Block 147, Block 148, Block 149, Block 150, Block 151; Block Group 2: Block 201, Block 202, Block 203, Block 204, Block 205, Block 206, Block 207, Block 208, Block 209, Block 210, Block 216, Block 222, Block 223, Block 224, Block 225, Block 226, Block 227, Block 228, Block 229, Block 230, Block 231, Block 232, Block 233, Block 234, Block 235, Block

236, Block 237; Block Group 3: Block 301, Block 302, Block 308, Block 311, Block 312, Block 314, Block 315, Block 316, Block 317, Block 318, Block 319, Block 320, Block 321; Block Group 4: Block 401, Block 402, Block 403, Block 404, Block 405; Tract 0057: Block Group 1: Block 101, Block 102, Block 103, Block 104, Block 105, Block 106, Block 107, Block 108, Block 109, Block 110, Block 111, Block 112, Block 113, Block 114, Block 115, Block 116, Block 117, Block 118, Block 124, Block 125, Block 126, Block 128, Block 129, Block 130, Block 131, Block 132, Block 133, Block 134, Block 135, Block 136, Block 137, Block 138, Block 139, Block 140, Block 141, Block 142, Block 143, Block 144, Block 145, Block 146, Block 147, Block 148, Block 149, Block 150, Block 151, Block 152, Block 153, Block 154, Block 155, Block 156, Block 157, Block 158, Block 159, Block 160, Block 161, Block 162, Block 163, Block 164, Block 165, Block 166, Block 167, Block 168, Block 169, Block 170, Block 171, Block 172, Block 173, Block 174, Block 175, Block 176, Block 177, Block 178, Block 179, Block 180, Block 181, Block 182, Block 183, Block 184, Block 185; Block Group 2: Block 201, Block 202, Block 203, Block 204, Block 205, Block 206, Block 207, Block 208, Block 209, Block 210, Block 211, Block 212, Block 213, Block 214, Block 215, Block 216, Block 217, Block 218, Block 219, Block 220, Block 221, Block 222, Block 223, Block 224, Block 225, Block 226, Block 227, Block 228, Block 229, Block 230, Block 231, Block 232, Block 233, Block 234, Block 235, Block 236, Block 237, Block 238, Block 239, Block 240, Block 241, Block 242, Block 243, Block 244, Block 245, Block 246, Block 247, Block 248, Block 249, Block 250, Block 251, Block 252, Block 253, Block 254, Block 255, Block 256, Block 257, Block 258, Block 259, Block 260, Block 261, Block 262, Block 263, Block 264, Block 265, Block 266, Block 267, Block 268; Tract 0058: Block Group 1: Block 101, Block 102, Block 108, Block 110, Block 111, Block 112, Block 113, Block 114, Block 115, Block 116, Block 117, Block 118, Block 124, Block 125, Block 126, Block 127, Block 128, Block 129, Block 130, Block 131, Block 132, Block 133, Block 134, Block 135, Block 136, Block 137, Block 138, Block 139, Block 140, Block 141, Block 142, Block 143, Block 144, Block 145, Block 146, Block 147, Block 148, Block 149, Block 150, Block 151; Block Group 2: Block 205, Block 207, Block 212, Block 213, Block 214, Block 215, Block 216; Block Group 3: Block 301, Block 315, Block 316, Block 317, Block 318, Block 319, Block 320, Block 321; Block Group 4: Block 403, Block 404, Block 405, Block 406, Block 407, Block 408, Block 409, Block 410, Block 411, Block 412, Block 413, Block 414, Block 415, Block 416, Block 417, Block 418, Block 419, Block 420, Block 421, Block 422, Block 423, Block 424, Block 425, Block 426, Block 427, Block 428, Block 429, Block 430, Block 431, Block 432, Block 433, Block 434, Block 435, Block 436, Block 437, Block 438, Block 439; Tract 0059.01: Block Group 1: Block 101, Block 102, Block 103, Block 104A, Block 104B, Block 105A, Block 105B, Block 106, Block 107, Block 108, Block 109, Block 110, Block 111, Block 112, Block 113, Block 114A, Block 114B; Block Group 2: Block 201A, Block 201B, Block 202, Block 203, Block 204, Block 205A, Block 205B, Block 206, Block 212, Block 213, Block 223, Block 229, Block 230, Block 231, Block 232, Block 233, Block 234, Block 235; Block Group 3: Block 301, Block 302, Block 303, Block 304, Block 305, Block 306, Block 307, Block 308, Block 309,

Block 310, Block 311, Block 312; Block Group 4: Block 401, Block 402, Block 403, Block 404, Block 405, Block 406, Block 407, Block 408, Block 409, Block 410, Block 411, Block 412, Block 413, Block 414, Block 415, Block 416, Block 417; Block Group 5: Block 501, Block 502, Block 503, Block 504, Block 505, Block 506, Block 507, Block 508, Block 509, Block 510, Block 511, Block 512, Block 513, Block 514, Block 515, Block 516, Block 517, Block 518, Block 519, Block 520, Block 521, Block 522, Block 523, Block 524, Block 525, Block 526, Block 527, Block 528, Block 529, Block 530, Block 531, Block 532, Block 533; Block Group 6: Block 601A, Block 601B, Block 602, Block 603, Block 604, Block 605, Block 606A, Block 606B, Block 607, Block 608, Block 609, Block 610, Block 611, Block 612, Block 613, Block 614, Block 615, Block 616, Block 617, Block 618, Block 619, Block 620, Block 621, Block 622, Block 623, Block 624, Block 625, Block 626, Block 627, Block 628, Block 629, Block 630, Block 631, Block 632, Block 633, Block 634, Block 635, Block 636, Block 637, Block 638, Block 639, Block 640, Block 641, Block 642, Block 643, Block 644, Block 645, Block 646; Block Group 7: Block 701, Block 702, Block 703, Block 704, Block 705A, Block 705B, Block 705C, Block 706, Block 707, Block 708A, Block 708B, Block 709, Block 710; Block Group 8: Block 801A, Block 801B, Block 802, Block 803, Block 804, Block 805, Block 806, Block 807, Block 808A, Block 808B, Block 809, Block 810A, Block 810B, Block 811, Block 812, Block 813, Block 814, Block 815; Tract 0059.02, Tract 0060.02, Tract 0060.85: Block Group 1: Block 101C, Block 102, Block 103, Block 104, Block 105A, Block 105B, Block 106A, Block 106B, Block 107A, Block 107B, Block 108A, Block 108B, Block 109, Block 110, Block 111, Block 112, Block 113, Block 114, Block 115, Block 116B, Block 119, Block 120, Block 121, Block 122, Block 123, Block 124, Block 125, Block 126, Block 127, Block 128, Block 129, Block 130, Block 131, Block 132, Block 133, Block 134, Block 136, Block 137, Block 138, Block 139, Block 140, Block 141, Block 142, Block 143, Block 144; Block Group 2: Block 201A, Block 201B, Block 202, Block 203; Block Group 3: Block 301A, Block 301B, Block 302, Block 303, Block 304, Block 305, Block 306, Block 307, Block 308, Block 309, Block 310, Block 311, Block 312, Block 313, Block 314, Block 315, Block 316, Block 317, Block 318, Block 319, Block 320, Block 321, Block 322, Block 323, Block 324, Block 325; Block Group 4: Block 401, Block 402A, Block 402B, Block 403, Block 404, Block 405, Block 406, Block 407, Block 408, Block 409, Block 410, Block 411, Block 412A, Block 412B, Block 413, Block 414; Block Group 5: Block 501A, Block 502, Block 503, Block 504, Block 505, Block 506, Block 507, Block 508, Block 509, Block 510, Block 511, Block 512, Block 513, Block 514; Perry County, Wilcox County. (Code 1852, § 31; Code 1867, § 34; Code 1876, § 29; Code 1886, § 29; Code 1896, § 969; Code 1907, § 99; Acts 1915, No. 75½, p. 875; Code 1923, § 154; Acts 1931, No. 59, p. 98; Code 1940, T. 17, § 425; Acts 1964, 1st Ex. Sess., No. 21, p. 42, § 1; Acts 1965, No. 564, p. 1050; Acts 1971, 3rd Ex. Sess., No. 120, p. 4359; Acts 1981, 1st Ex. Sess., No. 81-929, p. 78, § 1; Acts 1992, No. 92-63, p. 96, § 1.)

Constitutionality. — This section, as it read prior to its amendment in 1992, if applied to congressional elections in 1992, violated U.S. Const., Art. I, § 2. Wesch v. Hunt, 785 F. Supp. 1491 (S.D. Ala.), aff'd, 504 U.S. 902, 112 S. Ct. 1926, 118 L. Ed. 2d 535 (1992), — U.S. —, 113

S. Ct. 1233, 122 L. Ed. 2d 640 (1993).

Cited in Alsup v. Mayhall, 208 F. Supp. 713 (S.D. Ala. 1962), aff'd, 504 U.S. 902, 112 S. Ct. 1926, 118 L. Ed. 2d 535 (1992), — U.S. —, 113

S. Ct. 1233, 122 L. Ed. 2d 640 (1993).

Collateral references. — 29 C.J.S., Elections, §§ 1(2), 54.

25 Am. Jur. 2d, Elections, § 30.

§ 17-20-2. Election of congressional representative.

Each congressional district described in Section 17-20-1 is entitled to elect one representative in the Congress of the United States, who shall be chosen by the qualified electors of the district at the general election in each even-numbered year. (Code 1867, § 36; Code 1876, § 30; Code 1886, § 30; Code 1896, § 970; Code 1907, § 100; Code 1923, § 155; Code 1940, T. 17, § 426; Acts 1964, 1st Ex. Sess., No. 21, p. 42, § 2.)

Cross references. — See also § 17-2-10.

§ 17-20-3. Making returns to Secretary of State.

In all elections for representatives in Congress, the board of supervisors of each county must, within five days after making the statement of the county vote by precincts, return the result of the same to the Secretary of State. (Code 1876, § 343; Code 1886, § 436; Code 1896, § 1654; Code 1907, § 447; Code 1923, § 537; Code 1940, T. 17, § 223; Acts 1988, 1st Ex. Sess., No. 88-908, p. 482, § 6.)

§ 17-20-4. Governor to estimate returns and give notice of election.

Within 15 days after the time for making the returns, the Governor, in the presence of the Secretary of State and Attorney General, or either of them in the absence of the other, must estimate the returns, ascertain which candidates are elected and notify them by proclamation. (Code 1876, § 344; Code 1886, § 437; Code 1896, § 1655; Code 1907, § 448; Code 1923, § 538; Code 1940, T. 17, § 224.)

CHAPTER 21.

REIMBURSING COUNTIES FOR EXPENSES OF CERTAIN ELECTIONS.

§ 17-21-1. "Expenses" defined.

As used in this chapter, the term "expenses" shall include the following items, and no other:

(1) The per diem and mileage provided by law for election officials.

(2) The per diem provided by law for the clerk or register or other official acting in his stead for handling absentee ballots.

(3) The costs of ballots, supplies and other materials required by law to be furnished to election officials. In those counties and municipalities where voting machines are used, such voting machine shall not be considered as ballots, supplies or materials, as herein used.

(4) The costs of absentee ballots, supplies and other materials required by law to be furnished to the official handling absentee ballots.

(5) The cost of preparing and furnishing the lists of qualified electors to the election officials as required by law. (Acts 1955, No. 160, p. 406, § 1.)

§ 17-21-2. Both federal or state and county offices.

The State of Alabama shall reimburse a county for one half of all sums expended by the county in payment of expenses incurred in holding and conducting an election in which candidates for both federal or state and county offices are nominated or both federal or state and county officials are elected. (Acts 1955, No. 160, p. 406, § 2.)

§ 17-21-3. Only federal or state offices.

The State of Alabama shall reimburse a county for all sums expended by the county in payment of expenses incurred in holding and conducting an election in which only candidates for federal or state offices are nominated or federal or state officials are elected. (Acts 1955, No. 160, p. 406, § 3.)

§ 17-21-4. Constitutional amendments in general.

The State of Alabama shall reimburse a county for one half of all sums expended by the county in payment of expenses incurred in holding and conducting an election at which both amendments to the Constitution affecting one or more counties or subdivisions thereof and amendments affecting the State of Alabama as a whole are voted upon. (Acts 1955, No. 160, p. 406, § 4.)

§ 17-21-5. Constitutional amendments affecting state as a whole.

The State of Alabama shall reimburse a county for all sums expended by the county in payment of expenses incurred in holding and conducting an election at which only amendments to the Constitution affecting the State of Alabama as a whole are voted upon. (Acts 1955, No. 160, p. 406, § 5.)

§ 17-21-6. Appropriation.

There is hereby appropriated of any funds in the State Treasury not otherwise appropriated such sum or sums as may be necessary to carry out the provisions of this chapter. (Acts 1955, No. 160, p. 406, § 6.)

CHAPTER 22.

CORRUPT PRACTICES.

REPEALED.

§§ 17-22-1 through 17-22-15. Repealed by Acts 1988, 1st Ex. Sess., No. 88-873, p. 397, § 24, effective September 27, 1988.

Code Commissioner's note. — Section 26 of Acts 1988, 1st Ex. Sess., No. 88-873, which added Chapter 17-22A, provides: "This act shall become effective immediately upon its passage and approval by the Governor, or upon its otherwise becoming a law; provided, however, the reporting requirements provided for in this act shall have retroactive effect to July 1, 1988."

Cross references. — As to corrupt practices relating to elections, see § 17-22A-1 et seq.

CHAPTER 22A.

THE FAIR CAMPAIGN PRACTICES ACT.

Code Commissioner's note. — The act which added this chapter became effective September 27, 1988, and provided that reporting requirements provided for in this chapter shall have retroactive effect to July 1, 1988.

Acts 1988, 1st Ex. Sess., No. 88-873, which enacted Chapter 22A of Title 17, was named by Act No. 88-972 as the "Campbell-Bennett Act." Act No. 88-873, which enacted Chapter 22A of Title 17, was named by Act No. 88-972 as the "Campbell-Bennett Act."

Cross references. — As to filing by judges, parties, and attorneys of disclosure statements concerning contributions, and recusal of justice or judge, see Chapter 24 of Title 12. As to when a candidate, public official, or campaign committee may accept or solicit contributions, see § 36-25-6.

Chapter is mandatory if violation challenged prior to election, but directory if challenged after election. — Compliance with the Corrupt Practices Act is construed as mandatory if properly challenged prior to the election in a direct proceeding. If not so challenged, the provisions of that act are treated as directory only, after the election. Varner v. Long, 346 So. 2d 404 (Ala. 1977).

Cited in Lewis v. State ex rel. Evans, 387 So. 2d 795 (Ala. 1980).

Collateral references. — State regulation of the giving or making of political contributions or expenditures by private individuals. 94 ALR3d 944.

§ 17-22A-1. Short title.

This chapter shall be known and may be cited as the "Fair Campaign Practices Act." (Acts 1988, 1st Ex. Sess., No. 88-873, p. 397, § 1.)

§ 17-22A-2. Definitions.

For purposes of this chapter, unless a different meaning clearly appears in the context, the following terms shall have the meanings ascribed in this section:

(1) CANDIDATE. An individual who has:

a. Taken the action necessary under the laws of the state to qualify himself or herself for nomination or for election to any state office or local office or in the case of an independent seeking ballot access, on the date when he or she files a petition with the probate judge in the case of county offices or the Secretary of State in all other cases; or

b. Received contributions or made expenditures, or given his or her consent for any other person or persons to receive contributions or make expenditures, with a view to bringing about his or her nomination or election to any state office or local office. Provided, however, that no person shall be considered a candidate within the meaning of this subdivision until such time as he or she has either received contributions or expenditures as provided herein in the following amounts:

1. Ten thousand dollars or more, with a view toward bringing about nomination or election to any state office other than one filled by election of the registered voters of any circuit or district within the state;

2. Three thousand dollars or more, with a view toward bringing about nomination or election to any state office filled by election of the registered voters of any circuit or district; and

3. One thousand dollars or more, with a view toward bringing about nomination or election to any local office.

(2) CONTRIBUTION.

a. The following shall be considered contributions:

1. A gift, subscription, loan, advance, deposit of money or anything of value, a payment, a forgiveness of a loan, or payment of a third party, made for the purpose of influencing the result of an election;

2. A contract or agreement to make a gift, subscription, loan, advance, or deposit of money or anything of value for the purpose of influencing the result of an election;

3. Any transfer of anything of value received by a political committee from another political committee, political party or other source; or

4. The payment of compensation by any person for the personal services or expenses of any other person if such services are rendered or expenses incurred on behalf of a candidate, political committee or political party without payment of full and adequate compensation by such candidate, political committee or political party. Provided, however, that the payment of compensation by a corporation for the purpose

of establishing, administering or soliciting voluntary contributions to a separate, segregated fund as permitted by Section 10-1-2, shall not constitute a contribution.

b. The term "contribution" does not include:

1. The value of services provided without compensation by individuals who volunteer a portion or all of their time on behalf of a candidate or political committee;

2. The use of real or personal property and the cost of invitations, food or beverages, voluntarily provided by an individual to a candidate or political committee in rendering voluntary personal services on the individual's residential or business premises for election-related activities;

3. The sale of any food or beverage by a vendor for use in an election campaign at a charge to a candidate or political committee less than the normal comparable charge, if such charge to the political committee for use in an election campaign is at least equal to the cost of such food or beverage to the vendor;

4. Any unreimbursed payment for travel expenses made by an individual who on his or her own behalf volunteers personal services to a candidate or political committee; or

5. The payment by a state or local committee of a political party of the cost of preparation, display, or mailing or other distribution incurred by such committee with respect to a printed slate card or sample ballot, or other printed listing of two or more candidates for any public office for which an election is held in the state, except that this subparagraph shall not apply in the case of costs incurred by such committee with respect to a display of any such listing made on broadcasting stations, or in newspapers, magazines, or other similar types of general public political advertising.

6. The value or cost of polling data and voter preference data and information if provided to a candidate or political committee, unless such information was compiled with the advance knowledge of and approval of the candidate or the political committee.

(3) ELECTION. Unless otherwise specified, any general, special, primary or runoff election, or any convention or caucus of a political party held to nominate a candidate, or any election at which a constitutional amendment or other proposition is submitted to the popular vote.

(4) EXPENDITURE.

a. The following shall be considered expenditures:

1. A purchase, payment, distribution, loan, advance, deposit, or gift of money or anything of value, made for the purpose of influencing the result of an election;

2. A contract or agreement to make any purchase, payment, distribution, loan, advance, deposit, or gift of money or anything of value, for the purpose of influencing the result of an election; or

3. The transfer, gift or contribution of funds of a political committee to another political committee.

b. The term "expenditure" does not include:

1. Any news story, commentary, or editorial prepared by and distributed through the facilities of any broadcasting station, newspaper, magazine, or other periodical publication, unless such facilities are owned or controlled by any political party or political committee;

2. Nonpartisan activity designed to encourage individuals to register to vote, or to vote;

3. Any communication by any membership organization to its members or by a corporation to its stockholders and employees if such membership organization or corporation is not organized primarily for the purpose of influencing the result of an election;

4. The use of real or personal property and the cost of invitations, food or beverages, voluntarily provided by an individual in rendering voluntary personal services on the individual's residential or business premises for election-related activities;

5. Any unreimbursed payment for travel expenses made by an individual who, on his or her own behalf, volunteers personal services to a candidate or political committee;

6. Any communication by any person which is not made for the purposes of influencing the result of an election; or

7. The payment by a state or local committee of a political party of the cost of preparation, display, or mailing or other distribution incurred by such committee with respect to a printed slate card or sample ballot, or other printed listing of two or more candidates for any public office for which an election is held in the state, except that this subparagraph shall not apply in the case of costs incurred by such committee with respect to a display of any such listing made on broadcasting stations, or in newspapers, magazines, or other similar types of general public political advertising.

(5) IDENTIFICATION. The full name and complete address.

(6) LOAN. A transfer of money, property, or anything of value in consideration of a promise or obligation, conditional or not, to repay in whole or part.

(7) LOCAL OFFICE. Any office under the constitution and laws of the state, except circuit, district or legislative offices, filled by election of the registered voters of a single county or municipality, or by the voters of a division contained within a county or municipality.

(8) PERSON. An individual, partnership, committee, association, corporation, labor organization, or any other organization or group of persons.

(9) POLITICAL COMMITTEE. Any political committee, club, association, principal campaign committee, political party, or other group of one or more persons which receives or anticipates receiving contributions or makes or anticipates making expenditures to or on behalf of any elected official, proposition, candidate, principal campaign committee or other political committee. For the purposes of this chapter an individual who makes a personal political contribution (other than a candidate who makes a contribution to himself), shall not be considered a political committee.

(10) PRINCIPAL CAMPAIGN COMMITTEE. The principal campaign committee designated by a candidate under Section 17-22A-4. A political committee established primarily to benefit an individual candidate or an individual elected official shall be considered a principal campaign committee for purposes of this chapter.

(11) PROPOSITION. Any proposal for submission to the general public for its approval or rejection, including proposed as well as qualified ballot questions.

(12) STATE. The State of Alabama.

(13) STATE OFFICE. All offices under the constitution and laws of the state filled by election of the registered voters of the state of any circuit or district and shall include legislative offices. (Acts 1988, 1st Ex. Sess., No. 88-873, p. 397, § 2.)

Editor's note. — In light of the similarity of the provisions, decisions under former § 17-22-1 are included in the annotations for this section.

This chapter created a new offense, unknown to the common law. Finley v. State, 28 Ala. App. 151, 181 So. 123 (1938).

Effect of violation. — If the candidate or officeholder violates this chapter in a way which makes him ineligible or disqualified, by his terms, he thus becomes a usurper or intruder, or unlawful holder of the office, and may be removed by quo warranto. State ex rel.

Chambers v. Bates, 233 Ala. 251, 171 So. 370 (1936).

Improper remark of prosecuting attorney held harmless. — In prosecution for violation of this chapter, special prosecuting attorney's alleged improper remark in argument that one of the defendants may have been a candidate at the election was not error where trial court held that the remark was improper and not evidence, and no adverse ruling was made or exception reversed. Finley v. State, 28 Ala. App. 151, 181 So. 123 (1938).

§ 17-22A-3. Political committees; officers; segregation of funds; accounting and reporting; duties.

(a) Every political committee shall have a chairman and a treasurer.

(b) All funds of a political committee shall be segregated from, and shall not be commingled with, any personal funds of officers, members, or associates of such committee.

(c) It shall be the duty of the treasurer of a political committee to keep a detailed, exact account of:

(1) All contributions made to or for such committee;

(2) All expenditures made by or on behalf of such committee; and

(3) The identification of every person to whom an expenditure is made, the date and amount thereof, and the name of each candidate on whose behalf such expenditure was made or a designation of the election proposition the result of which the political committee will attempt to influence by making expenditures or receiving contributions.

(d) It shall be the duty of the treasurer to obtain and keep a receipted bill or cancelled check, stating the particulars for every expenditure made by or on behalf of a political committee greater than $100, and for any such expenditure in a lesser amount, if the aggregate amount of such expenditures to the same person during a calendar year is greater than $100. Provided, however, the treasurer of a political committee other than a principal campaign committee shall not be required under this chapter to report any expenditure not related to political contributions or expenditures or made as an administrative expense. The treasurer shall preserve all receipted bills and accounts required to be kept by this section for a period of two years from the date of any such expenditure. (Acts 1988, 1st Ex. Sess., No. 88-873, p. 397, § 3.)

§ 17-22A-4. Candidate to file statement showing principal campaign committee; candidate acting as own committee; duties and procedures; expenditures by candidate.

Within five days after any person becomes a candidate for office, such person shall file with the Secretary of State or judge of probate, as provided in Section 17-22A-9, a statement showing the name of not less than two nor more than five persons elected to serve as the principal campaign committee for such candidate, together with a written acceptance or consent by such committee, but any candidate may declare himself or herself as the person chosen to serve as the principal campaign committee, in which case such candidate shall perform the duties of chairman and treasurer of such committee prescribed by this chapter. If any vacancies be created by death or resignation or any other cause, such candidate may fill such vacancy, or the remaining members shall discharge and complete the duties required of such committee as if such vacancy had not been created. The principal campaign committee, or its treasurer, shall have exclusive custody of all moneys contributed, donated, subscribed or in any manner furnished to or for the candidate represented by such committee, and shall account for and disburse the same. No candidate shall expend any money in aid of his or her nomination or election except by contributing to the principal campaign committee designated by the candidate as aforesaid. (Acts 1988, 1st Ex. Sess., No. 88-873, p. 397, § 4.)

Applicability of statute of limitations. — The 20-day statute of limitations of § 17-15-22 applies to actions under the Fair Campaign Practices Act. Davis v. Reynolds, 592 So. 2d 546 (Ala. 1991).

Filing of statement. — All candidates are, of course subject to the five-day requirements of this section. If one fails to file a statement required by that section before the election, § 17-22A-21 applies the sanction: forfeiture of the election. If one files the statement required by this section before the election, but not within the five days required by that section,

§ 17-22A-22(b) applies. Davis v. Reynolds, 592 So. 2d 546 (Ala. 1991).

Removal of party's candidate for failure to timely file a statement naming his principal campaign committee created a vacancy, and the party's executive committee could exercise its prerogative under § 17-16-41 to fill the vacancy by such a method as the committee saw fit to pursue. Megginson v. Turner, 565 So. 2d 247 (Ala. 1990), overruled on other grounds, 592 So. 2d 546 (Ala. 1991).

Cited in City of Talladega v. Pettus, 602 So. 2d 357 (Ala. 1992).

§ 17-22A-5. Statement of organization by political committee other than principal campaign committee; report of material changes; notice of termination or dissolution of committee.

(a) Each political committee, other than a principal campaign committee, which anticipates either receiving contributions or making expenditures during the calendar year in an aggregate amount exceeding $1,000 shall file with the Secretary of State or the judge of probate as herein provided in Section 17-22A-9, a statement of organization, within 10 days after its organization or, if later within 10 days after the date on which it has information which causes the committee to anticipate it will receive contributions or make expenditures in an aggregate amount in excess of $1,000. Each such committee in existence at the date of enactment of this chapter shall file a statement of organization within 60 days after the effective date of this chapter.

(b) The statement of organization shall include:

(1) The name and complete address of the committee;

(2) The identification of affiliated or connected organizations, if any;

(3) The purposes of the committee;

(4) The identification of the chairman and treasurer;

(5) The identification of principal officers, including members of any finance committee;

(6) A description of the constitutional amendments or other propositions, if any, that the committee is supporting or opposing, and the identity, if known, of any candidate or elected official that the committee is supporting or opposing;

(7) A statement whether the committee is a continuing one, and if not, the expected termination or dissolution date; and

(8) The disposition of residual funds which will be made in the event of dissolution.

(c) Any material change in information previously submitted in a statement of organization, except for the information described in subdivision (6) above, shall be reported to the Secretary of State or judge of probate as provided in Section 17-22A-9, within 10 days following the change.

(d) A political committee, including a principal campaign committee, after having filed its initial statement of organization, shall continue in existence until terminated or dissolved as provided herein. When any political committee other than a principal campaign committee determines it will no longer receive contributions or make expenditures during any calendar year in an aggregate amount exceeding $1,000, or when any candidate through his or her principal campaign committee determines that he or she will not receive contributions or make expenditures in the amounts specified in Section 17-22A-2(1)b, the chairman or treasurer of such political committee may so notify the Secretary of State or judge of probate, as designated in Section 17-22A-9, of the termination or dissolution of such political committee. Such notice shall contain a statement by the treasurer of such committee of the intended disposition of any residual funds then held by the committee on behalf of a candidate. (Acts 1988, 1st Ex. Sess., No. 88-873, p. 397, § 5.)

Code Commissioner's note. — The act which added this chapter became effective September 27, 1988, and provided that reporting requirements provided for in this chapter shall have retroactive effect to July 1, 1988.

In 1995, the Code Commissioner inserted

"subdivision (6)" for "subdivision (f)" in subsection (c) to correctly implement a prior code hierarchy change.

§ 17-22A-6. Checking account; expenditures.

A political committee shall maintain a checking account and shall deposit any contributions received by such committee into such account. No expenditure of funds may be made by any such committee except by check drawn on such account, or out of a petty cash fund from which it may make expenditures not in excess of $100 to any person in connection with a single purchase or transaction. (Acts 1988, 1st Ex. Sess., No. 88-873, p. 397, § 6.)

§ 17-22A-7. Use of excess moneys received by principal campaign committee; solicitation or acceptance of contributions prohibited when Legislature convened.

(a) Amounts received by a principal campaign committee as contributions and any proceeds from investing such contributions that are in excess of any amount necessary to defray expenditures of the candidate represented by such committee, may be used by the candidate to defray any ordinary and necessary expenses, as defined in subsections (a), (b), and (e)(1) of Section 162 of Title 26 of U.S. Code, as it existed on May 5, 1993, incurred by him or her in connection with his or her duties as a holder of office, may be contributed by him or her to any organization described in Section 170(c), Section 501(c), or any other charitable, educational, or eleemosynary cause of Title 26 of U.S. Code, may be transferred to another political committee, or may be deposited into the State General Fund or the Alabama Special Educational Trust Fund or any department or agency therein funded. Contributions to an office holder shall not be converted to personal use. For purposes of this section, personal use shall not include room, telephones, office expenses and equipment, housing rental, meals, and travel expenses incurred in connection with the duties as a holder of office.

(b) Candidates for state offices and their principal campaign committees designated in the statement filed with the Secretary of State pursuant to Section 17-22A-4 on behalf of persons seeking or holding those offices, may not solicit or accept, or both, contributions during the period when the Legislature is convened in session. For the purposes of this section, the Legislature is considered convened in session at any time from the opening day of the special or regular session and continuing through the day of adjournment sine die for that session. This subsection (b) shall not apply within 120 days of any primary, run-off, or general election and shall not apply to the candidates or principal campaign committees participating in any special election called by the Governor. (Acts 1988, 1st Ex. Sess., No. 88-873, p. 397, § 7; Acts 1993, No. 93-762, p. 1528, § 1.)

The 1993 amendment, effective May 25, 1993, added the subsection (a) designation, and in subsection (a), in the first sentence, inserted "and any proceeds from investing such contri- butions," substituted "the candidate" for "such candidate," inserted "as defined in subsections (a), (b), and (e) of Section 162 of Title 26 of U.S. Code, as it existed on May 5, 1993," inserted

"Section 501(c), or any other other charitable, educational, or eleemosynary cause," deleted "used for any other lawful purpose" following "or may be," and added the language beginning "deposited into the State General Fund," and added the second and third sentences; and added subsection (b).

Funds solicited on behalf of a non-profit corporation, after governor had been elected,

were not "excess campaign funds". Hunt v. State, 642 So. 2d 999 (Ala. Crim. App. 1993), aff'd, sub nom. Ex parte Hunt, 642 So. 2d 1060 (Ala. 1994).

Using excess campaign funds for direct personal financial gain is a violation of the Ethics Law. Hunt v. State, 642 So. 2d 999 (Ala. Crim. App. 1993), aff'd, sub nom. Ex parte Hunt, 642 So. 2d 1060 (Ala. 1994).

§ 17-22A-8. Reports of contributions and expenditures by candidates, committees, and officials; filing; procedure.

(a) The treasurer of each principal campaign committee or other political committee shall file with the Secretary of State or judge of probate, as designated in Section 17-22A-9, reports of contributions and expenditures at the following times in any year in which an election is held:

(1) Forty-five days before and between 10 and five days before the date of any election for which a political committee receives contributions or makes expenditures with a view toward influencing such election's result;

(2) Provided, however, that a report shall not be required except between five and 10 days before a run-off election.

(b) All candidates, political committees, and elected state and local officials covered under the provisions of this chapter, shall annually file with the Secretary of State or judge of probate, as designated in Section 17-22A-9, reports of contributions and expenditures made during that year. The annual reports required under this subsection shall be made on or before January 31 of the succeeding year.

(c) Each report under this section shall disclose:

(1) The amount of cash or other assets on hand at the beginning of the reporting period; provided, however, that the initial report required by this chapter shall include cash and assets acquired from the date of July 1, 1988, and forward until the end of that reporting period and disbursements made from same;

(2) The identification of each person who has made contributions to such committee or candidate within the calendar year in an aggregate amount greater than $100.00, together with the amount and date of all such contributions; provided, however, in the case of a political committee, other than a principal campaign committee, identification shall mean the name and city of residence of each person who has made contributions within the calendar year in an aggregate amount greater than $100.00;

(3) The total amount of other contributions received during the calendar year but not reported under subdivision (c)(2) of this section;

(4) Each loan to or from any person within the calendar year in an aggregate amount greater than $100.00, together with the identification of the lender, the identification of the endorsers, or guarantors, if any, and the date and amount of such loans;

(5) The total amount of receipts from any other source during such calendar year;

(6) The grand total of all receipts by or for such committee during the calendar year;

(7) The identification of each person to whom expenditures have been made by or on behalf of such committee or elected official within the calendar year in an aggregate amount greater than $100.00, the amount, date, and purpose of each such expenditure, and, if applicable, the designation of each constitutional amendment or other proposition with respect to which an expenditure was made;

(8) The identification of each person to whom an expenditure for personal services, salaries, and reimbursed expenses greater than $100.00 has been made, and which is not otherwise reported or exempted from the provisions of this chapter, including the amount, date and purpose of such expenditure;

(9) The grand total of all expenditures made by such committee or elected official during the calendar year; and

(10) The amount and nature of debts and obligations owed by or to the committee or elected official, together with a statement as to the circumstances and conditions under which any such debt or obligation was extinguished and the consideration therefor.

(d) Each report required by this section shall be signed and filed by the elected official or on behalf of the political committee by its chairman or treasurer and, if filed on behalf of a principal campaign committee, by the candidate represented by such committee. There shall be attached to each such report an affidavit subscribed and sworn to by the official or chairman or treasurer and, if filed by a principal campaign committee, the candidate represented by such committee, setting forth in substance that such report is to the best of his or her knowledge and belief in all respects true and complete, and, if made by a candidate, that he or she has not received any contributions or made any expenditures which are not set forth and covered by such report. (Acts 1988, 1st Ex. Sess., No. 88-873, p. 397, § 8.)

Code Commissioner's note. — In 1995, the Code Commissioner translated the word "act" to "chapter" in subdivision (1) of subsection (c).

Editor's note. — In light of the similarity of the provisions, decisions under former § 17-22-5 are included in the annotations for this sections.

This section does not violate Constitution 1901, section 190, which requires uniformity in election laws. Jones v. Phillips, 279 Ala. 354, 185 So. 2d 378 (1966).

It is mandatory. Jones v. Phillips, 279 Ala. 354, 185 So. 2d 378 (1966).

Alabama courts uniformly, though at times reluctantly, have enforced violations of this section and former § 17-22-6 as mandatory if raised in a direct proceeding prior to the election, though only directory if raised after the election. Hadnott v. Amos, 295 F. Supp. 1003 (M.D. Ala. 1968), rev'd on other grounds, 394 U.S. 358, 89 S. Ct. 1101, 22 L. Ed. 2d 336 (1969).

And strictly construed. — The part of this section requiring candidates to designate committee to receive campaign expenditures should be strictly construed. Doughty v. Bryant, 226 Ala. 23, 145 So. 420 (1933).

This section is made applicable to primary elections by § 17-16-4. Kirksey v. Democratic Party, 495 So. 2d 638 (Ala. 1986).

It does not apply to candidate for city office. — The court has expressly held that a candidate for a city office is not within the requirements of this section. State ex rel. Chambers v. Bates, 233 Ala. 251, 171 So. 370 (1936).

The requirement that candidate for district office file names of committee designated to receive campaign expenditures held inapplicable to candidates for municipal offices. Doughty v. Bryant, 226 Ala. 23, 145 So. 420 (1933).

What constitutes "state office." — It is not the area or district from which a person is to be elected which determines whether an office is a "state office." It is the office itself which determines that. Kirksey v. Democratic Party, 495 So. 2d 638 (Ala. 1986).

Member of state board of education holds a "state office." Kirksey v. Democratic Party, 495 So. 2d 638 (Ala. 1986).

Unequal application of section in violation of United States Constitution. — The disqualification in the 1968 election of the national democratic party of Alabama candidates on the ground that they failed to meet requirements under the Alabama Corrupt Practices Act which their opponents did not have to meet constituted an unequal application of the law in violation of the equal protection clause of the fourteenth amendment. Hadnott v. Amos, 394 U.S. 358, 89 S. Ct. 1101, 22 L. Ed. 2d 336 (1969), rev'g 295 F. Supp. 1003 (M.D. Ala. 1968).

Compliance with it is a part of qualification as a candidate. — Compliance with this section is just as much a part of one's qualification as a candidate as is the paying of the qualification fee to the proper chairman of his party. Jones v. Phillips, 279 Ala. 354, 185 So. 2d 378 (1966).

And candidate's name is not allowed on ballot in event of noncompliance. — The penalty provided for failure to comply with this section is that the candidate's name shall not go on the ballot. Jones v. Phillips, 278 Ala. 354, 185 So. 2d 378 (1966).

The name of a candidate shall not be allowed to go on the ballot if the candidate fails to comply with the requirements of this section and former § 17-22-6 by filing a statement declaring the name of the committee to receive and disburse campaign funds within five days after the announcement of his candidacy. Herndon v. Lee, 281 Ala. 61, 199 So. 2d 74 (1967).

Where a candidate nominated by "mass meeting" did not comply with this section within five days after the certificate of the mass meeting was filed, former § 17-22-6 prevented his name from going on the ballot. Herndon v. Lee, 281 Ala. 61, 199 So. 2d 74 (1967).

A candidate for representative in the legislature from the thirty-sixth district, place No. 2, comprised of Butler, Crenshaw and Pike counties, who did not file the statement required by this section, with judge of probate of Pike county until February 11, 1966, with the judge of probate of Crenshaw county until February 15, 1966, or with the judge of probate of Butler county until February 28, 1966, all of these dates of filing being more than five days after his filing with the chairman of the state Democratic executive committee, was not entitled to have his name placed on the ballot at the primary election. Owens v. Heartsill, 279 Ala. 359, 185 So. 2d 382 (1966).

When announcement of candidacy is made. — See Jones v. Phillips, 279 Ala. 354, 185 So. 2d 378 (1966).

Announcement of candidacy occurs at the time of the filing of the certificate of nomination pursuant to § 17-7-1. Hadnott v. Amos, 320 F. Supp. 107 (M.D. Ala. 1970), aff'd, 401 U.S. 968, 91 S. Ct. 1189, 28 L. Ed. 2d 318 (1971), 405 U.S. 1035, 92 S. Ct. 1304, 31 L. Ed. 2d 576 (1972).

Collateral references. — 29 C.J.S., Elections, §§ 85-87, 216(2).

State regulation of the giving or making of political contributions or expenditures by private individuals. 94 ALR3d 944.

§ 17-22A-9. Filing procedure.

(a) All statements and reports required of principal campaign committees under the provisions of this chapter shall be filed with the Secretary of State in the case of candidates for state office or state elected officials, and in the case of candidates for local office or local elected officials, with the judge of probate of the county in which the office is sought.

(b) Political committees, except principal campaign committees, which seek to influence an election for local office or to influence a proposition regarding a single county, shall file all reports and statements with the judge of probate of the county affected. All other political committees, except as provided in subsection (a) above, shall file reports and statements with the Secretary of State. (Acts 1988, 1st Ex. Sess., No. 88-873, p. 397, § 9.)

Applicability to municipal elections. — Relator's replication to city commissioner's answer in quo warranto proceedings to oust commissioner, alleging that commissioner was disqualified for failure of campaign committee, allegedly designated by commissioner, to report amount of contributions to cause, and for commissioner's failure to make affidavit to such report as required by the following section, held demurrable, since requirement that candidate for district office file names of committee designated to receive campaign expenditures is in-

applicable to candidates for municipal offices. State ex rel. Chambers v. Bates, 233 Ala. 251, 171 So. 370 (1936).

§ 17-22A-10. Public inspection of reports; date of receipt.

(a) A copy of each report shall be preserved for public inspection by the Secretary of State or probate judge, whichever is applicable.

(b) The date of filing of a report or statement filed pursuant to this chapter shall be deemed to be the date of receipt by the Secretary of State or judge of probate, as the case may be; provided, that any report or statement filed by certified or registered mail shall be deemed to be filed in a timely fashion if the date of the United States postmark stamped on such report or statement is at least two days prior to the required filing date, and if such report or statement is properly addressed with postage prepaid. (Acts 1988, 1st Ex. Sess., No. 88-873, p. 397, § 10.)

§ 17-22A-11. Duties of Secretary of State and judge of probate.

The Secretary of State and the judge of probate shall have the following duties:

(1) To accept and file all reports and statements required by the provisions of this chapter to be filed with them and to accept any information voluntarily supplied that exceeds the requirements of this chapter;

(2) To make each statement and report filed by a principal campaign committee or other political committee or elected official available for public inspection and copying during regular office hours, any such copying to be at the expense of the person making copies; except that any information copied from such reports or statements may not be sold or used by any political party or any political committee for the purposes of soliciting contributions or for commercial purposes, without the express written permission of the candidate or political committee reporting such information.

(3) To furnish any forms to be used in complying with the provisions of this chapter. The expenses incurred by the Secretary of State in furnishing forms, accepting statements and reports, filing statements and reports, and making such statements and reports available to the public shall be paid from moneys designated to the distribution of public documents. (Acts 1988, 1st Ex. Sess., No. 88-873, p. 397, § 11.)

§ 17-22A-12. Paid advertisements to be identified as such.

Any paid political advertisement appearing in any print media or broadcast on any electronic media shall be clearly identified or marked as a paid advertisement. It shall be unlawful for any person, candidate, principal campaign committee or other political committee to broadcast, publish or circulate any campaign literature or political advertisement, without a notice appearing on the face or front page of any printed matter, or broadcast at the beginning or end of a radio or television spot, stating that the communication was a paid advertisement and giving the identification of the person, principal campaign committee or other political committee that paid for or otherwise authorized such communication. (Acts 1988, 1st Ex. Sess., No. 88-873, p. 397, § 12.)

Defendants who distributed on the night before municipal election printed matter which discussed people backing certain candidates and urged voters to vote against such candidates and did not contain names and addresses of persons circulating printed matter were guilty of violating this section. Finley v. State, 28 Ala. App. 151, 181 So. 123 (1938).

An indictment in language of this section charging that defendants printed, published or circulated municipal election bills, placards, posters or advertisements not bearing on their face the name and address of the person or committee causing them to be published is sufficient. Finley v. State, 28 Ala. App. 151, 181 So. 123 (1938).

Collateral references. — 29 C.J.S., Elections, § 216 et seq.

Validity and construction of state statute prohibiting anonymous political advertising. 4 ALR4th 741.

§ 17-22A-13. Cards, pamphlets, circulars, etc., to bear name of candidate, committee, etc.

It shall be unlawful for any person, candidate, principal campaign committee, or other political committee to publish or distribute or display, or cause to be published or distributed or displayed, any card, pamphlet, circular, poster, or other printed material relating to or concerning any election, which does not contain the identification of the person, candidate, principal campaign committee, or other political committee responsible for the publication or distribution or display of the same. (Acts 1988, 1st Ex. Sess., No. 88-873, p. 397, § 13.)

§ 17-22A-14. Establishment of political committee by corporation.

Notwithstanding any other provisions of this chapter or any other laws or parts of laws, a political committee may be established by a corporation. (Acts 1988, 1st Ex. Sess., No. 88-873, p. 397, § 14.)

§ 17-22A-15. Filing of copy of report filed with Federal Election Commission as compliance with chapter.

Notwithstanding any provision of this chapter to the contrary, political committees qualified with the Federal Election Commission established under 2 U.S.C. 437 shall file a copy of any report filed with the Federal Election Commission with the Secretary of State and such filing shall constitute compliance with the reporting requirements of this chapter. (Acts 1988, 1st Ex. Sess., No. 88-873, p. 397, § 15.)

§ 17-22A-16. Obstruction, intimidation, etc., of voting rights of others prohibited.

It shall be unlawful for any person to obstruct, intimidate, threaten or coerce any other person for the purpose of interfering with the right of such other person to vote or to vote as he or she may choose, or for the purpose of causing such other person to vote for, or not to vote for, any candidate for state or local office or any other proposition at any election. (Acts 1988, 1st Ex. Sess., No. 88-873, p. 397, § 16.)

Collateral references. — 29 C.J.S., Elections, §§ 118(6), 216 et seq. 26 Am. Jur. 2d, Elections, §§ 287, 288. Solicitation or receipt of funds by public officer or employee for political campaign expenses or similar purposes as bribery. 55 ALR2d 1137.

§ 17-22A-17. Paying, etc., or accepting payment for vote prohibited.

It shall be unlawful for any person to pay or offer to pay, or for any person to accept such payment, either to vote or withhold his or her vote, or to vote for or against any candidate. (Acts 1988, 1st Ex. Sess., No. 88-873, p. 397, § 17.)

§ 17-22A-18. Making or accepting contributions by one person in name of another prohibited; exception.

It shall be unlawful for any person to make a contribution in the name of another person, or knowingly permit his or her name to be used to effect such a contribution made by one person in the name of another person, or for any candidate or political committee to knowingly accept a contribution made by one person in the name of another person; provided, however, that nothing in this chapter would prohibit any person from soliciting and receiving contributions from other persons for the purpose of making expenditures to a candidate, political committee, or elected state or local official required to file reports pursuant to Section 17-22A-8. (Acts 1988, 1st Ex. Sess., No. 88-873, p. 397, § 18.)

Collateral references. — 29 C.J.S., Elections, §§ 118(6), 216(1), 216(5). 26 Am. Jur. 2d, Elections, §§ 287-290. State regulation of the giving or making of political contributions or expenditures by private individuals. 94 ALR3d 944.

§ 17-22A-19. Fraudulent misrepresentation as acting for candidate, etc., prohibited.

It shall be unlawful for any person to fraudulently misrepresent himself or herself, or any other person or organization with which he or she is affiliated, as speaking or writing or otherwise acting for or on behalf of any candidate, political committee or political party, or agent or employee thereof, in a manner which is damaging or is intended to be damaging to such other candidate, political committee or political party. (Acts 1988, 1st Ex. Sess., No. 88-873, p. 397, § 19.)

§ 17-22A-20. Solicitation by force, job discrimination, threats, etc., prohibited.

It shall be unlawful for any person or any political committee established pursuant to this chapter or for any person acting on behalf of such person or committee, to solicit or secure any money or anything of value by physical force, job discrimination or financial reprisals, or by threats thereof or by the imposition of dues, fees, or other moneys required as a condition of employment. (Acts 1988, 1st Ex. Sess., No. 88-873, p. 397, § 20.)

§ 17-22A-21. Failure to file required statement or report; nonissuance or revocation of certificate of election or nomination.

A certificate of election or nomination shall not be issued to any person elected or nominated to state or local office who shall fail to file any statement or report required by this chapter. A certificate of election or nomination already issued to any person elected or nominated to state or county office who fails to file any statement or report required by this chapter shall be revoked. (Acts 1988, 1st Ex. Sess., No. 88-873, p. 397, § 21.)

Revocation of certificate of election in municipal election. — The legislature deliberately made no provision for the revocation of a certificate of election in a municipal election. City of Talladega v. Pettus, 602 So. 2d 357 (Ala. 1992).

Sanctions and filing disclosure statements. — These two distinct sanctions in this section and § 17-22A-22, forfeiture of the election for those candidates who fail to file the disclosure statements required by the statute prior to the election, and criminal fines for candidates who file such disclosure statements prior to the election but not within the time prescribed by the statute, carry out the legislative intent of full disclosure before the election; but these sanctions do not require a candidate who discloses his contributions and expenditures before the election (but not within the time provided by the statute) to forfeit the election. Davis v. Reynolds, 592 So. 2d 546 (Ala. 1991).

Five-day requirement. — All candidates are, of course, subject to the five-day requirements of § 17-22A-4. If one fails to file a statement required by that section before the election, this section applies the sanction: forfeiture of the election. If one files the statement required by § 17-22A-4 before the election, but

not within the five days required by that section, § 17-22A-22(b) applies. Davis v. Reynolds, 592 So. 2d 546 (Ala. 1991).

Power of court. — A court can prevent the issuance of a certificate of election to a municipal office, but once the certificate is issued, the court is without authority to revoke it. City of Talladega v. Pettus, 602 So. 2d 357 (Ala. 1992).

Section 11-46-69 does not cover failure to timely file campaign disclosure forms. — Section 11-46-69 provides that a municipal election can be annulled because of the misconduct, fraud or corruption on the part of any election official, any marker, the municipal governing body or any other person, but the words "misconduct, fraud or corruption ... of any other person" are not broad enough to cover a failure to timely file campaign disclosure forms under the Fair Campaign Practices Act (FCPA), for which sanctions are imposed under the provisions of this section. City of Talladega v. Pettus, 602 So. 2d 357 (Ala. 1992).

Trial court lacked jurisdiction to revoke a certificate of election issued to the winner of a municipal election for mayor because of the candidate's failure to comply with the filing requirements of the Fair Campaign Practices Act relating to campaign contributions. City of Talladega v. Pettus, 602 So. 2d 357 (Ala. 1992).

§ 17-22A-22. Penalties; venue; time for prosecution.

(a) A person who violates any provision of this chapter other than a reporting requirement under Sections 17-22A-4, 17-22A-5 and 17-22A-8 is guilty of a Class A misdemeanor and subject to a fine of not more than $2,000.00, or imprisonment of not more than one year, or both such fine and imprisonment.

(b) A person who violates any reporting requirement of Sections 17-22A-4, 17-22A-5 and 17-22A-8 is guilty of a Class B misdemeanor, and subject to a fine of $1,000.00 or an amount not to exceed double the amount or value of the contributions or expenditures not reported, whichever is greater, or imprisonment of not more than six months, or both such fine and imprisonment;

provided, however, that this subsection shall not apply to contributions received or to expenditures made before the effective date of this chapter.

(c) The Attorney General may prosecute for violations of this chapter. Venue for cases involving violations of this chapter shall be in the county in which the alleged violator resides. No prosecution for violation of this chapter shall be commenced later than two years after the date of violation. (Acts 1988, 1st Ex. Sess., No. 88-873, p. 397, § 22.)

Code Commissioner's note. — The act which added this chapter became effective September 27, 1988, and provided that reporting requirements provided for in this chapter shall have retroactive effect to July 1, 1988.

Applicability of statute of limitations. — The 20-day statute of limitations of this section applies to actions under the Fair Campaign Practices Act. Davis v. Reynolds, 592 So. 2d 546 (Ala. 1991).

Willfulness is essential element. — He whose conduct is defined as criminal is one who "willfully" fails to do any of the acts denounced by the Corrupt Practices Law, and willfulness is an essential and constituent element of the charge in an indictment brought under said law. The indictment failing to so charge renders it fatally defective upon apt demurrer taking the point and must fall. Associated Indus. v. State, 55 Ala. App. 277, 314 So. 2d 879 (1975).

A person or organization charged with violating the Corrupt Practices Law must be charged with and proven to have willfully done or failed to do the acts defined as corrupt practices. Associated Indus. v. State, 55 Ala. App. 277, 314 So. 2d 879, cert. denied, 294 Ala. 281, 314 So. 2d 901 (1975).

A "willful" act may be described as one "done intentionally, knowingly, and purposely, without justifiable excuse, as distinguished from an act done carelessly, thoughtlessly, heedlessly or inadvertently." Associated Indus. v. State, 55 Ala. App. 277, 314 So. 2d 879, cert. denied, 294 Ala. 281, 314 So. 2d 901 (1975).

The word "corruptly" when used in a statute generally imports a wrongful design to acquire some unauthorized advantage. Associated Indus. v. State, 55 Ala. App. 277, 314 So. 2d 879 (1975).

The word "corruptly" is not synonymous with "willfully," since the former means viciously, wickedly, while the latter means with design or with some degree of deliberation.

Associated Indus. v. State, 55 Ala. App. 277, 314 So. 2d 879 (1975).

Failure of successful candidate to file expense account. — After the election there is nothing that can be done with reference to a failure of the successful candidate to file his expense account as required by former § 17-22-10, and mandamus will not lie to compel the striking of successful candidate's name from the ballot. McCutcheon v. Thomas, 261 Ala. 688, 75 So. 2d 649 (1954).

Sanctions and forfeiture of election. — These two distinct sanctions in § 17-22A-21 and this section, forfeiture of the election for those candidates who fail to file the disclosure statements required by the statute prior to the election, and criminal fines for candidates who file such disclosure statements prior to the election but not within the time prescribed by the statute, carry out the legislative intent of full disclosure before the election; but these sanctions do not require a candidate who discloses his contributions and expenditures before the election (but not within the time provided by the statute) to forfeit the election. Davis v. Reynolds, 592 So. 2d 546 (Ala. 1991).

Five-day requirement. — All candidates are, of course, subject to the five-day requirements of § 17-22A-4. If one fails to file a statement required by that section before the election, § 17-22A-21 applies the sanction: forfeiture of the election. If one files the statement required by § 17-22A-4 before the election, but not within the five days required by that section, subsection (b) of this section applies. Davis v. Reynolds, 592 So. 2d 546 (Ala. 1991).

Cited in Finley v. State, 28 Ala. App. 151, 181 So. 123 (1938); City of Talladega v. Pettus, 602 So. 2d 357 (Ala. 1992).

Collateral references. — 29 C.J.S., Elections, §§ 329, 343.

§ 17-22A-23. Construction of chapter.

It is the intention of the Legislature by the passage of this chapter that its provisions be construed in pari materia with other laws regulating political contributions, corporations, or political contributions by corporations. (Acts 1988, 1st Ex. Sess., No. 88-873, p. 397, § 23.)

Personal use of excess campaign funds constituted "direct personal financial gain." — Both the Ethics Act and the Fair Campaign Practices Act require that they be construed "in pari materia" with other related laws. Following this statutory mandate, the trial court's conclusion that the use of excess campaign funds for personal use constitutes the use of office for "direct personal financial gain" in violation of the Ethics Act is neither "unexpected" nor is it "indefensible." Hunt v. Tucker, 875 F. Supp. 1487 (N.D. Ala. 1995).

CHAPTER 23.

MISCELLANEOUS OFFENSES.

§ 17-23-1. Illegal voting or attempting to vote.

Any person who votes more than once at any election held in this state, or deposits more than one ballot for the same office as his vote at such election, or knowingly attempts to vote when he is not entitled to do so, or is guilty of any kind of illegal or fraudulent voting, must, on conviction, be imprisoned in the penitentiary for not less than two nor more than five years, at the discretion of the jury. (Code 1876, § 4289; Code 1886, § 4185; Code 1896, § 4692; Code 1907, § 6788; Code 1923, § 3906; Code 1940, T. 17, § 302.)

Scope of section. — The language of this section is broad enough to embrace, and in fact does in ipsis verbis embrace, "any election held in this state." Gandy v. State, 82 Ala. 61, 2 So. 465 (1887). See also Anderson v. State, 72 Ala. 187 (1882); Washington v. State, 75 Ala. 582 (1884).

"Election" defined. — The word "election" means the act of casting and receiving ballots, and the day and time of voting. State v. Tucker, 54 Ala. 205 (1875).

The words "illegal or fraudulent" as used in this section are merely descriptive of the intent necessary for the commission of the offense. Wilder v. State, 401 So. 2d 151 (Ala. Crim. App.), cert. denied, 401 So. 2d 167 (Ala.), 454 U.S. 1057, 102 S. Ct. 606, 70 L. Ed. 2d 595 (1981).

Clearly, the language of this section reflects a common understanding that "illegal or fraudulent voting" is voting more than one ballot for the same office, or attempting to vote when one is not entitled to do so. This section thus gives due notice of the criminal consequences of such action. Wilder v. State, 401 So. 2d 151 (Ala. Crim. App.), cert. denied, 401 So. 2d 167 (Ala.), 454 U.S. 1057, 102 S. Ct. 606, 70 L. Ed. 2d 595 (1981).

Mistake as to qualifications. — A minor, who is otherwise duly qualified, cannot be convicted of illegal voting because he was not of the requisite age, if he voted under the honest belief, induced by information from parents, relations or acquaintances having knowledge of the time of his birth, that he had attained his majority. Gordon v. State, 52 Ala. 308 (1875).

However, if one votes recklessly, or carelessly, when the facts are uncertain or doubtful, his ignorance will not excuse him. Gordon v. State, 52 Ala. 308 (1875). See also Carter v. State, 55 Ala. 181 (1876).

The poll lists are the highest and best evidence of who voted at an election. Wilson v. State, 52 Ala. 299 (1875). See also Hunter v. State, 55 Ala. 76 (1876).

Sufficiency of indictment. — A count of an indictment charging that the defendant, not being 21 years (now 18 years) of age, voted at a given general election held in this state is sufficient. Gordon v. State, 52 Ala. 308 (1875).

However, a mere general accusation of illegal voting, without specifying in what the illegal voting consisted, is not sufficient to support a conviction. Gordon v. State, 52 Ala. 308 (1875).

An indictment for dual voting is not demurrable because it fails to allege the names of the persons or officers for whom the accused voted. Wilson v. State, 52 Ala. 299 (1875). See also Carter v. State, 55 Ala. 181 (1876).

Cited in Gandy v. State, 82 Ala. 61, 2 So. 465 (1886); Gandy v. State, 86 Ala. 20, 5 So. 420 (1888).

Collateral references. — 29 C.J.S., Elections, § 325, n. 1.

§ 17-23-2. Illegal voting at municipal elections.

Any person who falsely impersonates another and thereby or otherwise fraudulently casts a vote to which he is not entitled, or having voted at such municipal election votes a second time, whether in the same ward or another, or having once obtained registration in any ward, shall cause himself to be registered a second time, or attempts to obtain a second registration, whether in the same or another name, or whether in the same or another ward, or shall aid or assist another not so entitled, knowing him not to be so entitled, to vote or to obtain registration as a voter, shall be guilty of a felony, and, on conviction in the circuit court, or court of like jurisdiction, of the county, shall be punished by imprisonment in the penitentiary for a period of not less than one nor more than two years. (Code 1907, § 6817; Code 1923, § 3935; Code 1940, T. 17, § 330.)

§ 17-23-3. Bribing or attempting to influence voter.

Any person who, by bribery or offering to bribe, or by any other corrupt means, attempts to influence any elector in giving his vote, or deter him from giving the same, or to disturb, or to hinder him in the free exercise of the right of suffrage, at any election, must, on conviction, be fined not less than $50.00 nor more than $500.00. (Code 1876, § 4292; Code 1886, § 4187; Code 1896, § 4694; Code 1907, § 6790; Code 1923, § 3908; Code 1940, T. 17, § 304.)

Collateral references. — 29 C.J.S., Elections, § 218.

26 Am. Jur. 2d, Elections, § 377.

§ 17-23-4. Buying votes.

Any person who buys or offers to buy any vote of any qualified elector at any election by the payment of money or the promise to pay the same at any future time, or by the gift of intoxicating liquors or other valuable thing, shall be deemed guilty of a misdemeanor, and, on conviction thereof, shall be fined not less than $50.00 nor more than $100.00. (Code 1907, § 6808; Code 1923, § 3926; Code 1940, T. 17, § 321.)

§ 17-23-5. Selling votes.

Any qualified elector at any election who takes or receives any money or other valuable thing, upon the condition that the same shall be paid at any future time, in exchange for the vote of such elector for any particular candidate, or the promise to vote for any particular candidate, shall be guilty of a misdemeanor, and, upon conviction thereof, shall be fined not less than $50.00 nor more than $500.00. No witness shall be prosecuted for any offense under this section as to which he testified before the grand jury. (Code 1907, § 6809; Code 1923, § 3927; Code 1940, T. 17, § 322.)

§ 17-23-6. Candidate barred by bribery.

Any candidate for office in any election, upon conviction of bribing or attempting to influence voter under Section 17-23-3, shall in addition to the fine, be declared ineligible for the office to which he was elected for that term. (Code 1907, § 368; Code 1923, § 458; Code 1940, T. 17, § 141.)

Collateral references. — 29 C.J.S., Elections, §§ 216(5), 325.

§ 17-23-7. Altering or changing vote of elector.

Any person who fraudulently alters or changes the vote of any elector, by which such elector is prevented from voting as he intended, must, on conviction, be fined not less than $100.00 nor more than $1,000.00, and imprisoned in the county jail for not less than 30 days nor more than six months. (Code 1876, § 4293; Code 1886, § 4188; Code 1896, § 4695; Code 1907, § 6791; Code 1923, § 3909; Code 1940, T. 17, § 305.)

Collateral references. — 29 C.J.S., Elections, § 340.

§ 17-23-8. Disturbing elector on election day.

Any person who, on election day, disturbs or prevents, or attempts to prevent, any elector from freely casting his ballot must, on conviction, be fined not less than $500.00 nor more than $1,000.00, and also sentenced to hard labor for the county, or imprisoned in the county jail for not less than six months nor more than one year. (Code 1876, § 4294; Code 1886, § 4189; Code 1896, § 4696; Code 1907, § 6792; Code 1923, § 3910; Code 1940, T. 17, § 306.)

Collateral references. — 29 C.J.S., Elections, § 340.

§ 17-23-9. Becoming intoxicated about voting place on election day.
    Repealed by Acts 1977, No. 607, p. 812, § 9901, effective January 1, 1980.

§ 17-23-10. Employer intimidating employee.

Any employer who attempts by coercion, intimidation, threats to discharge or to lessen the remuneration of an employee, to influence his vote in any election, or who requires or demands an examination or inspection by himself or another of an employee's ballot, shall be guilty of a misdemeanor, and, upon conviction, shall be fined not less than $500.00. (Code 1907, § 6804; Code 1923, § 3922; Code 1940, T. 17, § 317.)

Collateral references. — 29 C.J.S., Elections, §§ 334(2), 344.
26 Am. Jur. 2d, Elections, §§ 286, 383.

§ 17-23-11. Coercion of employees of corporations.

Any officer or agent of a corporation, or other person with authority to discharge employees, who shall attempt by coercion, intimidation, threats to discharge or to lessen the remuneration of any employee, to influence his vote in any election, or who requires or demands an examination or inspection by himself or another of any employee's ballot, shall be guilty of a misdemeanor, and, upon conviction, shall be fined not less than $500.00. (Code 1907, § 6805; Code 1923, § 3923; Code 1940, T. 17, § 318.)

Collateral references. — 29 C.J.S., Elections, § 334(2).

26 Am. Jur. 2d, Elections, §§ 286, 383.

"Golden parachute" defense to hostile corporate takeover. 66 ALR4th 138.

Lockup option defense to hostile corporate takeover. 66 ALR4th 180.

CHAPTER 24.

ELECTRONIC VOTE COUNTING SYSTEMS.

ARTICLE 1.

THE 1983 ELECTION REFORM ACT.

§ 17-24-1. Short title.

This chapter shall be known as The 1983 Election Reform Act. (Acts 1983, 2nd Ex. Sess., No. 83-200, p. 374, § 1.)

§ 17-24-2. Definitions.

For the purposes of this chapter, the following terms shall have the meanings respectively ascribed to them by this section:

(1) ELECTRONIC VOTE COUNTING SYSTEM. A system in which votes are recorded on a paper ballot or on a ballot card by means of marking or by means of punching, and such votes are subsequently counted and tabulated by automatic tabulating equipment at one or more counting locations.

(2) AUTOMATIC TABULATING EQUIPMENT. Such term shall include any apparatus necessary to examine and count automatically votes designated on ballots, and data processing machines which can be used for counting ballots and tabulating results.

(3) BALLOT. Such term shall include ballot cards, ballot labels, and paper ballots.

(4) BALLOT CARD. A ballot which is voted by the process of punching or marking.

(5) BALLOT LABEL. A card, paper, booklet, or other material which contains the names of the offices and candidates and statements of questions to be voted on.

(6) COMMITTEE. The Alabama Electronic Voting Committee. (Acts 1983, 2nd Ex. Sess., No. 83-200, p. 374, § 2.)

§ 17-24-3. Requirements for approval of system.

(a) The governing body of any county or municipality or other political subdivision of the state may, in its discretion, by adoption of an appropriate resolution, authorize, adopt, and direct the use of electronic vote counting systems for use in all elections held in such county or municipality or other political subdivision or any portion thereof; and such resolution, a copy of which shall be filed with the Secretary of State, shall specify the particular type of equipment to be used and a procedure for implementation.

(b) Provided, however, that no such electronic vote counting system shall be used unless it has been constructed so that it shall:

(1) Permit and require voting in secrecy.

(2) Permit each elector to vote at any election for all persons and offices for whom and for which he or she is lawfully entitled to vote; to vote for as many persons for an office as he or she is entitled to vote for; and to vote for or against any question upon which he or she is entitled to vote.

(3) Permit the voter at other than primary elections to vote a straight political party ticket in one operation.

(4) Permit such automatic tabulating equipment to be set to reject all votes for any office or question when the number of votes therefor exceeds the number which the voter is entitled to cast or when the voter is not entitled to cast a vote for the office or question.

(5) Be capable of correctly counting votes.

(6) When used in primary elections, the automatic tabulating equipment will count only votes for the candidates of one party, reject all votes for an office when the number of votes therefor exceeds the number which the voter is entitled to cast, and reject all votes of a voter cast for candidates of more than one party.

(7) At presidential elections to permit each elector, by one operation, to vote for all presidential electors of a party or independent candidates for president or vice president.

(8) Provide a method for write-in voting.

(9) Be capable of accumulating a count of the specific number of ballots tallied for a precinct; and accumulating total votes by candidate for each office, and accumulating total votes for and against each question for such precinct.

(10) Be capable of tallying votes from ballots of different political parties from the same precinct, in the case of a primary election.

(11) Be capable of automatically producing precinct vote totals in printed, marked, or punched form, or a combination thereof.

(12) Be capable of accurately and correctly tabulating each vote and to have the same so certified. (Acts 1983, 2nd Ex. Sess., No. 83-200, p. 374, § 3.)

§ 17-24-4. Electronic Voting Committee created; membership, compensation, etc.

There is hereby created the Alabama Electronic Voting Committee which shall consist of five members. The committee shall consist of Secretary of State, a representative appointed by the Attorney General and one judge of probate appointed by the chief justice of the Supreme Court who shall serve without pay or reimbursement for expenses. Additionally, one member from the House of Representatives and one member from the Senate, to be appointed by the presiding officer of each house who shall be entitled to his regular legislative compensation, his per diem and travel expenses for each day he attends a meeting of the committee which shall be paid out of any funds appropriated to the use of the Legislature, upon warrants drawn on the State Comptroller upon requisitions signed by the committee's chairman; provided, however, that members shall not receive additional legislative compensation or per diem when the Legislature is in session or if a member is being paid any other payments on the same dates for attendance of other state business. The judge of probate shall be chairman. The committee shall meet at the call of the chair or any three members. (Acts 1983, 2nd Ex. Sess., No. 83-200, p. 374, § 4.)

§ 17-24-5. Examination and certification of equipment.

It shall be the duty of the committee to ensure the examination, and certification of electronic vote counting systems in the following manner:

(1) By publicly examining all makes of electronic vote counting systems submitted and certifying whether such systems comply with the requirements of this section.

(2) By inviting any vendor or company interested in selling electronic vote counting system in Alabama to submit such equipment for examination. The vote counting system shall be certified after a satisfactory evaluation and testing has been performed according to electronic industry standards. For the purpose of assisting in examining such system, the committee shall employ not more than three individuals who are expert in one or more fields of data processing, mechanical engineering, and public administration, who may or may not be state employees and shall require from them a written report of their examination. The vendor submitting a system for certification shall pay to the State of Alabama by depositing with the State Treasury for distribution to reimburse the committee in an amount equal to the actual costs, if any, incurred in examining the system. Such reimbursement shall be made whether or not the system is certified. No member of the committee nor any examiner shall have any pecuniary interest in any voting equipment.

(3) After certification of any electronic vote counting system the Secretary of State shall make and maintain a report on the system, and as soon as practicable shall send a notice of certification and, upon request, a copy of the report to all governing bodies of the counties of the state. Any electronic vote counting system that does not receive certification shall not be adopted or used at any election. After an electronic vote counting system has been certified, any change or improvement in the system shall be certified by the committee prior to the adoption of such change or improvement by any county. The committee shall not re-examine or recertify the system in its

entirety. However, if any of the changes do not comply, the committee shall suspend all sales of the equipment or system in the state until such equipment or system complies with the requirements of this chapter. (Acts 1983, 2nd Ex. Sess., No. 83-200, p. 374, § 5.)

§ 17-24-6. Report of certification or rejection to be issued.

Examinations shall be conducted and a report of certification or rejection issued within 90 days following request by vendor or company. (Acts 1983, 2nd Ex. Sess., No. 83-200, p. 374, § 6.)

§ 17-24-7. Procedure for implementation of chapter.

(a) So far as practicable, the procedures for voting paper ballots and voting machines as prescribed in Chapters 8 and 9 of Title 17, shall apply to procedures followed pursuant to this chapter.

(b) It shall be the duty of the committee to prescribe other procedures where necessary to achieve and maintain the maximum degree of correctness and impartiality of voting, counting, tabulating, and recording votes, by electronic vote counting systems provided by this chapter. (Acts 1983, 2nd Ex. Sess., No. 83-200, p. 374, § 7.)

§ 17-24-8. Instructions to voters.

(a) If electronic vote counting systems are used, for the instruction of voters on election day, the election officials shall provide at each polling place one instruction model illustrating the manner of voting. Each such instruction model shall show the ballot arrangement of offices, candidates and questions to be voted on. Such model shall be located at a place which voters must pass to reach the official voting booth.

(b) If electronic voting systems are used, before entering the voting booth each voter shall be offered instruction in voting by use of the instruction model, and the voter shall be given ample opportunity to operate the model. In instructing voters, no precinct official may show partiality to any political party or candidate. (Acts 1983, 2nd Ex. Sess., No. 83-200, p. 374, § 8.)

§ 17-24-9. Testing of equipment.

(a) Not more than 10 days prior to the election the officials charged with the responsibility of conducting the election shall have the automatic tabulating equipment tested to ascertain that the equipment will correctly count the votes cast for all offices and on all questions. Public notice of the time and place of the test shall be given at least 48 hours prior thereto by written public service announcement, notices to newspapers and radio and television stations in the county and by filing such notice with the Secretary of State. The election officials shall convene, and each shall certify to the accuracy of the test. The test shall be open to the public.

(b) The test shall be conducted by processing a preaudited group of ballots so punched or marked as to record a predetermined number of valid votes for each candidate and on each question and shall include for each office one or more ballots which have votes in excess of the number allowed by law in order to test the ability of the automatic tabulating equipment to reject such votes. If any error is detected, the cause therefor shall be ascertained and corrected and an errorless count shall be made before the automatic tabulating equipment is approved. Such test shall be repeated immediately before the start of the official count of the ballots in the same manner as set forth above. After the completion of the count, the test shall be repeated. The programs and ballots used shall be sealed and retained under the custody of the election officials charged with the responsibility of conducting the election. (Acts 1983, 2nd Ex. Sess., No. 83-200, p. 374, § 9.)

§ 17-24-10. Provisions cumulative.

The provisions of this chapter are cumulative and shall not be construed to repeal or supersede any provision of Chapter 9, Title 17, relating to voting equipment, unless in direct conflict herewith. (Acts 1983, 2nd Ex. Sess., No. 83-200, p. 374, § 11.)

§ 17-24-11. Limitation on committee's authority.

The authority of the Alabama Electronic Voting Committee relative to voting equipment shall be limited to the electronic vote counting equipment authorized under the provisions of this chapter and such committee shall have no authority to examine, approve, disapprove or otherwise affect the use of voting equipment authorized under Chapter 9, Title 17. (Acts 1983, 2nd Ex. Sess., No. 83-200, p. 374, § 12.)

ARTICLE 2.

UNIFORM SYSTEM OF ELECTRONIC VOTING.

Cross references. — As to the Secretary of State establishing a pilot project designed to develop and test specifications for a uniform system of electronic voting in Alabama, see the Code Commissioner's note under Chapter 14 of Title 36.

Effective date. — The act which added this article became effective May 25, 1993.

§ 17-24-20. Secretary of State may implement uniform system of electronic voting in certain counties.

The Secretary of State may implement a uniform system of electronic voting in any county participating in the pilot project for establishing a uniform system of electronic voting provided for in Act No. 91-562. The Secretary of State may provide through the pilot project for the administration, and educational support of a uniform system to enable counties to immediately and electronically obtain all vote totals, and to enable a county to immediately transfer by electronic means all election vote totals, and other totals from a participating county directly to the office of the Secretary of State on a timely and economic basis. (Acts 1993, No. 93-766, p. 1531, § 1.)

§ 17-24-21. Counties participating in project may be eligible to receive state funding.

Any county participating in the pilot project may be eligible to receive funding from the state for 50 percent of the costs to lease purchase an electronic voting system for a period of not to exceed eight years from funds appropriated for election purposes which may accrue from savings in administrative and printing expense through the use of electronic voting. The Secretary of State may use as a guideline in determining the funds available for state reimbursement for the pilot project to a participating county the amount of the state reimbursement to the counties for election purposes and printing costs who had leased election systems during the 1988, 1990, and 1992 election years. Any county participating in the pilot project may receive funding from the state for 50 percent of the annual county lease purchase payment for the electronic system in lieu of reimbursement to the county for future voting machine ballot printing costs. (Acts 1993, No. 93-766, p. 1531, § 2.)

§ 17-24-22. Secretary of State may provide for orderly acceptance of counties requesting to participate; reimbursement.

After the establishment of the uniform system of electronic voting through the implementation of the pilot project, the Secretary of State may provide for the orderly acceptance of counties requesting to participate in the state uniform system. The Secretary of State may establish a list of counties requesting to participate in the state uniform system based on the order of receipt of the resolution of a county governing body. After the Secretary of State has accepted a county in the state uniform system, a county may be eligible for reimbursement of 50 percent of the costs of a lease purchase agreement or contract of not more than eight years in length to purchase an electronic voting system established by the pilot project. A county may be eligible for reimbursement only after the receipt of a voucher from the county governing body with a copy of a lease purchase agreement or contract meeting the specifications of this article attached. The state may continue to annually reimburse the county for 50 percent of the lease purchase agreement or contract which payment may be in lieu of voting machine ballot printing costs payments by the state to the participating county in the future. (Acts 1993, No. 93-766, p. 1531, § 3.)